KT-486-862

AROUND PARLIAMENT
See pages 104–119.

*Around
Városliget*

Central Pest

AROUND VÁROSLIGET
See pages 140–151.

CENTRAL PEST
See pages 120–139.

EYEWITNESS TRAVEL
BUDAPEST

EYEWITNESS TRAVEL
BUDAPEST

MAIN CONTRIBUTORS:
BARBARA OLSZAŃSKA, TADEUSZ OLSZAŃSKI

LONDON, NEW YORK,
MELBOURNE, MUNICH AND DELHI
www.dk.com

PRODUCED BY Wydawnictwo Wiedza i Życie, Warsaw SERIES EDITOR Ewa Szwagrzyk

CONSULTANTS András Hadik, Małgorzata Omilanowska,
Katalin Szokolay
EDITORS Joanna Egert, Anna Kożurno-Królikowska,
Bożena Leszkowicz
DESIGNER Paweł Pasternak

Dorling Kindersley Ltd
PROJECT EDITOR Jane Oliver
EDITORS Felicity Crowe, Nancy Jones

TRANSLATORS
Magda Hannay, Anna Johnson, Ian Wisniewski

PHOTOGRAPHERS
Gábor Barka, Dorota and Mariusz Jarymowiczowie

ILLUSTRATORS
Paweł Mistewicz, Piotr Zubrzycki

Printed and bound by South China Printing Co. Ltd., China

First published in Great Britain in 1999
by Dorling Kindersley Limited
80 Strand, London WC2R 0RL

Reprinted with revisions 2000, 2001, 2004, 2007, 2009, 2011 (001)

Copyright 1999, 2011 © Dorling Kindersley Limited, London
A Penguin Company

A CIP CATALOGUE RECORD IS AVAILABLE FROM THE BRITISH LIBRARY.
ISBN: 978 1 40535 851 4

FLOORS ARE REFERRED TO THROUGHOUT IN ACCORDANCE WITH BRITISH
USAGE; IE THE "FIRST FLOOR" IS THE FLOOR ABOVE GROUND LEVEL.

Front cover main image: Parliament Building, Budapest

MIX
Paper from
responsible sources
FSC
www.fsc.org   FSC™ C018179

**The information in this
DK Eyewitness Travel Guide is checked regularly.**
Every effort has been made to ensure that this book is as up-to-date
as possible at the time of going to press. Some details, however, are
liable to change. The publishers cannot accept responsibility for any
consequences arising from the use of this book, nor for any material
on third party websites, and cannot guarantee that any website
address in this book will be a suitable source of travel information.
We value the views and suggestions of our readers very highly.
Please write to: Publisher, DK Eyewitness Travel Guides,
Dorling Kindersley, 80 Strand, London WC2R 0RL, Great Britain,
or email: travelguides@dk.com.

CONTENTS

HOW TO USE
THIS GUIDE **6**

Pallas Athene on the Old Town Hall

INTRODUCING BUDAPEST

FOUR GREAT DAYS IN
BUDAPEST **10**

PUTTING BUDAPEST
ON THE MAP **12**

THE HISTORY OF
BUDAPEST **16**

BUDAPEST
AT A GLANCE **36**

BUDAPEST THROUGH
THE YEAR **58**

**Hungarian crest adorning a wall
close to the Tunnel (see p100)**

◁ **The Parliament building *(see pp108–9),* standing on the Danube**

A RIVER VIEW OF
BUDAPEST 62

BUDAPEST
AREA BY AREA

CASTLE DISTRICT 68

GELLÉRT HILL
AND TABÁN 86

NORTH OF THE
CASTLE 96

The Hungarian National Gallery (see pp74–7), in the former Royal Palace

AROUND
PARLIAMENT 104

FURTHER AFIELD
INCLUDING
EXCURSIONS 152

THREE GUIDED
WALKS 168

GETTING AROUND
BUDAPEST 236

STREET FINDER 242

TRAVELLERS'
NEEDS

WHERE TO STAY 178

RESTAURANTS, CAFÉS
AND BARS 190

View across the Danube towards
St Stephen's Basilica (see p116–17)

SHOPS AND
MARKETS 210

GENERAL INDEX 258

ACKNOWLEDGMENTS
269

PHRASE BOOK 271

ENTERTAINMENT IN
BUDAPEST 214

SURVIVAL GUIDE

PRACTICAL
INFORMATION 222

Barrel-organ player in the historic
Castle District (see pp68–85)

CENTRAL PEST 120

AROUND
VÁROSLIGET 140

GETTING TO
BUDAPEST 232

Porcelain in the Museum of
Applied Arts (see pp136–7)

The landmark domes and towers of four of Budapest's most striking places of worship

HOW TO USE THIS GUIDE

This Eyewitness Travel Guide helps you get the most from your stay in Budapest with the minimum of difficulty. The opening section, *Introducing Budapest*, locates the city geographically, sets modern Budapest in its historical context and describes events through the entire year. *Budapest at a Glance* is an overview of the city's main attractions. *Budapest Area by Area* starts on page 66. This is the main sightseeing

Plotting the route

section, which covers all of the important sights, with photographs, maps and illustrations. It also includes day trips from Budapest and three walks around the city. Information about hotels, restaurants, shops and markets, entertainment and sports is found in *Travellers' Needs*. The *Survival Guide* has advice on everything from using the postal service and telephones to Budapest's public transport system and medical services.

FINDING YOUR WAY AROUND THE SIGHTSEEING SECTION

Each of six sightseeing areas in Budapest is colour-coded for easy reference. Every chapter opens with an introduction to the area of the city it covers, describing its history and character, and has one or two *Street-by-Street* maps

illustrating typical parts of that area. Finding your way around the chapter is made simple by the numbering system used throughout. The most important sights are covered in detail in two or more full pages.

Each area has colour-coded thumb tabs.

Locator map

The area shaded pink is shown in greater detail on the Street-by-Street map.

A suggested route takes in some of the most interesting and attractive streets in the area.

1 Introduction to the area
For easy reference, the sights in each area are numbered and plotted on an area map. To help the visitor, this map also shows underground stations, main bus and tram stops and parking areas. The area's key sights are listed by category: Museums and Galleries; Churches; Historic Streets and Squares; Palaces and Historic Buildings; Hotels and Baths; and Parks and Gardens.

A locator map shows where you are in relation to the other areas in the city centre.

2 Street-by-Street map
This gives a bird's-eye view of interesting and important parts of each sightseeing area. The numbering of the sights ties up with the area map and the fuller description on the pages that follow.

The list of star sights recommends the places that no visitor should miss.

BUDAPEST AREA MAP

The coloured areas shown on this map *(see inside front cover)* are the six main sightseeing areas used in this guide. Each is covered in a full chapter in *Budapest Area by Area (pp66–167)*. They are highlighted on other maps throughout the book. In *Budapest at a Glance*, for example, they help you locate the top sights. They are also used to help you find the position of the three walks *(pp168–75)*.

Numbers refer to each sight's position on the area map and its place in the chapter.

Practical information provides everything you need to know to visit each sight. Map references pinpoint the sight's location on the Street Finder map *(pp242–53)*.

Façades of important buildings are often shown to help you recognize them quickly.

The **visitors' checklist** provides all the practical information needed to plan your visit.

3 Detailed information on each sight
All the important sights in Budapest are described individually. They are listed in order following the numbering on the area map at the start of the section. Practical information includes a map reference, opening hours, telephone numbers and admission charges. The key to the symbols used is on the back flap.

Stars indicate the features no visitor should miss.

4 Budapest's major sights
Historic buildings are dissected to reveal their interiors; museums and galleries have colour-coded floorplans to help you find important exhibits.

A timeline charts the key events in the history of the building.

INTRODUCING BUDAPEST

CONRAFACTVR. DER HAVBTSTAD OFEN IN VNGERN WIE DIE VON DEN CHRISTE BELEGERT GEWEST. AÑO. 1598

FOUR GREAT DAYS IN BUDAPEST 10–11

PUTTING BUDAPEST ON THE MAP 12–13

THE HISTORY OF BUDAPEST 16–35

BUDAPEST AT A GLANCE 36–57

BUDAPEST THROUGH THE YEAR 58–61

A RIVER VIEW OF BUDAPEST 62–65

FOUR GREAT DAYS IN BUDAPEST

The Fishermen's Bastion

It can be difficult to plan a visit to this historic, sprawling city, particularly if time is short. These four days provide a taste of Budapest, with a variety of sights and experiences, and together include much of the best in architecture, museums, shopping and fun that the city has to offer. The schedules are not meant to be rigid – all sights are cross-referenced to detailed entries in the guide to help you tailor your day, and are accessible by public transport. Costs are for two adults, or two adults and two children, with lunch but not dinner.

Passengers ride the antique Sikló funicular railway up Castle Hill

A DAY ON CASTLE HILL

- Art at the Royal Palace
- Lunch in a Castle courtyard
- Concert at Mátyás Church
- A subterranean Labyrinth

TWO ADULTS allow at least 10,000 HUF

Morning
Buda's **Castle District** *(see pp69–85)* towers over Pest. Winding paths lead up Castle Hill from Clark Ádám tér, but the traditional way up is by the **Sikló** *(see p239)*, a 100-year-old funicular railway. Start the day with a tour of the grounds of the **Royal Palace** *(see pp70–71)*. Take time to admire the Romantic design of **Mátyás Fountain** *(see pp72–3)*, and to visit the wonderful collection of 19th-century Hungarian paintings at the **National Gallery** *(see pp74–7)*. Leave the Palace area through the ornamental Habsburg Gate, then stop at **Rivalda** *(see p196)* for a splendid *al fresco* lunch.

Afternoon
A short walk along Tárnok utca into central Buda, past myriad souvenir shops, leads to **Fishermen's Bastion** *(see p80)*. From here there are glorious views of Pest, especially **Parliament** *(see pp108–9)* and **Chain Bridge** *(see p62)*, almost directly below. Do not fail to visit ancient **Mátyás Church** *(see pp82–3)* – where there are organ concerts some summer evenings – before walking along the wonderfully preserved streets of Buda's Old Town. Follow Fortuna utca round to Kapisztran tér and the lone, ruined tower of **St Mary Magdalene** *(see p84)*. Peerless **Lords' Street** *(see p85)*, with its Gothic details and peaceful courtyards, leads to the bizarre subterranean **Labyrinth** *(see p85)*. Nearby **Alabárdos** *(see p196)* is the perfect place for an early dinner in a medieval setting.

THE FINER SIDE OF LIFE

- A morning at the spa baths
- The Museum of Fine Arts
- A walk to the Opera House
- Dinner at Gresham Kávéház

TWO ADULTS allow at least 17,500 HUF

Morning
Start with coffee in **Gerbeaud Cukrászda** *(see p206)*, the city's most famous café. Then ride the beautifully preserved **Millennium Line** *(see p238)* to **Széchenyi Baths** *(see p151)*, and spend at least three hours indulging in bathing, sauna and massage in glorious imperial surroundings. Stop for lunch at **Gundel Étterem** *(see p204)*.

Afternoon
Walk off the effects of lunch in the **Museum of Fine Arts** *(see pp146–9)*, which houses

One of three outdoor pools at Széchenyi Baths, the hottest in Budapest

Hungary's finest collection of foreign art in a monumental building facing **Heroes' Square** (see pp142–3).

On leaving the museum, walk past the **Millennium Monument** (see p145) and down Andrássy út – a superb avenue of embassies and consulates, giving way to restaurants and shops – and stop at one of the many cafés on **Liszt Ferenc tér** (see p206). The highlight of Andrássy út is No. 22, the **State Opera House** (see pp118–19), which offers guided tours in the late afternoon. From here, walk along lower Andrássy út, over Erzsébet tér, to the **Gresham Palace** hotel (see p114), facing Chain Bridge. Finally, spend the evening dining at the informal **Gresham Kávéház** (see p200), famous for its "Three Foie Gras", a Hungarian speciality.

FAMILY FUN AL FRESCO

- A tour of the Buda Hills on the Children's Railway
- A walking safari round Budakeszi Wildlife Park
- Supper and folk music

FAMILY OF 4 allow at least 17,500 HUF

Morning
Head for the **Buda Hills** (see p161) by means of the Széchenyi Hill cog railway (5am–11pm, tel. 355 41 67), which begins at Szilagy Erzsébet fasor, just north of Moszkva tér metro station. At the top, a short walk leads to the TV tower (closed) and the terminus of the **Children's Railway** (open May–Aug: 10am–5pm). The steam engine departs on the hour and meanders through the Buda hills to Hűvösvölgy, passing the **Erszébet Look-Out Tower**. Disembark at Szép Juhászné station for lunch at the outdoor café.

Afternoon
A well-marked path runs from the café to **Budakeszi Wildlife Park** (open Mar–Oct: 9am–6pm; Nov–Feb: 9am–3pm.

Children relax at Budakeszi Wildlife Park in the Buda Hills

Tel. 023 45 17, 83). The park is set across 3 sq km (1 sq mile) and contains a wide variety of animals, from wild boar (which also roam the surrounding country-side), to wolves. There is a separate reserve for plants and flora. A walking safari tours the best of both areas. The on-site restaurant is a great place for supper, and offers folk music after 6pm. At going-home time the Children's Railway will be closed, but metro Line 1 takes you back to Deák Ferenc utca.

HISTORY AND SHOPPING

- The surviving monuments of the Jewish Quarter
- A Middle Eastern lunch
- Shopping on Váci utca and in Central Market

TWO ADULTS allow at least 8,700 HUF

Morning
Start at the **Hungarian National Museum** (see pp130–33), where Sándor Petőfi read his *National Song* in 1848 (see p31). Spend an hour amongst the treasures of Hungary's turbulent past, then go to another historic location – the **Jewish Quarter** (see p134). The **Great Synagogue** on Dohány utca is a splendid Byzantine-style building, attached to which is the **Jewish Museum**. The **Holocaust Memorial** is found

in the synagogue's courtyard. The rest of the quarter is known for its gift shops and book stores, and the less ostentatious synagogues on Rumbach S. utca and Kazinczy utca. On the same street, stop for a delicious but non-kosher lunch at **Carmel Étterem** (see p200).

Afternoon
Váci utca (see p127) offers great shopping at its northern end – for souvenirs, fashion and fine Hungarian porcelain at Goda (No. 9). Do visit the **Inner City Parish Church** (see pp124–5), then cross Kossuth Lajos út, and head south past the **Klotild Palaces** (see p127) and more shops, to Fővám tér. Rest here in a café. Across the road is the final retail challenge of the day – the huge, renovated **Central Market Hall** (see p211).

One of the many busy terrace cafés that line Váci utca

Putting Budapest on the Map

The capital of the Republic of Hungary, Budapest has over 1.8 million inhabitants, a fifth of the country's total population. The city is situated on the Danube and covers an area of 525 sq km (200 sq miles). One third of the city is taken up by hilly Buda and Óbuda, on the western bank of the Danube, and the remaining two thirds by flat Pest, on the eastern bank. Budapest has a pivotal location at the heart of central Europe. From here one can easily reach other major cities such as Vienna, Zagreb, Bratislava, Belgrade, Bucharest and Prague.

Hungary in Europe
Hungary is entirely landlocked within central Europe. Budapest's passenger airport, Ferihegy, has two terminals and there are numerous connections by road and rail to neighbouring countries (see pp232–5).

BUDAPEST AND ENVIRONS

ESZTERGOM

VÁC

SZENTENDRE

GÖDÖLLŐ

Ferihegy Airport

ÉRD

ÜLLŐ

SZÁZHALOMBATTA

| 0 kilometres | 15 |
| 0 miles | 15 |

Budapest and Environs

Most of the city's tourist attractions are found on Castle Hill in Buda and in the central part of Pest. These are described on pages 66–151. Sights outside the centre, including day trips, are covered on pages 152–67. Three suggested walk routes are given on pages 168–75.

KEY

Greater Budapest

Country boundary

✈ Airport

Motorway

Major road

Railway

| 0 kilometres | 50 |
| 0 miles | 25 |

Zakopane

TATRAS

RUDOHORIE

E50

E571

Salgótarján

Miskolc

BÜKK

Eger

MÁTRA

Tisza

26

25

35

3

33

34

32

E60

Szolnok

Kecskemét

Körös

Békéscsaba

47

44

44

E671

ROMANIA

Szeged

43 E68

Arad

E68

Mures

Subotica

E671

SERBIA AND MONTENEGRO

Novi Sad

E75

E70

E79

55

41

An aerial view over Castle Hill and central Budapest

Central Budapest

Detail on
the Stock
Exchange

The centre of town includes Castle Hill
(district I) on the western bank of the
Danube and districts V, VI, VII, VIII and
IX of Pest on the river's eastern bank,
bounded by the city's original tram line.
The Roman numerals denote the official
administrative districts. For the purposes of
this guide, the centre is divided into six
areas. Each area has its own chapter
containing a selection of sights that
convey its character and history. Sights
on the outskirts of the city, and suggested day trips
and walks, are covered in separate chapters.

Calvinist Church
*Situated close to the Danube,
this church is distinguished
by its eye-catching, poly-
chromatic roof (see p100).*

Royal Palace
*The Royal Palace has been
destroyed and pains-
takingly rebuilt many
times. It was last
meticulously recon-
structed after World
War II, to the form that
the Habsburgs had
given it (see pp70–71).*

Liberation Monument
*This statue of a woman hold-
ing aloft the palm of victory
was created by the Hungarian
sculptor Zsigmond Kisfaludi
Stróbl. Situated in a park on
Gellért Hill, the monument is
visible from all over the city.
It is now one of the symbols
of Budapest (see p92).*

NORTH OF
THE CASTLE

CASTLE
DISTRICT

GELLÉRT HILL
AND TABÁN

Budavári palota
Royal Palace

Mátyás templom
Mátyas Church

Szt. Anna templom
St Anne's Church

Danube

Gellért
hegy

0 metres   500

0 yards   500

Parliament
This magnificent building hosts the sessions of the Deputy Council Chamber. It is also the location of Hungary's most important government offices, including those of the prime minister (see pp108–9).

Váci Street
This pedestrianized street is a banking centre as well as a shopping venue with souvenir shops, cafés and pubs (see p127).

KEY

⬛	Major sight
Ⓜ	Metro station
🛥	River boat boarding point
🅿	Parking
ℹ	Tourist information
🚓	Police
✝	Church
✡	Synagogue

THE HISTORY OF BUDAPEST

As early as the Palaeolithic era, there were settlements in the area of Budapest: the narrowing of the Danube made the crossing of the river easy at this particular spot. In around AD 100, the Romans established the town of Aquincum here. Their rule lasted until the early 5th century AD, when the region fell to Attila the Hun. It was subsequently ruled by the Goths, the Longobards and, for nearly 300 years, by the Avars.

Crest of the Hunyadis

The ancestors of modern Hungarians, the Magyars, migrated from the Urals and arrived in the Budapest region in 896. They were led by Prince Árpád, whose dynasty ruled until the 13th century. At the turn of the first millennium, St István, whose heathen name was Vajk, accepted Christianity for the Hungarians. As their first crowned king, István I also laid the basis of the modern Hungarian state.

It was Béla IV who, in 1247, after the Mongol invasion, moved the capital to Buda. Much of the expansion of Buda took place under kings from the dynasty of the Angevins. Buda reached a zenith during the reign of Mátyás Corvinus in the 15th century, but further development was hindered by the advancing Turks, who took the region and ruled Buda for 150 years.

Liberation by the Christian armies resulted in the submission of the country as a whole to the Habsburgs. They suppressed all nationalist rebellions, but at the same time took care of economic development. Empress Maria Theresa and Archduke Joseph, the emperor's governor, made particular contributions to the modernization of both Buda and Pest. Yet, the slow pace of reforms led to an uprising in 1848, which was brutally crushed by Franz Joseph I. Compromise in 1867 and the creation of an Austro-Hungarian Empire stimulated economic and cultural life once more. Soon after, in 1873, Buda and Pest were united to create the city of Budapest.

Following World War I, the monarchy fell and Hungary lost two thirds of its territory. The desire to regain this contributed to its support of Germany in World War II. However, Budapest was taken by Russian troops in 1945 and large sections of it levelled. Under the subsequent Communist rule, the popular uprising of 1956 was ruthlessly suppressed by Soviet tanks but it initiated a crisis that shook the regime. Free elections took place in 1990, resulting in the victory of the democratic opposition, and the emergence of a new bourgeoisie.

Dating from 1686, when the Turks were expelled, this map shows the fortified towns of Pest and Buda

◁ Gyula Benczúr's *The Baptism of Vajk*, displayed in the Hungarian National Gallery *(see pp74–7)*

The City's Rulers

In the 13th century, Béla IV built a castle in Buda and designated the town as his new capital. Until that time, the Árpád dynasty, the first family of Hungarian kings, had ruled their domain from elsewhere. When, at the beginning of the 14th century, there were no male heirs to the Árpád throne, Hungary began a long period during which it was mainly ruled by foreign kings including the French Angevins and the Polish Jagiełłos. Under Mátyás Corvinus, a great Hungarian king, Buda became one of Europe's most impressive cities. The Habsburgs, while suppressing national insurrections, rebuilt Buda and Pest after the devastation left by the Turks, adding fine pieces of architecture.

1440–44
Władysław (Ulászló) I of Poland

1637–57
Ferdinand III

1301–5
Wenceslas II of Bohemia

1541–66
Sultan Süleyman, "the Magnificient"

1385–6
Charles II of Durazzo

1386–95
Maria (crowned)

1490–1516
Władysław (Ulászló) II

1608–19
Mátyás II

1272–90
Ladislas IV, "the Cuman"

1526–64
Ferdinand I

1270–72
István V

1437–9
Albert of Austria

1307–42
Charles I Robert of Anjou

1200	1300	1400	1500	1600
ÁRPÁDS	ANGEVINS		JAGIEŁŁOS	OTTOMANS
1200	1300	1400	1500	1600

1445–57
Ladislas V, "Posthumus"

1290–1301
András III

1382–5
Maria (uncrowned)

1235–70
Béla IV

1458–90
Mátyás I, "Corvinus"

1516–26
Louis II

1526–40
János I Szapolyai

1342–82
Louis I (Lajos), "the Great"

1564–76
Maximilian I

1576–1608
Rudolf I

1305–7
Otto Wittelsbach of Bavaria

1387–1437
Sigismund of Luxembourg (initially as Maria's consort)

1619–37
Ferdinand II

2005 President László Sólyom

1740–80
Maria Theresa

1919–44
Admiral
Miklós Horthy

1790–92
Leopold II

1848–9
Lajos Kossuth

1918–19
President
Mihály Károlyi

1950–56
Secretary
Mátyás
Rákosi

1705–11
Joseph I

1835–48
Ferdinand V

1700	1800	1900	2000

HABSBURGS   HEADS OF STATE

1700	1800	1900	2000

1711–40
Charles III

1792–1835
Franz I

1916–18
Charles IV

1946–8
President
Zoltán Tildy

2000
President
Ferenc Mádl

1657–1705
Leopold I

1948–50
President
Árpád
Szakasits

1990–2000
President Árpád Göncz

1780–90 Joseph II

1957–89
Secretary János Kádár

1848–1916
Franz Joseph I

Early Settlers

Traces of settlements in the region by the Scythians and the Celtic Eravi date from around 400 BC onwards. In the 1st century AD, the Romans conquered the area as their province of Pannonia and soon established Aquincum *(see pp162–3)* within the limits of the modern city. Little evidence remains of the next rulers, the Huns, who were followed by the Goths and the Longobards. For nearly three centuries, starting in around AD 600, the Avars were pre-eminent. In 896, the Magyars swept into the region and laid claim to what would later become the Hungarian state.

Bronze Age vessel

EXTENT OF THE CITY

▣ *AD 300*   ☐ *Today*

Bronze Decorations

In the 2nd century AD, Roman carts were often decorated with bronze plaques. This example depicts (from left): a satyr, Bacchus, god of wine and Pan, god of shepherds, under a palm frond. It was found in Somodor.

Workshops and shops, known as *tabernae*, were enclosed and faced onto the street.

The Sun God Mithras

The Persian god Mithras was adopted by the Eravi and his cult survived into the Roman period. This bronze image dates from 2nd–3rd centuries AD.

RECONSTRUCTION OF THE MACELLUM

This solidly built, square market hall was the focus for trade in the Roman town of Aquincum. At its centre was a courtyard with stalls, shops and workshops built around.

TIMELINE

10,000 BC Remains dating from the Palaeolithic era indicate the existence of a settlement in the Remeda Cave in Buda.	*Silver Celtic coin dating from the 4th century BC* **800 BC** Tombs with Iron Age urns at Pünkösdfürdő.	**c. 50 BC** Celtic Eravi settlement on Gellért Hill *(see pp88–9)* **400 BC** Scythians in the region	**c. AD 100** The town of Aquincum is established by the Romans
10,000	5000	1000	AD 1
5000 BC Stone Age settlements in Talxina and along the Danube *Scythian ornamental gold stag*		**AD 89** Romans establish a permanent army camp in modern-day Óbuda **AD 106** Aquincum becomes the capital of the Roman province of Lower Pannonia	

Sacrificial Altar
This altar, decorated with rams' heads, dates from the Neolithic era. It was found in Szeged.

Shell Necklace
Dating from the Neolithic era, some 5,000 years ago, this necklace was found in Kisköre. It provides evidence of the early migration of tribes and their developed trade activities.

Butchers' stalls faced onto the courtyard.

The rotunda housed the weights and measures.

Silver Augur's Rod
This instrument was used by Roman priests for divination purposes. This one was found near Komárom, the site of a 3rd-century Roman town.

WHERE TO SEE THE EARLY CITY

Some quite considerable relics of the Roman legions that were once stationed here can be seen in modern Óbuda. The remains of an amphitheatre are near an unusual underground museum (*see p170*), while magnificent mosaics adorn the Hercules Villa (*p171*). Further up the Danube are the ruins of Aquincum itself (*pp162–3*). Here visitors can wander around the remains of various buildings and enter a museum. On the Pest side of the river, just to the north of the Inner City Parish Church, there is a small, open-air section of remains from Contra Aquincum (*p122*).

This Roman amphitheatre, *one of two in Aquincum, indicates the status of the town.*

The mosaic of Hercules and Diana, *which survives at the Hercules Villa, was probably imported from Alexandria during the 2nd or 3rd century AD.*

c. 140–60 Two amphitheatres are built to serve Aquincum's growing population

409 The Huns, under Attila, conquer Aquincum

c. 600–896 The Avars rule the region

Ornate earring from the 7th century AD

| 200 | 400 | 600 | 800 |

194 Aquincum is promoted to the status of a Roman colony

294 Contra Aquincum is founded on the eastern bank of the Danube

453 Collapse of the Huns' domination

Carving of the Sun God Mithras

896 Magyar (Hungarian) tribes take over Pannonia

The Árpád Dynasty

Hair clasp from the 9th century

After a long journey beginning in the Urals region in Russia, nomadic tribes of Magyars eventually settled in Pannonia in AD 896. Following a period of internal disputes, the tribes made a blood-bonded alliance and chose one leader, Árpád. While Géza I made contact with missionaries, it was his son, István I, who accepted Christianity for his people. Their first crowned king, István organized the state according to the European, feudal model. Initially under the Árpáds, Esztergom (see p164) was the country's capital and later Székesfehérvár. The development of Buda, Pest and Óbuda began in the second half of the 12th century, but was interrupted by the Mongol invasion of 1241.

EXTENT OF THE CITY

◼ 1300   ☐ Today

Christ is depicted twice in the middle section of the coat; in each case He is larger than the surrounding figures.

Trinity of Hungarian Saints
The figures of three saints, King István, his son Imre and Bishop Gellért, are presented on this colourful triptych in the Chapel of St Imre in Mátyás Church (see pp82–3).

Figures of the Apostles

King Géza I
Géza I (1074–77), the father of King István, is represented on an enamel plaque decorating the Crown of the Árpáds.

CORONATION COAT
This silk coronation coat was made in 1031 for the Árpád kings. It has a pearl-beaded collar and is embroidered with the figures of Christ, Mary, the Apostles and the Prophets.

TIMELINE

c.900 Árpád settles on Csepel Island (in modern-day Budapest) and his brother Kurszán in Óbuda

Coronation sword

850	900	950	1000	1050

973 Prince Géza invites missionaries into the region

1046 Revolt by pagans and the martyr's death of Bishop Gellért, thrown in a barrel into the Danube

Sculpture of King István I by Imre Varga

1001 Coronation of István (Stephen) I

Crown of the Árpáds
This gold crown, ornamented with jewels, pearls and enamel, was created by joining two existing crowns. The lower, Byzantine one was known as the "Greek crown" and the upper one as the "Latin crown".

Bone artifacts
Bone items such as shepherds' staffs often had carved handles.

Figures of the Prophets

King István's coin
The first Hungarian coin, the denar, was produced soon after AD 1000, during King István's reign.

Tympanum
This 11th-century church tympanum, from Gyulafehérvár in modern Romania, is in the Hungarian National Gallery (see pp74–7).

WHERE TO SEE THE MEDIEVAL CITY

Only a few monuments survive from the Middle Ages. Among the notable ones that still remain are the crypts in Mátyás Church *(see pp82–3)*, and the elevations and cellars of some historic houses in the Castle District (a few of which are now converted into wine bars). The reconstructed lower chambers of the Royal Palace *(pp70–71)* and parts of its fortifications also date from the medieval era.

This 19th-century copy *of the Romanesque Ják Church (see p143) reveals how the Árpáds adopted European styles.*

Gothic niches *can be seen by the entrances to many houses in the Old Town (see pp78–9).*

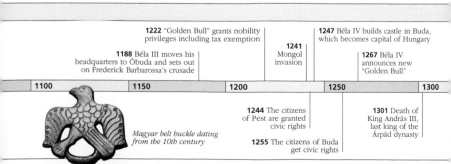

1188 Béla III moves his headquarters to Óbuda and sets out on Frederick Barbarossa's crusade

1222 "Golden Bull" grants nobility privileges including tax exemption

1241 Mongol invasion

1247 Béla IV builds castle in Buda, which becomes capital of Hungary

1267 Béla IV announces new "Golden Bull"

1100	1150	1200	1250	1300

Magyar belt buckle dating from the 10th century

1244 The citizens of Pest are granted civic rights

1255 The citizens of Buda get civic rights

1301 Death of King András III, last king of the Árpád dynasty

Gothic and Renaissance Eras

As a result of the efforts of the Angevins and Sigismund of Luxembourg, the Gothic style reached Buda in the 14th century. Buda's palace and the summer palace in Visegrád were both extensively rebuilt. Shortly after defeat by the Turks at Varna, Hungary regained control of Belgrade and, for a while at least, halted their invasion. Mátyás Corvinus, the son of hetman János Hunyadi, the victor of Belgrade, became king. Under Mátyás's rule Hungary was turned into the greatest monarchy of Middle Europe, and, as a result of his marriage to Beatrice, a Neapolitan princess, the Renaissance began to blossom in the country.

Tabernacle of the Inner City Parish Church

EXTENT OF THE CITY

■ c. 1480   □ Today

Castellan Ferenc Sárffy was the commander of Győr Castle.

Hungarian soldier

Illuminated letter from the Philostratus Codex
This letter depicts the son of King Mátyás I, Johannus Corvinus, after he took Vienna. It is housed in the Széchenyi National Library (see p72).

Royal Medallion
An unknown master from Lombardy commemorated King Mátyás I in this marble silhouette dating from the 1480s.

Gold Seal
This gold seal, which belonged to King Mátyás I, is indicative of the affluence enjoyed by Hungary while he was on the throne.

Ulrik Czettrich, an officer of the royal household, discovered the body of Louis II on the marshy bank of the Csele river.

TIMELINE

1355 Óbuda's citizens gain civic rights	**1370** Louis I enters a political union and becomes king of Poland	**1385** Sigismund of Luxembourg marries Maria	
Ciborium dating from the 14th century		**1395** University established in Óbuda	
1350	**1375**	**1400**	**1425**
	1342 Louis I, "the Great", becomes king	**1387–1437** Rule of Sigismund of Luxembourg. He enlarges the Royal Palace *(see pp70–71)*	
	1335 Treaty on co-operation and succession signed by the kings of Hungary, Poland and Bohemia in Visegrád	**1382** After death of Louis I, one daughter, Maria, becomes queen of Hungary and another, Jadwiga, queen of Poland	

Wine Cups

This pair of elaborate Renaissance wine cups, dating from the 16th century, is designed to fit together to form a covered receptacle.

Crest of King Mátyás Corvinus

Inscribed with the date 1470, this crest commemorates the building of significant additions to Mátyás Church (see pp82–3), which was then renamed after the king.

King Louis II

Hungarian knight

WHERE TO SEE THE GOTHIC AND RENAISSANCE CITY

The full bloom of the Gothic period took place in Hungary in the 14th century. Mátyás Church *(see pp82–3)* has portals that survive from this era. Renaissance art reached Hungary thanks to Italian masters brought by Mátyás's second wife, Beatrice. Both the Royal Palace *(pp70–71)* and the summer palace at Visegrád *(p164)* were outstanding pieces of Renaissance architecture. Since the storming of Buda by the Turks, only a few remnants of the former splendour have remained.

A chapel of the Royal Palace *from the period of Angevin rule can be seen in the Budapest History Museum (see p72).*

This portal of Mátyás Church *dates from the 14th century. In the 19th century, a Neo-Gothic porch was built around it.*

THE DISCOVERY OF LOUIS II'S BODY

At the Battle of Mohács, on 29 August 1526, King Louis II lost his life together with thousands of Hungarian and Polish knights. The tragic scene of the finding of his body was recreated by Bertalan Székely in 1859.

1440 Władysław III of Poland is Władysław I of Hungary

1456 Victory over Turks at the Battle of Belgrade

1473 *Chronica Hungarorum*, the first book to be published in Hungary, is printed by András Hess

1514 Peasant revolt under György Dózsa

Władysław II *(ruled 1490–1516)*

1450	1475	1500	1525	1550

1444 Władysław I is killed during the Battle of Varna

1458–1490 Reign of Mátyás Corvinus

1478 Law is passed threatening landlords who fail to maintain their buildings with dispossession

1526 Defeat by the Turks at the Battle of Mohács. King Louis II perishes during the fighting

Shield of soldier in the army of Mátyás Corvinus

The Turkish Occupation

Ottoman plate

After the battle of Mohács, the Turks razed Buda, but they temporarily turned their attention elsewhere and did not return to occupy it until 1541. When they then moved into the Royal Palace *(see pp70–71)*, Buda became the capital of Ottoman Hungary, while eastern Hungary and Transylvania were feudal suzerains. The Ottomans soon converted the city's churches, including Mátyás Church, into mosques and also built numerous Turkish baths *(see pp50–53)*. The Habsburgs tried relentlessly to recover Buda during this period. Their sieges destroyed the city progressively and when, in 1686, the Christian armies eventually recovered it the scene was one of devastation.

EXTENT OF THE CITY

◻ 1630   ◻ Today

Turkish fortress on Gellért Hill   **The Rudas and Rác Baths**

The Liberation of Buda in 1686
After a bloody siege, the Christian army, led by Prince Charles of Lorraine, entered Buda and liberated it from the Turks. This painting by Gyula Benczúr, dating from 1896, depicts the event.

Ottoman Tombstones
A few inscribed Ottoman tombstones, topped by distinctive turbans, remain to this day in Tabán (see p94).

PEST AND BUDA IN 1617
Georgius Hurnagel's copperplate print shows the heavily-fortified towns of Pest and Buda in a period when much of Hungary was firmly under Turkish rule.

TIMELINE

1526–41 Turks conquer Buda on three occasions

1529 János I Szapolyai, the Hungarian monarch, pays homage to Sultan Süleyman I

1541–66 Reign of Sultan Süleyman I, "the Magnificent", who considered himself the Turkish king of Hungary

1602–3 Austrians, led by General Herman Russworm, fail in attempts to storm Pest and Buda

1525	1545	1565	1585	1605

1530–40 János I Szapolyai rebuilds Buda

1542 The Austrians lay siege to Buda

Austrian siege of Buda

1594 Bálint Balassi, Hungary's first great lyric poet, is killed taking part in a battle against the Turks at Esztergom *(see p164)*

Campaign Tent
This Turkish leader's tent, decorated with appliqué work, was used during the siege of Vienna in 1683.

Mátyás Church *(see pp82–3)* was converted into a mosque.

Ottoman Coat
This 16th-century leather coat was supposedly taken from the battlefield of Mohács (see p25).

Ottoman Jug
Dating from the 17th century, this copper vessel was found in Buda during the reconstruction of the Royal Palace (see pp70–71).

WHERE TO SEE THE TURKISH CITY

Almost all Turkish buildings were razed by their successors, the Habsburgs, during or after the recapture of the city. Churches which the Turks had used as mosques were converted back again, although some *mihrabs*, the niches pointing towards Mecca, were left. These can be seen in the Inner City Parish Church *(see pp124–5)* and in the Capuchin Church *(p100)*. Among the few wonderful examples of classical Ottoman architecture to survive are the Rudas, Rác *(p95)* and Király Baths, and the Tomb of Gül Baba, a Turkish dervish *(p101)*.

The Király Baths, *built in the 16th century by Arshlan Pasha, remain an impressive Ottoman monument (see p101).*

The Rudas Baths *have an original Turkish dome covering their central chamber (see p93).*

Ottoman tablet with calligraphy

1634 György I Rákóczi, prince of Transylvania, joins an anti-Habsburg alliance with France and Sweden

1684 Start of ultimately successful siege of Buda by the Austrians

Viennese sword dating from the 17th century

1625	1645	1665	1685

1624 Signing of the Treaty of Vienna

1648 Death of György I Rákóczi

Gold five-ducat coin from 1603, showing the prince of Transylvania's crest

1686 Christian troops enter Buda. The end of Turkish rule in Hungary

Habsburg Rule

EXTENT OF THE CITY
■ 1770 □ Today

In order to gain control of Hungary, the Habsburgs encouraged foreign settlers, particularly Germans, to move into the country. This policy led to a national uprising in 1703–11, led by the prince of Transylvania, Ferenc II Rákóczi.

Only in the second half of the 18th century, particularly under Empress Maria Theresa, did the reconstruction of Buda, Óbuda and Pest begin in earnest. This was accompanied by economic development and a further increase in the country's population. The university at Nagyszombat (now Trnava in the Slovak Republic) moved to Buda in 1777, and subsequently to Pest in 1784, and was an important factor in their expansion.

Order created by Maria Theresa

Maria Theresa holds the infant Joseph, the successor to her throne.

The Return of the Crown to Buda *(1790)*
A vast ceremonial procession of commissioners marked the arrival in Hungary of royal insignias from Vienna, a sign of peace between the two countries.

Ferenc II Rákóczi
This fine portrait by Ádám Mányoki depicts Ferenc II Rákóczi, the leader of the national uprising of 1703–11 and a figure much loved by the Hungarian people.

"VITAM ET SANGUINEM"
In 1741, the Hungarian states swore on "life and blood" their loyalty to the Habsburg Empress Maria Theresa. This copperplate print by Joseph Szentpétery depicts the scene of the oath-taking.

TIMELINE

1687 Under Austrian pressure, the Hungarian parliament gives up its right to elect a king and accedes to the inheritance of the throne by the Habsburgs

1702 The Jesuits open a college and theological seminary

1703 The Prince of Transylvania, Ferenc II Rákóczi, leads a rebellion by the Hungarians against the Habsburgs

1729 The start of the reconstruction of Pest's suburbs

1690   **1705**   **1720**   **1735**

1689 Bubonic plague devastates the population of Buda and Pest

Royal postal carriage

1711 Suppression of Rákóczi's rebellion; a second bubonic plague decimates the city

1724 The population of Buda and Pest reaches 12,000 people

1723 Great Fire of Buda

Triple-jug of the Andrássy family
These silver jugs are joined by a miniature of the castle belonging to the Andrássy family, at what is now Krásna Hôrka in the Slovak Republic.

Hungarian aristocrats
swear on their lives to protect Maria Theresa's throne.

Dress *(c. 1750)*
This dress, typical of Hungarian style with its corset which was tightened by golden cords, was worn by a lady from the noble Majtényi family.

Ferenc II Rákóczi's Chair
Richly upholstered, this graceful 18th-century chair from Regéc Castle is typical of the style of the period.

WHERE TO SEE THE HABSBURG CITY

Having taken Buda and Pest from the Turks in the late 17th century, the Habsburgs set about rebuilding them in the 18th century, mainly in the Baroque style. Famous buildings from this era include the Municipal Council Offices, St Anne's Church *(see pp102–3)*, St Elizabeth's Church *(p101)* and the University Church *(p139)*.

St Anne's Church, *which was built between 1740–1805, astonishes visitors with its magnificent Baroque interior.*

The Municipal Council Offices
in the heart of Pest have a portico decorated with allegorical figures by Johann Christoph Mader (see p127).

1745–71 Building of the Habsburg Royal Palace

The magnificent Habsburg Royal Palace

1788 First Hungarian newspaper, *Magyar Merkurius*, begins printing

A hussar, or soldier

1778 Roman remains are discovered in Óbuda

1750	1765	1780	1795

1752 A regular postal service operates between Buda and Vienna

1766 A floating bridge links Buda and Pest

1792 Convocation of parliament and the coronation of Franz I

1746–57 Construction of the Zichy Palace in Óbuda *(see p171)*

1777 University moves from Nagyszombat to Buda; later relocates to Pest

1784 Establishment of Ferenc Goldberger's textile factory in Óbuda

National Revival and the "Springtime of Revolutions"

Hungarian crest

The dynamic economic development of Buda and Pest began at the start of the 19th century. Pest, in particular, benefited from favourable circumstances for the grain trade and became, in the Napoleonic Wars, an important centre for the Habsburg monarchy. A national revival and rekindling of cultural life took place after the Napoleonic Wars. The Hungarian National Museum and many other public and private buildings were built at this time. Yet, Hungarian reformers were hampered by the Viennese royal court and an uprising erupted in the spring of 1848. This rebellion was suppressed by the Habsburgs, with the help of the Russian army, and a period of absolutism followed.

EXTENT OF THE CITY

■ 1848   □ Today

Count György Andrássy, offered 10,000 forints towards the building of the Hungarian Academy of Sciences.

The Advance of the Hussars
In this watercolour, painted in 1850, Mór Than depicts fighting in the Battle of Tápióbicske of 1849. The Hungarian side was led by a Polish general, Henryk Dembiński.

The Great Flood
This bas-relief, made by Barnabás Holló in 1900, shows a heroic rescue by Count Miklós Wesselényi during the Great Flood of 1838.

THE FOUNDING OF THE ACADEMY

In 1825, István Széchenyi put up 60,000 forints towards the building of Hungarian Academy of Sciences (*see p114*), a move which led to a national effort to collect funds for it. Barnabás Holló created this bas-relief depicting the major donors.

TIMELINE

1802 Count Ferenc Széchenyi donates collections which will form the basis for Széchenyi National Library (*see p72*) and Hungarian National Museum (*see pp130–33*)

1809 Royal court moves from Vienna to Buda as Napoleon advances. Despite his offer of Hungarian independence, the Hungarians back the Habsburgs

1817 First steamboat sails on Danube in the environs of Buda and Pest

1800	1805	1810	1815	1820

1808 Establishment of the Embellishment Commission, led by Governor Archduke Joseph

Boats on the Danube

Lajos Batthyány Eternal Flame
This lamp, designed by Móric Pogány, has burnt since 1926 in Liberty Square (see p110). It was there that the Austrians shot Lajos Batthyány, the first prime minister of liberated Hungary, on 6 October 1849.

Count István Széchenyi, an energetic force for change, is regarded as the one of the greatest Hungarians.

National Song
The 1848 uprising was sparked on 15 March when Sándor Petőfi recited his poem, Nemzeti Dal (National Song), outside the Hungarian National Museum.

WHERE TO SEE THE NEO-CLASSICAL CITY

In the early 19th century, the Embellishment Commission, set up by Archduke Joseph and led by architect János Hild, prepared a plan for the development of Pest in which its centre was redesigned on a pattern of concentric streets. Monumental Neo-Classical buildings were built here and to this day they form the heart and the character of this area. Structures to look for in particular include the Hungarian National Museum, the Chain Bridge and several houses located on József Nádor Square (see p126).

The Hungarian National Museum, *which was built in 1837, is among Hungary's finest examples of Neo-Classical architecture (see pp130–31).*

The Chain Bridge, *the first permanent bridge over the Danube, was built by Adam Clark in 1839–49 (see p63).*

György Károlyi

Buda and Pest in 1838
Seen here in the year before the construction of the Chain Bridge, the Danube was an important means of transport.

1825–48 Period of major projects: establishment of the Hungarian Academy of Sciences, Hungarian National Museum and National Theatre

Poet Sándor Petőfi (1823–49)

1840 Language Act: Hungarian takes over from Latin as the official language of the nation

1847 Death of Archduke Joseph, emperor's governor

15 March 1848 Uprising begins

| 1825 | 1830 | 1835 | 1840 | 1845 |

1830 István Széchenyi publishes his book, On Credit. It is seen as the manifesto for the fight for modern Hungary

The Great Flood

1838 Catastrophic Great Flood results in destruction of half of Pest's buildings

1846 First railway line in the city, linking Pest and Vác

1849 After stout resistance, the Russian army, under the command of General Ivan Paskievicz, suppresses uprising

Compromise and the Unification of Budapest

After suffering a defeat by Prussia in 1866, the Habsburgs realized the necessity of reaching an agreement with Hungary and the Compromise brokered in 1867 proved to be of tremendous importance for the future of Buda, Óbuda and Pest, as it created political stability and prosperity and marked the beginning of rapid industrialization in the country. The option of uniting the three cities had been considered since the opening of the Chain Bridge in 1849. It eventually came about in 1873 and Budapest soon found itself among Europe's fastest growing metropolises. In 1896, Városliget was the focal point for Hungary's Millennium Celebrations *(see p142)*.

EXTENT OF THE CITY
■ *1873*   □ *Today*

The Citadel *(see p92)* on Gellért Hill

Castle District

Hungarian Wine Cup
This 19th-century wine cup is embellished with the Hungarian crest, which incorporates the Crown of the Árpáds (see p23).

Today's Boráros tér, where goods were once traded.

Ferenc Deák
(1803–76)
A great statesman, Deák was an advocate of moderate reforms. He argued persuasively in favour of accepting the Compromise reached with the Habsburgs in 1867.

Decorative Pipe *(1896)*
Made in the year of Hungary's Millennium Celebrations, this pipe of "heavenly peace" includes figures of the Árpád kings and Emperor Franz Joseph.

TIMELINE

1854 Martial law ends five years after 1848–9 uprising

1856 Tunnel *(see p100)* built by Adam Clark under Castle Hill

Entrance to the Tunnel

1875 Opening of the Franz Liszt Academy of Music *(see p129)*, with the composer as its principal

1850	1860	1870	1880

1859 Synagogue on Dohány utca *(see p134)* completed

1873 The unification of Buda, Óbuda and Pest as one city, with a total of 300,000 inhabitants

1864 Opening of the Great Market Hall *(see p203)*

1867 Compromise with Austria, giving Hungary independence in its internal affairs. Creation of the Dual Monarchy; Emperor Franz Joseph accepts the Hungarian crown

Monument to Hungarian Soldiers Killed in World War I
This bas-relief, by János Istók, commemorates the dead of World War I, in which Hungary fought on the German side. It is located next to the main entrance to the Servite Church (see p128).

"Handcuff" Bracelet
Following the defeat of the national uprising of 1848–9, Hungarians sought to symbolize their oppression even in pieces of jewellery.

WHERE TO SEE THE HISTORICIST CITY

Historicism had a profound influence on the form of the rapidly developing metropolis at this time. A wonderful example of the style is the Hungarian Academy of Sciences. Among others are Parliament *(see pp108–9)*, St Stephen's Basilica *(pp116–17)*, the Museum of Fine Arts *(pp146–7)*, the New York Palace *(p129)* and many of the buildings that stand on Andrássy Street *(p144)*.

The Hungarian Academy of Sciences *is housed in this fine Neo-Renaissance palace dating from 1864 (see p114).*

St Stephen's Basilica *was built over a period of 60 years by three architects. It was finished in 1905 (see pp116–17).*

TRADING ON THE PEST EMBANKMENT
Completed in 1887, this painting by Antal Ligeti shows the Pest embankment at a time when the city was booming. Manufactured goods and grain were sent along the Danube for sale in Germany and the Balkans.

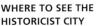

1894 Body of Lajos Kossuth *(see p106)* is returned from Turin

1904 Grand opening of Parliament *(see pp108–9)*

Old Upper House Hall in Parliament

1916 Franz Joseph dies and Charles IV becomes king of Hungary

1890	1900	1910	1920

1896 First metro line and several museums opened

1909 Airport opened in Rákos, now Kőbánya

1900 With a population of 773,000, Budapest is Europe's fastest growing city

1914 Hungary enters World War I on the German side

1918 Abdication of Charles IV marks end of the Austro-Hungarian Empire

Modern Budapest

Poster for Unicum liqueur *(see p195)*

Hungary paid a high price for its alliances first with Austria and later with Nazi Germany. Following defeat in both World Wars, the country had lost a large portion of its territory. As a result of the Yalta Agreement of 1945, it then found itself within the Soviet-controlled zone of Europe. Stalinism took on a particularly ruthless form here and led to the 1956 Uprising, which was brutally put down by Soviet tanks on the streets of Budapest. Efforts towards reform, undertaken by János Kádár, brought some changes but political opposition was not tolerated. In 1989, the Communists were ousted and Hungary at last regained control of its own affairs.

1960–66
Rebuilding of Castle District *(see pp68–85)*, including Royal Palace, and the Danube bridges

1919 Communists take over government and declare the Hungarian Soviet Republic

1941 Hungary enters World War II on Germany's side

1945 After a siege lasting six weeks, the Russian army takes Budapest

1939 Hungary neutral at beginning of World War II. Accepts refugees after capitulation of Poland

1946 Proclamation of Republic of Hungary. Smallholders' Party wins election

1922 Reopening of the State Opera House *(see pp118–19)* after World War I

1937 Sixth and last visit of author Thomas Mann

1928 Budapest is a free port on Danube

1949 Stalinist terror prevails. Cardinal Mindszenty *(see p111)* goes on trial. László Rajk, secret police chief, sentenced to death by Moscow loyalists

1920	1930	1940	1950	1960

1920	1930	1940	1950	1960

1935 Tabán *(see p94)* levelled and transformed into a park

1938 Eucharistic Congress

1953 The national football team beats England 6–3 at Wembley

1925 Radio Budapest broadcasts its first programme

1945–1 August 1946 Monetary reform. Banknotes valued at one billion pengő are printed during rampant inflation. There is not enough room for all the zeros to be shown on the notes

1958 The leader of the 1956 Uprising, Prime Minister Imre Nagy, is executed

1948 Mátyás Rákosi leads Hungarian Socialist Workers' Party, created by Communists

1919 Admiral Miklós Horthy enters Budapest; many killed in the period of "White Terror". Horthy becomes regent

1964 The Elizabeth Bridge *(see p63)* reopens, having been totally rebuilt

1944 Efforts to withdraw from World War II end with German troops entering the country. A ghetto is established in Budapest and the extermination of Hungarian Jews begins

1918 Democratic revolution; Hungary declared a republic. Mihály Károlyi selected as the country's first president

1947 After falsification of election results, Communists control the whole country

1970 Opening of a new metro line

October 1989 Republic of Hungary is proclaimed once more. The national emblem is changed

1991 Warsaw Pact is dissolved. Russian army leaves Hungary

1994 Election won by the Hungarian Socialist Party

1998 Election won by the Citizens' Party

1981 Director István Szabó receives an Oscar for his film *Mefisto*

2002 Election won by the Hungarian Socialist Party. Imre Kertész receives the Nobel prize for Literature

2010 Centre-right party Fidesz wins landslide majority in elections. Viktor Orbán is re-elected prime minister

February 1989 Round-table talks between opposition parties and ruling socialist government

2007 Hungary joins the Schengen open-borders agreement

| 1970 | 1980 | 1990 | 2000 | 2010 |

| 1970 | 1980 | 1990 | 2000 | 2010 |

1987 UNESCO places the historic Castle District and the Banks of the Danube on its list of world heritage sights

1993 Pope John Paul II visits Hungary

2004 Hungary becomes a member of the EU

June 1989 Ceremonial funeral for Imre Nagy and rehabilitation for other leaders of 1956 Uprising

September 1989 Hungary opens its borders to allow refugees to flee from East Germany to the West

1990 The Democratic Hungarian Forum wins free elections. József Antall becomes the first prime minister to be elected in a democratic process; Árpád Göncz is elected president

1968 Introduction of new economic system known as "goulash-Communism"

1991 Václav Havel, József Antall and Lech Walesa sign an agreement in Visegrád *(see p164)* between Czechoslovakia, Hungary and Poland

BUDAPEST AT A GLANCE

Often described as the "Little Paris of Middle Europe", Budapest is famous not only for the monuments reflecting its own 1,000-year-old culture, but also for the relics of others who settled here. Remains from both Roman occuption, and, much later, rule by the Turks can still be seen in the city. After Turkish rule, union with Austria had a particular influence on the city's form and style. Descriptions of nearly 150 places of interest can be found in the *Area by Area* section of the book. However, to help you make the most of your stay, the following 20 pages are a guide to the best Budapest has to offer. Museums and galleries, churches and synagogues, palaces and historic buildings, baths and pools are presented, together with the influence of Secession in the city. Each sight is is cross-referenced to its main entry. Below are the sights not to be missed.

BUDAPEST'S TOP TEN SIGHTS

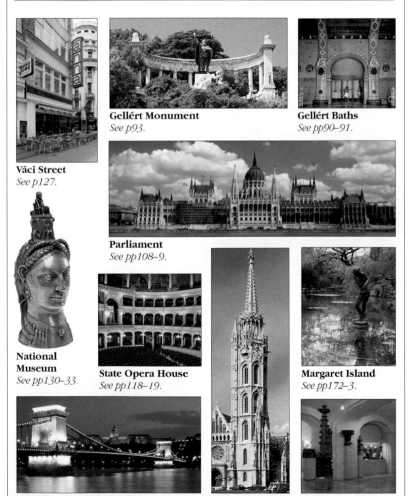

Gellért Monument
See p93.

Gellért Baths
See pp90–91.

Váci Street
See p127.

Parliament
See pp108–9.

National Museum
See pp130–33.

State Opera House
See pp118–19.

Margaret Island
See pp172–3.

Danube and Chain Bridge
See p62.

Mátyás Church
See pp82–3.

National Gallery
See pp74–7.

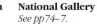

◁ The Neo-Renaissance façade of the City Council Chamber *(see p138)* in the centre of Pest

Budapest's Best: Museums and Galleries

Unlike many other European cities – such as
Paris with the Louvre and Madrid with the
Prado – Budapest does not have a museum
founded from a royal treasury because Hungary
was for so long ruled by foreign powers. In
the early 19th century, however, the modern
aristocracy, backed by an increasingly affluent
middle class, began to take an interest in pre-
serving historic objects for the nation. Today,
there are over 60 museums and galleries in
Budapest, ranging from those with collections
of international significance to others of much
more local interest. For more information on
museums and galleries see pages 40–41.

Museum of Military History
*This museum has interesting
displays illustrating the history of
Hungarian weaponry.*

Hungarian National Gallery
*The Hungarian art
displayed here dates
from the Middle Ages
right through to the
20th century. The
Yawning Apprentice
(1868), by the great
Mihály Munkácsy, is
among the highlights
of the collection.*

**North of
the Castle**

D A N U B E

Castle District

Budapest History Museum
*This Gothic work is one
of the medieval treasures
of the Budapest History
Museum. The oldest ex-
hibits are located in the
original, lower-floor
rooms of the Renais-
sance Royal Palace.*

**Gellért Hill
and Tabán**

0 metres	500
0 yards	500

**Semmelweis Museum of
Medical History**
*Doctor Ignác Semmelweis,
famous for his discovery of how to prevent
puerperal fever, was born in 1818 in the
house where the museum is now situated.*

Ethnographical Museum
Among the exhibits at this museum illustrating the material culture of the Hungarians is this jug, dating from 1864, made by György Mantl. There are also impressive displays concerning tribal societies in other parts of the world.

Museum of Fine Arts
The wonderful Portrait of a Man (c.1565), by Paolo Veronese, is one of many Old Masters in this splendid collection of paintings and sculpture.

Around Parliament

Around Városliget

Central Pest

Jewish Museum
Located in several rooms beside the Great Synagogue, this museum covers the Holocaust in this country and displays religious objects.

Hungarian National Museum
Beautiful frescoes by Károly Lotz and Mór Than decorate the elegant staircase of Hungary's oldest museum.

Museum of Applied Arts
Precious ceramics, porcelain and furnishings are housed in a building that is itself a work of art, surmounted by a magnificent, oriental-style dome.

Exploring the Museums and Galleries

Processional crucifix

Most of the city's museums and galleries are located in historic buildings. These include the spacious chambers of the restored Royal Palace, which in the 1970s and 1980s were designated as the premises of several museums, including the Hungarian National Gallery. The largest museums – including the Hungarian National Museum and Budapest History Museum – also stage temporary exhibitions that are popular with both locals and tourists.

Sculpture of Imre Varga at the gallery named after him *(see p171)*

HUNGARIAN PAINTINGS AND SCULPTURE

There are two important venues that should be on the itinerary of anyone interested in viewing the finest examples of Hungarian art.

At the **Hungarian National Gallery**, seven chronological sections present paintings and sculpture dating from the Middle Ages up until modern times. The sequence begins in the Lapidarium, where fragments of recovered medieval stone sculptures from the castles of the first Hungarian kings are exhibited.

As a rule, very few examples of Gothic and Renaissance art survive in Budapest because of the pillage inflicted by the Turks during their rule. However, a fine collection of altar retables from the 15th and 16th centuries are on display

in the Hungarian National Gallery. In the 19th century, Hungarian painting developed and flourished, at the same time reflecting all the major international modern art movements. The Hungarian style can be seen particularly in the works of Pál Szinyei-Merse, Mihály Munkácsy and László Paál. For sculpture, meanwhile, the main names to look out for are István Ferenczy, Zsigmond Kisfaludi Stróbl and Imre Varga.

It is portraits, rather than paintings and sculpture, that are shown at the **Hungarian National Museum**. These provide a fascinating insight into the country's history.

The **Vasarely Museum** has a collection of 300 works by Hungarian-born artist Victor Vasarely. He moved to Paris in 1930 and became famous as one of the main exponents of the Op Art movement.

EUROPEAN PAINTINGS AND SCULPTURE

Masterpieces by the finest European artists, from medieval times to the modern day, are also divided between two museums in Budapest.

The **Museum of Fine Arts** has a magnificent collection of Italian paintings, dating from the 14th century up to the Baroque period, by masters such as Titian, Antonio Correggio, Paolo Veronese, Giambattista Tiepolo and Jacopo Tintoretto. However, it is the *Esterházy Madonna* (1508) by Raphael, that is the jewel of the Italian collection. Equally splendid is the exhibition of Spanish paintings, which is one of the largest in the world. Works by Goya include *The Water Carrier* (c.1810). There are seven canvases by El Greco and others by Francisco de Zurbarán and Bartolomé Esteban Murillo. Other galleries within the museum represent artists of the Netherlands and Germany, as well as British, French and Flemish masters. The museum also owns more than 100,000 drawings and engravings by the Old Masters, while its modern art collection includes some notable works.

Modern European paintings can also be viewed in the **Ludwig Museum of Contemporary Art**. All the canvases belong to the Peter Ludwig Foundation of Germany. Highly prized works here include two paintings by Pablo Picasso, *Mother and Child* and *Musketeer*.

Pablo Picasso's *Musketeer* (1967), in the Ludwig Collection

The Jewish Museum, located beside the Great Synagogue

HISTORY

The history of Budapest, and that of Hungary as a whole, is illustrated in several museums. Relics from the Roman era can be found at the **Aquincum Museum** and at a handful of museums, including the **Roman Camp Museum**, in Óbuda.

The most important national historic treasures are housed in the **Hungarian National Museum**. The Coronation Mantle, dating back to the 11th century, is included in this collection.

Medieval seals and Gothic statuary are among the exhibits at **Budapest History Museum**. At the **Museum of Military History**, displays chart various Hungarian struggles for liberty, including the 1956 Uprising (see p34).

The **Jewish Museum** has a room covering the Holocaust, as well as many ritual objects. The collection of the **Lutheran Museum**, situated next to the Lutheran Church, includes a copy of Martin Luther's will.

MUSIC

Two of the museums featured in this book, the **Franz Liszt Museum** and the **Zoltán Kodály Museum**, are dedicated to internationally renowned composers. In each case, the setting is the apartment where the composer lived and worked, and on display are the instruments they played, musical scores and photographs.

A more general view of Hungarian music is on offer at the **Museum of Musical History**, located in a Baroque palace on Mihály Táncsics Street. Displays feature the development of instruments and music in the 18th and 19th centuries; a special section is dedicated to Béla Bartók.

ETHNOGRAPHY AND ORIENTAL CRAFTS

Lavish folk costumes, as well as many other everyday items that belonged to the people of the region, can be viewed in the beautiful interiors of the **Ethnographical Museum**. The museum also has a section that focuses on the primitive tribes of Africa, America and, particularly, Asia. It is in Asia that the Hungarians seek their roots as it is from there that the Magyars are thought to have come.

This fascination with the Orient has led to the foundation of two other museums displaying Eastern artifacts. The **Ferenc Hopp Museum of Far Eastern Art** has assorted Indian objects; its Chinese and Japanese collections are displayed at the **Ráth György Museum**.

DECORATIVE ARTS

Housed in an extraordinary building designed by Ödön Lechner (see p56), the **Museum of Applied Arts** gives an impressive overview of the development of crafts from the Middle Ages onwards. Meissen porcelain is exhibited alongside oriental carpets and

Stained-glass window at the Museum of Applied Arts

Hungarian pieces. The display relating to the Secession (see pp54–7) is striking. The museum's permanent collection was founded in 1872. Major exhibitions tend to change each year, while smaller national and foreign displays change monthly.

SPECIALIST MUSEUMS

The **Semmelweis Museum of Medical History** explores the work of a doctor called Ignác Semmelweis, who discovered how to prevent puerperal fever. This affliction had previously been a serious threat for women who had recently given birth. The **Golden Eagle Pharmacy Museum** is situated in a building that first opened as a pharmacy in 1681. Many original fixtures are intact and pharmaceutical exhibits are displayed.

Railway enthusiasts of all ages will appreciate the **Transport Museum** on Hermina Street, with its enormous collection of model trains and exhibits on the evolution of air, sea, road and rail transport.

WHERE TO FIND THE MUSEUMS AND GALLERIES

Aquincum Museum pp162–3
Budapest History Museum p72
Ethnographical Museum p110
Ferenc Hopp Museum, p145
Franz Liszt Museum p144
Golden Eagle Pharmacy Museum, p80
House of Terror Museum, p144
Hungarian National Gallery pp74–7
Hungarian National Museum pp130–33
Jewish Museum pp134
Ludwig Museum, Palace of Arts p156
Lutheran Museum, p128
Museum of Applied Arts pp136–7
Museum of Fine Arts pp146–9
Museum of Military History p85
Museum of Musical History p81
Palace of Arts, p156
Rath György Museum, p145
Semmelweis Museum of Medical History, p95
Transport Museum, p151
Vasarely Museum p171
Zoltán Kodály Museum p144

Budapest's Best: Churches and Synagogues

There are very few medieval and Renaissance churches still standing in Budapest. This is mainly due to the fact that the Turks, during their 150-year rule, turned all churches into mosques, which were later destroyed during the attacks on Buda and Pest by the Christians. The reconstruction of old churches and the building of new ones started in the late 17th century, hence the prevalence of Baroque and Neo-Classical styles.

Capuchin Church
Two Turkish windows remain from the time when this church was used as a mosque, alongside fragments of its medieval walls.

St Anne's Church
Built in the mid-18th century, this is one of the most beautiful Baroque churches in the city. The joined figures of St Anne and Mary decorate the centre of its façade.

North of the Castle

DANUBE

Castle District

Mátyás Church
Romanesque and Gothic styles are both evident in the coronation church of the Hungarian kings. The Neo-Gothic altar dates from the 19th century.

Gellért Hill and Tabán

Rock Church
In the rocky interior of St István's Cave, on the south side of Gellért Hill, the priests of the Pauline order established a church in 1926. It was designed to imitate the holy grotto at Lourdes.

| 0 metres | 500 |
| 0 yards | 500 |

St Stephen's Basilica
A bas-relief by Leó Feszler, representing the Virgin Mary surrounded by Hungarian saints, decorates the main tympanum of St Stephen's Basilica. This imposing church was built between 1851–1905.

Lutheran Church
This Neo-Classical church was completed by Mihály Pollack in 1808. The impressive façade was added half a century later by József Hild.

Around Városliget

Around Parliament

Central Pest

Great Synagogue
Two Moorish-style minarets, each topped by an onion-shaped dome, dominate the exterior of the largest synagogue in Europe.

Franciscan Church
The magnificent 19th-century paintings that decorate the interior of this Baroque church are by Károly Lotz.

Inner City Parish Church
Dating from 1046, this church is Pest's oldest building. A figure of St Florian, the patron saint of fire fighters, was placed on the wall beside the altar after the church survived the great fire of 1723.

Exploring the Churches and Synagogues

Detail on St Elizabeth's Church

Most of the city's churches are found around the centres of Buda and Pest. Only a few sacred buildings of architectural interest are situated on the outskirts of the city. The greatest period of construction took place in the 18th century, after the final expulsion of the Turks. Another phase occurred in the second half of the 19th century, producing two of Budapest's grandest places of worship: St Stephen's Basilica and the Great Synagogue. Religious buildings were neglected after World War II, but thanks to restoration some have now regained their former splendour.

Reconstructed Gothic window of the Church of St Mary Magdalene

MEDIEVAL

Both **Mátyás Church** and the **Inner City Parish Church** date originally from the reign of Béla IV in the 13th century. Glimpses of their original Romanesque style can be seen, although each church was subsequently rebuilt in the Gothic style. After being sacked by the Turks in 1526,

Mátyás Church was given a Baroque interior by the Jesuits who had at that time taken it over. Finally, the church was returned to a likeness of its medieval character between 1874–96, when all Baroque elements were systematically removed and it was given a Neo-Gothic shape.

The **Church of St Mary Magdalene**, built in 1274 in the Gothic style, was almost completely destroyed in 1945. All that remains intact today is the 15th-century tower with its two chapels. A Gothic window has also been rebuilt.

St Michael's Church, founded in the 12th century on Margaret Island, was completely destroyed by the Turks. However, in 1932 it was reconstructed from its original Romanesque plans.

BAROQUE

In the 18th century, 17 churches were built in Pest, Buda and Óbuda, all of them in the Baroque style. The influence of the Italian architectural school is visible in many of them, although only

University Church was built by an Italian architect, Donato Allio. Under Habsburg rule, the leading architects working in the city, András Meyerhoffer, Mátyás Nepauer and Kristóf Hamon, often chose to follow Austrian examples.

University Church and **St Anne's Church** are generally considered to be the most beautiful buildings in the city dating from this era. The former astonishes visitors with its beautifully carved stalls and pulpit, and with the paintings by Johann Bergl adorning its vaults. St Anne's Church has a magnificent Baroque façade and reveals the influence of southern German Baroque in its oval floor plan. Inside, there is a lavish altar and pulpit designed by Károly Bebó.

The **Franciscan Church**, which is situated in the centre of Budapest and dates from 1758, has a wide Baroque nave and a main altar created by Antal Grassalkovich.

The interior of the Servite Church (1725), with its Baroque altar

SPIRES AND DOMES

The Gothic spire belonging to the Church of St Mary Magdalene and the Neo-Gothic spire of Mátyás Church are among Budapest's main landmarks. The twin Baroque towers of St Anne's Church and the soaring spire of the Calvinist Church rise above the Danube in Buda. On the Pest side, the dome of St Stephen's Basilica and the minarets of the Great Synagogue dominate.

Gothic spire of the Church of St Mary Magdalene

Baroque towers of St Anne's Church

Neo-Gothic spire of the Calvinist Church

NEO-CLASSICAL AND HISTORICIST

In 1781, Joseph II passed an edict permitting the building of Protestant churches. The city already had many Catholic churches and Protestant communities now started to build their own places of worship in the prevailing style of the time, Neo-Classicism.

One of the first to go up was the **Lutheran Church**, on Deák Ferenc tér, completed in 1808 by Mihály Pollack, a gifted master of Neo-Classical architecture. The white, ascetic interior of the church, with its two-floor gallery, was ideally suited to the nature of this place of worship. The majesty and simplicity of the Neo-Classical style corresponded with the more austere nature of Protestant belief. József Hild, another master of the style, later extended the church. He added the portico with its Doric columns, linking the church with the presbytery and a school. The complex as a whole is one of the best examples of Neo-Classical architecture in Budapest.

On a more modest scale is the **Calvinist Church**, built in the Neo-Gothic style between 1893–6.

When plans for it were drawn up by József Hild in 1845, **St Stephen's Basilica** was intended to be the pinnacle of Neo-Classical architecture. However, several delays, including the collapse of its dome at one point, meant

that the realization of the original design was impossible. Following Hild's death in 1867, Miklós Ybl continued the project. He departed from Hild's plan, incorporating Renaissance-style features. The Basilica was finally completed by a third architect, József Kauser, in 1905.

LATE 19TH- AND 20TH-CENTURY

The two most stunning synagogues in Budapest were designed by Viennese architects in the second half of the 19th century.

Ludwig Förster constructed the **Great Synagogue** in Byzantine-Moorish style in 1859 and Otto Wagner, an important Secession architect (*see pp54–7*), realized one of his first projects in 1872. This was the **Orthodox Synagogue** on Rumbach utca, which also incorporated Moorish ideas. Closely linked to the Secession style is the Hungarian National Style, based on an idiosyncratic combination of ethnic motifs and elements from folk art. This style is most visible in two churches by Hungarian architects. Ödön Lechner, the originator of the Hungarian National Style, completed **Kőbánya Parish Church**, on the outskirts of Budapest, in 1900. Meanwhile, Aladár Árkay built **Városliget Calvinist Church** in 1913. These two churches display a striking combination of

The Byzantine-Moorish interior of the Great Synagogue

colourful ceramics, Eastern-style ornamentation and also Neo-Gothic elements.

WHERE TO FIND THE CHURCHES AND SYNAGOGUES

Buda Lutheran Church
  p84
Calvinist Church *p100*
Capuchin Church *p100*
Chapel of St Roch *p135*
Church of St Mary Magdalene
  p85
Cistercian Church of
  St Imre *p157*
Franciscan Church *p139*
Great Synagogue
  pp134–5
Inner City Parish Church
  pp124–5
Józsefváros Parish Church
  p155
Kőbánya Parish Church
  p156
Lutheran Church *p128*
Mátyás Church *pp82–3*
Orthodox Synagogue,
  Jewish Quarter *p134*
Rock Church *p92*
St Anne's Church
  pp102–3
St Elizabeth's Church *p101*
St Michael's Church,
  Margaret Island *p173*
St Stephen's Basilica
  pp116–17
Serbian Church *p138*
Servite Church *p128*
Tabán Parish Church *p95*
Újlak Parish Church
  p154
University Church *p139*
Városliget Calvinist Church,
  Városligeti Avenue *p144*

Baptismal font at the Lutheran Church

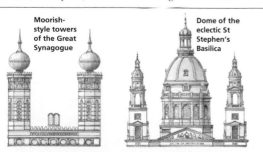

Moorish-style towers of the Great Synagogue

Dome of the eclectic St Stephen's Basilica

Budapest's Best: Palaces and Historic Buildings

Detail on the façade of Károly Palace

Budapest boasts historic buildings and palaces in a broad range of architectural styles. The majority represent the Neo-Classicism, Historicism and Secession of the 19th and early 20th centuries, when a dynamic development of the capital took place. All but a few Gothic and Renaissance details were lost in the destruction of Buda and Pest by Christian troops in 1686, but some examples of its Baroque heritage remain. This map gives some highlights, with a more detailed look on pages 48–9.

Royal Palace
This palace has a turbulent history dating back to the 13th century. Its present form, however, reflects the opulence of the 19th century. Today the palace houses some of the city's finest museums.

North of the Castle

Castle District

Houses on Vienna Gate Square
This charming row of four houses was built in the late 18th and early 19th centuries on the ruins of medieval dwellings. The houses are adorned with decorative motifs in the Baroque, Rococo and Neo-Classical styles.

Gellért Hill and Tabán

Sándor Palace
The original friezes that decorated this 19th-century palace were recreated by Hungarian artists as part of its restoration. The palace is now the headquarters of the President of the Republic of Hungary.

Várkert Casino
This Neo-Renaissance pavilion was built by Miklós Ybl (see p119) as a pump house for the Royal Palace. It now houses the luxurious Várkert Casino.

Hungarian Academy of Science
The façade of the academy is adorned with statues by Emil Wolff and Miklós Izsó, symbolizing major fields of knowledge: law, natural history, mathematics, philosophy, linguistics and history.

Gresham Palace
Now housing a Four Seasons Hotel, this splendid example of Secession design was built in 1905–7 by Zsigmond Quittner.

Around Parliament

Around Városliget

Central Pest

0 metres	500
0 yards	500

Pallavicini Palace
Gustáv Petschacher built this Neo-Renaissance mansion on Kodály körönd in 1882. The inner courtyard was copied from the Palazzo Marini in Milan.

DUBE

Ervin Szabó Library
The grand, Neo-Baroque palace that now houses this library was originally built in 1887 for the Wenckheims, a family of rich industrialists.

Péterffy Palace
This plaque, commemorating a flood of 1838, was placed on one of the few Baroque mansions that remain in Pest. The house was built in 1756.

Exploring the Palaces and Historic Buildings

Little more than fragments remain of Budapest's Gothic and Renaissance past. However, some Baroque buildings have survived in Buda's Castle District and Víziváros. Neo-Classicism, on the other hand, has a much wider presence; there are many apartment buildings, palaces and secular monuments built in this style, especially around the old fortification walls of Pest on the eastern side of the Danube. Historicism dominated the architecture of the second half of the 19th century. It played a vital role in the enlargement of the city as it expressed and celebrated the optimism of the era.

BAROQUE PALACES AND BUILDINGS

Many buildings in the Castle District and neighbouring Víziváros, around Fő utca, have retained their original Baroque façades. The main entrance of the **Hilton Hotel**, formerly a 17th-century Jesuit college, is a fine example.

Other outstanding instances of this style are the four houses on **Vienna Gate Square, the Batthyány Palace** on Parade Square and the **Erdődy Palace** on Mihály Táncsics Street, now the Museum of Musical History.

The **Zichy Palace** in Óbuda is a splendid Baroque edifice, and the buildings of the former **Trinitarian Monastery**, now the Kiscelli Museum, stand as significant models of the style.

There are only two Baroque monuments remaining in Pest. The **Péterffy Palace**, a mansion that stands below the current street level, dates from 1755. Pest's other Baroque edifice was, however, the first to be built in either Buda or Pest. The huge complex of the **Municipal County Offices**, formerly a hospital for veterans of the Turkish wars, was constructed by the Italian master Anton Erhard Martinelli. It was greatly admired by Empress Maria Theresa, who declared it to be more beautiful than the Schönbrunn Palace in Vienna.

Façade of the Gross Palace, built by József Hild in 1824

NEO-CLASSICAL PALACES AND BUILDINGS

Neo-classicism, influenced by ancient Greco-Roman design, was popular in the first half of the 19th century as it reflected the confidence of this period of national awakening and social reform. Many monumental Neo-Classical structures were produced, including the **Chain Bridge**, built in 1839–49. The leading Neo-Classical architect was Mihály Pollack, who built the **Hungarian National Museum**.

Two stunning Neo-Classical palaces deserve particular mention – **Sándor Palace** in Buda and **Károlyi Palace** in Pest. The first stands on Castle Hill, by the top of the funicular railway, and impresses visitors with its harmonious elegance. The second, now housing the Petőfi Literary Museum, gained its present form in 1834 after considerable reconstruction.

A group of particularly attractive Neo-Classical houses is situated on **József Nádor Square**. Some of their features, such as the pillars, projections and tympanums, merit individual attention.

In 1808, the Embellishment Commission was set up by the Austrian architect János Hild to develop Pest. He and his son, József Hild, who built the **Gross Palace** in 1824, were both involved in the general restoration of the city. Having studied architecture in Rome, they created many splendid Italianate buildings.

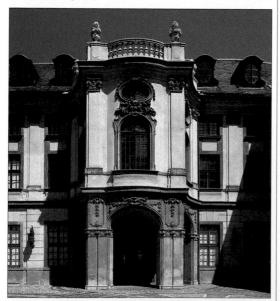

The outstanding Baroque façade of Erdődy Palace, Museum of Musical History

HISTORICIST PALACES AND BUILDINGS

In the second half of the 19th century, Historicism took precedence over Neo-Classicism. After the unification of Buda, Óbuda and Pest in 1873, Historicism had a significant influence on the city's architectural development. In this period Budapest gained an eclectic mix of new apartment buildings and palaces, as Historicist architects sourced different genres for inspiration. Miklós Ybl, whose work includes the **State Opera House** and the expansion of the **Royal Palace**, looked to the Renaissance, while Imre Steindl designed a Neo-Gothic **Parliament** (to which a Neo-Renaissance dome was added). Frigyes Schulek's **Fishermen's Bastion** features

Sculptures on the Vigadó façade

Neo-Gothic and Neo-Romanesque designs.

The **Vigadó**, a concert hall built by Frigyes Feszl between 1859 and 1864, is often thought of as the most magnificent Historicist building, with its façade richly decorated with relief sculptures and busts of the great Hungarians. However, the complex of three French-style, Neo-Renaissance palaces, Festetics, Károly and Esterházy, in **Mihály Pollack Square**, is also considered by many to be a fine example.

The **Drechsler Palace** in Andrássy út is a marvellous model of Neo-Renaissance design, while **Páris Nagyáruház** (Paris department store) features Lotz's Hall, stunningly decorated with paintings and gold. The twin apartment buildings known as the **Klotild Palaces** incorporate Spanish-Baroque

Beautiful Neo-Baroque interior of the New York Palace

motifs and can be admired near the Elizabeth Bridge. Perhaps one of the most extravagant examples of Historicism is the Neo-Baroque **New York Palace** by Alajos Hauszmann, which has a luxurious interior of marble columns and rich colour.

DECORATIVE FEATURES

The façades of many palaces and buildings still display the rich sculptural decoration characteristic of the various styles of architecture prevalent in the city. These features include coves, cartouches, finials, relief sculptures and ornamental window frames.

Regrettably, almost no original Gothic detail remains in Budapest, but niches or pointed arches decorating old apartment buildings can be spotted in the Old Town.

Baroque elements are still evident in fine buildings such as the Zichy Palace and the Erdődy Palace. Decorative Neo-Classical features,

such as borders and tympanums, are visible on many buildings from the first half of the 19th century.

A finial with cartouche on the Neo-Classical Károlyi Palace

Relief on the Hungarian National Bank (1905)

Cove detail on the façade of the Staffenberg House

Ornate window frame adorning the house at 21 József Nádor utca

WHERE TO FIND THE PALACES AND HISTORIC BUILDINGS

Batthyány Palace *p80*
Chain Bridge *pp62–3*
Drechsler Palace *p115*
Erdődy Palace *p81*
Ervin Szabó Library *p135*
Fishermen's Bastion *p80*
Gellért Hotel *pp90–91*
Golden Stag House *p95*
Gresham Palace *p114*
Gross Palace *p126*
Hilton Hotel *p81*
Hungarian Academy of Sciences *p114*
Hungarian National Museum *pp130–33*
József Nádor Square *p126*
Károlyi Palace *p139*
Klotild Palaces *p127*
Mihály Pollack Square *p135*
Municipal County Offices *p128*
New York Palace *p129*
Parliament *p108–9*
Péterffy Palace *p122*
Royal Palace *pp70–71*
Sándor Palace *p73*
State Opera House *pp118–19*
Várkert Kiosk, Miklós Ybl Square *p95*
Vienna Gate Square *p84*
Zichy Palace *p171*

Budapest's Best: Baths and Pools

Budapest is one of the great spa cities of Europe. Numerous natural hot springs pour out over 80 million litres (18 million gal) of richly mineralized water every day. The greatest concentrations of natural springs are situated in Óbuda, near Gellért Hill, on the Buda embankment near Margaret Bridge and on Margaret Island itself. Baths have existed here since Roman times, but it was the Turks who best exploited Budapest's natural resources. Today there is a wide choice of therapeutic and recreational baths and pools.

Palatinus Strand
With seven swimming pools, hot springs, water slides and a restful location on Margaret Island, this spa is perhaps the most beautiful in Europe.

Hajós Olympic Pool
The pool was designed by Alfréd Hajós, who won Hungary's first Olympic gold medal for swimming in 1896, and on the walls of the swimming hall hang gold-engraved marble plaques citing Hungary's numerous Olympic champions.

North of the Castle

Castle District

DANUBE

Lukács Baths
These 19th-century thermal pools are open all year round, and attract both tourists and the locals of Budapest.

Gellért Hill and Tabán

Király Baths
Dating from 1566, these baths were built by the Turks and have many authentic Ottoman features.

Rác Baths
The original Ottoman pool and cupola are hidden behind a 19th-century façade, and adjacent to a luxury hotel.

BUDAPEST AT A GLANCE

Dagály Strand
Half a century ago, it was discovered that the water in a pond on this site was beneficial to health. Now a huge open-air complex of swimming pools, children's pools and a hydrotherapy and fitness centre is located here.

Around Városliget

Széchenyi Baths
This spa has the hottest thermal baths in Budapest and the added attraction of magnificent Neo-Baroque architecture. The warmth of the water is such that these baths are popular even during the winter season.

Around Parliament

Central Pest

Rudas Baths
The most famous of the Turkish baths were constructed during the 16th century. They still have an original Ottoman cupola and octagonal pool.

Gellért Baths
The main indoor swimming pool of this popular Buda spa delights bathers with its beautiful Secession interior, marble columns and colourful mosaics.

0 metres	500
0 yards	500

Exploring Budapest's Baths and Pools

Heated deep inside the earth, the waters of the mineral-rich hot springs which bubble up through fractures in the rocky hills of Buda and Óbuda have given the city a Turkish-influenced bathing culture which has survived even the rigours of Communism. A total of 31 spa-water pools and thermal baths, with entrance fees kept low by generous government subsidies, make taking the waters an unmissable treat for visitors to Budapest.

THE TURKISH INFLUENCE

Although the ruins of Roman thermal baths dating from the 2nd century AD have been found in Óbuda, it was only under the Ottoman occupation of the 16th–17th centuries *(see pp 26–7)*, that the bathing culture really took hold in Budapest.

Four stunning Turkish-built baths, some of the few remaining examples of Ottoman architecture in Budapest, are still in operation. The **Rudas**, the **Rác**, the **Király** and the **Komjády** (formerly known as Császár) were all built in the 16th century, and are constructed on a single model. A marble staircase leads into a chamber containing a dome-topped, octagonal thermal pool, which is surrounded by smaller dome-covered pools at temperatures ranging from icily cold to roastingly hot. The most beautiful are almost certainly the Rudas Baths, followed closely by the Király Baths. The Rác Baths have undergone extensive restoration work and reopened in 2010 as a spa

and hotel complex. The Császár Baths have been absorbed into the Lukács Baths complex *(see below)*.

Many of the city's newer baths are for both men and women. The Turkish baths, however, remain resolutely single-sex, though the Rudas Baths are open to men during the week and women at weekends; and the Rác and the Király Baths open to men and women on alternate days. There is no need to wear a bathing suit, as a small apron is provided.

AFTER THE TURKS

The late 19th and early 20th century was a new golden age for Budapest *(see pp32–3)*, and saw the building of a number of splendid baths. Many have spring-water swimming pools attached.

Opened in 1894 the Neo-Classical **Lukács Baths** offer two outdoor swimming pools as well as the 16th-century Császár thermal pool. The **Széchenyi Baths**, opened 20 years later on the Pest side of the river, make up the biggest

bathing complex in Europe. In addition to the usual indoor thermal pools, they also boast outdoor thermal and swimming pools, complete with sun terraces. With the hottest spa-water in the city, the outdoor thermal pool is popular even in the depths of winter.

As well as the thermal pools, Budapest's bathing establishments also include a steam room and sauna. Professional massages are almost always available for a small fee. Some places offer medicinal mud and sulphur baths. You will be invited to take a shower, and a short nap in the rest room before you leave.

Swim in style at the Rudas Baths

SPA HOTELS

Nestling at the foot of Gellért Hill, the beautiful **Gellért Hotel and Baths Complex** is the oldest and most famous of a handful of luxury hotels in Budapest offering swimming and thermal pools, steam rooms, sauna and massage. The renowned Gellért Baths were opened to the general public in 1927, and include a fabulous, marble-columned indoor swimming pool, a labyrinth of thermal baths (one set for men and one for women), single-sex nudist sun-bathing areas and an outdoor swimming pool. A hugely popular wave machine is switched on in the latter for ten minutes in every hour.

A second wave of spa-hotels were built in the 1970s and '80s. Set on Margaret Island, the modern, squeaky-clean and extremely luxurious **Danubius Health Spa Resort Margitsziget**, is linked by an underground passage to the older **Danubius Grand Hotel Margitsziget**. In addition to the usual range of baths and pools, treatments

Outdoor pool at the Gellért Hotel and Baths Complex

include manicure, pedicure and a solarium. The late 1980s saw the arrival of two new spa hotels, the **Danubius Health Spa Resort Helia** not far from the Pest riverbank and, on the Buda side, the **Ramada Plaza Budapest**, facing north towards Óbuda. The spa hotel Continental Zara *(see p185)*, in the 7th district, shares the magnificent façade of Hungária Fürdő (Hungarian Baths).

Széchenyi Baths, the biggest bathing complex in Europe

THE HEALING WATERS

The citizens of Budapest are great believers in the social, psychological and medical benefits of the thermal baths. Office workers will often visit the public baths as early as 6am, to prepare for the day. Others like to visit at the end of the day, at 6pm, to relax, recharge and work up an appetite. Most of the baths employ staff who can offer advice on the most appropriate pools and special treatments for a particular ailment. The warm, mineral-rich spa waters are extremely good for general relaxation. They can also be helpful in the relief of a number of specific complaints, including post-traumatic stress, joint and muscle damage, rheumatism and menstrual pain. Budapest's public baths are also extremely good value for money. Admission is usually no more than 500 forints, and a 15-minute massage costs the same. All baths employ expert masseurs.

An ornamental tap, typical of the architectural detail found in Budapest's historic baths

SWIMMING AS SPORT

Many Hungarians are excellent swimmers, and the country has achieved great success in competitive water sports. In addition to Budapest's many recreational pools, sports pools include the **Hajós Olympic Pool** complex on Margaret Island. The complex consists of three sports pools, two outdoor, including one at full Olympic size, and one indoor. The pools are used for professional training, but are also open to the public. Together with the Komjádi Béla Swimming Stadium on Árpád Fejedelem útja, the Hajós Olympic Pool is the place to go to see professional swimming, diving or water polo.

A DAY AT THE STRAND

Designed as a complete bathing day out, the strands of Budapest are a phenomenon not to be missed. A total of 12 strands in the city testifies to their popularity. Outdoor swimming and thermal pools are surrounded by grassy sunbathing areas. Trampolines and ping-pong and pool tables offer a change from the water, while ice creams, beers and hot dogs add to the summer-holiday atmosphere.

The lovely **Palatinus Strand**, set in a large area of parkland on Margaret Island, boasts seven outdoor pools, some thermal and some for swimming, complete with water slides and wave machines. Just east of the Pest river bank is the vast, modern **Dagály Strand** complex. Built after World War II, it includes 12 pools, with space for up to 12,000 people. Other strands worth visiting include **Római Strand** in Óbuda in the north of the city. Three pools have been carefully rebuilt here, on the site of some Roman baths, together with a not-so-Roman water chute. To the north of the city at Csillaghegy on the HÉV suburban train line, **Csillaghegy Strand** consists of four pools set in picturesque grounds, and includes a popular south-facing nudist beach.

Sculpture at the Római Strand

WHERE TO FIND THE BATHS AND POOLS

Danubius Grand Hotel Margitsziget *pp173, 189*
Danubius Health Spa Resort Helia *p189*
Danubius Health Spa Resort Margitszieget *p189*
Gellért Hotel and Baths Complex *pp90–91*
Hajós Olympic Pool *p172*
Király Baths *p101*
Komjádi Baths *p101*
Lukács Baths *p101*
Palatinus Strand *p172*
Rác Baths *p95*
Ramada Plaza Budapest *p189*
Rudas Baths *p93*
Széchenyi Baths *p151*

Budapest's Best: the Secession

Visitors to Budapest are often impressed by its wonderful late 19th and early 20th century buildings. The majority of these are found in central Pest and around Városliget; Buda was already developed at this stage and so boasts few examples. The

Decoration on a house on Áldás utca

movement started among groups of avant-garde artists in Paris and Vienna, from where the term Secession comes. In Budapest, the Secession style was also the inspiration for the development of the Hungarian National Style. Further details are given on pages 56–7.

The School on Rose Hill
Károly Kós and Dezső Zrumeczky used motifs from village houses in Transylvania to give this building on Áldás utca its character.

Woman with a Birdcage (1892)
This painting by József Rippl-Rónai has an atmosphere of mystery and intimacy typical of Hungarian art of the period. It hangs in the Hungarian National Gallery (see p77) today.

North of the Castle

Castle District

DANUBE

Ironwork Gates of Gresham Palace
Two peacocks, a classic Secession motif, decorate the wrought-iron gates of the Four Seasons Gresham Palace hotel. The building was built by Zsigmond Quittner and the Vágó brothers between 1905–7.

Gellért Hill and Tabán

Gellért Hotel and Baths Complex
Supported by flattened arches, a glass roof adds to the tranquil appeal of this hall in the famous spa at the Gellért Hotel. The Secession interiors created here are among the most splendid to be found in Budapest.

Post Office Savings Bank
The main staircase of this building by Ödön Lechner is embellished by fine balusters, rounded lamps and decorative windows.

Entrance to the Zoo
Kornél Neuschloss made ingenious use of elements of Hindu architecture when he created this amusing gate guarded by two elephants.

Around Parliament

Around Városliget

Central Pest

Sipeky Balázs Villa
Built between 1905–6, this fanciful villa is perhaps the most representative example of the Secession style in Budapest. It was designed by Ödön Lechner.

Philanthia Florist's
This extraordinary florist's is on Váci utca. The interior of the shop is in the Secession style, while the building itself is Neo-Classical.

0 metres	500
0 yards	500

Apartments on Bartók Béla utca
Ödön Lechner was the leading exponent of the Hungarian National Style. He built this apartment block, with a studio for himself on the fourth floor, in 1899. The block is at 40 Bartók Béla utca.

Exploring Secession Budapest

The Secession movement crossed artistic boundaries, influencing painting and the decorative arts as well as architecture. Colourful, sometimes fantastical designs are instantly recognizable hallmarks of the style. The Hungarian National Style drew heavily on this general trend, incorporating motifs from old Hungarian architecture, particularly that of Transylvania, folk art and even oriental features.

Secession ornament

Vase designed by István Sovának, in the Museum of Applied Arts

József Rippl-Rónai's *Woman in White-Spotted Dress* (1899), in the Hungarian National Gallery

PAINTINGS AND DRAWINGS

The main exponents of Secession art in Hungary were József Rippl-Rónai, János Vaszary and Lajos Gulácsy.

Rippl-Ránai spent many years in Paris, at the time when the Art Nouveau movement was beginning to flourish. *Lady in Red*, which he painted in 1899, was the first Hungarian painting in the Secession style. Many of Rippl-Rónai's works are on show in the **Hungarian National Gallery**. There is also a tapestry version of *Lady in Red* in the **Museum of Applied Arts**.

The work of János Vaszary was heavily influenced by both German and English art. His finest pictures, which include *Golden Age* and the mysterious *Adam and Eve*, can be admired in the Hungarian National Gallery. Lajos Gulácsy was influenced by the Pre-Raphaelite movement and his pictures are often symbolic. Many of his paintings, too, can now be viewed in the Hungarian National Gallery. The artists' colony based at Gödöllő was an important centre for painters working in the new Secession style. Its founder, Aladár Körösfői-Kriesch, created numerous works, including a fresco entitled *The Fount of Youth* which decorates the **Franz Liszt Academy of Music**.

DECORATIVE ARTS

New ideas in the decorative arts at this time were closely related to architectural developments. Ödön Lechner began to make use of colourful ceramic tiles, acquired from his father-in-law's brickyard in Pécs in southern Hungary, not only to cover roofs but also as a decorative element.

The owner of this brickyard, Vilmos Zsolnay, discovered an innovative method of glazing tiles and ceramics. This proved so successful that the the brickyard was turned into a factory specializing in their production. Zsolnay's factory eventually made most of the vivid and distinctive ceramic tiles covering the Secession buildings in the city.

Zsolnay also employed leading designers to create ranges of dinner services, vases and candlesticks. For these he was awarded the Gold Medal of the Legion of Honour at the World Fair in Paris. And at an exhibition organized in 1896, to mark the millennial anniversary of the Hungarian Kingdom, the

ÖDÖN LECHNER (1845–1914)

The most influential architect of the Hungarian Secession, Ödön Lechner trained in Berlin before completing his apprenticeship by working in both Italy and France. His quest was to create an identifiable Hungarian National Style, by combining Secession motifs with elements from Hungarian folk art and Hindu designs. The colourful ceramics that he often used became his signature. Among the buildings that Budapest owes to him are the Museum of Applied Arts, the Post Office Savings Bank and the Institute of Geology. Behind the ingenious and fantastical exteriors, Lechner's buildings have wonderfully simple, functional and superbly lit interiors.

Portrait of Lechner

factory introduced its most beautiful pieces.

Gresham Palace and the **Gellért Hotel and Baths Complex** are among the many buildings in the city that are embellished by ornamental wrought-iron gates, gratings and banisters that incorporate Secession motifs.

INTERIOR DECORATION

Among the interiors of the era, those of the **New York Palace** *(see p129)* are a real jewel. Decked out in the best materials, including bronze and marble, they retain the splendour of their original, Neo-Baroque form.

Also worth visiting are the **Hungarian National Bank** and the **Post Office Savings Bank**, with their furnished secure rooms and ornate door and window frames. The interior of Philanthia, a florist's shop, is another wonderfully

Window created by Miksa Róth, at the Hungarian National Bank

preserved example of decor from the Secession.

Exhibitions of attractive Secession furniture are a feature of both the Museum of Applied Arts and also the **Nagytétény Palace**.

ARCHITECTURE

Hungarian architecture of the *fin de siècle* is characterized not only by decorative forms using glazed ceramics, but, more fundamentally, by the implementation of modern technical solutions. Reinforced concrete, steel and glass were used together, and large, light-filled interiors were often achieved. The central hall of the Museum of Applied Arts is a fine example of this.

Aside from Ödön Lechner, the most important of the Hungarian Secession architects, others who contributed significant buildings in the prevailing style included Béla Lajta, Aladár Árkay, Károly Kós and István Medgyaszay.

Béla Lajta, a pupil of Lechner, designed the **Rózsavölgyi Building**, with its distinctive geometrical ornamentation, on Martinelli tér. Also among his buildings is the extraordinary former **Jewish Old People's Home**, at No. 57 Amerikai út. With sophisticated ornamental details based on folk designs, **Városliget Calvinist Church** was the creation of Aladár Árkay. Károly Kós was a highly original member of this set. Fascinated by the traditional architecture of Transylvania, he trawled the whole of that region, making drawings of the village churches and manor houses he encountered. Motifs from these buildings were later transferred to the aviary at Budapest's **Zoo** and the houses of the **Wekerle Estate**.

Frieze on the Rózsavölgyi Building

WHERE TO FIND SECESSION BUDAPEST

Franz Liszt Academy of Music *p129*
Gellért Hotel and Baths Complex *pp90–91*
Gresham Palace *p114*
Hungarian National Bank, Liberty Square *p110*
Hungarian National Gallery *pp74–7*
Institute of Geology *p154*
Museum of Applied Arts *pp136–7*
Nagytétény Palace *p161*
New York Palace *p129*
Philanthia Florist's, Váci Street *p55*
Post Office Savings Bank *p111*
Turkish Bank *p128*
Városliget Calvinist Church *p144*
Wekerle Estate *p157*
Zoo *p150*

A Secession cabinet, displayed in the Museum of Applied Arts

DECORATIVE MOTIFS

Stylized folk motifs derived from embroidery and also oriental patterns were often employed in Budapest's decorative arts during this period. Secession motifs such as feline forms, based on Viennese and Parisian examples, also feature.

Sunflower motif adorning the Post Office Savings Bank

Secession lettering on the sign of Philanthia Florist's

Colourful mosaic at No. 3 Aulich utca

BUDAPEST THROUGH THE YEAR

S et in the middle of Hungary, Budapest enjoys a continental climate with sharply defined seasons, each of which brings its own attractions, from traditional feast days to cultural and sporting events. Historically a centre of cultural, and especially musical, activity, Budapest continues the tradition with many musical events including the

Spring Festival logo

Spring Festival, an international celebration of classical music and ballet, and the smaller Budapest Contemporary Music Weeks, devoted to contemporary classical music. Many hotels and tourist offices provide a programme of the events taking place in the city, as do the English-language weeklies.

SPRING

Spring makes a welcome return to the city in March, with sunshine and fresh, warm days. Budapest turns green and the Spring Festival sees the arrival of some of the year's first tourists.

MARCH

The Spring Uprising *(15 Mar)*. A public holiday marks the day in 1848 when the youth of Buda, led by the poet Sándor Petőfi, rebelled against the Habsburg occupation of Hungary *(see pp30–31)*. Thousands of people take to the streets to lay wreaths and light eternal flames, wearing the national colours of red, white and green. There are speeches and street theatre, especially in front of the Hungarian National Museum *(see pp130–33)*.
Spring Festival *(the last two weeks of Mar–mid-Apr)*.
www.festivalcity.hu

Parade in the Castle District during the Spring Festival

Top national and international musicians gather for several weeks of music and dance in churches and concert halls all over the city. The emphasis of the festival is on the classical tradition, but also in evidence are folk music and dance, as well as pop and jazz.

APRIL

Easter is an important religious event in Hungary and the Easter service is well worth attending in one of the city's many churches. On the

morning of Easter Monday young men spray their female friends and relatives with perfume or water, a ritual which is said to keep the recipients beautiful until the following year. Painted eggs are given in return.
Festival Celebrating the Day of Dance *(end Apr)*.
www.nemzetitancszinhaz.hu
The National Dance Theatre and the Association of Hungarian Dance Artists organize this festival every year, with participation from top Hungarian dance groups and foreign guest artists.
Horse Racing *(Sun, Apr–Oct)*. April sees the beginning of the flat-racing season. Place your bets at the busy and charmingly down-at-heel Kincsem Park race course on Albertsirai út.
Budapest International Book Festival.
www.bookfestival.hu
Organised in co-operation with the Frankfurt Book Fair, this festival is the most important event in Hungary's publishing year, both for the publishing industry and for the general public. It is held at a modern venue in the Millenáris Park.

MAY

May Day *(1 May)*. No longer a compulsory display of patriotism, May Day celebrations take place in public parks all over the city and involve craft markets, street performers and sausage and beer tents. A dip in the local thermal bath or swimming pool *(see pp50–53)*, is another popular May Day activity.

Springtime magnolia blossom on Margaret Island

AVERAGE DAILY HOURS OF SUNSHINE

Sunshine Chart
Budapest enjoys some of the sunniest weather in Europe, with an average of eight hours of sunshine each day from April to September. During the sticky months of high summer (June, July and August), the Buda hills provide a welcome refuge from the heat of the city.

SUMMER

The long hot days of summer are made for relaxing on Margaret Island or sun-bathing at some of the city's twelve open-air pools.

JUNE

Open-Air Theatre Festival *(Jun–Aug).* **www**.szabadter.hu
Margaret and Óbuda Islands provide two of the major venues for this summer-long, open-air arts festival.
Budapesti Búcsú *(last weekend in Jun).* **www**.festivalcity.hu
A mixture of music, dance and theatre celebrates the departure from Hungary of Soviet troops in 1991.
Danube Carnival International Cultural Festival
www.dunaart.com
Various venues host music and dance events.

Formula One racing in the Hungarian Grand Prix

JULY

Hungarian Grand Prix *(end Jul).* **www**.hungaroring.hu
The biggest event in the Hungarian sporting calendar takes place east of the city, at Mogyoród race track.
Chain Bridge Festival *(weekends in Jul & Aug).*
www.festivalcity.hu
A lively series of free events including concerts and dance,

traditional arts and crafts, street theatre, parades and activities for children.
Concerts in St Stephen's Basilica *(Jul–Aug).* Monday evening organ concerts in the city's largest church *(see pp116–17)* provide a perfect opportunity to study the lavish interior decoration of this extraordinary building.
Budafest Summer Music Festival *(Jul or Aug).*
www.viparts.hu
Look out for the series of shows at the State Opera House *(see pp118–19).*

AUGUST

St István's Day *(20 Aug).*
St István, the patron saint of Hungary, is celebrated with mass in St Stephen's Basilica followed by a huge procession. The day ends with fireworks on Gellért Hill *(see pp88–9)* and along the Danube.
Sziget Festival *(Aug).*
www.sziget.hu
Ten stages and a camp site are set up on Óbuda Island for this popular week-long festival of rock, folk and jazz, which features top bands such as REM and Iron Maiden.

Fireworks on Gellért Hill to celebrate St István's Day

AVERAGE MONTHLY RAINFALL

Rainfall Chart
Budapest is a fairly dry city. Typically, it rains very heavily for two days or so, then is dry for several weeks. June is the wettest month, with May, July, August and November only slightly dryer. Autumn is usually the dryest season, while there is some snowfall in the winter months.

AUTUMN

One of the many treats of autumn in Budapest is a visit to one of the city's fruit and vegetable markets, where you can feast your eyes on a vast array of jewel-coloured vegetables and fruit.

SEPTEMBER

Jewish Summer Cultural Festival *(end Aug–beg Sep)*.
www.zsidonyarifesztival.hu
This multicultural festival includes a Jewish book fair, an Israeli film festival, art exhibitions, and cuisine presentations.

Budapest Wine Festival *(2nd week of Sep)*.
www.aborfesztival.hu Wine makers set up stalls for wine tastings and folk dancing on Buda's Castle Hill *(see p69)*.

OCTOBER

Plus Budapest International Marathon and Running Festival *(Oct)*. There is a marathon, a relay race, a mini-marathon and a family running competition for participants. Concerts and events are held for spectators.
Autumn Festival *(mid-Oct)*. Several weeks of contemporary film, dance and theatre at venues across the city.

A colourful food stall in one of Budapest's covered markets

Vienna-Budapest Super Marathon Running Competition. This competition aims, through sport, to strengthen ties between central European countries, particularly those of Austria and Hungary, and celebrates open European borders.
www.szupermarathon.hu.
Remembrance Day *(23 Oct)*. This is a national day of mourning to remember the 1956 Uprising, when 2,500 people were killed by Soviet tanks and 200,000 fled the country. Wreaths are laid in Municipal Cemetery *(see pp158–9)*, on the grave of the executed leader Imre Nagy *(see p34)*.

NOVEMBER

Budapest Christmas Fair *(26 Nov–24 Dec)*. The Budapest Christmas Market transforms Vörösmarty Square into a festive marketplace, where Hungarian artists and craftsmen display their work and national dishes are served.
www.budapestinfo.hu

Performers take part in the Open-Air Theatre Festival

AVERAGE MONTHLY TEMPERATURE

Temperature Chart
Seasons in Budapest are sharply defined. Daytime temperatures rise rapidly from March onwards. By June, the thermometer often reaches 30°C (90°F) and more. September sees cooler weather, with temperatures falling rapidly to lows of well below freezing in January.

WINTER

Despite the cold weather, winter can be an exciting time to visit Budapest. Open-air ice-skating takes place from November, roast-chestnut sellers appear on the streets and a Christmas tree is erected in Mihály Vörösmarty Square.

DECEMBER

Budapest Christmas Fair *(26 Nov–24 Dec)* continues.
Silver and Gold Sunday *(2nd-to-last Sunday before Christmas)*. All the city's shops stay open for this Sunday of serious Christmas shopping.
Mikulás *(6 Dec)*. On *Mikulás*, or St Nicholas Day, children leave their shoes on the window sill for Santa Claus to fill.
Christmas *(25–26 Dec)*. The city shuts down for two days. Celebrations begin with a family meal of carp on 24 Dec.
Szilveszter *(31 Dec)*. Budapest celebrates in style on New Year's Eve, with music in Vörösmarty and Nyugati Squares until dawn, and fireworks. Public transport is free and runs all night.

Seeing in the New Year, a stylish affair in Budapest

Christmas tree in Mihály Vörösmarty Square

JANUARY

New Year's Gala Concert *(1 Jan)*. This cheerful occasion is an excellent way to start the new year. Outstanding Hungarian and foreign artists perform excerpts from European opera and musicals, providing a lively evening of music. **www**.viparts.hu

FEBRUARY

Hungarian Film Festival *(early Feb)*. This two-day celebration of Hungarian film has been run by the *Magyar Filmszemle* since 1969, to attract funding to a hard-pressed industry. Many films are subtitled. **www**.szemle.film.hu
Masked-Ball Season *(Feb)*. Budapest forgets the cold weather to welcome the coming of spring, and the arrival of the *farsang*, or fancy dress masked-ball season. The climax of the season is the spectacular Opera Ball and a masked procession, on the last Saturday and Sunday before Lent, respectively. **www**.operabal.com

Shopping for Christmas

PUBLIC HOLIDAYS

Public holidays mainly follow the Christian calendar. Two days mark cataclysmic events in Magyar history, while one, May Day, is a reminder of the country's socialist past.

New Year's Day (1 Jan)
Spring Uprising (15 Mar)
Easter Sunday (variable)
Easter Monday (variable)
Whit Monday (variable)
May Day (1 May)
St István's Day (20 Aug)
Remembrance Day (23 Oct)
All Saints' Day (1 Nov)
Christmas Day (25 Dec)
Boxing Day (26 Dec)

Margaret Bridge to Elizabeth Bridge

Crown on Elizabeth Bridge

A trip on a river boat along the Danube provides a unique panorama of the city. Most major cities have a river at their heart. However, the Danube historically played a different role in this case, for centuries dividing the separate towns of Buda and Pest. Several road bridges today link the two halves of the modern city. All had to be reconstructed this century after being destroyed by the retreating Nazi army towards the end of World War II.

Centenary Monument
This monument was erected in 1973 to commemorate the centenary of the joining of Buda, Óbuda and Pest as Budapest. It stands on Margaret Island (see pp172–3), close to Margaret Bridge.

MARGIT I

St Francis's Wounds Church
This Baroque church, built for an order of nuns, has its front facing away from the Danube. The hospital and hostel run by the sisters face the river (see p101).

BATTHYÁNY
TÉR

Mátyás Church
With medieval origins, the tower of this church has been rebuilt several times. It overlooks the Hilton Hotel and the Fishermen's Bastion (see pp82–3).

St Anne's Church
can be recognized by its twin, slender Baroque towers.

LÁNCHÍ

Chain Bridge was built between 1839–49 at the inititiative of Count István Széchenyi *(see p31)*. It was designed by Englishman William Tierney Clark and built by the unrelated Scot, Adam Clark. The bridge extends for 380 m (1,250 ft), supported by two towers – a major feat of engineering at the time.

KEY

M	Metro
⚓	River boat boarding point

Margaret Bridge was built by the French engineer Ernest Gouin, at the point where the Danube becomes a single body once more after dividing to flow around Margaret Island. The bridge is distinguished by its unusual chevron shape. It was erected in 1872–6, and between 1899–1900 access from the bridge onto the island was added. Sculptures by Adolphe Thabart decorate its columns.

Parliament
The magnificent, high dome of the Parliament building is visible from every point along the Danube in central Budapest (see pp108–9).

Much of the eastern bank of the river is characterized by fairly uniform architecture. Variation is provided here by the dome and towers of St Stephen's Basilica *(see pp116–17).*

0 metres	300
0 yards	300

Hungarian Academy of Sciences

Elizabeth Bridge, constructed in 1897–1903, was at that time the longest suspension bridge in the world. Destroyed in 1945, it was rebuilt in its current form by Pál Sávolya.

The bridgehead of Chain Bridge is guarded by two vast stone lions sculpted by János Marschalkó. According to an anecdote János was heartbroken because he forgot to give the lions any tongues, so he drowned himself in the river. In fact the lions do have tongues, but they are not easily visible.

Piers, from which passenger cruises operate daily in summer, are spaced frequently along the Danube in central Budapest.

Elizabeth Bridge to Lágymányosi Bridge

Like Paris, Budapest has fully exploited the opportunities given by its river. The most important and beautiful buildings of Buda and Pest crowd along the banks of the Danube. These include the Royal Palace, churches, historic palaces and the Gellért Hotel and Baths Complex.

VÖRÖSMARTY TÉR M

FERENCIEK TERE

ERZSÉBET HÍD

SZABADS

Royal Palace
The monumental Habsburg Royal Palace that once occupied this spot was destroyed during World War II, then reconstructed to reveal defensive walls and royal chambers that date from the Middle Ages (see pp70–71) .

Inner City Parish Church
This church was built in the 12th century on the ruins of Roman Contra Aquincum's walls. The spot was, from early times, an important place for crossing the river (see pp124–5).

Gellért Hotel and Baths Complex
The architects of this hotel maximized its river façade to make it as imposing as possible (see pp90–91) .

Technical University
The university campus occupies almost the entire space between Liberty Bridge (Szabadság híd) and Lágymányosi híd (see p157).

The embankment walk near Petőfi Bridge extends along the length of the Danube on the Pest side. It is a favourite place to meet or to go for a stroll, and is lined by smart hotels and restaurants.

Little Princess (1989), perched by the tram rails on the Pest side of the Danube, was so liked by Charles, Prince of Wales, on his visit here that he invited its designer, László Marton, to exhibit in London.

Liberty Bridge was built between 1894–9 by Hungarian engineer János Feketeházy. Opened by Emperor Franz Joseph, it initially took his name. All its original features were retained when it was rebuilt after World War II: on top of the bridge there are legendary Hungarian *turul* birds and royal crests.

Corvinus University
Formerly a customs' headquarters, this building has an elegant façade decorated with ten allegorical figures. These are the work of German sculptor August Sommer (see p138).

Lágymányosi Bridge, Budapest's most modern and southernmost bridge was built in 1995 for a planned world exhibition that never happened. It carries traffic on a ring road bypassing the city centre.

KÁLVIN TÉR
PETŐFI HÍD
LÁGYMÁNYOSI HÍD

Exterior detailing of Ödön Lechner's Post Office Saving Bank *(see p111)* ▷

BUDAPEST AREA BY AREA

CASTLE DISTRICT 68–85

GELLÉRT HILL AND TABÁN 86–95

NORTH OF THE CASTLE 96–103

AROUND PARLIAMENT 104–119

CENTRAL PEST 120–139

AROUND VÁROSLIGET 140–151

FURTHER AFIELD 152–163

EXCURSIONS 164–167

THREE GUIDED WALKS 168–175

CASTLE DISTRICT

The hill town of Buda grew up around its castle and Mátyás Church from the 13th century onwards. At 60 m (197 ft) above the Danube, the hill's good strategic position and natural resources made it a prize site for its earliest inhabitants. In the 13th century, a large settlement arose when, after a Tartar invasion, King Béla IV decided to build his own defensive castle and establish his capital here. The reign of King Mátyás Corvinus in the 15th century was an important period in the evolution of

Bas-relief on the Eugene of Savoy monument

Buda, but it suffered neglect under Turkish rule during the next century and was then destroyed by Christian troops. The town was reborn, however, and assumed an important role during the 18th and 19th centuries under the Habsburgs. By the end of World War II, the Old Town had been almost utterly destroyed and the Royal Palace burnt to the ground. Since the war the Royal Palace and Old Town have been reconstructed, restoring the original allure of this part of the city.

SIGHTS AT A GLANCE

Churches
Buda Lutheran Church **17**
Church of St Mary Magdalene **18**
Mátyás Church pp82–3 **11**

Museums and Galleries
Budapest History Museum **1**
Golden Eagle Pharmacy Museum **8**
House of Hungarian Wines **10**
Hungarian National Gallery pp74–7 **4**

Labyrinth of Buda Castle **22**
Museum of Military History **20**
Széchenyi National Library **2**

Historic Streets and Squares
András Hess Square **14**
Holy Trinity Square **9**
Lords' Street **21**
Mihály Táncsics Street **15**
Parade Square **5**
Parliament Street **19**
Vienna Gate Square **16**

Palaces, Historic Buildings and Monuments
National Dance Theatre **7**
Fishermen's Bastion **12**
Hilton Hotel **13**
Mátyás Fountain **3**
Sándor Palace **6**

GETTING THERE

Castle Hill and the Old Town are largely pedestrianized, but there are a couple of car parks where cars and coaches can park for a fee, allowing visitors to walk to the area. Bus 16 runs from Clark Ádám tér to Dísz tér, and a funicular railway (Sikló) connects Clark Ádám tér to Szent György tér. There is also a minibus (Várbusz) that arrives at this square from Moszkva tér to the north.

0 metres 400
0 yards 400

KEY

■ Street-by-Street map
   See pp70–71

■ Street-by-Street map
   See pp78–9

ℹ Tourist information

◁ **Fountain on Tárnok utca in the Old Town**

Street-by-Street: The Royal Palace

The Royal Palace has borne many incarnations during its long life. Even now it is not known exactly where King Béla IV began building his castle, though it is thought to be nearer the site of Mátyás Church (see pp82–3). The Holy Roman Emperor Sigismund of Luxembourg built a Gothic palace on the present site, from which today's castle began to evolve. In the 18th century, the Habsburgs built their monumental palace here. The current form dates from the rebuilding of the 19th-century palace after its destruction in February 1945. During this work, remains of the 15th-century Gothic palace were uncovered. Hungarian archeologists decided to reveal the recovered defensive walls and royal chambers in the reconstruction.

An ornamental gateway, dating from 1903, leads from the Habsburg Steps to the Royal Palace. Nearby, a bronze sculpture of the mythical turul bird guards the palace. This statue marks the millennium anniversary of the Magyar conquest in 896.

★ **Mátyás Fountain**

In the northwest courtyard of the Royal Palace stands the Mátyás Fountain. It was designed by Alajos Stróbl in 1904 and depicts King Mátyás Corvinus and his beloved Ilonka ❸

Lion Gate, leading to a rear courtyard of the Royal Palace, gets its name from the four lions that watch over it. These sculptures were designed by János Fadrusz in 1901.

TIMELINE

1255 First written document, a letter by King Béla IV, refers to building a fortified castle	c.1400 Sigismund of Luxembourg builds an ambitious Gothic palace on this site	1541 After capturing Buda, the Turks use the Royal Palace to stable horses and store gunpowder	1719 The building of a small palace begins on the ruins of the old palace, to a design by Hölbling and Fortunato de Prati	1881 Miklós Ybl (see p119) begins programme to re-build and expand the Royal Palace
1200	**1400**	**1600**	**1800**	
c.1356 Louis I builds a royal castle on the southern slopes of Castle Hill		1686 The assault by Christian soldiers leaves the palace completely razed to the ground	1849 Royal Palace is destroyed again, during an unsuccessful attack by Hungarian insurgents	Turul *bird*
1458 A Renaissance palace evolves under King Mátyás		1749 Maria Theresa builds a vast palace comprising 203 chambers		

The dome of the Royal Palace was rebuilt in the Neo-Classical style after the Neo-Baroque dome, designed by Alajos Hauszmann, was destroyed in the razing of the palace in World War II.

LOCATOR MAP
See Street Finder, maps 1, 3 & 9

NORTH OF THE CASTLE

CASTLE DISTRICT

GELLÉRT HILL AND TABÁN

0 metres 50

0 yards 50

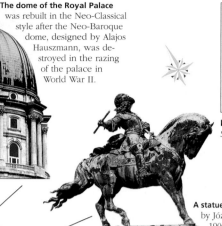

A statue of Prince Eugene of Savoy, by József Róna, was unveiled in 1900. It commemorates the battle of Zenta in 1697, victory at which was a turning point in the Turkish war. The bas-reliefs on the base depict scenes from the battle. Two Turkish prisoners cower by the feet of the prince.

★ **Hungarian National Gallery**
Artworks depicting Hungary's turbulent history are displayed here. Periods of both foreign domination and patriotic home rule are brought to life through the gallery's extensive collection ❹

KEY

– – – Suggested route

BUILDING THE ROYAL PALACE

In the 15th century, a Gothic Royal Palace was built on the site, but it was rebuilt in the Renaissance style by King Mátyás in 1458. After the Turkish occupation it was razed and reborn on a smaller scale. Maria Theresa further developed the palace and it was rebuilt again after World War II to a design originally completed in 1905.

■ 15th century ■ 1749
■ 1719 ■ 1905

STAR SIGHTS

★ Hungarian National Gallery

★ Mátyás Fountain

Renaissance majolica floor from the 15th century, uncovered during excavations on Castle Hill and displayed at the Budapest History Museum

Budapest History Museum **①**

Budapesti Történeti Múzeum

Szent György tér 2. **Map** 3 C1 (9 B4). **Tel** 487 88 00. 5, 16, 78, Várbusz. ☐ Mar–Oct: 10am–6pm Tue–Sun; Nov–Feb: 10am–4pm Tue–Sun. www.btm.hu

Since the unification of Budapest in 1873, historic artifacts relating to Hungary's capital have been collected. Many are now on show at the Budapest History Museum (also called the Castle Museum).

During the rebuilding that followed the destruction suffered in World War II, chambers dating from the Middle Ages were uncovered in the south wing (wing E) of the Royal Palace. They provide an insight into the character of a much earlier castle within today's Habsburg reconstruction.

These chambers, including a tiny prison cell and a chapel, were recreated in the basement of the palace. They now house an exhibition, the Royal Palace in Medieval Buda, which displays authentic weapons, seals, tiles and other early artifacts.

On the ground floor, Budapest in the Middle Ages illustrates the evolution of the town from its Roman origins to a 13th-century Hungarian settlement. Also on this level are reconstructed defensive walls, gardens, a keep, and

Gothic Statues from the Royal Palace dating from the 14th and 15th centuries. The statues were uncovered by chance in the major excavations of 1974. On the first floor, Budapest in Modern Times traces the history of the city from 1686 to the present.

Széchényi National Library **②**

Nemzeti Széchényi Könyvtár

Szent György tér 6. **Map** 3 C1 (9 B4). **Tel** 224 37 00. 5, 16, 78, Várbusz. ☐ 10am–9pm Tue–Sat. www.oszk.hu

A magnificent collection of books has been housed, since 1985, in wing F of the Royal Palace, built in 1890–1902 by Alajos Hauszmann and Miklós

Corviniani illuminated manuscript in the Széchényi National Library

Ybl *(see p119)*. Previously, the library was part of the Hungarian National Museum *(see pp130–33)*.

Among the library's most precious treasures is the *Corviniani*, a collection of ancient books and manuscripts that originally belonged to King Mátyás Corvinus *(see p24–5)*. His collection was one of the largest Renaissance libraries in Europe. Also of importance are the earliest surviving records in the Hungarian language, dating from the early 13th century.

The library was established by Count Ferenc Széchenyi in 1802. He endowed it with 15,000 books and 2,000 manuscripts. The collection now comprises five million items; everything that has been published in Hungary, in the Hungarian language or that refers to Hungary is here.

Crest on the Lion Gate in a courtyard at the Royal Palace

Mátyás Fountain **③**

Mátyás Kút

Royal Palace. **Map** 1 C5 (9 B3). 5, 16, 78, Várbusz.

The ornate fountain in the northwest courtyard of the Royal Palace (situated between wings A and C) was designed by Alajos Stróbl in 1904. The statue is dedicated to the great Renaissance king, Mátyás, about whom there are many popular legends and fables.

The Romantic design of the bronze sculptures takes its theme from a 19th-century ballad by the poet Mihály Vörösmarty. According to the tale, King Mátyás, while on a hunting expedition, meets a beautiful peasant girl, Ilonka, who falls in love with him. This representation shows King Mátyás disguised as hunter, standing proudly with his kill. He is accompanied by his chief hunter and several hunting dogs in the central part of the fountain. Beneath the left-hand columns sits Galeotto Marzio, an Italian court poet, and the figure of the young Ilonka is beneath the columns on the right.

In keeping with the romantic reputation of King Mátyás, a new tradition has grown up concerning this statue. The belief is that anyone wishing to revisit Budapest should throw some coins into the fountain to ensure their safe return.

The western elevation of the Neo-Classical Sándor Palace

Hungarian National Gallery ❹

Magyar Nemzeti Galéria

See pp74–7.

Batthyány Palace on Parade Square retains its original Baroque façade

Parade Square ❺

Dísz Tér

Map 1 B5 (9 A3). 🚌 Várbusz.

Parade Square is named after the military parades that were held here in the 19th century. At the northern end of the square is the Honvéd Monument, built in 1893 by György Zala. It honours and commemorates those who died during the recapture

of Buda from Austria in the 1848 revolution.

The house at No. 3 was built between 1743–8, by József Giessl. This two-floor Baroque palace was the home of the Batthyány family until 1945. Although the building has been frequently remodelled, the façade remains intact.

A few houses on Parade Square incorporate medieval remains. Such houses can be seen at Nos. 4–5 and No. 11, built by Venerio Ceresola. The former has seat niches dating from the 13th century.

Sándor Palace ❻

Sándor Palota

Szent György tér 1–3. **Map** 1 C5 (9 A3). 🚌 5, 16, 78, Várbusz. ⬤ to the public. **www**.keh.hu

By the top of the cog-wheel railway stands the grand Neo-Classical mansion, Sándor Palace. It was commissioned in 1806 by Count Vincent Sándor from architects Mihály Pollack and Johann Aman.

The bas-reliefs that decorate the palace are the work of Richárd Török, Miklós Melocco and Tamás Körössényi. The decoration on the western elevation depicts Greek gods on Mount Olympus. The southern elevation shows Count Sándor being knighted and the northern elevation features a 1934 sculpture of Saint George by Zsigmond Kisfaludi Stróbl.

Sándor Palace functioned as the prime minister's official residence from 1867 to 1944,

when it was severely damaged in World War II. The building has been completely restored, and it is now the official residence of the President of Hungary.

National Dance Theatre ❼

Nemzeti Táncszínház

Színház utca 1–3. **Map** 1 C5 (9 A3). **Tel** 201 44 07 or 375 86 49. 🚌 5, 16, 78, Várbusz. **Box Office** 🕙 1–6pm Mon–Sun. **www**.nemzetitancszinhaz.hu

An unlikely assortment of institutions have stood on this site. The church of St John the Evangelist, founded by King Béla IV, stood here in the 13th century. This church was then used as a mosque under Ottoman rule, and in 1686 it was demolished by the Christian armies that retook the city. In 1725 the Carmelite order built a Baroque church in its place and this building was first converted into a theatre in 1786, during the reign of Emperor Joseph II. Farkas Kempelen, a famous Hungarian designer added a Rococo façade and seats for 1,200 spectators. The first plays were in German and it was not until 1790 that any work was staged in Hungarian. Beethoven's concert of 1800 is commemorated by a plaque.

The building was damaged in World War II and restored in 1978. The National Dance Theatre now performs here.

Hungarian National Gallery ❹

Established in 1957, the Hungarian National Gallery houses a comprehensive collection of Hungarian art from medieval times to the 20th century. Gathered by various groups and institutions since 1839, these works had previously been exhibited at the Hungarian National Museum (see pp130–33) and the Museum of Fine Arts (see pp146–9). The collection was moved to the Royal Palace (wings B, C and D) in 1975. There are now six permanent exhibitions, presenting the most valuable and critically acclaimed Hungarian art in the world.

Sisters by Erzsébet Schaár

St Anne Altarpiece (c.1520)
Elaborately decorated, this folding altarpiece from Kisszeben is one of the Gothic highlights in the gallery.

First floor

Madonna of Toporc (c. 1420)
This is a captivating example of medieval wood sculpture in the Gothic style. It was originally crafted for a church in Spiz (now part of Slovakia).

Madonna of Bártfa (1465–70)
This painting of a Madonna and Child is from a church in Bártfa (now in Slovakia). It is thought to have been painted in Cracow, Poland.

★ **The Visitation** (1506)
This painting by Master MS is a delightful example of late Gothic Hungarian art. It is a fragment of a folding altarpiece from a church in Selmecbánya in modern-day Slovakia.

Ground floor

Main entrance

STAR EXHIBITS

★ The Visitation

★ Picnic in May

KEY

- ☐ Stone sculptures and artifacts
- ☐ Gothic works
- ☐ Late Gothic altarpieces
- ☐ Renaissance and Baroque works
- ☐ 19th-century works
- ☐ Early 20th-century works
- ☐ Temporary exhibitions

Luischen *(1884)*
One of the earliest works by the sculptor Alajos Stróbl is this marble bust of Luischen on display on the first floor.

Second floor

Woman Bathing *(1901)*
This painting by Károly Lotz, better known for his frescoes, is the best example of Neo-Classical painting in Hungary. It reflects his fascination for the work of the French painter, Ingres.

GALLERY GUIDE
Early stone and Gothic exhibits are on the ground floor. Late Gothic, Renaissance and Baroque works and 19th-century works share the first floor. Works from the 20th century are on the second floor, and temporary exhibits are displayed on the top floor.

Third floor

Churning Woman *(1872–73)*
This painting is by Mihály Munkácsy, Hungary's most internationally celebrated artist. The tiredness of the woman's features with her worn hands show the reality of a life of poverty.

★ Picnic in May *(1873)*
The captivating colours of this landscape scene were painted by Pál Szinyei Merse. He was influenced by two works of Edouard Manet and Claude Monet, both entitled Le Déjeuner sur l'Herbe.

Exploring the Hungarian National Gallery

Secession poster

The works are displayed in six permanent exhibitions and give a thorough insight into Hungarian art from the early Middle Ages to the present day. Although one-and-a-half centuries of Turkish occupation and wartime destruction interrupted the development of Hungarian art, the birth of national pride in the 19th century allowed a new indigenous style to develop. Among the most interesting are the Hungarian paintings of the late 19th century, when a greater diversity of styles came to the fore.

The Habsburg Crypt, with the sarcophagus of Palatine Archduke Joseph

THE LAPIDARIUM

On the ground floor, to the left of the main entrance, is a display of stone objects discovered during the reconstruction of the Royal Palace *(see p70)*. Called the Lapidarium, it includes sculptures and fragments of architectural features, such as balustrades and windows, that decorated the royal chambers during the Angevin and Jagiełło eras *(see p18)*. The most valuable exhibit, however, is a sculpture of King Béla III's head, which dates from around 1200.

Also in this first section are two marble bas-reliefs of King Matthias and his wife Beatrice, by an unknown Renaissance master from Lombardy.

The second section exhibits late Gothic and Renaissance artifacts from other palaces in Hungary. There are pillars and balustrades from the palace at Visegrád and bas-reliefs from a chapel in Esztergom.

GOTHIC WORKS

A collection of painted panels, sculptures and fragments of altar decoration is opposite the Lapidarium. Note, however, the image of the *Madonna of Bártfa*, which is a rare complete example from the Gothic period.

The sculptures of the "Beautiful Madonnas" are executed in the Soft Style. This style

King's head sculpted from red marble

is characterized, as its name suggests, by the sentimental and gentle imagery of the Madonna playing with the Christ child.

The Visitation, a magnificent late Gothic work by Master MS, is, in fact, only the main section of an altar; the other pieces are now in Esztergom *(see p164).*

RENAISSANCE AND BAROQUE WORKS

The exhibition begins with a still life by Jakab Bogdány (1660–1724) and portraits by Ádám Mányoki (1673–1757) *(see p28),* who actually settled outside Hungary. As a result of the powerful influence of the Habsburgs during this period *(see pp28–9),* Baroque art was overwhelmingly dominated by Austrian artists. Painters such as Joseph Dorfmeister and Franz Anton Maulbertsch and sculptors Georg Raphael Donner and Philipp Jakob Straub were the acknowledged masters. Jan Kupetzky's portraits are also exemplary models of this era. The sculptures by Donner and the sacred paintings of Dorfmeister conclude this section of the gallery.

LATE GOTHIC ALTARPIECES

One of the star exhibits of this collection is the imposing late Gothic altarpiece. Arranged in the Great Throne Room, the majority of these vast altarpieces date from the 15th and early 16th centuries.

The Great Throne Room, displaying the collection of folding altarpieces

Architecturally these altarpieces are pure Gothic, while adorned with sculptures and paintings revealing a Renaissance influence. This is evident in the altars of St Anne and St John the Baptist from a church in Kisszeben (now Sabinov in Slovakia), which date from 1510–16. The most recent altarpiece dates from 1643 and is from the church of Our Lady Mary in Csíkmenaság.

Christmas (1903) by Jozsef Rippl-Ronai, a leading Hungarian artist

Bertalan Székely's *Women of Eger* (1867), depicting the Turkish wars

19TH-CENTURY WORKS

The wonderful collection of works from this period reflects the rise of fine art in Hungary in the 19th century. Historicist art developed during this period. Among those distinguishing themselves in particular were Gyula Benczúr and Bertalan Székely, who produced the epic works *The Recapture of Buda in 1686* (1896) and *Women of Eger* (1867) respectively. The latter depicts the women of the town defending the Castle of Eger against the Turks.

Viktor Madarász's work *The Mourning of László Hunyadi* (1859) refers to the execution of László Hunyadi by the Habsburgs in 1457. It alludes, too, to the execution of many Hungarians after the crushing of the uprising against Austria in 1849 *(see pp30–31).*

European developments in fine art can also be seen in Hungarian painting from the late-19th century. The influence of Impressionism, for example, is best seen in Pál Szinyei Merse's *Picnic in May* (1873).

Hungarian Realism is expressed in the work of László Paál and Mihály Munkácsy, the latter being widely regarded as the country's greatest artist. Paintings by Munkácsy which deserve particular attention are *The Yawning Apprentice* (1869), *Dusty Road* (1874), the still life *Flowers* (1881), and – most notably – *Woman Carrying Brushwood* (1870), which was painted at the zenith of his career.

It is also worth spending a few moments seeing the paintings of the Neo-Classical artists. The work of Károly Lotz, who is perhaps better known for his frescoes that can be seen on walls and ceilings around Budapest, is exhibited here.

20TH-CENTURY WORKS

Examples of work from the Secession era through to Expressionism and Surrealism, and even contemporary art are exhibited here. They provide a comprehensive review of 20th-century Hungarian art.

József Rippl-Rónai studied in France with Gaugin and Toulouse-Lautrec. His work shows the influence of the Secession style in *The Palace in Körtyvélyes* and *Woman with a Birdcage*. But one of the most engaging artists from the early-20th century is Károly Ferenczy whose *The Paintress* (1903) exemplifies the serene qualities of his work.

Tivadar Kosztka Csontváry is an artist whose work did not follow any conventional style but was greatly admired,

even by Pablo Picasso. One of his paintings in particular, the *Ruins of the Greek Amphitheatre in Taormina* (1905), captures his abstract interpretation of the world.

The Eight, a group of artists who set up the first Hungarian avant-garde school, were active between the two world wars. Notable examples of their work are *Young Girl with a Bow* by Béla Czóbel, *Woman Playing a Doublebass* by Róbert Berény, *The Oarsmen* by Ödön Marffy, *Landscape* by Lajos Tihanyi and *Riders at the Edge* by Károly Kernstok.

The best works of Hungarian Expressionism can be seen in the paintings *Along the Tracks*, *For Bread* and *Generations,* by Gyula Derkovits.

Among the sculptures on display, the most interesting are *Raising Oneself* and *The Sower,* by Ferenc Medgyessy, and *Standing Girl,* by Béni Ferenczy. The exhibition is completed by a section featuring contemporary artists.

The Paintress by Károly Ferenczy (1903), a typically peaceful work

Street-by-Street: the Old Town

Bas-reliefs on a house on Fortuna utca

Buda's old town has been a barometer of Hungary's changing fortunes. It developed, to the north of the Royal Palace, from the 13th century. Under kings such as Sigismund, it flourished, and wealthy German merchants set up shops in Lords' Street (Úri utca) to supply the court. The area was later destroyed by the Turks and again by their evictors. It was rebuilt after World War II, but genuine relics can be hunted out in its cobbled streets and squares.

Mihály Táncsics Street
During the Middle Ages, this street was inhabited by Jews. A museum at No. 26, on the site of an old synagogue, displays finds such as tombstones ⓯

The State Archive of Historic Documents, located in a Neo-Romanesque building, houses items that were transferred to Buda in 1785 from the former capital of Hungary, Bratislava.

Surviving tower of the Church of St Mary Magdalene

Defensive walls

0 metres   50
0 yards   50

Labyrinth of Buda Castle
This 1,200-metre long system of dungeons, springs, caves and cellars that runs beneath Castle Hill also includes exhibitions on early Hungarian history and legend ㉒

★ Lords' Street
Once the homes of aristocrats and merchants, the houses on Úri utca have medieval foundations. Many have Gothic details and peaceful courtyards ㉑

KEY
– – – Suggested route

LOCATOR MAP
See Street Finder, maps 1 & 9

★ Mátyás Church
Although with much earlier parts, this church is mainly a Neo-Gothic reconstruction dating from 1874–96. A picturesque vestibule on the church's southern façade covers an original Gothic portal dating from the 14th century ⑪

Fishermen's Bastion
Designed by Frigyes Schulek in 1895, this fantastical structure never had the role of a defensive building, despite its name. It serves instead as a viewing terrace. The conical towers are an allusion to the tribal tents of the early Magyars ⑫

This statue of St Stephen, or István, the first crowned king of Hungary *(see pp22–3)*, was erected in 1906. Its pedestal includes a bas-relief showing scenes from the king's life.

Holy Trinity Square
In 1713, after an epidemic of the plague was overcome, a column representing the Holy Trinity was raised in this square ⑨

Golden Eagle Pharmacy Museum
From the 18th century a pharmacy called "Under the Golden Eagle" traded in this medieval house, now a museum ⑧

The House of Hungarian Wines offers wine-tasting tours detailing the wine-growing regions of Hungary.

STAR SIGHTS
★ Lords' Street (Úri utca)
★ Mátyás Church

Golden Eagle Pharmacy Museum ❽

Aranysas Patikamúzeum

Tárnok utca 18. **Map** 1 B5 (9 A2).
Tel 375 97 72. 🚌 16, Várbusz.
🕐 mid-Mar–Oct: 10:30am–5:30pm
Tue–Sun; Nov–mid-Mar:
10:30am–3:30pm Tue–Sun.

This pharmacy was opened in 1688 by Ferenc Ignác Bösinger and traded under the name the "Golden Eagle" from 1740. It moved to this originally Gothic building, with its Baroque interior and Neo-Classical façade, in the 18th century. The museum opened here in 1974. It displays pharmaceutical items from the Renaissance and Baroque eras.

Holy Trinity Square ❾

Szentháromság Tér

Map 1 B4 (9 A3).
🚌 Várbusz from Moszkva tér.

This square is the central point of the Old Town. It takes its name from the Baroque Holy Trinity Column, originally sculpted by Philipp Ungleich in 1710–13, and restored in 1967. The column commemorates the dead of two outbreaks of the plague, which struck the inhabitants of Buda in 1691 and 1709.

The pedestal of the column is decorated with bas-reliefs by Anton Hörger. Further up are statues of holy figures and at the summit is a magnificent composition of the figures of the Holy Trinity. The central section of the column is decorated with angelic figures surrounded by clouds.

Buda's Old Town Hall, a large Baroque building with two courtyards, was also built on the square at the beginning of the 18th century. It was designed by the imperial court architect, Venerio Ceresola, whose architectural scheme incorporated the remains of medieval houses. In 1770–74 an east wing was built, and bay windows and a stone balustrade with Rococo urns, by Mátyás Nepauer, were also added. The corner niche, opposite Mátyás Church, houses a small statue by Carlo Adami of Pallas Athene.

At No. 6 is the House of Hungarian Wines with an extensive selection of wines to sample and buy.

House of Hungarian Wines ❿

Magyar Borok Háza

1014 Szentháromság tér 6.
Map 1 B4 (9A2). **Tel** 212 10 31.
🚌 Várbusz from Moszkva tér.
🕐 noon–8pm daily. 🎫
www.magyarborokhaza.hu

At No. 6 on the square, opposite the Hilton Hotel, the House of Hungarian Wines represents all 22 of the country's wine-producing regions and stocks approximately 700 different wines. Some 55 of these are made available to visitors for tasting. The wider aim of the House is to stock the complete range of wines produced in Hungary in a single location, to aid appreciation and understanding. The House also aims to raise the profile of Hungarian wines both nationally and internationally.

Mátyás Church ⓫

Mátyás Templom

See pp82–3.

A statue of St István stands in front of the Fishermen's Bastion

Fishermen's Bastion ⓬

Halászbástya

Szentháromsag tér. **Map** 1 B4 (9 A2).
🚌 Várbusz from Moszkva tér.
🕐 9am–11pm daily. 🎫 Mar–Oct.

Frigyes Schulek designed this Neo-Romanesque monument to the Guild of Fishermen in 1895. It occupies the site of Buda's old defensive walls and a medieval square where fish was once sold. The bastion is a purely aesthetic addition to Castle Hill and boasts beautiful views of the Danube and Pest. In front of it stands a statue of St István, the king who introduced Hungary to Christianity.

Buda's Old Town Hall, its clock tower crowned with an onion-shaped dome, on Holy Trinity Square

Bas-relief depicting King Mátyás on the façade of the Hilton Hotel

Hilton Hotel ⑬
Hilton Szálló

Hess András tér 1–2. **Map** 1 B4 (9 A2). **Tel** 889 66 00. 🚌 Várbusz. ♿ **www.**hilton.com

Built in 1976, the Hilton Hotel is a rare example of modern architecture in the Old Town. Controversial from the outset, the design by the Hungarian architect Béla Pintér combines the historic remains of the site with contemporary materials and methods.

From 1254 a Dominican church, to which a tower was later added, stood on this site, followed by a late-Baroque Jesuit monastery. The remains of both these buildings are incorporated into the design. For example, the remains of the medieval church, uncovered during excavations in 1902, form part of the Dominican Courtyard, where concerts and operettas are staged during the summer season.

The main façade comprises part of the façade of the Jesuit monastery. To the left of the entrance is St Nicholas's Tower. In 1930, a replica of the 15th-century German bas-relief of King Mátyás, considered to be his most authentic likeness, was added to this tower.

András Hess Square ⑭
Hess András Tér

Map 1 B4 (9 A2).
🚌 Várbusz frov m Moszkva tér.

This square is named after the Italian-trained printer who printed the first Hungarian book, *Chronica Hungarorum*, in a printing works at No. 4 in 1473. The house was rebuilt at the end of the 17th century as an amalgamation of three medieval houses, with quadruple seat niches, barrel-vaulted cellars and ornamental gates.

The former inn at No. 3 was named the Red Hedgehog in 1696. This one-floor building has surviving Gothic and Baroque elements.

The square also features a statue by József Damkó of Pope Innocent XI, who was involved in organizing the armies who recaptured Buda from the Turks. It was built to mark the 250th anniversary of the liberation, in 1936.

Hedgehog on the façade of No. 3 András Hess Square

Mihály Táncsics Street ⑮
Táncsics Mihály Utca

Map 1 B4 (9 A2). 🚌 Várbusz.
Museum of Musical History
Tel 214 67 70. ⬜ 10am–4pm Tue–Sun. **www.**ztl.hu

Standing at No. 7 is Erdődy Palace, built in 1750–69 for the Erdődy family by Mátyás

Nepauer, the leading architect of the day. It features outstanding Baroque façades. Like many houses on this street, it was erected on the ruins of medieval houses.

In 1800, Ludwig van Beethoven, who was then giving concerts in Budapest, resided here for a short period.

The palace now houses the Museum of Musical History and the Béla Bartók archives. A permanent exhibition illustrates musical life in Budapest from the 18th to 20th centuries, and includes the oldest surviving Hungarian musical instruments. The Royal Mint stood on the site of No. 9 during the Middle Ages, and, in 1810, the Joseph Barracks were built here. These were later used by the Habsburgs to imprison leaders of the 1848–9 uprising, including Mihály Táncsics himself.

An original mural has survived on the façade of the house at No. 16, which dates from around 1700. It depicts Christ and the Virgin Mary surrounded by saints. The bas-reliefs on the gateway are, however, from a Venetian church.

Relics of Buda's Jewish heritage can be found at Nos. 23 and 26. The remains of a 15th-century synagogue stand in the garden of the mansion at No. 23. During archeological excavations, tombs and religious items were also found in the courtyard of No. 26.

The Museum of Musical History on Mihály Táncsics Street

Mátyás Church ⑪

The Parish Church of Our Lady Mary was
built on this site between the 13th and
15th centuries. Some of the existing
architectural style dates from the reign of
Sigismund of Luxembourg, but its name
refers to King Mátyás Corvinus, who
greatly enlarged and embellished the
church. Much of the original detail was
lost when the Turks converted the church
into the Great Mosque in 1541. During the
liberation of Buda the church was almost
totally destroyed, but was rebuilt in the
Baroque style by Franciscan Friars. The
church sustained more damage in 1723,
and was restored in the Neo-Gothic style
by Frigyes Schulek in 1873–96. The crypt
houses the Museum of Ecclesiastical Art.

Rose Window
*Frigyes Schulek faithfully repro-
duced the medieval stained-glass
window that was in this position
during the early Gothic era.*

Béla Tower
*This tower is named after
the church's founder,
King Béla IV. It has
retained several of its
original Gothic features.*

★ Baroque Madonna
*According to legend, the original
statue was set into a wall of the
church during the Turkish occupation. When the church was virtually
destroyed in 1686, the Madonna
made a miraculous appearance. The
Turks took this as an omen of defeat.*

Main Portal
*Above the arched west
entrance is a 19th-
century bas-relief of
the Madonna and
Child, seated between
two angels. The work
is by Lajos Lantai.*

STAR FEATURES

- ★ Baroque Madonna
- ★ Mary Portal
- ★ Tomb of King
  Béla III and Anne
  de Châtillon

★ Tomb of King Béla III and Anne de Châtillon

The remains of this royal couple were transferred from Székesfehérvár Cathedral to Mátyás Church in 1860. They lie beneath an ornamental stone canopy in the Trinity Chapel.

VISITORS' CHECKLIST

Szentháromság tér 2. **Map** 1 B4.
Tel 355 56 57. 🚌 Várbusz. 🕐
9am–5pm Mon–Fri, 9am–1pm
Sat, 1–5pm Sun. ♿ ✓ 📷
Museum 🕐 9am–5pm Sun–Fri.

The roof is decorated with multicoloured glazed tiles.

Pulpit
The richly decorated pulpit includes the carved stone figures of the four Fathers of the Church and the four Evangelists.

The main altar was created by Frigyes Schulek and based on Gothic triptychs.

Stained-Glass Windows
Three arched windows on the south elevation have 19th-century stained glass. They were designed by Frigyes Schulek, Bertalan Székely and Károly Lotz.

★ Mary Portal
This depiction of the Assumption of the Blessed Virgin Mary is the most magnificent example of Gothic stone carving in Hungary. Frigyes Schulek reconstructed the portal from fragments.

TIMELINE

c.1387 Church redesigned as Gothic hall-church by Sigismund of Luxembourg

1458 Thanksgiving mass following the coronation of Mátyás Corvinus

1541 Turks convert church into a mosque

1686 After liberation of Buda from Turkish rule, church is almost destroyed. New church built with a Baroque interior

Holy figures on the pulpit

1250	1350	1450	1550	1650	1750	1850	1950

1309 Coronation of the Angevin king Charles Robert

1255 Church originally founded by King Béla IV after the Mongol invasion

1526 Cathedral burnt in the first attack by Turks

1470 Mátyás Tower is completed after its collapse in 1384

1896 Frigyes Schulek completes the reconstruction of the church in the Neo-Gothic style

1945 Church is severely damaged by German and Russian armies

1970 Final details are completed in post-war rebuilding programme

Vienna Gate, rebuilt in 1936, commemorating the liberation of Buda

Vienna Gate Square **16**

Bècsi Kapu Tér

Map 1 B4.
🚌 Várbusz from Moszkva tér.

The square takes its name from the gate that once led from the walled town of Buda towards Vienna. After being damaged several times, the old gate was demolished in 1896. The current gate, based on a historic design, was erected in 1936 on the 250th anniversary of the liberation of Buda from the Turks.

The square has a number of interesting houses. Those at Nos. 5, 6, 7 and 8 were built on the ruins of medieval dwellings. They are Baroque and Rococo in design and feature sculptures and bas-reliefs. The façade of No. 7 has medallions with the portraits of Classical philosophers and poets; Thomas Mann, the German novelist, lodged here between 1935–6. No. 8, meanwhile, is differentiated by its bay windows, attics and the restored medieval murals on its façade.

On the left-hand side of the square is a vast Neo-Romanesque building with a beautiful multicoloured roof, built in 1913–20 by Samu Pecz. This building houses the National Archive, which holds documents dating from before the battle of Mohács in 1526 and others connected with the Rákóczi and Kossuth uprisings (see pp 25, 31 and 38).

Behind the Vienna Gate Square is a monument built in honour of Mihály Táncsics, the leader of the Autumn Uprising. It was unveiled in 1970.

Buda Lutheran Church **17**

Budavári Evangélikus Templom

Bécsi kapu tér. **Map** 1 B4.
Tel 356 97 36. 🚌 Várbusz. ♿

Facing the Vienna Gate is the Neo-Classical Lutheran church, built in 1896 by Mór Kallina. A plaque commemorates pastor Gábor Sztéhló, who saved 2,000 children during World War II.

At one time, a painting by Bertalan Székely, called Christ Blessing the Bread, adorned the altar, but it was unfortunately destroyed during the war.

Church of St Mary Magdalene **18**

Mária Magdolna Templom Tornya

Kapisztrán tér 6. **Map** 1 A4.
🚌 Várbusz.

Now in ruins, this church was built in the mid-13th century. During the Middle Ages, Hungarian Christians worshipped here because Mátyás Church was only for use by the town's German population. The church did not become a mosque until the second half of the Turkish occupation, but it was severely damaged in 1686, during the liberation of Buda from the Turks. An

order of Franciscan monks subsequently took possession and added a Baroque church and tower.

After World War II, all but the tower and the gate were pulled down. These now stand in a garden, together with the reconstructed Gothic window.

Parliament Street **19**

Országház Utca

Map 1 A4 & 1 B4.

This street was once inhabited by the Florentine artisans and craftsmen who were working on King Mátyás' Royal Palace (see pp70–71), and it was known for a time as Italian Street. Its present name comes from the building at No. 28, where the Hungarian parliament met from 1790–1807. This building was designed in the 18th century by the architect Franz Anton Hillebrandt as a convent for the Poor Clares. However, Emperor Joseph II dissolved the order before the building was completed.

Numerous houses on Parliament Street have retained attractive Gothic and Baroque features. No. 2, now with a Neo-Classical façade, is the site of the Alabárdos Étterem (see p196), but its history dates back to the late 13th century. In the 15th century, Sigismund of Luxembourg built a Gothic mansion here and some details, such as the colonnade around the courtyard and the murals on the second floor, have survived until the present day. The entrance to No. 9 features the Gothic traceried seat niches that were popular in Buda at this time. In front of the Neo-Classical house at No. 21 is a statue of Márton Lendvay (1807–58), who was a famous Hungarian actor and member of the National Theatre.

The reconstructed Baroque tower of the Church of St Mary Magdalene

Museum of Military History ❷⓪
Hadtörténeti Múzeum

Tóth Árpád Sétány 40.
Map 1 A4. *Tel* 356 95 22.
🚌 *Várbusz.* ⏱ *Apr–Sep: 10am–6pm Tue–Sun; Oct–Mar: 10am–4pm Tue–Sun.* 🖼

The museum is located in a wing of the former Palatine barracks. It houses a wide range of military items relating to the skirmishes and wars that have afflicted Budapest from before the Turkish occupation to the 20th century. Uniforms, flags, weapons, maps and ammunition from as far back as the 11th century give an insight into the long, turbulent history of Budapest.

Of particular interest is the exhibit concerning the 1956 Uprising. Photographs illustrate the 13 days of demonstrations that ended in a Soviet invasion, and a huge civilian death toll.

Lords' Street ❷①
Úri Utca

Map 1 A4, 1 B4 and 1 B5 (9 A2).
🚌 *Várbusz.* **Telephone Museum**
Tel 201 81 88. ⏱ *10am–6pm Tue–Sun.*

The buildings in Lords' Street were destroyed first in 1686 and again in 1944. Reconstruction in 1950–60 restored much of their original medieval character. Almost all have some remnant of a Gothic gateway or hall, while the façade is Baroque or Neo-Classical.

An excellent example of a Gothic façade can be seen on Hölbling House at No. 31. Enough of its original features survived the various wars and renovations to enable architects to reconstruct the façade in considerable detail. The first-floor window is a particularly splendid Gothic feature. The houses opposite are also examples of this restoration work.

The building at No. 53 was rebuilt between 1701–22 as a Franciscan monastery, but in 1789 it was restyled for use by Emperor Joseph II. In 1795, Hungarian Jacobites, led by Ignác Martinovics, were

imprisoned here; a plaque records this event. A well featuring a copy of a sculpture of Artemis, the Greek goddess of hunting, by Praxiteles, was set in front of the house in 1873.

There are two museums on Lords' Street. The Telephone Museum, at No. 49, is a former telephone exchange and one of the most fun and interactive museums in the city. At No. 9 is the entrance to the Labyrinth, one of the seven underground wonders of the world.

Labyrinth of Buda Castle ❷❷
Budavári Labirintus

Úri utca 9 & Lovas út 4. **Map** 1 B5.
Tel 489 32 81, 212 02 87.
🚌 *Várbusz.* ⏱ *9:30am–7:30pm daily; oil lamps lit 6–7:30pm.* 🖼
English, German; personal tours from 8pm. 🖼 **www**.labirintus.com

The haunt of prehistoric man some half a million years ago, the Labyrinth of Buda Castle comprises a 1,200-metre (1,000-yard) section of the impressive complex of caves, cellars, dungeons and springs that run beneath Castle Hill to a depth of several storeys. The complex, which was created by the action of hot spring water on calcareous rock, has

One of many tufa-clad caves in the ancient, subterranean Labyrinth

been used variously as a storage area, a refuge and a secret military installation. Now it contains a series of imaginative and unusual themed exhibits. "Prehistoric Labyrinth" contains copies of the most celebrated cave paintings in Europe; "Historical Labyrinth" is populated by figures from Hungarian myth and legend; and "Gallery" is a collection of reconstructions and representations of labyrinths from various ages and cultures. From 6pm, oil lamps are lit. Personal tours, conducted in the dark, "for those who are not afraid of themselves", can be arranged.

Lords' Street, which runs the full length of the Old Town

GELLÉRT HILL AND TABÁN

Rising steeply beside the Danube, Gellért Hill is one of the city's most attractive areas. From the top, at a height of 140 m (460 ft), a beautiful view of the whole of Budapest unfolds. The Celtic Eravi, who preceded the Romans, formed their settlement on the hill's northern slope (see p94). Once called simply Old Hill, many superstitions and tales are connected

Carving on the altar in the Rock Church

with it. In 1046, heathen citizens threw a sealed barrel containing Bishop Gellért, who was trying to convert them to Christianity, from the hill to his death. Afterwards, the hill was named after this martyr. Gellért Hill bulges out slightly into the Danube, which narrows at this point. This made the base of the hill a favoured crossing place, and the settlement of Tabán evolved as a result.

SIGHTS AT A GLANCE

Museums
Semmelweis Museum of Medical History **12**

Churches
Rock Church **2**
Tabán Parish Church **10**

Historic Buildings
Citadel **4**
Golden Stag House **13**

Hotels and Baths
Gellért Hotel and Baths Complex pp90–91 **1**
Rác Baths **9**
Rudas Baths **6**

Districts, Squares and Monuments
Liberation Monument **3**
Miklós Ybl Square **11**
Queen Elizabeth Monument **7**
Statue of St Gellért **5**
Tabán **8**

KEY

■ Street-by-Street map
See pp88–9

M Metro station

⊞ Police station

⊠ Post office

| 0 metres | 300 |
| 0 yards | 300 |

GETTING THERE
The easiest ways to ascend Gellért Hill are to drive up, or to take bus 27, which makes its way from Móricz Zsigmond körtér right up to the top of the hill. Tram 19 travels to Tabán along the Danube from the tram station at Batthyány tér, while bus 86 stops there on its route from Óbuda. Buses 5, 7, 8, 112, 178 and 239, all originating in Pest, also make stops in Tabán.

◁ **The Statue of St Gellért, dedicated to a murdered 11th-century bishop**

Street-by-Street: Gellért Hill

The hill to the south of Castle hill was long regarded as a notorious spot. In the 11th century, Prince Vata, brother of King István, incited a heathen rebellion here that resulted in the death of Bishop Gellért. During the Middle Ages, witches were even reputed to celebrate their sabbath here. Under the Turks, a small stronghold was first built on the hill to protect Buda. In 1851, the Austrians placed their own bleak and intimidating Citadel at the summit. Not until the end of the 19th century did the popular image of Gellért Hill begin to change, when it became a venue for picnicking parties. In 1967, the area around the Citadel was made into an attractive park.

Queen Elizabeth Monument
Close to the entrance to Elizabeth Bridge stands this statue of Emperor Franz Joseph's wife, who was popular with the Hungarians **7**

HEGYALJA ÚT

★ **Statue of St Gellért**
Blessing the city with his uplifted cross, the martyred Bishop Gellért is regarded as the patron saint of Budapest **5**

Citadel
Once a place to inspire terror, the Citadel now hosts a hotel, restaurant and wine bar, where people can relax and enjoy the view **4**

0 metres	500
0 yards	500

KEY

— — — Suggested route

Liberation Monument
At the foot of the Liberation Monument, towering above the city, are two sculptures, one representing the battle with evil **3**

STAR SIGHTS

★ Rock Church

★ Statue of St Gellért

Rudas Baths
These famous Turkish baths, which date from the 16th century, have a characteristic Ottoman cupola **6**

The observation terraces on Gellért Hill provide those who climb up to them with a beautiful panorama over the southern part of Buda and the whole of Pest

LOCATOR MAP
See Street Finder, maps 3, 4 & 9

THE RESERVOIR
In 1978, a reservoir for drinking water was established close to the Uránia Observatory on Gellért Hill. The surface of the reservoir is covered over and provides a point from which to observe the Royal Palace *(see pp70–71)* to the north. A sculpture by Márta Lessenyei decorates the structure.

★ Rock Church
This church was established in 1926 in a holy grotto. Under the Communists, the Pauline order of monks was forced to abandon the church, but it was reopened in 1989 **2**

Sculpture by Márta Lessenyei on Gellért Hill's reservoir

SZENT GELLÉRT RAKPART

Gellért Hotel and Baths Complex
One of a number of bath complexes built at the beginning of the 20th century, this magnificent spa hotel was erected here to exploit the natural hot springs **1**

Gellért Hotel and Baths Complex **0**

Stained-glass window by Bózó Stanisits

Between 1912–18, this hotel and spa was built in the modernist Secession style *(see pp54–7)* at the foot of Gellért Hill. The earliest reference to the existence of healing waters at this spot dates from the 13th century, during the reign of King András II and in the Middle Ages a hospital stood on the site. Baths built here by the Ottomans were referred to by the renowned Turkish travel writer of the day, Evliya Çelebi. The architects of the hotel were Ármin Hegedűs, Artúr Sebestyén and Izidor Sterk. Destroyed in 1945, it was rebuilt and modernized after World War II. The hotel has several restaurants and cafés. The baths include an institute of water therapy, set within Secession interiors, but with modern facilities.

Outdoor Wave Pool
An early swimming pool with a wave mechanism, built in 1927, is situated at the back of the complex, looking towards Gellért Hill behind.

★ **Baths**
Two separate baths, one for men and one for women, are identically arranged. In each there are three plunge pools, with water at different temperatures, a sauna and a steam bath.

Balconies
The balconies fronting the hotel's rooms have fanciful Secession balustrades that are decorated with lyre and bird motifs.

★ **Entrance Hall**
The interiors of the hotel, like the baths, have kept their original Secession decor, with elaborate mosaics, stained-glass windows and statues.

Sun Terraces
Situated in the sunniest spot, these terraces are a popular place for drying off in the summer.

VISITORS' CHECKLIST

Szent Gellért tér. **Map** 4 E3.
Tel 466 61 66. 🚌 7, 7A, 86.
🚋 18, 19, 47, 49. 🚫 ♿ ⊡
🍴 **Baths** Kelenhegyi út.
⏰ 6am–8pm daily. 📷 🚫 ♿
www.gellertbath.com

Hot pool with medicinal spa water

Eastern-Style Towers
The architects who designed the hotel gave its towers and turrets a characteristically oriental, cylindrical form.

Main Staircase
The landings of the main staircase have stained-glass windows by Bózó Stanisits, added in 1933. They illustrate an ancient Hungarian legend about a magic stag, recorded in the poetry of János Arany.

Restaurant Terrace
From this first-floor terrace, diners can appreciate a fine view of Budapest. On the ground and first floors of the hotel there are a total of four cafés and restaurants.

★ Main Façade
Behind the hotel's imposing façade are attractive recreational facilities and a health spa that is also open to non-guests. The entrance to the baths is around to the right from the main entrance, on Kelenhegyi út.

STAR FEATURES

★ Baths

★ Entrance Hall

★ Main Façade

Gellért Hotel and Baths Complex ❶

Gellért Szálló és Fürdő

See pp90–91.

Rock Church ❷

Sziklatemplom

Gellért rakpart 1a. **Map** 4 E3.
Tel *385 15 29.* ⬤ *9am–8pm daily.*
🚎 *7, 7A, 86.* 🚋 *18, 19, 47, 49.*

On the southern slope of
Gellért Hill, the entrance to
this grotto church is a short
walk from the Gellért Hotel
and Baths Complex. Based on
the shrine at Lourdes, the
church, designed by Kálmán
Lux, was established in 1926.

The church was intended
for the Pauline order of monks,
which was founded in the
13th century by Eusebius of
Esztergom. In 1934, 150 years
after Joseph II had dissolved
the order in Hungary,15
friars arrived back in the city
from exile in Poland. However,
their residence lasted only
until the late 1950s, when the
Communist authorities suspended the activities of the
church, accusing the monks
of treasonable acts, and sealed
the entrance to the grotto.

The church and adjoining
monastery were reopened on
27 August 1989, when a papal
blessing was conferred on its
beautiful new granite altar,
designed by Győző Sikot. To
the left within the grotto is a
copy of the *Black Madonna of
Czestochowa* and a depiction
of a Polish eagle. Visitors will
also see a painting of St Kolbe,

a Polish monk who gave his
life to protect other inmates at
Auschwitz concentration
camp. A memorial plaque lists
the names of the camps
where Polish soldiers were
interned during World War II,
together with the towns and
schools where Polish refugees
were sheltered in those years.

At the entrance to the church
stands a statue of St István. The
monastery can be reached
through the Chapel of St István
inside. Here, it is worth
pausing to look at Béli Ferenc's
exquisite wooden sculptures.

Liberation Monument ❸

Felszabadulási Emlékmű

Map 4 D3. 🚎 *27.*

Positioned high on Gellért
Hill, this imposing monument
towers over the rest of thc
city. It was designed by the
outstanding Hungarian sculptor
Zsigmond Kisfaludi Stróbl and
set up here to commemorate
the liberation of Budapest by
the Russian army in 1945 *(see
p34)*. The monument was
originally intended to honour
the memory of István, son of
the Hungarian Regent Miklós
Horthy, who disappeared in
1943 on the eastern front.
However, after the liberation
of the city by Russian troops,
Marshal Klimient Woroszyłow
spotted it in the sculptor's
workshop and reassigned it to
this purpose.

The central figure on the
monument is a woman holding

The Liberation Monument, standing at the top of Gellért Hill

aloft a palm leaf. Standing on
its pedestal, this reaches a
height of 14 m (46 ft). At the
base of the monument there
are two allegorical compositions, representing progress
and the battle with evil.

The arrival of the Russians
in Budapest was a liberation
but also the beginning of
Soviet rule. After Communism's
fall, a figure of a Russian
soldier was removed from
the monument to Statue
Park *(see p160)*.

Citadel ❹

Citadella

Map 4 D3. 🚎 *27.* ⬤ *daily.*
🏨 **Hotel Citadella** ***Tel*** *466 57 94.*
Citadella Restaurant ***Tel*** *386 48
02.* ⬤ *11am–11pm daily.*
www.citadellarestaurant.com

After the suppression of the
uprising of 1848–9 *(see
pp30–31)*, the Habsburgs
decided to build a fortification
on this strategically important
site. Constructed in 1850–54,
the Citadel housed 60 cannons,
which could, in theory, fire on
the city at any time. In reality,
from its very inception the
Citadel did not fulfil any real
military requirements, but
served rather as a means of
intimidating the population.

The Citadel is some 220 m
(720 ft) long by 60 m (200 ft)
wide, and has walls 4 m (12 ft)
high. After peace was agreed
with the Habsburgs, Hungarian
society continually demanded
the destruction of the Citadel,
but it was not until 1897 that
the Austrian soldiers left their
barracks here. A section of its

Entrance to the Rock Church, run by the Pauline order of monks entrance gateway was then symbolically ripped out.

After much discussion in the early 1960s, the Citadel was converted into a leisure complex. A restaurant *(see p196)*, hotel *(see p182)* and even a nightclub now attract customers up Gellért Hill. From the old defensive walls of the Citadel there is a spectacular panorama of the city.

Statue of St Gellért ❺
Szent Gellért Emlékmű

Map 4 D2. 🚌 27. *(And a long walk. Go via the steps by Elizabeth Bridge.)*

In 1904 a vast monument was established on the spot where Bishop Gellért was supposedly murdered in the 11th century. It is said the bishop was thrown into the Danube in a barrel, by a mob opposed to the adoption of Christianity. St Gellért holds a

The main plunge pool at the Rudas Baths, covered by a Turkish cupola

cross in his outstretched hand and a Hungarian convert to Christianity kneels at his feet.

The statue was designed by Gyula Jankovits; the semi-circular collonade behind it is by Imre Francsek. A spring that bubbles up here was used to create the fountain.

Overlooking the Elizabeth Bridge, the monument can be seen from throughout the city.

Rudas Baths ❻
Rudas Gyógyfürdő

Döbrentei tér 9. **Map** 4 D2 (9 C5). *Tel* 356 13 22. **Spa Baths** ☐ *6am–8pm Sun–Thu, 10am–4pm Fri & Sat.* **Swimming pool** ☐ *6am–6pm Mon–Fri, 6am–2pm Sat & Sun.* **www**.budapestspas.hu

Dating originally from 1550, these baths were extended in 1566 by Sokoli Mustafa, an Ottoman pasha. The main part of the baths, dating from this period, have an octagonal plunge pool and four small corner pools with water of varying temperatures.

The baths have been modernized and now include a mixed swimming pool. The spa pools are mixed on weekends, but Tuesdays are reserved for women and the rest of the week for men.

Queen Elizabeth Monument ❼
Erzsébet Királyné Szobra

Döbrentei tér. **Map** 4 D2 (9 C5).

This monument to Queen Elizabeth, wife of Habsburg Emperor Franz Joseph, was created by György Zala.

The statue was erected in its present location in 1986. It stands close to the Elizabeth Bridge *(see p63)*, which was also named after the empress, who showed great friendship to the Hungarians. The statue stood on the opposite side of the river from 1932 until 1947, when the Communists ordered it to be taken down.

The landmark Gellért Monument overlooking the Elizabeth Bridge

Tabán ⑧

Map 3 C1, C2, C3 (9B5).
🚊 18, 19. 🚌 5, 78, 112.

The Tabán now consists of a pleasant park and a few historic buildings, but was once very different. In the early 20th century this district, nestling in between Castle Hill and Gellért Hill, was a slum which was cleared as part of a programme to improve the city. Only a few buildings, including Tabán Parish Church, escaped the demolition.

Natural conditions ensured that this was one of the first places in the area where people chose to live. The Celtic Eravi were the first to make a settlement here, while the Romans later built a watchtower from which they could observe people using a nearby crossing point over the river. The first reference to bathing in thermal waters in Tabán dates from the 15th century. The Turks took advantage of this natural asset and built two magnificent baths here, the Rác Baths and the Rudas Baths *(see p93)*, around which a blossoming town was established. Apart from the baths, virtually everything was destroyed in the recapture of Buda in 1686 *(see p26)*.

In the late 17th century, a large number of Serbs, referred to in Hungarian as Rács, moved into the Tabán after fleeing from the Turks. They were joined by Greeks and Gypsies. Many of the inhabitants of the Tabán at this stage were tanners or made their living on the river. On the hillside above grapevines were cultivated. By the early 20th century, though picturesque, the district was still without proper sanitation. The old, decaying Tabán, with its numerous bars and gambling dens, was demolished and the present green space established in its place.

A statue of Miklós Ybl,
*the 19th-century architect,
was erected here in 1894.
It was designed by
Ede Mayer.*

Gardens with terraces, *decorative stairways and arcades designed by Miklós Ybl were established here to connect the Royal Palace (see pp70–71) with the banks of the Danube.*

Several Ottoman tombstones *stand here. They are the remnants of a cemetery in which the Turks who died defending Buda in 1686 were buried.*

**Golden
Stag House**

YBL MIKLÓS TÉR

GROZA PÉTER RAKPART

DÖBRENTEI UTCA

ÁRPÁD UTCA

0 metres 150
0 yards 150

Rác Baths ❾

Rác Gyógyfürdő

Hadnagy utca 8–10. **Map** 4 D2 (9 B5). **Tel** 487 03 13. ⛟ 18, 19. ◯ 7am–10pm daily.

Taking their name from the Serbian, or Rác, people who once lived here, the baths date back to the Turkish era (see pp26–7). This is not clear from the outside, as the baths were redeveloped in 1869 to a design by Miklós Ybl. Inside, however, original Ottoman features include an octagonal pool and cupola. The baths have been redeveloped into a modern, luxurious spa and hotel complex, including 11 pools as well as saunas and treatment rooms.

The façade of the Rác Baths

Tabán Parish Church ❿

Tabáni Plébániatemplom

Attila út 11. **Map** 4 D1 (9 C5). **Tel** 375 54 91. ⛟ 18, 19.

A temple is thought to have stood on this site even in the reign of Prince Árpád. In the Middle Ages a church was built here, which was converted into a mosque by the Turks and subsequently destroyed. In 1728–36, after the Habsburgs had taken control of the city, a second church was erected to a design by Keresztély Obergruber. Mátyás Nepauer added the tower in the mid-18th century. In 1881 the façade was extended and the tower crowned by a Neo-Baroque dome.

Inside the church, on the right-hand side under the choir gallery, is a copy of a

Tabán Parish Church, with its Neo-Baroque domed tower

12th-century carving entitled *Christ of Tabán*; the original is now in the collection of the Budapest History Museum (see p72). The altar, pulpit and several paintings adorning the walls of the church all date from the 19th century.

Miklós Ybl Square ⓫

Ybl Miklós Tér

Map 4 D1 (9 C4). ⛟ 19.

It is no coincidence that the important architect Miklós Ybl (see p119) is commemorated by a statue in this square, close to many of his buildings. Among Ybl's most monumental projects were the State Opera House (see pp118–19), St Stephen's Basilica (see pp116–17) and also a large-scale rebuilding of the Royal Palace (see pp70–71).

The Várkert Kiosk, on the square, was also built by Ybl. Initially it pumped water up to the Royal Palace, but in 1903 it was converted into a café. The building also contains the Casino-Valentine Restaurant.

Semmelweis Museum of Medical History ⓬

Semmelweis Orvostörténeti Múzeum

Apród utca 1–3. **Map** 4 D1 (9 B4). **Tel** 375 35 33. ⛟ 18, 19. ◯ Mar–Oct: 10:30am–6pm daily; Nov–Feb 10.30am–4pm. 📷 🎫 🚫

This museum is located in the 18th-century house where Dr Ignáz Semmelweis was born in 1818. He is renowned for his discovery of an antiseptic-based prevention for puerperal fever, a fatal condition common among women who had recently given birth.

The history of medicine from ancient Egypt onwards is portrayed in the museum, which includes a replica 19th-century pharmacy. Semmelweis's surgery can also be seen with its original furniture. In the courtyard is a monument called *Motherhood* by Miklós Borsos.

Golden Stag House ⓭

Szarvas Ház

Szarvas tér 1. **Map** 3 C1 (9 B4). **Tel** 375 64 51. ⛟ 19.

Standing at the foot of Castle Hill is this distinctive early 19th-century house. It received its name from the inn that opened here called "Under the Golden Stag" – above the entrance you will see a bas-relief depicting a golden stag pursued by two hunting dogs. The building still accommodates a restaurant of that name, Aranyszarvas, which specializes in game dishes. There is also a separate wine bar located in the cellar.

Bas-relief above the entrance to Golden Stag House

NORTH OF THE CASTLE

Decoration on the Millacher Fountain

Between Castle Hill and the western bank of the Danube, extending north from the Chain Bridge towards Margit körút, is the area known as Víziváros or Water Town. This area gained its name in the Middle Ages due to constant flooding. It was originally an area inhabited by artisans and fishermen who, consequently, remained poorer than their neighbours on Castle Hill. Today,

the church towers of Víziváros create a wonderful vista along the western bank of the Danube.

In the Middle Ages and during the 150 years of Turkish occupation this area north of Castle Hill was fortified by a system of walls. A short section of these walls still exists by No. 66 Margit körút, and is commemorated by a plaque. The tomb of Gül Baba, a Turkish dervish, is in the north of the area. It is one of the few surviving Ottoman monuments.

SIGHTS AT A GLANCE

Churches
Calvinist Church ❸
Capuchin Church ❷
St Anne's Church pp102–3 ❹
St Francis's Wounds Church ❻

Historic Buildings and Monuments
Tomb of Gül Baba ❽
Tunnel ❶

Squares
Batthyány Square ❺

Baths
Király Baths ❼
Lukács Baths ❾

GETTING THERE
This area is well served by Public transport. Buses 4, 16, 86 and 105 run to Clark Ádám tér (next to the Chain Bridge). Tram 19, metro line M2 (red) and the HÉV suburban train converge at Batthyány tér. The tram and HÉV run parallel with the Danube, the tram from the south, the HÉV from the north. The M2 metro links the area with Pest to the east.

0 metres 300
0 yards 300

KEY
- ▬ Street-by-Street map
  See pp98–99
- 🅷 HÉV station
- Ⓜ Metro station
- ⊠ Post office
- ⛴ River boat boarding point

◁ The Calvinist Church, viewed from the Danube, beautifully illuminated at night

Street-by-Street: Víziváros

Fő Utca, the main street of
Víziváros (Water Town), runs
the length of the neighbourhood. Numerous cafés and
restaurants, spectacular Baroque
monuments, and a promenade
along the Danube give this area
a charming atmosphere. A fine
array of churches, in an interesting assortment of architectural
styles, reflect the history of the
area as far back as the Middle
Ages. From the Danube promenade the panorama of Pest
opposite, with Parliament *(see
pp108–9)* in the foreground,
can best be viewed.

★ **St Francis's Wounds Church**
*The Baroque pulpit in this church
was carved by the Franciscans, for
whom the church was built in the
mid-18th century* ❻

The Hikisch House was
built on top of medieval
walls. The façade, dating
from 1795, features bas-
reliefs of cherubs carrying
out different tasks. Other
reliefs depict allegories
of the four seasons.

The White Cross Inn,
one of Budapest's
earliest inns, was est-
ablished in 1770. Its
asymmetrical façade
was created by joining
two houses together.
Among those reputed
to have stayed here
are Emperor Joseph II
and also Casanova.

0 metres   100

0 yards   100

STAR SIGHTS

★ Bathyány Square

★ St Anne's Church

★ St Francis's Wounds
Church

★ **Batthyány Square**
*A monument to Ferenc Kölcsey
(1790–1838) overlooks this
square. He was a literary critic
and political commentator of the
early 19th century, and also wrote
the prayer* Lord, Bless Hungary,
*which is used as the lyrics for the
Hungarian national anthem* ❺

KEY

– – – Suggested route

★ St Anne's Church

Characteristic of the late Baroque period, the interior of this church is quite stunning. The main portal is decorated with allegorical sculptures of Faith, Hope and Charity ❹

LOCATOR MAP
See Street Finder, maps 1 & 9

Calvinist Church

The roof of this church, built in 1893–6, is covered with colourful ceramic tiles from the Zsolnay factory (see p56). They are a strong focal point in the panorama of Buda ❸

BEM RAKPART

A Monument to Samu Pecz stands beside one of his most important buildings, the Calvinist Church. Pecz was a follower of the Neo-Gothic movement and constructed many other important buildings in the city.

Capuchin Church

In its original medieval form, this church underwent conversion into a mosque at the hands of the Turks. Many Gothic elements have survived, however. Its present structure dates from 1854–6 ❷

FŐ UTCA

To Clark Ádám tér and the Chain Bridge

Kapisztory House, at No. 20 Fő utca, was built in 1811 for the Greek merchant, Joseph Kapisztory. Its unusual turretted cylindrical window is an attractive feature of this street.

The imposing entrance to the Tunnel on Clark Ádám tér

Tunnel ❶

Alagút

Clark Ádám tér. **Map** 1 C5 (9 B3).
🚌 16, 105.

The Scottish engineer Adam
Clark settled in Hungary after
completing the Chain Bridge
(see p62). One of his later
projects, in 1853–7, was
building the Tunnel that runs
right through Castle Hill, from
Clark Ádám tér to Krisztin-
aváros. The Tunnel is 350 m
(1,150 ft) long, 9 m (30 ft)
wide and 11 m (36 ft) in
height.

The entrance on Clark Ádám
tér is flanked by two pairs of
Doric columns. This square is
the city's official centre
because of the location here
of the Zero Kilometre Stone,
from which all distances from
Budapest are calculated.

The Tunnel's western
entrance was originally ornamented with Egyptian motifs.
However, it was rebuilt without these details after it was
damaged in World War II.

Capuchin Church ❷

Kapucinus Templom

Fő utca 32. **Map** 1 C4 (9 B2). *Tel*
201 47 25. 🕐 *by arrangement.*

The origins of this church
date from the 14th century,
when the mother of Louis I,
Queen Elizabeth, decided to
establish a church here. Fragments of walls on the northern
façade survive from this time.

During the Turkish occupation *(see pp26–7)*, the church
was converted into a mosque.
Features from this period, such

as the window openings and
and the doorway on the southern façade, have remained
despite the fighting of 1686.

Between 1703–15 the
church was rebuilt, following
a Baroque design created by
one of the Capuchin Fathers.

In 1856 the church was again
restyled, by Ferenc Reitter and
Pál Zsumrák, who linked the
differently styled façades har-
moniously together. The statue
of St Elizabeth on the mid-
19th-century Romantic façade
also dates from 1856.

The altar of the Capuchin Church

Calvinist Church ❸

Református Templom

Szilágyi Dezső tér 3. **Map** 1 C4 (9
B2). *Tel 457 01 09.*

One of Budapest's more
unusual churches, the Calvinist
Church was built by Samu
Pecz between 1893–6 on the
site of a former medieval market. It is one of the major examples of his work.

Despite the use of modern
tiles on the roof, the church is

Neo-Gothic in style. It is also
interesting to note that Pecz
used this traditional design of
medieval Catholic churches
for a Calvinist church, which
has very different liturgical
and ecclesiastical needs.

St Anne's Church ❹

Szent Anna Templom

See pp102–3.

Batthyány Square ❺

Batthyány Tér

Map 1 C3 (9 B1). Ⓜ *Batthyány tér.*

Batthyány Square is one
of the most interesting
squares on the Danube's western bank. Beautiful views of
Parliament and Pest on the opposite bank unfold from here.

In 1905, the square was
renamed after Count Lajos
Batthyány, the prime minister
during the Hungarian uprising
of 1848–9 *(see pp30–31)*, who
was shot by the Austrian army.

The square features buildings
in many different styles. The
Hikisch House, at No. 3, dating
from the late 18th century, is
late Baroque. It is notable for
the bas-reliefs on its façade
depicting the four seasons. The
White Cross Inn, at No. 4, also
late Baroque, features Rococo
decoration. On the western
side of the square is the first
covered market in Buda,
dating from 1902. Though
damaged in World War II, it
is now fully restored.

The Hikisch House, with bas-reliefs
representing the four seasons

St Francis's Wounds Church ⑥

Szent Ferenc sebei-templom

Fő utca 41–43. **Map** 1 C3 (9 B1). **Tel** 201 80 91. Ⓜ Batthyány tér.

In 1731–57 a church was built for the Franciscan order on the ruins of a former mosque, to a design by Hans Jakab. In 1785, after he had dissolved the Franciscan order, Emperor Joseph II gave the church to St Elizabeth's Convent.

The Baroque interior is adorned with late 19th-century frescoes, including one of St Florian protecting Christians from a fire in 1810. Their resonance is due to their skilful restoration. The original pulpit and pews, carved by the friars, have remained intact.

In the early 19th century, a hospital and hostel were built adjacent to the church. These were run by the Elizabeth Sisters.

Király Baths ⑦

Király Gyógyfürdő

Fő utca 84. **Map** 1 C2. **Tel** 202 36 88. Ⓜ Batthyány tér. ◯ 8am–8pm Mon & Wed (women); 8am–8pm Tue, Thu, Fri & Sat (men); 8am–8pm Sun (mixed). ▨

The Ottoman Király Baths are one of the city's four remaining Turkish baths *(see p50–53)*. Built from 1566–70, with 19th-century neo-classical additions, they retain many original features, the most beautiful being the central cupola hall with its octagonal pool. From here radiate out the smaller pools of different temperatures, the steam rooms and saunas.

At the end of Fő utca, in the square that bears his name is the monument to the Polish general József Bem. The hero of the 1848–9 uprisings, he is depicted with his arm in a sling. It was in this state, in the front line of the Battle of Pisk, that he inspired the Hungarian troops to attack the bridge and achieve victory over the Habsburg armies. Memorable words, which he uttered during the battle, are engraved on the base of the monument.

Tiles on the Tomb of Gül Baba

Tomb of Gül Baba ⑧

Gül Baba Türbéje

Mecset utca 14. **Map** 1 B1. ▥ 91. ◯ May–Sep: 10am–6pm Tue–Sun; Oct–Jan: 10am–4pm Tue–Sun. ▨

Gül Baba was a Muslim dervish and member of the Bektashi order, who died in 1541, just after the capture of Buda. He was one of the few Turks who was respected and revered by the people of Hungary. His remains now lie in a tomb built between 1543 and 1598.

According to legend, it was Gül Baba who introduced roses to Budapest. From this came both the name of this area, Rózsadomb, meaning Rose Hill, and Gül Baba's own name, which in English means Father of Roses. Fittingly, his tomb is surrounded by a lovely rose garden.

A 400-year-old dome covers the octagonal tomb. Inside, the sarcophagus is draped in green cloth with gold citations from the Koran. Pictures, religious items and beautiful rugs also adorn the tomb.

It is a well-known place of pilgrimage for Muslims.

Lukács Baths ⑨

Lukács Gyógyfürdő

Frankel Leo út 25–9. **Map** 1 C1. **Tel** 326 16 95. ◯ 6am–8pm daily. ▨ ▤ 17. **www**.budapestspas.hu

This famous spa is named after St Luke. Although the Neo-Classical complex was established in 1894, the baths are one of a number still operating in the city *(see pp50–53)* that date back to the period of Turkish rule.

Set in peaceful surroundings, the complex comprises the 16th-century Komjády (Császár) thermal baths and two outdoor swimming pools. Natural hot springs keep these pools heated all year round; bathing is comfortable even in winter.

It is also worth entering the overgrown courtyard to see a statue of St Luke, dating from 1760, and the plaques inscribed with thanks by bathers from around the world who benefited from the healing waters.

Lukács Baths, with beautiful old plane trees growing outside

St Anne's Church ➍

Budapest is home to many churches, but the twin-towered parish church of Víziváros is one of its most beautiful Baroque examples. Initially a Jesuit church, the architect who first designed it is unknown. Building was begun in 1740 by Kristóf Hámon and completed after his death by Mátyás Nepauer. In 1763 an earthquake seriously damaged the building and the dissolution of the Jesuit order ten years later further delayed the completion of the church. Thus it remained unconsecrated until 1805. The rectory now houses the Angelika café.

Crucifix on the St Cross altar

The twin towers are crowned by magnificent Baroque spires.

Façade
Buda's coat of arms appears in the centre of the tympanum. The symbol of the Trinity is above this, between two kneeling angels.

★ Pulpit
This magnificent, late Baroque pulpit was created by Károly Bebó in 1773. It features gilded details and angels that embody theological virtues. The reliefs were added at a later date.

Main entrance

Organ
The organ case from a former Carmelite church on Castle Hill was transferred to St Anne's Church in the late 18th century, after the dissolution of the order by Emperor Joseph II.

★ **Painted Ceiling**
The painted ceiling in the cupola of the chancel depicts the Holy Trinity. It was painted in 1771 by Gergely Vogl. There are also Neo-Baroque frescoes in the nave dating from 1938.

VISITORS' CHECKLIST

Batthyány tér 7. **Map** 1 C3 (9 B1).
Tel *201 34 04.* M *Batthyány tér.* 🚌 *Only for services.*
🚇 *daily.* **Angelika café**
🕐 *9am–noon daily (till 11pm Nov–Mar).*

★ **High Altar**
The sculptures depict Mary, as a child, being brought into the Temple of Jerusalem by St Anne, her mother. Completed in 1773, it is regarded as one of the most beautiful works of Károly Bebó.

Church Pew
The choir pews are decorated with intricately carved wooden panels which feature figurative scenes.

Baptismal Font
Concealed behind a pillar, this baptismal font has a carved pedestal and a simply, but beautifully, decorated cover.

Side Altar
This late Baroque altar of St Francis the Saviour, like the altar of St Cross on the opposite side of the church, is the work of Antal Eberhardt and dates from 1768. The picture in the centre was, however, executed by Franz Wagenschön.

STAR FEATURES

★ High Altar
★ Painted Ceiling
★ Pulpit

AROUND PARLIAMENT

Towards the end of the 18th and throughout the 19th century Pest underwent a series of huge changes. In 1838 a flood destroyed most of the rural dwellings that had occupied the area until that time. The unification of Budapest in 1873 and the 1,000-year anniversary, in 1896, of the Magyar conquest also boosted the city's development. The medieval walls that originally marked Pest's limits were crossed as the area was gradually urbanized. This period produced a number of the most important buildings in Hungary, including St Stephen's Basilica, Parliament and the Hungarian Academy of Sciences, which were built in a variety of revivalist styles. Many Neo-Classical residences were also built, particularly on Nádor utca, Akadémia utca and Október 6 utca.

An ornate lantern on the Parliament

SIGHTS AT A GLANCE

Historic Buildings and Palaces
Central European University **6**
Drechsler Palace **12**

Gresham Palace **8**
Hungarian Academy of Sciences **9**
Ministry of Agriculture **3**
Parliament pp108–9 **1**
Post Office Savings Bank **5**
Radisson Béke Hotel **13**

Museums
Ethnographical Museum **2**

Squares
Liberty Square **4**
Roosevelt Square **7**

Theatres
Budapest Operetta Theatre **14**
State Opera House pp118–19 **11**

Churches
St Stephen's Basilica pp116–17 **10**

GETTING THERE
The M2 metro line (red) runs to Kossuth Lajos tér and the M3 metro line (blue) runs to Arany János utca. Tram 2 runs north along the Danube and terminates past Parliament at Margaret Bridge.
Trolley buses 70 and 78 also serve this area.

KEY

▇	Street-by-Street map *See pp106–7*
▇	Street-by-Street map *See pp112–13*
M	Metro station
⊠	Post office
i	Tourist information

0 metres 500
0 yards 500

◁ **Neo-gothic spires, flying buttresses and stained-glass windows on Hungary's Parliament**

Street-by-Street: Kossuth Square

Brigadier Woroniecki

This square expresses well the pomp and pride with which Pest was developed during the 19th and early 20th centuries. Parliament dominates the square on the Danube side, but equally imposing are the Ministry of Agriculture and the Ethnographical Museum on the opposite side. Several monuments commemorate nationalist leaders and provide a visual record of Hungary's political history.

★ **Ethnographical Museum**
Among 170,000 exhibits amassed in the museum's collection is a captivating collection of folk costumes representing the various nationalities and ethnic groups in Hungary ❷

★ **Parliament**
This building has become the recognized symbol of democracy in Hungary, despite the dome being crowned by a red star during the Communist period ❶

Attila József was a radical poet whose work sensitively explored the human condition. In 1937 he committed suicide, aged 32. This statue by László Marton dates from 1980.

LAJOS KOSSUTH (1802–94)

The popularity of Lajos Kossuth among the Hungarian people is immense. He led the 1848–9 uprising against Austrian rule *(see pp30–31)*, and was one of the most outstanding political figures in Hungary. He was a member of the first democratic government during the uprising, and briefly became its leader before being exiled after the revolt was quashed in 1849.

Stained-glass window depicting Lajos Kossuth

BALASSI BÁLINT U

LAJOS

| 0 metres | 150 |
| 0 yards | 150 |

Ferenc II Rákóczi, the prince of Transylvania, led one of the earliest revolts for independence against the Habsburgs in 1703–11. This bronze equestrian monument can be seen in front of Parliament. It was completed by János Pásztor in 1937.

LOCATOR MAP
See Street Finder, maps 4 & 7

Ministry of Agriculture
A massive Corinthian collonade, supporting an entablature, lends this Neo-Classical building a dignified character ❸

This monument to Imre Nagy symbolizes the insurgent prime minister's 1956 defection from the side of Communism to the side of the people – a protest that cost him his life.

The Hungarian TV headquarters were designed in the Late Eclectic style by Ignác Alpár. Constructed in 1905, the building originally housed the Stock Exchange.

LAY U

VECSEY UTCA

ARIBALDI UTCA

NADOR UTCA

Plaque commemorating Brigadier Woroniecki, hero of the uprising of 1948–9

KEY

– – – Suggested route

STAR SIGHTS

★ Ethnographical Museum

★ Parliament

Parliament ❶

One of the pair of lions at the main entrance

Hungary's Parliament is the country's largest building and has become a symbol of Budapest. A competition was held to choose its design, the winner being Imre Steindl's rich Neo-Gothic masterpiece built between 1885–1902. Based on the Houses of Parliament in London, completed by Charles Barry in 1835–6, it is 268 m (880 ft) long and 96 m (315 ft) high, and comprises 691 rooms.

Aerial View
The magnificent dome marks the central point of the Parliament building. Although the façade is elaborately Neo-Gothic, the ground plan follows Baroque conventions.

★ **Domed Hall**
Adorning the massive pillars that support Parliament's central dome are figures of some of the rulers of Hungary.

Danube façade

★ **Deputy Council Chamber**
Formerly the lower house, this hall is now where the National Assembly convenes. Two paintings by Zsigmond Vajda hang on either side of the Speaker's lectern. These were especially commissioned for the building.

South wing

Gables
Almost every corner of the Parliament building features gables with pinnacles based on Gothic sculptures.

Lobby
Lobbies, the venues for political discussions, are to be found along the corridors beneath stained-glass windows.

Dome
The ceiling of the 96-m (315-ft) high dome is covered in an intricate design of Neo-Gothic gilding combined with heraldic decoration.

Gobelin Hall
This hall is decorated with a Gobelin tapestry illustrating Prince Árpád, with seven Magyar leaders under his command, signing a peace treaty and blood oath.

North wing

Old Upper House Hall
The Old Upper House Hall is now used for holding international conferences. It is virtually a mirror image of the National Assembly Hall.

The Royal Insignia, excluding the Coronation Mantle *(see p132),* are kept in the Domed Hall.

The main entrance on Kossuth Lajos tér

Main Staircase
The best contemporary artists were invited to decorate the interior. The sumptuous main staircase features ceiling frescoes by Károly Lotz and sculptures by György Kiss.

STAR FEATURES

★ Deputy Council Chamber

★ Domed Hall

The magnificent façade of the Ethnographical Museum

Parliament ❶

Országház

See pp108–9.

Ethnographical Museum ❷

Néprajzi Múzeum

Kossuth Lajos tér 12. **Map** 2 D3 (9 C1). **Tel** 473 24 00. Ⓜ Kossuth Lajos tér. ⬜ 10am–5pm Tue–Sun. 🖼 🖼 💻 www.neprajz.hu

This building, designed by Alajos Hauszmann and constructed between 1893–6, was built as the Palace of Justice and, until 1945, served as the Supreme Court.

The building's design links elements of Renaissance, Baroque and Classicism. The façade is dominated by a vast portico crowned by two towers. It also features a gable crowned by the figure of the Roman goddess of justice in a chariot drawn by three horses, by Károly Senyei. The grand hall inside the main entrance features a marvellous staircase and frescoes by Károly Lotz.

The building was first used as a museum in 1957, housing the Hungarian National Gallery (see pp74–7), which was later transferred to the Royal Palace. The Ethnographical Museum has been here since 1973.

The museum's collection was established in 1872 in the Department of Ethnography at the Hungarian National Museum (see pp130–33). There are now around 170,000 exhibits,

although most are not on display. The collection includes artifacts reflecting the rural folk culture of Hungary from the prehistoric era to the 20th century. A map from 1909 shows the settlement of the various communities who came to Hungary. Ethnic items relating to these communities, as well as primitive objects from North and South America, Africa, Asia and Australia, can also be seen.

The museum has two very informative permanent displays: Traditional Culture of the Hungarian Nation, and From Primeval Communities to Civilization.

Ministry of Agriculture ❸

Földművelésügyi Minisztérium

Kossuth Lajos tér 11. **Map** 2 D3 (9 C1). Ⓜ Kossuth Lajos tér. www.fvm.hu

On the southeast side of Kossuth Square is this huge building, bordered by streets on all its four sides. It was built for the Ministry of Agriculture by Gyula Bukovics at the end of the 19th century.

The façade is designed in a manner typical of late Historicism, drawing heavily on Neo-Classical motifs. The columns of the colonnade are echoed in the fenestration above the well-proportioned pedimented windows.

On the wall to the right of the building two commemorative plaques can be seen. The first is dedicated to the commanding officer of the Polish Legion, who was also a hero of the 1948–9 uprising

(see p30–31). Brigadier M Woroniecki, who was renowned for his bravery, was shot down on this spot by the Austrians in October 1849.

The second plaque honours Endre Ságvári, a Hungarian hero of the resistance movement, who died in 1944.

The two sculptures in front of the building are by Árpád Somogyi. The *Reaper Lad* dates from 1956 and the *Female Agronomist* from 1954.

Liberty Square ❹

Szabadság Tér

Map 2 E4 (10 D1). Ⓜ Kossuth Lajos tér, Arany János utca.

After the enormous Neugebäude Barracks were demolished in 1886, Liberty Square was laid out in its place. The barracks, built for the Austrian troops, once dominated the southern part of Lipótváros (Leopold Town). It was here that Hungary's first independent prime minister, Count Lajos Batthyány was executed on 6 October 1849. Since 1926, an eternal flame (see p31) has been burning at the corner of Aulich utca, Hold utca and Báthory utca to honour all those executed during the uprising.

Two particularly impressive buildings by Ignác Alpár are on opposite sides of the square. The former Stock Exchange, now the Hungarian TV headquarters (Magyar Televízió székháza), dates from 1905 and shows the influence of the Secession style. The Hungarian National Bank (Magyar Nemzeti Bank) is decorated in a pastiche of Historicist styles and also dates from 1905.

Bas-reliefs on the former Stock Exchange

tendrils and icons taken from nature. The bees climbing up the gable walls represent the bank's activity and the pinnacles, which look like hives, represent the accumulation of savings. These features were intended to be accessible to the people who banked here.

The building is not officially open to the public, but it is possible to see the Cashiers' Hall during office hours.

Central European University 6
Közép-Európai Egyetem

Nádor utca 9. **Map** 2 E5 (10 D2). **Tel** 327 30 00. Ⓜ Kossuth Lajos tér www.ceu.hu

This Neo-Classical palace on Nádor utca, in the direction of Roosevelt Square, was built in 1826 by Mihály Pollack for Prince Antal Festetics. Since 1993 it has housed the Central European University.

Founded by the American millionaire George Soros, who was born in Budapest, this international educational establishment is open to students from central and eastern Europe and the former USSR.

The university offers postgraduate courses in subjects ranging from history and law to political and environmental sciences. In Budapest, the Soros Foundation finances numerous other ventures and it has branches in all the central European countries.

Beautiful Secession interior of the Post Office Savings Bank

An obelisk by Károly Antal stands at the northern end of the square commemorating the Red Army soldiers who died during the siege of Budapest in 1944–5. A second statue is to the US general Harry Hill Bandholtz. He led the allied forces that thwarted the Romanian troops looting the Hungarian National Museum.

Post Office Savings Bank 5
Postatakarék Pénztár

Hold utca 4. **Map** 2 E4 (10 D1). Ⓜ Kossuth Lajos tér.

A masterpiece by Ödön Lechner, the former Post Office Savings Bank was built between 1900–1901. Chiefly a Secession architect, Lechner (see p56) combined the curvilinear motifs of that style with motifs from Hungarian folk art to produce a unique visual style for his work.

Approaching the Post Office Savings Bank, one can see glimpses of the details that

have made this building one of Pest's most unusual sights. The construction methods, interior design and exterior detailing of the building are remarkable. Lechner commissioned the tiles used in the design, including the vibrant roof tiles, from the Zsolnay factory (see p56). The façades are decorated with floral

THE AMERICAN EMBASSY

Plaque commemorating Joseph Mindszenty

This beautiful house, at No. 12 Liberty Square, was designed by Aladár Kálmán and Gyula Ullmann and built between 1899–1901. The façade is decorated with bas-reliefs featuring motifs typical of the Secession style.

By the entrance to the embassy is a plaque with an image of the Catholic Primate, Cardinal Joseph Mindszenty, who was part of the movement seeking to liberate Hungary from the Communists after World War II. He was imprisoned by the regime in 1949 and was mistreated for many years. Released during the 1956 uprising, he asked for political asylum in the embassy. He lived here for 15 years in internal exile until, in 1971, the Vatican finally convinced him to leave Hungary.

Street-by-Street: Roosevelt Square

In 1867, a cermonial mound was made of earth from
all over the country to celebrate the coronation of
Franz Joseph as king of Hungary. Today, the historic
earth has been dug into the ground where Roosevelt
Square now stands. At the head of the Chain Bridge on
the eastern bank of the Danube, it features many of
Pest's most beautiful buildings, such as the Hungarian
Academy of Sciences, to the north of the square, and
Gresham Palace, to the east. The square was named
after American president Franklin D Roosevelt in 1947.

No. 1 Akadémia utca was
built in the Neo-Classical
style by Mátyás Zitterbarth
the younger, in 1835.
A plaque shows that in
November 1848 General
József Bem *(see p101)*
stayed here when it was
the Prince Stephen Hotel.

★ Gresham Palace
*One of the most expressive
examples of Secession architecture in Budapest, now a
Four Seasons hotel* **8**

**House
designed by
József Hild
in 1836**

**★ Hungarian Academy
of Sciences**
*The debating hall of the Hun-
garian Academy of Sciences
is decorated with sculptures
by Miklós Izsó and ceiling
paintings by Károly Lotz* **9**

**The Chain
Bridge** *(see p62)*
was built between
1839–49 and was the
city's first permanent
river crossing. It was
destroyed by the
German forces in
World War II and
was reopened in
1949, 100 years after
it was first finished.

NÁDOR UTCA

AKADÉMIA UTCA

ROOSEVELT
TÉR

The Pichler House is an unusual building. It was completed by Ferenc Wieser between 1853–7 in the style of a Venetian Gothic palace.

LOCATOR MAP
See Street Finder, maps 2, 9 & 10

★ St Stephen's Basilica
The interior of this church was decorated by leading Hungarian artists, such as Alajos Stróbl and Károly Lotz. It was seriously damaged in World War II, and renovation began in the 1980s **⑩**

No. 7 Nádor utca is a Neo-Classical building completed in 1830. It has a modest but well-balanced façade accented by pilasters with decorative capitals, and the large first-floor windows are crowned with elegant arches.

No. 8 József Attila utca, an impressive five-floor office building, was erected in 1898 by Artúr Meinig. It is an attractive example of the use of the Secession style *(see pp 54–7)*.

KEY

- - - Suggested route

0 metres   100
0 yards   100

STAR SIGHTS

★ Gresham Palace

★ Hungarian Academy of Sciences

★ St Stephen's Basilica

Monument to Ferenc Deák, dating from 1887, in Roosevelt Square

Roosevelt Square ⑦
Roosevelt tér

Map 2 D5 (9 C3). 🚎 16. 🚋 2.

Previously, Roosevelt Square was known by several different names – Franz Joseph Square and Unloading Square among others – but it received its current title in 1947. It is located at the head of the Pest side of the Chain Bridge, and is home to many beautiful and important buildings.

At the beginning of the 20th century the square was lined with various hotels, the Diana Baths and the Lloyd Palace designed by József Hild. The only building from the previous century still standing today is the Hungarian Academy of Sciences. The other buildings were demolished and replaced by the Gresham Palace and the Bank of Hungary, on the corner of Attila József utca. Two large modern hotels, the Sofitel Atrium Budapest *(see p184)* and the Inter-Continental Budapest *(see p186)*, stand on the southern side of the square.

There is a statue to Baron József Eötvös (1813–71), a reformer of public education, in front of the Inter-Continental. Situated in the centre of the square are monuments to two politicians who espoused quite different ideologies: Count István Széchenyi (1791–1860), the leading social and political reformer of his age, and Ferenc Deák (1803–76), who was instrumental in the Compromise of 1867, which resulted in the Dual Monachy *(see p32)*.

Gresham Palace ⑧
Gresham Palota

Roosevelt tér 5–7. **Map** 2 D5 (9 C3). *Tel* 268 60 00. 🚎 16. 🚋 2.
www.fourseasons.com/budapest

This Secession palace aroused both controversy and praise from the moment it was built. One of Budapest's most distinctive pieces of architecture, it was commissioned by the London-based Gresham Life Assurance Company from Zsigmond Quittner and the brothers József and László Vágó, and completed in 1907.

This enormous edifice enjoys an imposing location directly opposite the Chain Bridge. The façade features characteristic Secession motifs *(see pp54–7)*, such as curvilinear forms and organic themes. The ornately carved window surrounds appear as though they are projecting from the walls, blending seamlessly with the architecture. The bust by Ede Telcs, at the top of the façade, is of Sir Thomas Gresham. He was the founder of the Royal Exchange in London and of Gresham's Law: "bad money drives out good".

On the ground floor of the palace there is a T-shaped arcade, covered by a multi-coloured glazed roof. The entrance to the arcade is marked by a beautiful wrought-iron gate with peacock motifs. Still the original gate, it is widely regarded as one of the most

Bust of Sir Thomas Gresham on the façade of the Gresham Palace

splendid examples of design from the Secession era. Inside the building, the second floor of the Kossuth stairway has a stained-glass window by Miksa Róth, featuring a portrait of Lajos Kossuth *(see p106)*.

In 2004 the palace opened as a Four Seasons Hotel, the second in Central Europe, and the first in Hungary. Visitors can wander in and admire its many splendours.

Miklós Izsó's sculptures inside the Hungarian Academy of Sciences

Hungarian Academy of Sciences ⑨
Magyar Tudományos Akadémia

Roosevelt tér 9. **Map** 2 D4 (9 C2). *Tel* 411 61 00. 🚎 16. ☐ 11am–4pm Mon–Fri. 🖼 by appointment. www.mta.hu

Built between 1862–4, this Neo-Renaissance building was designed by the architect Friedrich August Stüler.

The statues adorning the façade represent six disciplines of knowledge – law, history, mathematics, sciences, philosophy and linguistics – and are the works of Emil Wolf and Miklós Izsó. On the Danube side are allegories of poetry, astronomy and archeology, and on the corners of the building are statues of renowned thinkers including Newton, Descartes and Révay. Inside are more statues and the library, which has a priceless collection of academic books.

The Neo-Renaissance façade of the Drechsler Palace

St Stephen's Basilica ⑩
Szent István Bazilika

See pp116–17.

State Opera House ⑪
Magyar Állami Operaház

See pp118–19.

Drechsler Palace ⑫
Drechsler Palota

Andrássy út 25. **Map** 2 F4 (10 E2). Ⓜ Opera.

Formerly the State Ballet Institute, the Drechsler Palace was originally built as Neo-Renaissance apartments for the Hungarian Railways Pension Fund in 1883. It was designed by Gyula Pártos and Ödön Lechner to harmonize with the façade of the State Opera House (see pp118–19).

Its name derives from the Drechsler Café, which occupied the ground floor in the 1890s and early 1900s. A photo of the café's patrons at outdoor tables has since graced countless postcards.

Radisson SAS Béke Hotel ⑬
Radisson SAS Béke Hotel

Teréz körút 43. **Map** 2 F3. **Tel** 889 39 00. Ⓜ Oktogon. **www**.danubiushotels.wm/beke

This elegant hotel was built in 1896 as an apartment building, and in 1912 was restyled by Béla Málnai as the Hotel Brittania. A mosaic of György Szondi, a Hungarian captain who fought against the Turks in the 16th century, was added to the façade at this time.

In 1978 the hotel was taken over by the Radisson group, which restored the rich interiors. Notable features are the stained-glass windows in the Szondi Restaurant, by Jenő Haranghy, illustrating the works of Richard Wagner. The Romeo and Juliet conference room and the Shakespeare Restaurant are named after the murals that decorate them. The café serves cake and coffee on porcelain from the Pécs factory (see p56).

Budapest Operetta Theatre ⑭
Budapesti Operett Színház

Nagymező utca 17. **Map** 2 F4 (10 F1). **Tel** 472 20 30. 🚊 4, 6. **www**.operettszinhaz.hu

Budapest has a good reputation for musical entertainment, and its operetta scene (see p216) is over 100 years old. Operettas were first staged on this site in the Orfeum Theatre, designed in the Neo-Baroque style by the Viennese architects Fellner and Helmer, in 1898. The project was financed by the impressario Károly Singer-Somossy.

In 1922, the American entrepreneur Ben Blumenthal redeveloped the building and opened the Capital Operetta Theatre, which then specialized in the genre. After 1936, this theatre became the only venue for operetta in Budapest.

The repertoire of the theatre includes the works of both international and Hungarian composers of this genre, including Imre Kálmán, Ferenc Lehár and Pál Ábrahám, who wrote the Csárdás Princess.

Entrance to the Budapest Operetta Theatre on Nagymező utca

St Stephen's Basilica ⑩

St István's coronation

Dedicated to St Stephen, or István, the first Hungarian Christian king *(see p22)*, this church was designed by József Hild in the Neo-Classical style, using a Greek cross floor plan. Construction began in 1851 and was taken over in 1867 by Miklós Ybl *(see p119)*, who added the Neo-Renaissance dome after the original one collapsed in 1868. József Kauser completed the church in 1905. It received the title of Basilica Minor in 1938, the 900th anniversary of St István's death.

St Matthew
St Matthew is one of the four Evangelists represented in the niches on the exterior of the dome. They are all the work of the sculptor Leó Feszler.

Dome
Reaching 96 m (315 ft), the dome is visible from all over Budapest.

Observation point

Tower
A bell, weighing 9,144 kg (9 tons) is housed in this tower. It was funded by German Catholics to compensate for the original bell, which was looted by the Nazis in 1944.

Main Portal
The massive door is decorated with carvings depicting the heads of the 12 Apostles.

Mosaics
The dome is decorated with mosaics designed by Károly Lotz.

VISITORS' CHECKLIST

Szent István tér. **Map** 2 E4 (10 D2).
Tel 317 28 59. M *Deák Ferenc tér.* **Treasury** ⬚ *9am–5pm Mon–Fri (till 2pm Sat), 1–5pm Sun.* 🈲 🚺 ♿

★ **Main Altar**
In the centre of the altar there is a marble statue of St István by Alajos Stróbl. Scenes from the king's life are depicted behind the altar.

★ **Holy Right Hand**
Hungary's most unusual relic is the mummified forearm of King István. It is kept in the Chapel of the Holy Right Hand.

Figures of the 12 Apostles, by Leó Feszler, crown the exterior colonnade at the back of the church.

St Gellért and St Emericus
This portrayal of St Gellért and his pupil, St Emeryka, is the work of Alajos Stróbl.

★ **Painting by Gyula Benczúr**
This image shows King István, left without an heir, dedicating Hungary to the Virgin Mary, who became Patrona Hungariae, the country's patron.

STAR FEATURES

★ Main Altar

★ Holy Right Hand

★ Painting by Gyula Benczúr

State Opera House ⑪

Opened in September 1884, the State Opera House in Budapest was built to rival those of Paris, Vienna and Dresden. Its beautiful architecture and interiors were the life's work of the great Hungarian architect, Miklós Ybl. The interior also features ornamentation by Hungarian artists, including Alajos Stróbl and Károly Lotz. During its lifetime, the State Opera House has seen some influential music directors, including, Ferenc Erkel, composer of the Hungarian opera *Bánk Bán*, Gustav Mahler and Otto Klemperer.

Decorative lamp with putti

Façade
The decoration of the symmetrical façade follows a musical theme. In niches on either side of the main entrance there are figures of two of Hungary's most prominent composers, Ferenc Erkel and Franz Liszt (see p144). Both were sculpted by Alajos Stróbl.

Murals
The vaulted ceiling of the foyer is covered in magnificent murals by Bertalan Székely and Mór Than. They depict the nine Muses.

★ Foyer
The foyer, with its marble columns, gilded vaulted ceiling, murals and chandeliers, gives the State Opera House a feeling of opulence and grandeur.

Main entrance
Wrought-iron lamps illuminate the wide stone staircase and the main entrance.

★ Main Staircase
Going to the opera was a great social occasion in the 19th century. A vast, sweeping staircase was an important element of the opera house as it allowed ladies to show off their new gowns.

Chandelier
The main hall is decorated with a bronze chandelier that weighs 3,050 kg (3 tons). It illuminates a magnificent fresco, by Károly Lotz, of the Greek gods on Olympus.

Central Stage
This proscenium arch stage employed the most modern technology of the time. It featured a revolving stage and metal hydraulic machinery.

The side entrance has a loggia that reflects the design of the main entrance.

★ Royal Box
The royal box is located centrally in the three-storey circle. It is decorated with sculptures symbolizing the four operatic voices – soprano, alto, tenor and bass.

MIKLÓS YBL (1814–91)
The most prominent Hungarian architect of the second half of the 19th century, Miklós Ybl had an enormous influence on the development of Budapest. He was a practitioner of Historicism, and tended to use Neo-Renaissance forms. The State Opera House and the dome of St Stephen's Basilica are examples of his work. Ybl also built apartment buildings and palaces for the aristocracy in this style. A statue of the architect stands on the western bank of the Danube, in Miklós Ybl Square *(see p95).*

Bust of Miklós Ybl

STAR FEATURES
★ Foyer
★ Main Staircase
★ Royal Box

CENTRAL PEST

Bas-relief on the façade of the City Council Chamber

At the end of the 17th century much of Pest was in ruins and few residents remained. Within the next few decades, however, new residential districts were established, which are today's mid-town suburbs. In the 19th century, redevelopment schemes introduced grand houses and apartment blocks, some with shops and cafés, as well as secular and municipal buildings. Perhaps the most prominent example of this work is the Hungarian National Museum. At this time Pest surpassed Buda as a centre for trade and industry. This was partly due to the area's Jewish community, who played an active role in its development.

SIGHTS AT A GLANCE

Churches
Calvinist Church ㉒
Chapel of St Roch ⑱
Franciscan Church ㉛
Great Synagogue ⑰
Inner City Parish Church pp124–5 ①
Lutheran Church ⑪
Serbian Church ㉖
Servite Church ⑩
University Church ㉘

Museums
Hungarian National Museum pp130–33 ⑳
Museum of Applied Arts pp136–7 ㉓

Historic Buildings and Monuments
City Council Chamber ㉕
Danube Fountain ⑫
Ervin Szabó Library ㉑
Franz Liszt Academy of Music ⑭
Károlyi Palace ㉙
Klotild Palaces ⑥
Lóránd Eötvös University ㉗
Municipal Council Offices ⑧
New Theatre ⑬
New York Palace ⑮
Pest County Hall ⑦
Turkish Bank ⑨
University Library ㉚
University of Economics ㉔

Streets and Squares
Jewish Quarter ⑯
József Nádor Square ③
Mihály Pollack Square ⑲
Mihály Vörösmarty Square ④
Váci Street ⑤
Vigadó Square ②

KEY
▢	Street-by-Street map See pp122–3
Ⓜ	Metro station
ℹ	Tourist Information
✉	Post Office

0 metres	400
0 yards	400

◁ The well of Danaid, who was condemned to carry water to a leaking barrel, in Szomory Dezső tér

Street-by-Street: Around Váci Street

Váci Street has been Budapest's fashionable area for walking, meeting in cafés and shopping in elegant boutiques since the early 19th century. Its attractive promenade is an enjoyable place for an evening stroll, when it is stylishly illuminated.

Gerbeaud Cukrászda is one of the best patisseries in town *(see p206)*.

Servite Church
Holy figures adorn the 19th-century façade of this Baroque church ⑩

Vigadó concert hall

Mihály Vörösmarty Square
A Carrara marble monument to the poet Mihály Vörösmarty stands in this square. It was created by Ede Telcs and symbolizes the Hungarian nation united in the poets's words: "Your homeland, Hungary, serve unwaveringly" ❹

Thonet House was built in 1888–90 by Ödön Lechner *(see p56)* and Gyula Pártos. It stands today in its original form, featuring Zsolnay ceramics from Pécs.

Péterffy Palace, now the Százéves Étterem *(see p203)*, is Pest's only Baroque house. It was built by András Meyerhoffer in 1755 for the magistrate, János Péterffy. Above the gateway there is a beautiful balcony supported by atlantes.

Remains of Contra Aquincum *(see p21)*

0 metres	50
0 yards	50

LOCATOR MAP
See Street Finder, maps 2, 7, 8, 10

★ Váci Street
Budapest's most elegant promenade and shopping area is lined with fashion boutiques, cafés, fountains and statues. Off the street there are old courtyards and shopping arcades ❺

Párizsi Udvar *(see p212)* is found on the corner of Kígyó utca and Petőfi Sándor utca. The arcade, which features shops, bookshops and a cafe, is decorated with beautiful wrought-iron work.

★ Klotild Palaces
This beautifully decorated block is one of two buildings, which together form a magnificent gateway to the Elizabeth Bridge ❻

KEY

 Suggested route

STAR SIGHTS

★ Inner City
  Parish Church

★ Klotild Palaces

★ Váci Street

★ Inner City Parish Church
This white limestone and red marble tabernacle, in the church, dates from the early 16th century ❶

Inner City Parish Church ❶

This church is the oldest building in Pest. It was first established during the reign of St István, the first king of Hungary (see pp22–3), on the burial site of the martyred St Gellért. In the 14th century, a large Gothic church was built, which was used as a mosque under the Turks. Damaged by the Great Fire of 1723, the church was partly rebuilt in the Baroque style by György Pauer in 1725–39. The interior also features Neo-Classical elements by János Hild, as well as some 20th-century works.

The south tower includes one of the surviving walls of the Romanesque church.

★ **Pulpit**
This Neo-Gothic pulpit is beautifully carved from wood. It was produced in 1808 by Fülöp Ungradt.

Main Portal
The late Baroque portal is crowned by a sculpture of the Holy Trinity, inlaid with gold.

A fragment of a wall from the Romanesque church is visible in the lower section of the façade.

Nave
The interior of the church reflects the Gothic and Baroque periods in which it was built. The nave, in the western section of the church, is Baroque in design.

STAR FEATURES

★ Fresco

★ Gothic Chapel

★ Pulpit

★ Fresco
This fragment of a 15th-century Italianate fresco depicts the crucifixion of Christ. It was transferred from the cloister to its current location in the choir.

VISITORS' CHECKLIST

Március 15 tér 2. **Map** 4 E1 (10 D5). *Tel* 318 31 08.
M Ferenciek tere.
9am–7pm daily. daily.

Reconstructed Gothic tabernacle

Main Altar
The original altar was destroyed in World War II, and the current one, by Károly Antal and Pál C Molnár, dates from 1948.

Turkish Prayer Niche
One of the few remnants of the Turkish occupation (see pp26–7) is this mihrab, or prayer niche, indicating the direction of Mecca.

★ Gothic Chapel
This vaulted chapel is entered through a painted archway. It features recreated tracery windows.

Crest of Pest
The crest of Pest adorns the pedestal of a Renaissance tabernacle, which was commissioned by Pest's city council in 1507. It is the work of a 16th-century Italian artist.

HISTORICAL FLOORPLAN OF THE CHURCH

Nothing remains of the first church: the oldest sections date from the 12th-century Romanesque church.

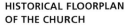

KEY

■	Romanesque church
■	Gothic church
■	Baroque church

The opulent façade of the Vigadó concert hall, decorated with figures and busts of statesmen, leaders and other prominent Hungarians

Inner City Parish Church ❶
Belvárosi Plébánia Templom

See pp124–5.

Vigadó Square ❷
Vigadó Tér

Map 4 D1 (10 D4). 🚋 2. **Tel** 354 37 55. ☐ 10am–6pm Tue–Sun.

The Vigadó concert hall, incorporating a cultural centre and gallery, dominates the square with its mix of eclectic forms. It was built by Frigyes Feszl in 1859–64 to replace a predecessor destroyed by fire during the uprising of 1848–9 *(see pp30–31)*. The façade includes features such as folk motifs and busts of former monarchs, rulers and other Hungarian personalities. An old Hungarian coat of arms is also visible in the centre.

The Budapest Marriott Hotel *(see p185)*, located on one side of the square, was designed by József Finta in 1969. It was one of the first modern hotels to be built in Budapest.

On the Danube promenade is a statue of a childlike figure on the railings: *Little Princess (see p65)*, by László Marton. The square also has craft stalls, cafés and restaurants.

József Nádor Square ❸
József Nádor Tér

Map 2 E5 (10 D3). Ⓜ *Vörösmarty tér.*

Archduke József, after whom this square is named, was appointed as the emperor's Palatine for Hungary in 1796 at the age of 20. He ruled the country for 51 years until his death in 1847. One of the few Habsburgs sympathetic to the Hungarian people, he was instrumental in the development of Buda and Pest and, in 1808, he initiated the Embellishment Commission *(see p30)*.

A statue of Archduke József, by Johann Halbig, stands in the middle of the square. It was erected in 1869.

Some of the houses on the square are worth individual mention. The Neo-Classical Gross Palace at No. 1 *(see p48)* was built in 1824 by József Hild. Once a café, it now houses a bank. The building at Nos. 5–6,

Sculpture in Vigadó Square

which overlooks the southern end of the square, dates from 1859 and was built by Hugó Máltás. At No. 11 is a shop run by the Herend company *(see p212)*. Its factory has produced world-renowned porcelain for almost 200 years.

Mihály Vörösmarty Square ❹
Vörösmarty Mihály Tér

Map 2 E5 (10 D3). Ⓜ *Vörösmarty tér.*

In the middle of the square stands a monument depicting the poet Mihály Vörösmarty (1800–55). Unveiled in 1908, it is the work of Ede Telcs.

Behind the monument, on the eastern side of the square, is the former Luxus department store, which used to be one of the rare places in the Socialist era where you could buy fashionable clothes.

On the northern side of the square there is a renowned pâtisserie, opened by Henrik Kugler in 1858. It was taken over by the Swiss *patissière* Emil Gerbeaud, who was responsible for the richly decorated interior which survives to this day.

The elegant interior of the Gerbeaud pâtisserie, on Mihály Vörösmarty Square

A tempting selection of coffee, cakes, pastries and desserts are on offer. In summer, these can be taken on a terrace overlooking the square.

Thonet House, decorated with Zsolnay tiles, at No. 11 Váci Street

Váci Street ⑤
Váci Utca

Map 4 E1–F2 (10 E5).
Ⓜ Ferenciek tere.

Once two separate streets, which were joined at the beginning of the 18th century, Váci Street still has two distinct characters. Today, part of the southern section is open to traffic, while the northern end is pedestrianized and has long been a popular commercial centre. Most of the buildings lining the street date from the 19th and early 20th centuries. More recently, however, modern department stores, banks and shopping arcades have sprung up among the older original buildings.

Philantia, a Secession style florist's shop opened in 1905, now occupies part of the Neo-Classical block at No. 9, built in 1840 by József Hild. No. 9 also houses the Pest Theatre, where classic plays by Anton Chekhov, among others, are staged. The building was once occupied by the Inn of the Seven Electors, which had a large ballroom-cum-concert hall. It was here that a 12-year-old Franz Liszt performed.

Thonet House, at No. 11, is most notable for the Zsolnay tiles *(see p56)* from Pécs, which decorate its façade.

No. 13 is the oldest building on Váci Street and was built in 1805. In contrast, the post-modern Fontana department store at No. 16, was built in 1984. Outside the store there is a bronze fountain with a figure of Hermes, dating from the mid-19th century.

The Nádor Hotel once stood at No. 20 and featured a statue of Archduke Palatine József in front of the entrance. Today the Mercure Hotel *(see p185)*, designed by József Finta and opened in 1987, stands here.

In a side street off Váci Street, at No. 13 Régiposta utca, is a building from the Modernist period. An unusual sight in Pest, this Bauhaus-influenced building dates from 1937 and is by Lajos Kozma.

Klotild Palaces ⑥
Klotild Paloták

Szabadsajtó utca. **Map** 4 E1 (10 E5).
Ⓜ Ferenciek tere.

Flanking Szabadsajtó utca, on the approach to the Elizabeth Bridge, stand two massive apartment blocks built in 1902. The buildings were commissioned by the daughter-in-law of Palatine József, Archduchess Klotild, after whom they were named.

They were designed by Flóris Korb and Kálmán Giergl in the Historicist style, with

One of the twin Klotild Palaces, from 1902, by the approach to the Elizabeth Bridge *(see p63)*

elements of Rococo decoration. The Palace to the right houses apartments and the Buddha Bar Hotel *(see p185)*, while the left side houses the Casino Lido, a restaurant and a café.

Pest County Hall ⑦
Pest Megyei Önkormányzat

Városház utca 7. **Map** 4 F1 (10 E4).
Tel 485 68 00. Ⓜ Ferenciek tere.
◷ 8am–4:30pm Mon–Thu, 8am–2pm Fri.

Built in several stages, this is one of Pest's most beautiful, monumental Neo-Classical civic buildings. It was erected during the 19th century, as part of the plan for the city drawn up by the Embellishment Commission.

A seat of the Council of Pest has existed on this site since the end of the 17th century. By 1811, however, the building included two conference halls, a prison and a prison chapel. In 1829–32, a wing designed by József Hofrichter was added on Semmelweis utca, which was used to accommodate council employees.

In 1838 another redevelopment programme was begun, this time employing designs by Mátyás Zitterbarth Jr, a highly regarded exponent of Neo-Classical architecture. Completed in 1842, it included an impressive façade, which overlooks Városház utca. This features a portico with six Corinthian columns supporting a prominent tympanum.

Pest County Hall was destroyed in the course of World War II. During post-war rebuilding it was enlarged, with the addition of three internal courtyards, the first of which is surrounded by atmospheric cloisters. Due to the excellent acoustics, concerts are often held here during the summer.

Between Pest County Hall and the Municipal Council Offices building *(see p128)*, in the small Kamermayer Károly tér, there is a monument to the first mayor of Budapest. Károly Kamermayer (1829–97) took office in 1873 after the unification of Óbuda, Buda and Pest. The aluminium monument was designed in 1942 by Béla Szabados.

Municipal Council Offices ❽

Fővárosi Önkormányzat

Városház utca 9–11. **Map** 4 E1 & F1 (10 E4). **Tel** 327 10 00. Ⓜ *Ferenciek tere.* ◗ *8am–4:30pm Mon–Thu, 8am–12:30pm Fri.* **www**.budapest.hu

The largest Baroque building in Budapest, this edifice was completed in 1735 to a design by the architect Anton Erhard Martinelli. It was originally a hospital for veterans of the war between the Christians and Turks at the end of the 17th century *(see pp26–7)*.

In 1894 the city authorities bought the building in order to convert it into council offices. Ármin Hegedűs was commissioned to refurbish the building.

Most notable are the bas-reliefs decorating the gates on the Városház utca side of the building. The scenes depicted in the bas-reliefs commemorate a victory of Charles III *(see p19)* and Prince Eugene of Savoy's role in the war against the Turks *(see p71)*. These are thought to be the work of the Viennese sculptor Johann Christoph Mader.

Turkish Bank ❾

Török Bankház

Szervita tér 3. **Map** 4 E1 (10 D4). Ⓜ *Deák Ferenc tér.*

Dating from 1906 and designed by Henrik Böhm and Ármin Hegedűs, the building that formerly housed the Turkish Bank is a wonderful example of the Secession style.

The exterior used modern construction methods to create the glass façade, which is set in reinforced concrete. Above the fenestration, in the gable, is a magnificent colourful mosaic by Miksa Róth. Entitled *Glory to Hungary*, it depicts Hungary paying homage to the Virgin Mary, or *Patrona Hungariae (see p117)*. Angels and shepherds surround the Virgin, along with figures of Hungarian political heroes, such as Prince Ferenc Rákóczi *(see p28)*, István Széchenyi *(see pp30–31)* and Lajos Kossuth *(see p106)*.

Glory to Hungary, the mosaic on the façade of the Turkish Bank

Servite Church ❿

Szervita Templom

Szervita tér 7. **Map** 4 E1 (10 D4). Ⓜ *Deák Ferenc tér.*

This Baroque church was built between 1725–32 to a design by János Hölbling and György Pauer. In 1871, the façade was rebuilt and the tower was covered with a new roof, designed by József Diescher.

Above the doorway there are figures of St Peregrin and St Anne, and above them sit St Philip and St Augustine. To the right of the entrance there is a bas-relief by János Istók, dating from 1930. It is dedicated to the heroes of the VIIth Wilhelm Hussar Regiment who gave their lives in World War I.

Lutheran Church ⓫

Evangélikus Templom

Deák tér 4. **Map** 2 E5 (10 E3). **Tel** 317 34 13. Ⓜ *Deák Ferenc tér.* ♿ **National Lutheran Museum Tel** 483 21 50. ◗ *10am–6pm Tue–Sun.* 📷 ✔ *by arrangement.*

Mihály Pollack designed this Neo-Classical church, built between 1799–1808. A portico, which features a tympanum supported by Doric columns, was added to the façade in 1856 by József Hild.

The church's simplicity is typical of early Neo-Classicism.

It also reflects the notion of minimal church decoration, which was upheld by this branch of Protestantism. Above the modest main altar is a copy of Raphael's *Transfiguration* by Franz Sales Lochbihler, made in 1811. Organ recitals are often held in the church, which has excellent acoustics.

Another Neo-Classical building adjoins the church. Constructed as a Lutheran school, it is now the National Lutheran Museum. The museum illustrates the history of the Reformation in Hungary, with the most interesting exhibit being a copy of Martin Luther's last will and testament. The original document, dating from 1542, is held in the Lutheran Archives.

Neo-Classical main altar in the Lutheran Church

The Danube Fountain, built in 1880–83 by Miklós Ybl

Danube Fountain ⓬
Danubius Kút

Erzsébet tér. **Map** 2 E5 (10 D3). Ⓜ *Deák Ferenc tér.*

This fountain, which once stood in Kálvin tér, was designed and built by Miklós Ybl *(see p94)* in 1880–83. It is decorated with copies by Dezső Győri of original sculptures, by Béla Brestyánszky and Leó Feszler, which were damaged in World War II.

The figure at the top of the fountain is Danubius, representing the Danube. The three female figures below symbolize Hungary's three principal rivers after the Danube: the Tisza, the Dráva and the Száva.

New Theatre ⓭
Új Színház

Paulay Ede utca 35. **Map** 2 F4 (10 E2). *Tel* 269 60 21. Ⓜ *Opera.*

Originally completed in 1909, this building has undergone many transformations. It was designed by Béla Lajta in the Secession style, and, as the home of the cabaret troupe Parisian Mulató, became a shrine to frivolity.

In 1921 it was completely restyled by László Vágó, who turned it into a theatre. After World War II, the theatre gained a glass-and-steel façade, and a children's theatre company was based here.

Between 1988–90 the building was returned to its original form using Lajta's plans. Gilding, stained glass and marble once more adorn this unusual building. Hungary's New Theatre is now in residence.

Franz Liszt Academy of Music ⓮
Liszt Ferenc Zeneakadémia

Liszt Ferenc tér 8. **Map** 7 A1 (10 F2). *Tel* 462 46 00. 🚎 *4, 6 to Király utca.* **www**.liszt.com

The academy is housed in a late Historicist palace, built between 1904–7 by Kálmán Giergl and Flóris Korb. Above the main entrance there is a statue of Franz Liszt, by Alajos Stróbl. The six bas-reliefs above its base are by Ede Telcs, and depict the history of music.

The Secession interiors of this building deserve particular attention. The *Fount of Youth* fresco, in the first floor foyer, is by Aladár Körösfői-Kriesch, who was a member of the Gödöllő school. The academy has two auditoriums. The first seats 1,200 people and features allegories of musical movements. The second seats 400 and is used for chamber music.

New York Palace ⓯
New York Palota

Erzsébet körút 9–11. **Map** 7 B2. *Tel* 886 61 11. Ⓜ *Blaha Lujza tér.* 🔟 🖥 **www**.boscolohotels.com

Built between 1891–5 to a design by the architect Alajos Hauszmann, the building was initially the offices of an American insurance firm.

This five-floor edifice displays an eclectic mix of Neo-Baroque and Secession motifs. The decorative sculptures that animate the façade are the work of Károly Senyei.

On the ground floor is the renowned New York Café. The beautiful, richly gilded Neo-Baroque interior, with its chandeliers and marble pillars, now attracts tourists, just as it once attracted the literary and artistic circles in its heyday. The New York Palace hotel *(see p187)* has 112 rooms, a luxurious spa, and a restaurant serving international haute cuisine.

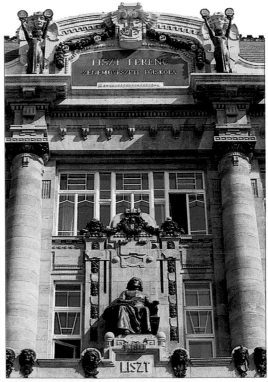

Statue of Franz Liszt above the entrance to the Academy of Music

Hungarian National Museum ❷

Seal from Esztergom

The Hungarian National Museum is the country's richest source of art and artifacts relating to its own turbulent history. Founded in 1802, the museum owes its existence to Count Ferenc Széchényi, who offered his collection of coins, books and documents to the nation. The museum's constantly expanding collection of art and documents is exhibited in an impressive Neo-Classical edifice built by Mihály Pollack.

Placing the Cornerstone *(1864)*
This painting by Miklós Barabás shows the ceremony that marked the beginning of construction of the Chain Bridge (see p62) in 1842.

Campaign Chest
This carved Baroque campaign chest features the prince regent's decoration and the Hungarian crest. It dates from the insurrection led by Ferenc II Rákóczi (see p28).

Armchair
Adorned with multi-coloured fruit and floral ornamentation, this armchair dates from the early 18th century. It is the work of Ferenc II Rákóczi, who learnt carpentry during his exile in Turkey.

★ **Coronation Mantle**
This textile masterpiece, made of Byzantine silk, was donated to the church in Székesfehérvár by St Stephen in 1031. It became the Coronation Mantle in the 12th century.

KEY

☐	Coronation Mantle
☐	Archaeological exhibition
☐	11th–17th-century exhibition
☐	18th–19th-century exhibition
☐	20th-century exhibition

MUSEUM GUIDE
On the first floor is the Coronation Mantle and the archaeological exhibition. Second floor exhibits comprise Hungarian artifacts from 11th–20th centuries. The Roman Lapidary is found in the basement.

Main entrance

VISITORS' CHECKLIST

Múzeum körút 14–16. **Map** 7 A4
(10 F5). **Tel** *338 21 22 (327 77 73*
for guided tours in English).
47, 49. M *Kálvin tér, Astória.*
9, 15. 10am–6pm Tue–Sun.
www.hnm.hu

★ Funeral Crown
This magnificent 13th-century golden
crown was found in the ruins of the
Dominican Church and Convent on
Margaret Island in the Danube
(see pp172–3).

Second
floor

Pelisse
This short jacket is typical of
Hungarian national costume.
It belonged to Gábor Bethlen, a
prince of Transylvania, and
dates from around 1620.

First
floor

Gothic Well
These recon-
structed fragments are
part of a well from
the Royal Palace at
Visegrád (see
p164). The well
dates from the 14th-
century rule of the
Angevin dynasty.

★ Golden Stag
This hand-forged Iron Age figure dates
from the 6th century BC. It was originally
part of a Scythian prince's shield.

STAR EXHIBITS

★ Coronation Mantle

★ Funeral Crown

★ Golden Stag

Exploring the Museum's Collection

A 13th-century seal

The steps of the Hungarian National Museum were the scene of a major event in Hungary's history. It was from these steps that, in 1848, the poet Sándor Petőfi first read his *National Song*, which sparked the uprising against Habsburg rule *(see p30–31)*. This moment is commemorated each year on 15 March, when the museum is decorated in the national colours and a re-enactment is performed. Items from the museum's rich collection, including works of art and craft, historical documents and photographs, vividly illustrate this and other events from Hungary's varied and fascinating past.

Remarkably, the royal insignia, which includes a sceptre and golden crown, have survived Hungary's dramatic history. Discovered by the American forces during World War II, they were removed and stored in Fort Knox before being returned to Hungary in 1978.

In 2000, these other treasures of the royal insignia were transferred to the Domed Hall of Parliament *(see pp108–9)*, where they can also be visited.

ARCHAEOLOGICAL EXHIBITION

The archaeological display was opened in 2002 to celebrate the 200th anniversary of the museum's foundation. The visitor is taken through a display of Hungary's heritage, spanning the period between 400 BC and AD 804, from the first inhabitants of the country at Vértesszölős until the end of the Early Medieval period, immediately preceeding the Hungarian Conquest.

The exhibition presents some of the latest and important archaeological finds, and abounds in authentic recon-structions of the past.

11TH–17TH-CENTURY EXHIBITION

The exhibition begins in the Árpád era and features one of the museum's most valuable exhibits, the crown of Constantine IX Monomachus, decorated with enamel work. Also on display in this section are the funeral decorations of

Monument to poet János Arany in front of the Neo-Classical façade

MUSEUM BUILDING

Built between 1837–47, according to a design by Mihály Pollack, this imposing Neo-Classical building is one of the finest manifestations of that architectural epoch.

The façade is preceded by a monumental portico, which is crowned by a tympanum designed by Raffael Ponti. The composition depicts the figure of Pannonia *(see p20)* among personifications of the arts and sciences.

In the gardens surrounding the museum there are a num-ber of statues of prominent figures from the spheres of literature, science and art. A monument to the poet János Arany, author of the *Toldi Trilogy*, stands in front of the main entrance. This bronze

and limestone work dates from 1893 and is by Alajos Stróbl. The notable features of the interior include the magnificent paintings by Mór Than and Károly Lotz in the main staircase.

CORONATION MANTLE

One of the most important Hungarian treasures, the Coronation Mantle *(see pp22–3)*, is currently on display in a separate hall of its own in the museum. Made of Byzantine silk, it was originally donated to the church by St Stephen in 1031. The magnificent gown was then refashioned in the 13th century. The now much faded cloth features an intricate embroidered design of fine gold thread and pearls.

Carved base of a chalice dating from the 15th century

Béla III, Romanesque sacred vessels, weapons and an interesting collection of coins.

The period of Angevin rule (see p18) coincided with the birth of the Gothic style, which is represented here by some excellent examples of gold work. The next two halls explore the reign of Sigismund of Luxembourg (see p24) and the achievements of János Hunyadi (see p24). On display here are copies of portraits of King Sigismund by Albrecht Dürer and a richly decorated ceremonial saddle. There are also several platinum and gold pieces, illuminated manuscripts and documents. The lifestyle of peasants from this era is illustrated, as well as the history of the royal court.

The reign of Mátyás Corvinus (see pp24–5) and the Jagiełło dynasty (see p18) marks the decline of the Gothic period and the birth of the Renaissance. Exhibits from this era include a 15th-century glass goblet belonging to King Mátyás, late Gothic pews from a church in Bártfa, armour and weapons, as well as a 16th-century dress belonging to Maria Habsburg.

Magnificent examples of sculpture, art and artifacts from the 16th and 17th centuries follow. Of interest are items that survived the Turkish occupation (see pp26–7), especially the everyday objects and weapons.

A separate hall is dedicated to the Transylvanian principality and the important historical role that it played. Exhibited here are vessels and jewellery elaborately crafted in gold, 17th-century costumes, and original ceramics produced by the people of Haban, who settled there in the early 17th century. This last section of the exhibition ends in 1686, at the time of the liberation of Buda by the Christian armies after the Turkish occupation. In this part of the museum there are also portraits of influential Hungarians from the period, and an interesting exhibition of jewellery dating from the 17th century.

Printing press used in 1848 to print nationalist propaganda

18TH–19TH-CENTURY EXHIBITION

This part of the museum covers Habsburg rule, a period of great civil unrest. The exhibition begins with artifacts connected to the Rákóczi insurrection of 1703–11 (see pp28–9). Weapons, as well as furniture from Ferenc II Rákóczi's palace, are exhibited here. One item of particular interest is the armchair produced by Rákóczi himself. The next hall is dedicated to 18th-century Hungarian art and culture.

Brooch from the 18th-century

The following rooms portray the Hungarian history of the first half of the 19th century. Artworks, including magnificent portraits and historic paintings, such as Placing the Cornerstone of the Chain Bridge, are assembled along with important documents and memoirs from that time.

The central section, dedicated to the uprising of 1848–9 (see pp30–31), features a printing press on which were printed leaflets outlining the 12 demands in Hungary's fight for independence from Austria.

The exhibits from the second half of the 19th century include collections of masonic items, official decorations, coins and historic manuscripts. Items relating to the coronation of Franz Joseph in 1867 and the Millennium Celebrations of 1896 are also displayed here.

20TH-CENTURY EXHIBITION

Reflecting the technical developments of this century, Hungary's recent history is presented in a documentary style. Photographs, and documents are widely used to illustrate this period. Artifacts relating to World War I and the era of revolution between the wars, and shocking documents from World War II can be found here. The post-war history of Hungary is depicted mainly from a political perspective. Emphasis is placed on significant episodes, such as the uprising of 1956 and the events of 1989, which signalled the end of Communism in Eastern Europe (see p35).

Guild chest from the 20th century

Jewish Quarter ⑯
Zsidó Negyed

Király utca, Rumbach Sebestyén utca,
Dohány utca & Akácfa utca. **Map** 2 F5
& 7 A2 (10 F3). 🅜 Deák Ferenc tér.

Jews first came to Hungary in
the 13th century and settled in
Buda and Óbuda. In the 19th
century, a larger Jewish
community was established
outside the Pest city boundary,
in a small area of Erzsébetváros.
In 1251, King Béla IV gave
the Jews of Buda certain privil-
iges, including freedom of

HOLOCAUST MEMORIAL

This sculpture of a weeping willow, designed by Imre
Varga, was unveiled in 1991 in memory of the 600,000
Hungarian Jews killed by the Nazis in World War II. It was
partly funded by the Hungarian-American actor Tony Curtis.

Window of the Orthodox Synagogue

religion. The Jewish community became well integrated
into Hungarian society, until
in 1941, a series of Nazi anti-
Semitic laws were passed and
the wearing of the Star of
David was made compulsory.
In 1944, a ghetto was created
in Pest and the deportation of
thousands of Jews to camps,
including Auschwitz, was imp-
lemented. After heavy fighting
between the Russian and German armies, the Soviet Red
Army liberated the ghetto on
18 January 1945. In total,
600,000 Hungarian Jews were

victims of the Holocaust. This
persecution is commemorated
by a plaque at the Orthodox
Synagogue on Rumbach utca.
In the late 19th century, three
synagogues were built and
many Jewish shops and workshops were established. Kosher
establishments, such as the
Hanna Étterem (see p200) in
the courtyard of the Orthodox
Synagogue, and the butcher
at No. 41 Kazinczy utca, were
a common feature. Shops are
now being reconstructed to
recreate the pre-ghetto character of the Jewish Quarter.

Great Synagogue ⑰
Zsinagóga

Dohány utca 2. **Map** 4 F1 (10 F4).
Tel 342 89 49. 🅜 Astoria. **Jewish
Museum** ⃝ Mar–Oct: 10am–
5:30pm Sun–Thu, 10am–3:30pm Fri;
Nov–Feb: 10am–3:30pm Sun–Thu,
10am–1:30pm Fri. 🖼 🅲

This synagogue is the
largest in Europe. It was built
in a Byzantine-Moorish style
by the Viennese architect
Ludwig Förster between
1854–9. It has three naves
and, following orthodox
tradition, separate galleries for
women. Together the naves
and galleries can accommodate up to 3,000 worshippers.
Some features, such as the
position of the reading plat-
form, reflect elements of
Judaic reform. The interior
has valuable decorative
fittings, particularly those on
the Ark of the Law, by
Frigyes Feszl. In 1931, a

museum was established; a
vast collection of historical
relics, Judaic devotional items
and everday objects, from
ancient Rome to the present

A large rose window is the
façade's main ornamentation. It
is located between two richly
decorated towers crowned with
distinctive onion domes.

The façade is composed
of white and red brick
and intricately designed
ceramic friezes.

day, has been assembled. It
includes the book of Chevra
Kadisha from 1792. There is
also a moving Holocaust
Memorial Room.

A Hebrew inscription from
the second book of Moses is
situated under the rose window.

Chapel of St Roch **①**
Szent Rókus Kápolna

Gyulai Pál u 2. **Map** 7 A3. **Tel** *338 35 15.* Ⓜ *Astoria or Blaha Lujza tér.*

Pest town council built this chapel in what was then an uninhabited area. It was dedicated to St Roch and St Rosalie, who were believed to provide protection against the plague, which afflicted Pest in 1711.

In 1740 the chapel was extended to its present size, and a tower was added in 1797. The façade is decorated with Baroque figures of saints, although the originals were replaced with copies in 1908.

Inside, on the right-hand wall of the chapel's nave, is a painting of the Virgin Mary from 1740. A painting by Jakab Warsch, depicting the Great Flood of 1838, is in the oratory.

Mihály Pollack Square **①**
Pollack Mihály Tér

Map 7 A4 (10 F5). Ⓜ *Kálvin tér.* **Festetics Palace Tel** *266 52 22.* 🖼 *by prior arrangement.*

At the rear of the Hungarian National Museum *(see pp130–33)* is a square named after Mihály Pollack, the architect of several Neo-Classical buildings such as the museum and Sándor Palace *(see p73).*

In the late 19th century, three palaces were built side by side on this square for the aristocratic elite of Hungary: Prince Festetics, Prince Eszterházy and Count Károlyi. The beautiful façades makes this one of the city's most captivating squares.

Miklós Ybl *(see p94)* built the French-Renaissance style palace at No. 6 for Lajos Károlyi, in 1863–5. The façade is decorated with sculptures by Károly Schaffer. There is also a covered driveway for carriages. Next door, at No. 8, is a small palace, which was built in 1865 for the Eszterházy family by Alajos Baumgarten. At No. 10 is the palace built for the Festetics family in 1862, again by Miklós Ybl. The interior, especially the Neo-Baroque staircase, is splendid.

Magnificent staircase inside the Festetics Palace on Mihály Pollack Square

Hungarian National Museum **②**
Nemzeti Múzeum

See pp130–33.

Ervin Szabó Library **②**
Szabó Ervin Könyvtàr

Szabó Ervin tér 1. **Map** 7 A4 (10 F5). **Tel** *411 50 00.* Ⓜ *Kálvin tér.* ⏰ *10am–8pm Mon–Fri, 10am–4pm Sat.* **www**.fszek.hu

In 1887, the wealthy industrialist Wenckheim family commissioned the architect Artur Meining to build a Neo-Baroque and Rococo style palace. The result was the former Wenckheim Palace, regarded as one of the most beautiful palaces in Budapest. The magnificent wrought-iron

Spiral staircase in one of the rooms of the Ervin Szabó Library

gates, dating from 1897, are the work of Gyula Jungfer. Also worth particular attention are the richly gilded salons on the first floor, as well as the dome above an oval panel of reliefs.

In 1926, the city council acquired the building and converted it into a public lending library, whose collection focuses on the city itself and the social sciences.

The Ervin Szabó Library was named after the politician and social reformer Ervin Szabó (1877–1918), who was the library's first director. It has over a hundred branches throughout Budapest and some three million books.

Calvinist Church **②**
Református Templom

Kálvin tér 7. **Map** 4 F2. **Tel** *217 67 69.* Ⓜ *Kálvin tér.* ⏰ *6pm Thu; 10am, 11:30am, 6pm Sun.*

This single nave church was designed by József Hofrichter and built between 1816–30. In 1848 József Hild designed the four-pillared façade and tympanum, and a spire was added in 1859. Inside the church, the pulpit and choir gallery were designed by Hild in 1831 and 1854 respectively. The stained-glass windows are the work of Miksa Róth. Sacred artifacts from the 17th and 18th centuries are kept in the church treasury.

Museum of Applied Arts ㉓

A Lalique pendant

Opened in 1896 by Emperor Franz Joseph for the Millennium Celebrations, this collection is housed not within a Neo-Classical building, but in an outstanding Secession building designed by Gyula Pártos and Ödön Lechner *(see p56)*. The exterior incorporated elements inspired by the Orient as well as the Zsolnay ceramics characteristic of Lechner's work. Damaged in 1945 and again in 1956, the building has now regained its original magnificence. The collection, founded in 1872, includes many examples of arts and crafts workmanship.

18th-Century Perfumer
The base of this decorative perfumer comes from Paris, the porcelain figure from Meissen in Germany.

Turkish Rug
Part of a large collection of Turkish Ottoman rugs, this carpet is from the period of Turkish occupation of Transylvania, and dates to around 1600.

Second floor

Ground floor

Inner Courtyard
This courtyard, covered by a glazed roof, is surrounded by cloisters with arcades designed in an Indian-Oriental style.

MUSEUM GUIDE
The museum is home to various temporary exhibitions on both floors. Pieces from the permanent collections, which include furniture, textiles, precious metals, ceramics and glassware, are illustrated here. The major exhibitions change each year, while the smaller national and foreign displays change monthly. The library, dating from 1872, is located on the first floor and contains around 50,000 books.

Main entrance

KEY

■	Library
□	Temporary exhibitions
□	Non-exhibition space
■	Permanent collections

Renaissance Tile
This tile, which dates from around 1530, depicts Queen Anne, wife of Ferdinand I.

VISITORS' CHECKLIST

Üllői út 33–37. **Map** 7 B5.
Tel 456 51 07. M Ferenc körút.
10am–6pm Tue–Sun.
www.imm.hu

Seahorses
Part of the Goldsmiths' Collection, two trident-wielding sea satyrs ride seahorses in this fanciful piece from Germany, circa 1590.

First floor

Astronomical Clock
Medieval craftsmanship distinguishes this ornate astronomical clock from 1566, which displays the relative positions of the sun, moon and constellations.

Holics Dish
Animal and plant-shaped kitchen ceramics in the Holics style were manufactured in Hungary in the mid-18th century.

Devotional Tablet
This csóktábla or "kiss tablet" was crafted in Limoges, France, at the beginning of the 16th century.

Central Market Hall 24

Központi Vásárcsarnok

Vámház körút 1-3. **Map** 4 F3.
Tel 366 33 00. 🚋 *47, 49.* Ⓜ *Kálvin tér.* ⏲ *6am–5pm Mon, 6am–6pm Tue–Fri, 6am–2pm Sat.* ◉ *Sun.*

Rebuilt in 1999, Budapest's main produce market is a great place to find local delicacies such as spicy *kolbász* salami and sheep's cheese. There are numerous farmers' stalls selling meat, sausage, fruit, vegetables and fish. The upper floor has a dozen or so food booths and souvenir stalls selling paprika, caviar, Hungarian dolls, T-shirts and chessboards. The basement level has a small grocery store selling imported delicacies.

Sausages for sale at the Central Market Hall

Decorative element on the façade of the City Council Chamber

City Council Chamber 25

Új Városháza

Váci utca 62–64. **Map** 4 F2 (10 E5).
Ⓜ *Deák tér.* *Tel 235 17 00.*
⏲ *8am–noon Fri* 🔲 *compulsory*

This three-floor edifice was built between 1870–75 as offices for the newly unified city of Budapest *(see p32)*. Its architect, Imre Steindl, was also responsible for designing Parliament *(see pp108–9)*.
The building is a mix of styles. The exterior is a Neo-Renaissance design in brick, with grotesques between the

windows, while the interior features cast-iron Neo-Gothic motifs. The Great Debating Hall is decorated with mosaics designed by Károly Lotz.
Many antiquarian bookshops and galleries have now opened around here. Fashionable bars, restaurants and cafés, and pedestrianization of the streets, make this a charming area.

Serbian Church 26

Szerb Templom

Szerb utca 2–4. **Map** 4 F2 (10 E5).
Ⓜ *Kálvin tér, Ferenciek tere.*
⏲ *10am–6pm Tue–Sun.*

Serbs settled in the now largely residential area around the church as early as the 16th century. The end of the 17th century brought a new wave of Serb immigrants, and by the early 19th century Serbs comprised almost 25 per cent of Pest's home-owners.
In 1698, the Serb community replaced an earlier church on the site with this Baroque one. The church gained its final appearance after a rebuilding project that lasted until the mid-18th century, probably undertaken by András Meyerhoffer.
The interior of the church is arranged according to Greek Orthodox practice. A section of the nave, which is entered from the vestibule, is reserved for

Ceramic tile from the Serbian Church

women. This area is divided from the men's section by a partition, and the division is further emphasized by the floor, which has been lowered by 30 cm (1 ft). The choir gallery is enclosed by an iconostasis that divides it from the sanctuary. This iconostasis dates from around 1850. The carving is by Serb sculptor Miahai Janic; Renaissance-influenced paintings are by Greek artist Károly Sterio.

Lóránd Eötvös University 27

Eötvös Lóránd Tudomány Egyetem Központja

Egyetem tér 1–3. **Map** 4 F2 (10 E5).
Ⓜ *Ferenciek tere, Kálvin tér.*
Tel 411 65 00. www.elte.hu

In 1635, Cardinal Péter Pázmány, the leader of the Counter-Reformation, established a university in Nagyszombat (now Trnava in Slovakia). It moved to Buda in 1777, nearly a century after the end of the Turkish occupation *(see pp26–7)*, during the reign of Maria Theresa. Emperor Joseph II transferred the university to Pest, to the environs of the Pauline Church, now called the University Church. It was not until 1889 that the university was endowed with a permanent home. This Neo-Baroque building, now the Law Faculty, was designed by architects including Sándor Baumgarten and Fülöp Herzog.

The university is named after the noted physicist Lóránd Eötvös (1848–1919).

University Church 28

Egyetemi Templom

Papnövelde utca 9. **Map** 4 F2 (10 E5). *Tel* 318 05 55. M Kálvin tér. ⬚ 7am–6pm Mon–Sat, 8am–7:30pm Sun.

This single-nave church is considered one of the most impressive Baroque churches in the city. It was built for the Pauline Order in 1725–42, and was probably designed by András Meyerhoffer. The tower was added in 1771. The Pauline Order, founded in 1263 by Canon Euzebiusz, was the only religious order to be founded in Hungary.

The magnificent exterior features a tympanum and a row of pilasters that divide the façade. Figures of St Paul and St Anthony flank the emblem of the Pauline Order, which crowns the exterior. The carved-wood interior of the main vestibule is also worth particular mention.

Inside the church a row of side chapels stand behind unusual marble pilasters. In 1776 Johann Bergl painted the vaulted ceiling with frescoes depicting scenes from the life of Mary. Sadly, these frescoes are now in poor condition.

The main altar dates from 1746, and the carved statues behind it are the work of József Hebenstreit. Above it, a copy of the painting *The Black Madonna of Czestochowa*, is thought to date from 1720. Much of the Baroque interior detail of the church is the work of the Pauline monks, such as the balustrade of the organ loft and the carved pulpit on the right.

Sculptures decorating the pulpit in the University Church

Tympanum adorning the façade of the University Library

Károlyi Palace 29

Károlyi Palota

Károlyi Mihály utca 16. **Map** 4 F2 (10 E5). *Tel* 317 36 11. M Ferenciek tere, Kálvin tér. **Petőfi Exhibition** ⬚ 10am–6pm Tue–Sun (until 4pm Nov–Feb). 📷 317 36 11.

In 1696 there was a small Baroque palace on this site, which was extended by András Mayerhoffer between 1759–68. Subsequent rebuilding, which gave the palace a Neo-Classical appearance, was undertaken between 1832–41 by Anton Riegl. It is named after Mihály Károlyi, leader of the 1918–19 Hungarian Republic *(see p34)*, who was born here in 1875.

The palace now houses the Hungarian Museum of Literature and the Petőfi Exhibition, dedicated to the poet Sándor Petőfi *(see p31)*. Other poets remembered are Atilla József, Endre Ady and Mór Jókai.

University Library 30

Egyetemi Könyvtár

Ferenciek tere 6. **Map** 4 F1 (10 E5). *Tel* 266 58 66. M Ferenciek tere, Kálvin tér. ⬚ 9am–3:30pm Mon–Fri.

This Neo-Renaissance Edifice, by Antal Szkalniczyky and Henrik Koch, was built from 1873–6. It is distinguished by the dome on the corner tower. The library's two million works include 11 *Corviniani (see p72)* and 160 medieval manuscripts and miniatures. The reading room has sgraffiti by Mór Than and frescoes by Károly Lotz.

Franciscan Church 31

Belvárosi Ferences Templom

Ferenciek tere 9. **Map** 4 F1 (10 E4). *Tel* 317 33 22. M Ferenciek tere. ⬚ 7am–8pm daily. ⬤ noon–4pm.

A Franciscan church and monastery have stood on this site, beyond the old city walls, since the 13th century. In 1541 the Turks rebuilt the church as the Mosque of Sinan, but after the liberation *(see pp26–7)* the monks regained the building. Between 1727–43 they remodelled the church in the Baroque style, which it still retains today.

The façade features a magnificent portal incorporating sculptures of Franciscan saints, and the Franciscan emblem crowned by a figure of Mary being adored by angels.

The interior of the church is decorated with frescoes, dating from 1894–5, by Károly Lotz and paintings by Viktor Tardos Krenner, from 1925–6. The jewel of this church is the Baroque main altar with sculptures that date from 1741 and 1851. The side altars and the pulpit date from 1851–2.

AROUND VÁROSLIGET

Városliget, or City Park, was once an area of marshland, which served as a royal hunting ground. Leopold I gave the land to the town of Pest, but it was in the mid-18th century, under Maria Theresa, that the area was drained and planted. Today's park was designed towards the end of the 19th century in the English style, which was the fashion of the

Statue of János Hunyadi

day. Városliget was chosen as the focus of the Millennium Celebrations in 1896 *(see p142)*, which marked the 1,000-year anniversary of the conquest of the Carpathian basin by the Magyars. A massive building programme was undertaken, which included the Museum of Fine Arts, Vajdahunyad Castle and the impressive monument in Heroes' Square.

SIGHTS AT A GLANCE

Museums

Ferenc Hopp Museum of Far Eastern Art **6**
Franz Liszt Museum **2**
House of Terror Museum **1**
Museum of Fine Arts pp146–9 **9**
Műcsarnok Art Gallery **8**
Kodály Memorial Museum **4**

Parks and Zoos

Funfair **12**
Zoo **11**

Streets and Monuments

Hermina Street **14**
Millennium Monument **7**
Városligeti Avenue **5**

Historic Buildings

University of Fine Art **3**
Erkel Theatre **15**
Széchenyi Baths **13**
Vajdahunyad Castle **10**

GETTING THERE

The M1 metro line runs under Andrássy út from Bajcsy-Zs Út to Hősök tere, while bus 104 runs along the street above. Trams, buses and the metro operate in the south of the area, around Thököly út.

KEY

■ Street-by-Street map
  See pp142–3
Ⓜ Metro station
⊠ Post office
🚊 Train station

0 metres 400
0 yards 400

◁ **The ornate neo-Baroque ceiling at Széchenyi Baths**

Street-by-Street: Around Heroes' Square

Heroes' Square is a relic of a proud era in Hungary's history. It was here that the Millennium Celebrations opened in 1896. A striking example of this national pride is the Millennium Monument. Its colonnades feature statues of renowned Hungarian leaders and politicians, and the grand central column is crowned by a figure of the Archangel Gabriel. Vajdahunyad Castle was built in Városliget, or City Park, adjacent to the square. Probably the most flamboyant expression of the celebrations, it is composed of elements of the finest architectural works found throughout Hungary.

Árpád, leader of the Magyars

★ Museum of Fine Arts
This monumental museum building has an eight-pillared portico supporting a tympanum ❾

Entrance to the Zoo

Millennium Monument
Dominating Heroes' Square, this monument includes a figure of Rydwan, the god of war, by György Zala.

Műcsarnok Art Gallery
The crest of Hungary decorates the façade of this building – the country's largest venue for artistic exhibitions ❽

Secession pavilion

THE HUNGARIAN MILLENNIUM CELEBRATIONS

The Millennium Celebrations in 1896 marked a high point in the development of Budapest and in the history of the Austro-Hungarian monarchy. The city underwent modernization on a scale unknown in Europe at that time. Hundreds of houses, palaces and civic buildings were constructed, gas lighting was introduced and continental Europe's first underground transport system was opened.

Archangel Gabriel

| 0 metres | 200 |
| 0 yards | 200 |

KEY

– – – Suggested route

★ Széchenyi Baths
This is the largest complex of spa baths in Europe. Its hot springs, discovered in 1876, bubble up from a depth of 970 m (3,180 ft) and are reputed to have considerable healing properties ⑬

LOCATOR MAP
See Street Finder, maps 5 & 6

Városliget

Ják Church
This church faithfully reproduces the portal of a Benedictine church, dating from 1214, which can be found in the area of Ják, near the border with Austria. It is part of the Vajdahunyad Castle complex.

Statue of Anonymous
Completed in 1903 by Miklós Ligeti, this is one of Budapest's most famous monuments.

★ Vajdahunyad Castle
This Baroque section of the castle houses the Museum of Agriculture ⑩

STAR SIGHTS

- ★ Museum of Fine Arts
- ★ Széchenyi Baths
- ★ Vajdahunyad Castle

The former headquarters of the secret police on Andrássy Avenue

House of Terror Museum ❶
Teror Háza Múzeum

Andrássy út 60. **Map** 2 F5 (10 E2). **Tel** 374 26 00. Ⓜ *Vörösmarty utca,* 🚍 *4,6 to Oktogon.* 🕐 *10am–6pm Tue–Sun.* 🈳 www.terrorhaza.hu

The museum is located in the former headquarters of the secret police of both the Nazi and Communist governments. It records the grim events and practices of the "double occupation" of Hungary at the end of World War II.

Franz Liszt Museum ❷
Liszt Ferenc Emlékmúzeum

Vörösmarty út 35. **Map** 5 A5. **Tel** 322 98 04. Ⓜ *Vörösmarty utca.* 🕐 *10am–6pm Mon–Fri, 9am–5pm Sat.* 🈳 ✚ www.lisztmuseum.hu

This Neo-Renaissance corner house was designed in 1877 by Adolf Lang. Above the windows of the second floor are bas-reliefs depicting famous composers – J S Bach, Wolfgang Amadeus Mozart,

Joseph Haydn, Ferenc Erkel, Ludwig van Beethoven, and Franz Liszt himself. Liszt not only lived in this house, but also established an Academy of Music in the city *(see p129)*.

In 1986, 100 years after Liszt's death, this museum was established in his house. Various items were assembled here, including documents, furniture and two pianos on which he composed and practised.

University of Fine Art ❸
Képzőművészeti Egyetem

Andrássy út 69–71. **Map** 5 A5. **Tel** 342 17 38. Ⓜ *Vörösmarty utca.* **Barcsay Gallery** 🕐 *10am–6pm Mon–Fri, 10am–1pm Sat (seasonal).* 🈳 www.mke.hu

The university began as a drawing school, later becoming a Higher School of Art. Since 1876, it has occupied these adjacent buildings on Andrássy Street.

The two-floor Neo-Renaissance building at No. 71 was designed in 1875, by Lajos Rauscher. Its façade is decorated with sgrafitti by Robert Scholtz. The Italianate Renaissance exterior of No. 69, designed by Adolf Lang from 1875–7, is distinguished by Corinthian pilasters and a full-length balcony. The entrance hall and first-floor corridor feature frescoes by Károly Lotz. Only the Barcsay Gallery is open to visitors, but the interior can be glimpsed from here.

Sgrafitto by Robert Scholtz

Kodály Memorial Museum ❹
Kodály Zoltán Emlékmúzeum

Kodály Körönd 1. **Map** 5 B5. **Tel** 342 84 48. Ⓜ *Kodály Körönd.* 🕐 *10am–4pm Wed, 10am–6pm Thu–Sat, 10am–2pm Sun.* ⬤ *Mon, Tue.* 🈳 🈳 www.kodaly.hu

Zoltán Kodály (1881–1967) was one of the greatest Hungarian composers of the 20th century. His profound knowledge of Hungarian folk music allowed him to use elements of it in his compositions, which reflected the fashion for Impressionism and Neo-Romanticism in music.

This museum was established in 1990 and occupies the house where he lived and worked from 1924 until his death in 1967. A plaque set into one of the walls of the house bears testimony to this fact. The museum consists of three rooms that have been preserved in their original style, and a fourth room that is used for exhibitions. An archive has also been created here, for the composer's valuable handwritten music scores and correspondence.

Worthy of attention are the composer's piano in the salon and a number of folklore ceramics which Kodály collected in the course of his ethnographical studies. Portraits and busts of Kodály by Lajos Petri can also be viewed.

Városligeti Avenue ❺
Városligeti Fasor

Map 5 C5. Ⓜ *Hősök tere.*

This beautiful street, lined with plane trees, leads from Lövölde tér to Városliget.

At the beginning of the avenue is a Calvinist church built in 1912–13 by Aladár Árkay. This stark edifice is virtually bereft of any architectural features. However, stylized, geometric folk motifs

Original furnishings in the salon in the Franz Liszt Museum

Chinese gate at the Ráth György Museum on Városligeti Avenue

have been used as ornamentation and harmonize with the interior Secession decoration.

In front of the church is the Ráth György Museum, part of the Ferenc Hopp Museum of Far Eastern Art, displaying artifacts from China and Japan collected in the 19th century.

Further along the avenue is a Lutheran church. It was constructed between 1903–5 to a Neo-Gothic design by Samu Pecz, who also designed the interior detail. Worthy of note is the painting on the high altar, by Gyula Benczúr, entitled *The Adoration of the Magi.*

Ferenc Hopp Museum of Far Eastern Art ❻

Hopp Ferenc Kelet-ázsiai Művészeti Múzeum

Andrássy út 103. **Map** 5 B4.
Tel *322 84 76.* Ⓜ *Bajza utca.*
◯ *10am–6pm Tue–Sun.*
For guided tours call 456 51 10.
Ráth György Museum *Városligeti Fasor 12.* ***Tel*** *342 39 16.*
◯ *10am–6pm Tue–Sun.*
www.hoppmuzeum.hu

Ferenc Hopp (1833–1919), a wealthy merchant and the proprietor of an opthalmic shop, was the first great Hungarian traveller, amassing a collection of more than 20,000 items from countries such as India, China and Vietnam. The collection's smaller

examples of art and handicrafts can be seen in his former home, while its garden features large stone sculptures.

The Chinese and Japanese collection is displayed in the **Ráth György Museum**.

Millennium Monument ❼

Milleniumi Emlékmű

Map 5 C4. Ⓜ *Hősök tere.*

This monument was designed by György Zala and Albert Schikedanz to commemorate Hungary's Millennium Celebrations in 1896, but was not completed until 1929.

At the centre of the monument is a 36-m (120-ft) high Corinthian column, upon which stands the Archangel Gabriel holding St István's crown and the apostolic cross. These objects signify Hungary's conversion to Christianity under King István *(see p22).* At the base of the column there are equestrian statues of Prince Árpád and six of the conquering Magyar warriors.

A stone tile set in front of the column marks the Tomb of the Unknown Soldier.

The column is embraced by two curved colonnades, featuring allegorical compositions at both ends. Personifications of War and Peace are nearest the column, while Knowledge and Glory crown the far end of the right-hand colonnade, and Labour and Prosperity crown the far end of the left. Statues of great Hungarians, including statesmen and monarchs, are arranged within the colonnades.

The right-hand colonnade of the Millennium Monument on Heroes' Square, completed in 1929

Museum of Fine Arts ❾

The origins of the Museum of Fine Arts' comprehensive collection date from 1870, when the state bought a magnificent collection of paintings from the aristocratic Esterházy family. The museum's collection was enriched by donations and acquisitions, and in 1906 it moved to its present location.

The building, by Fülöp Herzog and Albert Schickedanz, is Neo-Classical with Italian-Renaissance influences. The tympanum crowning the portico is supported by eight Corinthian columns. It depicts the Battle of the Centaurs and Lapiths, and is copied from the Temple of Zeus at Olympia, Greece.

Grimani jug

First floor

The Water Carrier
(c. 1810)
La Aquadora *demonstrates the full range of Francisco de Goya's artistic talent.*

The Fall of Man
(c. 1620)
The Flemish artist, Jacob Jordaens, worked alongside van Dyck and was Rubens' principal associate.

★ **Esterházy Madonna**
(c. 1508)
This unfinished picture by Raphael is so named because it became the property of the Esterházy family at the beginning of the 19th century.

Lower ground floor

St James Conquers the Moors *(1750)*
Giambattista Tiepolo portrayed the miraculous appearance of the saint during a battle at Clavijo in 844.

KEY

- ☐ Egyptian artifacts
- ☐ Classical artifacts
- ☐ German art
- ☐ Dutch and Flemish art
- ☐ Italian art
- ☐ Spanish art
- ☐ French and British art
- ☐ Drawings and graphic art
- ☐ 19th- and 20th-century works
- ☐ Temporary exhibitions

View of Amsterdam
(c. 1656)
Jacob van Ruisdael was a master of Dutch realist landscape painting. He greatly influenced the development of European landscape painting in the 19th century.

Second floor

Mother and Child
(1905)
The rare subtlety of this intensely intimate picture, by Pablo Picasso, is achieved using watercolour.

Renaissance Hall

Baroque Hall

★ St John the Baptist's Sermon *(1566)*
In this wonderful painting, Pieter Bruegel the Elder, a renowned observer of daily life, depicts a preacher addressing a group of peasants from Flanders.

Ground floor

These Women in the Refectory *(1894)*
This pastel sketch by the artist Henri de Toulouse-Lautrec, an observer and protagonist in the Parisian demi-monde, depicts prostitutes in a bar.

MUSEUM GUIDE
As a result of continuous renovation work on the building, not all the rooms are currently open to the public. The works displayed may be moved as restoration work progresses.

STAR PAINTINGS

★ Esterházy Madonna

★ St John the Baptist's Sermon

Exploring the Museum of Fine Arts

The museum's collection encompasses international art dating from antiquity to the 20th century. As well as Egyptian, Greek and Roman artifacts, the museum houses galleries dedicated to a variety of modern art. Alongside its interesting collection of sculptures, there are priceless drawings and works of graphic art. Over the next few years the museum will be undergoing a process of redevelopment. In spite of this, exhibits will continue to be open to the public throughout the duration of the restoration work. Individual collections will simply be moved to different locations as building work progresses.

Egyptian head (c. 1200 BC)

Albrecht Dürer's simple yet beautiful *Portrait of a Young Man*

EGYPTIAN ARTIFACTS

Egyptian artifacts have been exhibited in the museum since 1939. Principally, they are the result of 19th-century excavations that involved Hungarian archaeologists.

The rich collection includes stone sculptures from each historic period, from the Old Kingdom to the Ptolemy dynasty. A nobleman's head of a votive statue dates from the New Kingdom and is a particularly beautiful example.

Also worthy of note is the collection of small bronze figures, which also date mainly from the New Kingdom, together with domestic objects that illustrate everyday life.

CLASSICAL ARTIFACTS

The collection of Classical artifacts is rather varied. It encompasses works of Greek, Etruscan, and Roman works.

The collection of Greek vases ranks as one of the best of its kind in Europe. A black-figure amphora by Exekias and a kylix from the studio of the painter Andokides are very fine examples of this work.

Bronze work, which dates from various epochs, including the famous Grimani jug from the 5th century BC, gold jewellery, and marble and terracotta sculptures are all exquisite artifacts from this era.

SCULPTURE

This collection is located throughout the museum. The most valuable element by far is a small bronze sculpture by Leonardo da Vinci (1452–1519). This is an unusually dynamic representation of King François I of France on his horse. Other superb examples of Italian sculpture, by masters such as Andrea Pisano of the Ronni family, can also be seen.

Leonardo da Vinci's figure of François I

GERMAN ART

Among the most valuable works in the collection are the *Portrait of a Young Man*, by Albrecht Dürer, and the carefully composed painting of *The Dormition of Mary*, by Hans Holbein. The work of such masters as Hans Baldung

Grien and Lucas Cranach are worth seeing, as is the collection of German and Austrian Baroque painting, which includes work by Franz Anton Maulbertsch.

DUTCH AND FLEMISH ART

The museum's Dutch and Flemish collection features works by the finest masters, including influential landscape artist, Jacob van Ruisdael, with *View of Amsterdam (see p147)*. The subtle *Nativity* by Gerard David and Pieter Bruegel's detailed masterpiece *St John the Baptist's Sermon (see p147)*, depicting Flemish peasants listening to the saint's words, are exemplary exhibits. The museum also boasts canvases attributed to Rembrandt, including *St Joseph's Dream*, portraits by Frans Hals and Jan Vermeer's *Portrait of a Lady*. Not to be missed are the magnificent 17th-century Dutch paintings by artists including Adrian van Ostade, Jacob Ruisdael, Jan Steen and others.

The highlight of the Flemish collection is the 17th-century *Mucius Scaevola before Porsenna* by Peter Rubens and his assistant, Anthony van Dyck. The latter was responsible for the picture of St John the Evangelist, also on display.

Also important is the painting of Adam and Eve in *The Fall of Man* by Jacob Jordaens, who also worked as an assistant to Rubens.

Detail of a hunting scene on a 3rd-century AD Greek sarcophagus

ITALIAN ART

This valuable collection of Italian art, which was the core of the Esterházy family's collection, is often considered the museum's biggest attraction. All the schools of Italian painting, from the 13th to the 18th centuries, are on display here. The Renaissance period is perhaps the best represented.

Of particular note is the captivating *Esterházy Madonna (see p146)*, an unfinished painting by Raphael. Another great work by this outstanding artist is the *Portrait of Pietro Bembo*.

There is no shortage of work by famous 16th-century Venetian artists among the paintings collected here. Important works by Titian, Bonifazio Veronese, Antonio Correggio, Jacopo Tintoretto, Giorgione and Giovanni Boltraffio are all exhibited here. An excellent example of Baroque art is Giambattista Tiepolo's vast late 18th-century painting, *St James Conquers the Moors (see p146)*.

Giovanni Boltraffio's *Madonna and Child* (c. 1506)

SPANISH ART

The most important features of this collection are seven paintings by El Greco, including *The Annunciation, Christ in the Garden of Gethsemane* and *The Penance of St Mary Magdalene*, a subtle though fully expressive work.

The dramatic *Martyrdom of St Andrew* by Jusepe de Ribera should not be missed, nor the work of artists such as Diego

El Greco's *The Penance of St Mary Magdalene* (c. 1576)

Velázquez, Bartolomé Murillo and Francisco Zurbarán. Francisco de Goya's observations of daily life produced paintings such as *The Water Carrier (see p146)*, which also deserves special attention.

FRENCH AND BRITISH ART

Works by French and British artists are not as numerous as Italian works, for example, but represent the various styles of the two countries.

French works include the well-composed *Resting on the Journey to Egypt* by Nicolas Poussin, the grandly majestic *Finding of Moses*, also by Poussin, and the bucolic landscape of *Villa in the Roman Countryside* by Claude Lorrain.

The collection of British paintings includes portraits by artists of the calibre of Joshua Reynolds, William Hogarth and Thomas Gainsborough.

DRAWINGS AND GRAPHIC ART

The collection of drawings and graphic art combines the work of old masters, including drawings by Leonard da Vinci, Raphael, Albrecht Dürer and Rembrandt, with pieces from artists of the 19th and 20th centuries. The collection is one of Europe's best.

19TH- AND 20TH-CENTURY WORKS

French painting makes up the largest constituent of the collection of 19th- and 20th-century art. The visitor can admire works by all the major painters of the time, including Pablo Picasso's *Mother and Child (see p147)*, Henri de Toulouse-Lautrec's *These Women in the Refectory (see p147)*, Gustave Courbet's *Wrestlers*, Edouard Manet's *Woman with a Fan* and Camille Pissarro's *Pont-Neuf*. Paul Gauguin's *Black Pigs*, one of his first Tahitian canvases, is also on display here. To complete the collection, the likes of Eugène Delacroix, Claude Monet, Pierre Bonnard, Pierre Renoir and Paul Cézanne are also represented.

Austrian and German 19th- and 20th-century art is represented with works by Waldmüller, Amerling, Lenbach, Leibl and Menzel.

Paul Cézanne's still life, *Credenza*, dating from 1874–7

The façade of the Palace of Art, featuring a six-columned portico

Műcsarnok Art Gallery ❽

Műcsarnok

Hősök tere. **Map** 5 C4. **Tel** *460 70 00*. Ⓜ *Hősök tere.* ○ *10am–6pm Tue–Sun, noon–8pm Thu.* 🅿 ⚡ 📷 **www.**mucsarnok.hu

Situated on the southern side of Heroes' Square, opposite the Museum of Fine Arts *(see pp146–9)*, is Hungary's largest exhibition space. Temporary exhibitions of mainly contemporary painting and sculpture are held here.

The imposing Neo-Classical building, which was designed by Albert Schickedanz and Fülöp Herzog in 1895, is fronted by a vast six-columned portico. The mosaic, depicting St István as the patron saint of fine art, was added to the tympanum between 1938–41. Behind the portico is a fresco in three parts by Lajos Deák Ébner: *The Beginning of Sculpture*, *The Source of Arts* and *The Origins of Painting*.

Museum of Fine Arts ❾

Szépművészeti Múzeum

See pp146–9.

Vajdahunyad Castle ❿

Vajdahunyad Vára

Városliget. **Map** 6 D4. **Tel** *363 19 73*. **Museum of Agriculture Tel** *363 19 73*. ○ *Mar–Oct: 10am–5pm Tue–Sun; Nov–Feb: 10am–4pm Tue–Sun.* 🅿 ⚡ 📷 **www.**mmgm.hu

This fairytale-like building is located among the trees at the edge of the lake in Városliget. Not a genuine castle but a complex of buildings reflecting various architectural styles, it was designed by Ignác Alpár for the 1896 Millennium Celebrations *(see p142)*.

Alpár's creation illustrated the history and evolution of architecture in Hungary. Originally intended as temporary exhibition pavilions, the castle proved so popular with the public that, between 1904–6, it was rebuilt using brick to create a permanent structure.

The pavilions are grouped in chronological order of style: Romanesque is followed by Gothic, Renaissance, Baroque and so on. The individual styles were linked together to give the impression of a single, cohesive design. Each of the pavilions either uses authentic

details copied from Hungary's most important historic buildings or is a looser interpretation of a style inspired by a specific architect of that historic period.

The Romanesque complex features a copy of the portal from a church in Ják *(see p143)* as well as a monastic cloister and palace. The details on the Gothic pavilion have been taken from castles like those in Vajdahunyad and Segesvár (both now in Romania). The architect Fischer von Erlach was the inspiration for the Renaissance and Baroque complex. The façade copies part of the Bakócz chapel in the cathedral at Esztergom *(see p164)*.

The Museum of Agriculture can be found in the Baroque section. It has exhibits on cattle breeding, wine-making, hunting and fishing.

The entire complex reflects more than 20 of Hungary's most renowned buildings. The medieval period, often considered to be the most glorious time in Hungary's history, is given greatest emphasis, while the controversial Habsburg era is pushed into the background.

Zoo ⓫

Fővárosi állat-és Növénykert

Állatkerti körút 6–12. **Map** 5 C3. **Tel** *363 37 10*. Ⓜ *Széchenyi fürdő.* ○ *Daily, phone for opening hours.* 🅿 **www.**zoobudapest.com

Budapest's zoo is one of the city's great attractions. It was established in 1866 by the Hungarian Academy of Sciences *(see p114)*. In 1907 it was bought by the State and totally redeveloped, between 1909–11, by Károly

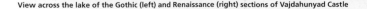

View across the lake of the Gothic (left) and Renaissance (right) sections of Vajdahunyad Castle

Kós and Dezső Zrumeczky. The animals are housed in enclosures, most of which strive to mimic their natural habitat. The elephant house, however, by Kornél Neuschloss-Knüsli, is a fine example of Secession style. Károly Kós, on the other hand, adopted a folk style for the aviary, in which a wide variety of birds fly freely. There is also a popular children's zoo.

Funfair ⓬

Vidámpark

Állatkerti körút 14–16. **Map** 6 D2. *Tel* 363 83 10. Ⓜ *Széchenyi fürdő.* ◗ *Apr & Oct: noon–6pm daily; May & Sep: noon–8pm daily; Jun–Aug: 10am–8pm daily.* 🎫 www.vidampark.hu

In 1878 there was already a carousel here, along with games and theatrical shows. Today it is a charmingly unsophisticated amusement park with an assortment of old-fashioned rides. Next door is a smaller funfair for toddlers.

There are numerous kiosks, bars and restaurants serving food, so it is easy to spend the entire day here. The circus is also close by *(see p219)*.

Széchenyi Baths ⓭

Széchenyi Strandfürdő

Állatkerti körút 11. **Map** 6 D3. *Tel* 363 32 10. Ⓜ *Széchenyi fürdő.* ◗ **Thermal Pool:** *6am–7pm daily.* **Swimming pool and group thermal pool:** *6am–10pm daily.* 🎫 www.szechenyibath.com

A statue stands at the main entrance to the Széchenyi Baths depicting geologist Vilmos Zsigmond, who discovered a hot spring here while drilling a well in 1879.

The Széchenyi Baths are the deepest and hottest baths in Budapest – the water reaches the surface at a temperature of 74–5° C (180° F). The springs, rich in minerals, are distinguished by their alleged healing properties. They are recommended for treating rheumatism and disorders of the nervous system, joints and muscles.

One of the outdoor pools at the beautiful Széchenyi Baths

The spa, housed in a Neo-Baroque building by Győző Cziegler and Ede Dvorzsák, was constructed in 1909–13. In 1926, three open-air swimming pools were added. The pools are popular all year due to the water's high temperature. Bathing caps are required.

Hermina Street ⓮

Hermina út

Map 6 E3, 6 E4 & 6 F4. 🚎 *70.* **Transport Museum** *Tel* 273 38 40. ◗ *Apr–Oct: 10am–5pm Tue–Fri, 10am–6pm Sat & Sun; Nov–Mar: 10am–4pm Tue–Fri, 10am–5pm Sat & Sun.* ● *Mon.* 🎫 ♿ 🎟

This beautiful street is worth walking along to experience the romantic atmosphere of the historic, elegant villas in this area. Particularly notable is the unusual Secession building at No. 47, Sipeky Balázs Villa *(see p55)*, built in 1905–6 by architects Ödön Lechner, Marcell Komor and Dezső Jakab. The asymmetric design of the villa's façade includes features such as a domed glass conser-

A steam train exhibited at the Transport Museum, just off Hermina Street

vatory, an ironwork porch and a tall, narrow side tower. The villa's exterior decoration is inspired by national folk art.

Hermina Chapel at No. 23, by József Hild, was built in 1842–6 in memory of Palatine József's daughter, Hermina Amália, who died in 1842.

Backing onto Hermina Street, at No. 11 Városligeti körút, is the Transport Museum with exhibits on the evolution of air, sea, road and rail transport. Among the trains, helicopters and aeroplanes are some pre-World War II right-hand-drive cars and the first trams in Budapest.

Poster for a gala ballet performance at the Erkel Theatre

Erkel Theatre ⓯

Erkel Színház

Köztársaság ter 30. **Map** 7 C3. *Tel* 333 01 08. Ⓜ *Keleti pu.*

An alternative venue of the National Opera Company, this is the largest theatre in Hungary, seating 2,500 people. Designed in 1911 by Marcell Komor, Dezső Jakab and Géza Márkus, its current form dates from the 1950s. Concerts and operas are performed here.

FURTHER AFIELD

Budapest is a sprawling city and several sights on its periphery are well worth a visit. North from the centre of Buda are the fascinating ruins of Aquincum, a town founded by the Romans in approximately AD 100. To the west, the city is skirted by wooded hills, which offer walks around beautiful nature reserves and exciting cave visits. Out

Roman urn from Aquincum

to the east of Pest is Kerepesi Cemetery, where a host of famous Hungarians are buried. To the south of the city is the Nagytétény Palace, one of the most beautiful Baroque palaces in all of Hungary. The setting for Socialist-era statues, Memento Park, is not far from the palace. All the sights can be reached easily using public transport.

SIGHTS AT A GLANCE

Museums and Theatres
Aquincum ㉗
Gizi Bajor Theatre Museum ㉑
Holocaust Memorial Center ⑩
National Theatre ⑯
Palace of Arts ⑪

Historic Buildings and Monuments
Geology Institute ④
Ludovika Academy ⑨
Nagytétény Palace Museum ㉕
Raoul Wallenberg Monument ①
Memento Park ㉓
Technical University ⑱
Törley Mausoleum ㉔
Wekerle Estate ⑰

Parks and Recreation Areas
Buda Hills ㉖
Congress and World Trade Centre ⑳
Eagle Hill Nature Reserve ㉒
Ferenc Puska's Stadium ⑤
Railway History Park ⑫
Szemlő-hegy and Pál-völgy Caves ②
University Botanical Gardens ⑧

Cemeteries
Jewish Cemetery ⑮
Kerepesi Cemetery ⑥
Municipal Cemetery ⑭

Churches
Cistercian Church of St Imre ⑲

Józsefváros Parish Church ⑦
Kőbánya Parish Church ⑬
Újlak Parish Church ③

KEY

▓	City centre
░	Greater Budapest
✈	Airport
🚇	Train station
▭	Motorway
▬	Main road
—	Railway

◁ The huge 19th-century Catholic cathedral at Esztergom, overlooking the Danube *(see p164)*

Raoul Wallenberg Monument ❶

Raoul wallenberg szobor

Szilágyi Erzsébet fasor.
🚋 56.

Tucked away at the junction of Szilágyi Erzsébet fasor and Nagyajtai utca, is this monument to an heroic but little known figure of World War II. Raoul Wallenberg was a Swedish diplomat who used his position to save over 20,000 Hungarian Jews from the extermination camps. He set up safe houses in the city and obtained fake Swedish documents for them.

Following the liberation of Budapest by the Soviet army, Wallenberg disappeared. It is thought he was arrested by the KGB and sent to a prison camp where he died. The memorial, by sculptor Imre Varga, was erected in 1987.

Szemlő-hegy and Pál-völgy Caves ❷

Szemlő-hegyi-barlang és Pál-völgyi-cseppkőbarlang

Szemlő-hegy Cave Pusztaszeri út 35. *Tel* 325 60 01. 🚌 29. ☐ 10am–4pm Wed–Mon. 🖼 ♿ 📷
Pál-völgy Cave Szépvölgyi út 162. *Tel* 325 95 05. 🚌 65. ☐ 10am–4pm Tue–Sun. 🖼 📷

To the north of Budapest lies the Pilis mountain range, formed of limestone and dolomite. Natural geological processes which occur within these mountains have created some picturesque caves, two of which are unusual tourist attractions.

Szemlő-hegy Cave features extraordinary formations called "cave pearls", produced when hot spring waters penetrate its limestone walls. There are guided tours every hour.

In Pál-völgy Cave, strange formations protruding from the rock face resemble animals.

It is a good idea to wear warm clothes when visiting the caves as they are cold and damp. Some claim, however, that the atmosphere in the caves has a therapeutic effect on the respiratory system.

The Baroque interior of Újlak Parish Church, dating from 1756

Újlak Parish Church ❸

Újlaki plébániatemplom

Bécsi út 32.
🚋 17.

Bavarian settlers first built a small church here early in the 18th century. The present church, designed by Kristóf Hamon and Mátyás Nepauer, was finished in 1756. Its tower was added some years later.

In the Baroque interior there is a depiction of the Madonna, a gift from the inhabitants of Passau to the church. The main altar, dating from 1798, also includes

a painting entitled *The Visitation*, which was the work of Francis Falkoner.

Not far away, at Zsigmond tér, stands the Holy Trinity Column, built in 1691 as a memorial to the city's earliest plague epidemic. The Baroque monument was moved from central Buda to Újlak in 1712.

Geology Institute ❹

Földtani Intézet

Stefánia út 14. **Map** 8 F1. *Tel* 251 09 99. 🚋 75, 77. **Museum** ☐ 10am–4pm Thu, Sat & Sun. 🖼 www.mafi.hu

This beautiful and unusual building, housing the Geology Institute, dates from 1898–9 and was designed by Ödön Lechner (*see p56*).

Lechner's very individual Secession style, also known as the Hungarian National Style, is on show here including motifs drawn from Hungarian Renaissance architecture.

On the picturesque elevations and gables of the building pale yellow plaster walls form a striking contrast to the brick-work quoins and window frames. Here and there Zsolnay blue glazed ceramic ornaments adorn the walls and harmonize with the blue roof tiles. The central pitched roof is topped by three human figures bent under the weight of a large globe. Inside the Geology

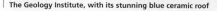
The Geology Institute, with its stunning blue ceramic roof

Institute is a small museum with rock and mineral exhibits. Lechner's Secession interiors have been carefully preserved – the central hall is particularly grand, and can be seen when visiting the museum or with the caretaker's permission.

Ferenc Puskás Stadium ❺

Puskás Ferenc stadion

Istvánmezei u. 3-5. **Map** 8 F1. **Tel** 471 43 21. 🚋 23, 24, 36. ⬜ 8am–2pm Mon–Thu, 8am–noon Fri.

Hungary's biggest sports stadium, named after a national football hero, was built between 1948–53 to a design by Károly Dávid. The roofless structure seats 78,000, but generally only fills to capacity for major events. The entrance is at the end of the "Avenue of Youth", which is lined with Stalinist-era statues, depicting various sports, by well-known Hungarian sculptors.

Kerepesi Cemetery ❻

Kerepesi temető

Fiumei út 16–20. **Map** 8 E3. 🚋 23, 24, 36.

Since 1847, the Kerepesi Cemetery has provided the resting place for many of Hungary's most prominent citizens. Fine tombstones mark the graves of some, while others were interred here inside large mausoleums.

The mausoleum of the leader of the 1848–9 uprising, Lajos Kossuth *(see p106)* and Lajos Batthyány, the first prime minister of Hungary *(see p31)* are found here. Ferenc Deák, who formulated the Compromise with Austria *(see p32)*, is buried here.

Also at the cemetery are the graves of poets Endre Ady and Attila József *(see p106)*, writers Kálmán Mikszáth Zsigmond Móricz and actors such as Lujza Blaha, whose tomb is particularly beautiful. Sculptors, painters and

composers are buried close to great architects.

Hungarian Communists who were sentenced to death in the show trials of 1949, were buried here. Their funerals inspired a revolutionary spirit which, a few years later, led to the 1956 Uprising *(see p34)*.

Józsefváros Parish Church ❼

Józsefváros plébániatemplom

Horváth Mihály tér 7. **Map** 7 C4. **Tel** 313 63 13. 🚋 83. 🚌 9, 17.

Building work on this Baroque church began in 1797, but it was not completed until 1814. The main altar is by József Hild. A formidable architectural composition, it is based on a triumphal arch. This frames a magnificent painting, *The Apotheosis of St Joseph*, by Leopold Kupelwieser. The church also has two beautiful, late Baroque side altars.

University Botanical Gardens ❽

Egyetemi Botanikus kert

Illés utca 25. **Map** 8 D5. **Tel** 314 05 35. Ⓜ Klinikák. **Garden** ⬜ Nov–Mar: 9am–4pm; Apr–Oct: 9am–5pm. **Glasshouses** ⬜ 9am–noon, 1pm–3pm. 🎟️ 📷

Gardens were first established on this 3-ha (8-acre) site by the Festetics family. Their modest,

The late Baroque façade of Józsefváros Parish Church

early Neo-Classical villa is now the administration centre for the gardens. It was built in 1802–3, probably to a design by Mihály Pollack. The smoking room in the villa houses a huge collection of tropical plants, including the striking *Victoria regia*, which flowers once a year. The author Ferenc Molnár (1878–1952) used the gardens as a setting in his novel, *The Paul Street Boys*, although the lake mentioned in the book no longer exists. Not far away are Pál utca (Paul Street) and Mária utca, the scene of a battle the boys fought.

Ludovika Academy ❾

Ludovika Akadémia

Ludovika tér 2–6. Ⓜ Klinikák. 🚋 4. **Tel** 210 10 85. ⬜ 10am–6pm Wed–Mon. **National History Museum** ⬜ 10am–5pm Wed–Sun. 🎟️ ♿ www.nhmus.hu

The huge Ludovika Academy is in district IX, east of the city centre. It was designed in the 1830s by Mihály Pollack, the famous architect of the Hungarian National Museum *(see pp130–33)*. A military academy until 1945, it is an impressive example of Neo-Classical style, with many original features intact. It is now the city's Natural History Museum, with a rich paleontological collection.

The tomb of actress Lujza Blaha at Kerepesi Cemetery

Holocaust Memorial Center ⑩
Holokauszt Emlékközpont

Pava út 39. Ⓜ *Ferenc korut.*
🚃 *4, 6.* **Tel** *455 33 33.* ⏰ *10am–6pm Tue–Sun.* 🔲 ♿ www.hdke.hu

The Center was founded in order to collect and study material relating to the history of the Holocaust, and to honour its victims. The building complex is a mix of classical and modern architecture, and its asymmetrical outline and dislocated walls all symbolize the distorted and twisted time of the Holocaust.

A permanent exhibition examines the history of the suffering of Hungarian Jews and Roma during the Holocaust.

The impressive open-space interior of the Palace of Arts, a cultural hub

Palace of Arts ⑪
Művészetek Palotája

Komor Marcell utca 1. 🚋 *1, 2, 2A, 24.* **Tel** *555 30 01, 555 30 02 or 555 30 05.* ⏰ *10am–10pm daily.* www.mupa.hu **Ticket Office** (for all events) ⏰ *1–6pm Mon–Sat, 10am–6pm Sun.* www.jegyelado.hu

The Palace of Arts in the Millennium City Centre, located on the Pest side of the Danube between the Lágymányos bridge and the National Theatre, brings together the different branches of the arts under one roof. Permanent residents include the Ludwig Museum of Contemporary Art, the National Philharmonic Orchestra and the National Dance Theatre.

Railway History Park ⑫
Vasúttörténeti Park

Tatai út 95. 🚇 *Vintage diesel shuttle from Nyugati station 9:45am, 10:45am, 1:45pm, 3:45pm.* **Tel** *450 14 97.* ⏰ *Mid–end Mar & Nov–Dec: 10am–3pm Tue–Sun; Apr–Sep: 10am–6pm.* ● *19 Dec–mid-Mar.* 🔲 ♿ www.mavnosztalgia.hu

This open-air museum of railway history is one of Europe's largest. It boasts around 100 locomotives – most fully functioning – dating from the early days of steam to modern times. Visitors have the opportunity to drive a steam train, play with a model railway and ride in a line-inspection car. Every year, the legendary *Orient Express* makes several visits here. The park is popular with families as well as enthusiasts, and there is a full programme of events for children.

Kőbánya Parish Church ⑬
Kőbányai Plébániatemplom

Szent László tér. 🚋 *13, 28.*
🚃 *17, 32, 62, 185.* ♿

An industrial suburb on the eastern side of Pest, Kőbánya is the unexpected home of the beautiful Kőbánya Parish Church. Designed by Ödön Lechner *(see p56)* in the 1890s, the church makes magnificent use of the architect's favourite materials, including vibrant roof tiles developed and produced at the now-famous Zsolnay factory in the town of Pécs. Like much of Lechner's work, including the Museum of Applied Arts *(see pp136–7),* the church combines motifs and colours from Hungarian folk art with Neo-Gothic elements. Inside the church, both the altar and the pulpit are superb examples of early 20th-century wood

Schmidl family tomb at the Jewish Cemetry

Gleaming ceramic tiles on the roof of Kőbánya Parish Church

carving. Somehow surviving heavy World War II bombing, a number of Miksa Roth's original stained-glass windows are still in place.

Municipal Cemetery ⑭
Rákoskeresztúr

See pp158–9.

Jewish Cemetery ⑮
Izraelita Temető

Kozma út. 🚃 *37.*

Next door to the Municipal Cemetery is the Jewish Cemetery, opened in 1893. The many grand tombs here are a vivid reminder of the vigour and success of Budapest's pre-war Jewish community. At the end of the 19th century, nearly a quarter of the city's inhabitants were Jewish. Tombs to look out for as you stroll among the graves include that of the Wellisch family, designed in 1903 by Arthur Wellisch, and that of Konrád Polnay, which was designed five years later by Gyula Fodor. Perhaps the most eye-catching of all belongs to the Schmidl family. The startlingly flamboyant tomb, designed in 1903 by Ödön Lechner and Béla Lajta, is covered in vivid turquoise ceramic tiles. The central mosaic in green and gold tiles represents the Tree of Life.

National Theatre ⑯
Nemzeti Színház

*Bajor Gizi Park 1. **Tel** 476 68 68. 🚋 1, 2, 2A, 24. **www**.nemzetiszinhaz.hu*

The theatre, built in 2002, stands at the foot of Lágymányosi Bridge. The architect, Mária Siklós, designed a Neo-Eclectic building surrounded by a park containing statues of Hungary's best actors.

Wekerle Estate ⑰
Wekerle Telep

*Kós Károly tér. **Tel** 280 01 14. Ⓜ Határ út, then 🚌 194.*

Out in district XIX, the Wekerle Estate was built between 1909 and 1926, and represents a bold and successful experiment in 20th-century social planning. Named after Prime Minister Sándor Wekerle, the estate was

Façade of the Technical University, as seen from the Danube

originally known as the Kispest Workers and Clerks Settlement and was built to provide better housing for local workers.

Designed by a group of young architects, students of Ödön Lechner, the buildings have a uniquely Hungarian style. Other key influences were the English Arts and Crafts movement, and early English new towns such as Hampstead Garden Suburb in London.

Fanning out around Kós Károly tér, 16 types of family house and apartment block are separated by tree-lined streets. Wooden gables and balconies, and sharply pitched, brightly tiled roofs, contribute to the estate's lively and eclectic atmosphere.

Technical University ⑱
Budapesti Műszaki Egyetem

*Műegyetem rakpart 3. **Map** 4 F4. **Tel** 463 11 11. 🚋 4, 6, 18, 19, 47, 49. 🚌 7, 86. **www**.bme.hu*

Founded in 1857, the city's Technical University moved to its present site in 1904. Built on reclaimed marshland, the imposing building overlooks the Danube just south of Gellért Hill *(see pp88–9)*. Extended at the end of World War II, it is now the largest higher education establishment in Hungary. Former students include Imre Steindl, the architect of the Parliament building *(see pp108–9)*, and the richest and most widely known graduate to date, Ernő Rubik, inventor of the Rubik Cube.

Cistercian Church of St Imre ⑲
Cisztercita Szent Imre Plébániatemplom

*Villányi út 25. **Map** 3 C4. 🚋 61. 🚌 27, 40. ♿*

Not far from the Technical University is the Cistercian Church of St Imre. The vast Neo-Baroque structure with its double tower was built in 1938 and is typical of the grand and rather sombre architecture in vogue in Budapest during the inter-war years.

Inside the church are relics of St Imre, canonized at the end of the 11th century. Other patron saints of the Cistercian order are depicted above the church's main entrance.

A police station on the early 20th-century Wekerle Estate

Municipal Cemetery 🅔

A new, historic significance was gained by the Municipal Cemetery following the 1956 Uprising *(see p35)*. Here, at Budapest southeastern limits, the leaders and victims of this bloody revolution against the oppressive Stalinist government were secretly buried in mass graves. During the 1970s, the country's democratic opposition began placing flowers on the site, at the far side of the cemetery. In 1990, after the fall of Communism, the revolutionary heroes were given a ceremonial funeral and reburied, and several memorials were set up to them.

View of Plot 300
Until 1989, the state militia guarded access to a thicket which covered the communal graves of the heroes of the 1956 Uprising.

Campanile
A wooden campanile is the type of decoration often found in old Hungarian cemeteries. It stands in front of panels listing the names of over 400 victims of the 1956 Uprising, giving the exact locations of their graves.

Plot 300

PLAN OF THE CEMETERY

In 1886, the city authorities opened a vast, new municipal cemetery in Rákoskeresztúr, on the outskirts of town. It became the largest cemetery in Budapest, occupying 30 sq km (12 sq miles).

Plots 300 and 301

Main entrance

0 metres 500
0 yards 500

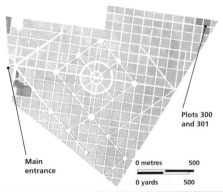

★ Transylvanian Gate
The 1956 Uprising Combatants' Association erected the carved Transylvanian Gate which stands at the beginning of one of the paths leading into plot 300. It is inscribed with the words: "Only a Hungarian soul may pass through this gate".

★ Imre Nagy's Grave
A marble slab bears the modest inscription: "Imre Nagy, Prime Minister of Hungary, 1956". Arrested after the uprising, Nagy was interned and shot dead on 16 June 1956 in Budapest, following a bogus political trial.

Plot 301

VISITORS' CHECKLIST

Kozma utca 8–10, Kőbánya.
95 from Zalka Máté tér.
Plots 300 and 301 *30 mins walk from the main gate. Fee charged for cars.*

Christ the Sorrowful
A figure of Christ the Sorrowful is traditionally placed in a plot containing Protestant graves.

★ Heroes' Monument
This simple monument symbolizes the passage through purgatory. It was created by the leading modern Hungarian sculptor, György Jovánovics.

Protestant Graves
The tradition of Hungarian Protestants is to place a simple wooden post to mark each grave.

STAR SIGHTS

★ Heroes' Monument

★ Imre Nagy's Grave

★ Transylvanian Gate

View from Eagle Hill Nature Reserve, down across the smart residential quarter below

Congress & World Trade Centre ⓴

Kongresszusi és Világkereskedelmi Központ

Jagelló út 1–3. *Tel* 372 57 00. 🚎 61. ☐ For events. **www**.bcwtc.hu.

Opened in 1975, this large arts complex houses a concert hall, a cinema, conference rooms and several restaurants. It hosts international conferences and events, as well as the annual Hungarian Film Festival *(see p61)*. It was designed, with the neighbouring Novotel Budapest Congress *(see p189)*, by the architect József Finta. The *Tree of Life* decorating the main wall of the Congress Hall is by József Király.

Gizi Bajor Theatre Museum ⓤ

Bajor Gizi Színészmúzeum

Stromfeld Aurél út 16. *Tel* 225 31 61. 🚎 102, 105. ☐ 2–6pm Thu–Sun. 🖼 🗗

This museum was opened in 1952, in a garden villa which once belonged to Gizi Bajor, a leading Hungarian actress of her day. Its exhibits, which include furniture, portraits, theatrical props, fans and velvet gloves, transport visitors to the world of the theatre in the 19th century.

In 1990, the 200th anniversary of theatre in Hungary, the museum's collection was further extended, to include mementoes of well-known contemporary Hungarian actors, after whom some of the museum's rooms are named.

The garden features the busts of several writers, together with a number of other leading figures in Hungary's cultural history.

Eagle Hill Nature Reserve ⓦ

Sashegy Természetvédelmi Terület

Tájék utca 26. *Tel* 06 304 084 370. 🚎 8, 8A. ☐ Mar–Oct: 10am–6pm Thu, Sat & Sun. 🗗 available.

A nature reserve more or less in the centre of a city of nearly two million inhabitants is a remarkable phenomenon.

Access to the summit of this steep, 266-m (872-ft) high hill to the west of Gellért Hill *(see pp88–9)* is strictly regulated to protect the extremely rare animal and plant species found here. A smart residential quarter, which lies on the lower slope of Eagle Hill, extends almost to the fence of the reserve and the craggy 30-ha wilderness that it encloses.

It is well worth taking a guided walk, particularly in spring or early autumn. Only here is it possible to see *centaurea sadleriana*, a flower resembling a cornflower but much bigger. The reserve is also home to a type of spider not found anywhere else in the world, as well as to extraordinary, colourful butterflies and to *ablebharus kitaibeli*, a rare lizard.

Memento Park ⓦ

Memento Park

Balatoni út & Szabadkai utca. *Tel* 424 75 00. 🚎 50. ☐ 10am–dusk daily. 🖼 **www**.mementopark.hu

In 1991, Budapest's City Council decided to gather in one place Communist monuments which had formerly occupied prestigious locations in the city.

The park, which has been enlarged and renamed, features gigantic monuments of the Communist regime. Statues of Karl Marx, Friedrich Engels, VI Lenin and Hungarian Communist heroes stand side by side, headed by the leader of the 1919 revolution in Hungary *(see p34)*, Béla Kun.

Stalin's Tribune is a replica of the original grandstand from which Communist leaders greeted the crowds. Above the tribune stood an 8m- (26 ft-) high bronze of Stalin, but it was pulled down during the national Uprising in 1956 and only the boots remain.

The Barakk Museum has exhibitions on everyday life under the Communist regime, and a cinema has a screening of the special methods used by the Communist secret services.

Cubist-style statues of Marx and Engels in the Statue Park

The marble Törley Mausoleum

Törley Mausoleum ㉔

Törley Mauzoleum

Sarló utca 6. 🚊 3.

Until 1880 Budafok had a number of vineyards, but their cultivation was destroyed in that year by a plague of phylloxera (American aphid). It was then that József Törley, who had studied wine-making in Reims, started to produce sparkling wine in Budafok using the French model (see p194). His wines sold well abroad and he quickly expanded his enterprise, storing the wines in the local cellars.

József Törley died in 1900 and was laid to rest in this monumental mausoleum designed by Rezső Vilmos Ray. Constructed of white marble, it is adorned with Eastern motifs and bas-reliefs by József Damkó.

Nagytétényi Palace Museum ㉕

Nagytétényi Kastély Múzeum

Kastélypark utca 9–11. **Tel** 207 00 05. 🚊 41. ⬜ Mar–Dec: 10am–6pm Tue–Sun; Jan–Feb: 10am–6pm Sat & Sun. 🈺 🎫 In period costume, by arrangement. **www**.nagytetenyi.hu

This is one of the best known Baroque palaces in Hungary. It was built in the mid-18th century, incorporating the remains of a 15th-century Gothic building. The work was started by György Száraz and completed by his son-in-law,

József Rudnyánszky, acquiring its final shape in 1766. Based on the typical Baroque layout, it includes a main block and side wings. The coping features the Száraz and Rudnyánszky family crests.

The palace suffered severe damage during World War II, but the original wall paintings and furnishings survived. In 1949, the palace was rebuilt and turned into an interior design museum. Now it is a department of the Museum of Applied Arts (see pp136–7). On display are fine pieces of Hungarian and European furniture from the 15th–18th centuries, early 19th-century paintings and more functional items, such as tiled stoves.

Standing close to the palace is an 18th-century Baroque church, built on the remains of a medieval church. Original Gothic features incorporated in it include the window openings in its tower and three supports on the outer wall of the presbytery. In 1760, the Austrian artist Johann Gfall created the painting in the dome which features illusory galleries. The altars, pulpit and baptistries also date back to the mid-18th century.

Buda Hills ㉖

Budai-hegység

Ⓜ Moszkva tér, then 🚌 18 or 56, then cog-wheel railway and chair lift.

To the west of the city centre are the wooded Buda Hills where Budapesters come to walk and relax.

The first station of a cog-wheel railway, built in 1874, is on Szilágyi Erzsébet fasor. This runs up Sváb Hill – named after the Germanic Swabians, who settled here under the Habsburgs (see p28) – and then Széchenyi Hill.

From Széchenyi Hill a narrow-gauge railway covers a 12-km (7-mile) route to the Hűvös Valley. As in the days of the Soviet Young Pioneers movement, the railway is entirely staffed by children, apart from the adult train drivers. At the top of János Hill stands the Erzsébet Look-Out Tower, designed by Frigyes Schulek in 1910. A chair lift also connects the summit of János Hill with Zugligeti út and is a good way of making the descent.

Aquincum ㉗

Aquincum

See pp162–3.

The Erzsébet Look-Out Tower at the summit of János Hill

Aquincum ㉗

The remains of the Roman town of Aquincum *(see p20–21)* were excavated at the end of the 19th century. Visitors are free to stroll along its streets, viewing the outlines of temples, shops, baths and houses, in what was once the centre of the town. This civilian town was founded at the beginning of the 2nd century AD, a couple of decades after a legionary fortress *(see pp170–71)* was established to its south. In the centre of the site there is a Neo-Classical museum display-ing the most valuable Roman archaeological finds. On the other side of the road are the remains of an amphitheatre, where Aquincum's in-habitants once sought entertainment.

Roman Column

View Towards the Museum
The area opened to visitors is only a fragment of a much bigger town.

★ Public Baths
The walls of the thermal baths are immaculately preserved. Visiting the baths was a social event for the Romans.

Central Heating System
Archaeologists have here unearthed the Roman ver-sion of central heating, an under-floor system in which hot air was circu-lated under mosaic floors.

★ Macellum
This was the covered mar-ket hall. Having stalls positioned around a cool inner courtyard kept the produce fresh and made shopping comfortable all year round (see pp20–21).

STAR SIGHTS

★ Macellum

★ Museum

★ Public Baths

★ Museum
This Neo-Classical Lapidarium is part of the museum, which houses an exhibition of objects found at Aquincum and at other Roman sites nearby. These include weapons and inscribed stone monuments.

VISITORS' CHECKLIST

Szentendrei út 139. **Tel** 250 16 50.
🚊 Aquincum. ⬜ 9am–5pm Tue–Sun 🖼 **Museum** ⬜ 10am–5pm Tue–Sun ⬛ Mid-Oct–mid-Apr. 🏷 www.aquincum.hu

Thoroughfare
Paving stones can still be seen on the network of streets that run across the town at right angles.

Double Baths
Built mainly of stone, the baths were once richly decorated. Traces of wall paintings and mosaics can still be seen in some places.

Drain Cover
Aquincum had a water supply system. Carefully crafted drain covers, such as this one, cut into the stone paving slabs, provided the required drainage.

Peristyle House
Surrounded by a colonnade, this courtyard once stood at the centre of a large town house.

Excursions from Budapest

Budapest is ten times bigger than any other Hungarian city. Sleepy and charming, the towns and villages on these pages are ideal for day or overnight trips. Coaches *(see p234)* and trains *(see p239)* are cheap and reliable. Esztergom, Visegrád and Szentendre to the north of the city can all be reached by boats *(see p235)*, which run throughout the summer along this beautiful stretch of the Danube. More off the beaten track, the towns and villages to the south offer a fascinating glimpse of traditional life.

Overlooking the Danube, the vast cathedral at Esztergom

Esztergom ❶

46 km (28 miles) NW of Budapest.
🏃 30,000. 🚇 from Árpád híd.
🚇 from Nyugati pu. 🚤 from
Vigadó tér (summer only), take local
buses 1-6 and get off at Béke tér
stop. 🛈 Lőrinc utca **Cathedral**
Szent István tér 1. **Tel** (0633) 41 18
95. ◯ Daily 🔆 **Treasury Tel**
(0633) 40 23 54. ◯ Mar–Oct:
8am–5pm daily; Nov–Feb: 8am–4pm
Tue–Sun. 🔖 🖼 **Castle Tel** (0633)
41 59 86. ◯ Daily 🔖 🔆
www.esztergom.hu

St István, Hungary's first Christian King, was baptized in Esztergom and crowned here

on Christmas Day 1000 AD. Almost completely destroyed by the Mongol invasion 250 years later, the city was gradually rebuilt in the 18th and 19th centuries.

Esztergom today is still the country's most sacred city, the seat of the archbishop of Hungary. Dominating the skyline is the huge Catholic **cathedral**, built in the early 19th century. By the southern entrance, built by 16th-century Florentine craftsmen, is the red marble Bakócz burial chapel. On the northern side is the **treasury** containing a collection of ecclesiastical treasures

rescued from the ruins of the 12th-century church that existed on the cathedral site.

Below the cathedral are the remains of the 10th-century **castle**, rebuilt several times. It features a 12th-century chapel. The picturesque old town is also well worth exploring. At its heart is the town square, home to several cafés.

SIGHTS AT A GLANCE

Esztergom ❶
Fót ❺
Gödöllő ❻
Kecskemét ❼
Kiskunfélegyháza ❽

Martonvásár ❿
Ráckeve ❾
Szentendre ❸
Vác ❹
Visegrád ❷

KEY

■ City centre

▢ Greater Budapest

▬ Motorway

▬ Main road

25 kilometres = 15 miles

Visegrád ②

40 km (25 miles) N of Budapest.
🏛 *1,800.* 🚆 *from Árpád híd.*
🚢 *from Vigadó tér (summer only).*
ℹ️ *Rév utca 15.* **Tel** *(0626) 39 81 60.*
Castle Tel *(0626) 39 81 01.* ⬤ *Mar–
Sep: 9:30am–6pm Mon–Sun; Oct–
Nov: 9:30am–4pm Mon–Sun; Dec–
Feb: 9:30am–4pm Sat & Sun.* 📷 ♿
**Mátyás Museum & Visegrád Palace
Tel** *(0626) 39 80 26.* ⬤ *9am–5pm
Tue–Sun.* 📷 📸 *by arrangement.*
www.visegrad.hu

Set on the narrowest stretch
of the Danube, the village of
Visegrád is a popular tourist
destination, thanks to its
spectacular ruined **castle**.

A 25-minute walk, or a
short bus or taxi ride will take
you up to the castle from
Visegrád. Built in the 13th
century by King Béla IV, this
was once one of the finest
royal palaces ever built in
Hungary. The massive outer
walls are still intact, and offer
stunning views over the
surrounding countryside.

Halfway down the hill, in
the Salamon Tower, is the
Mátyás Museum, a collection
of items excavated from the
ruins of the **Visegrád Palace**.
Built by King Béla IV at the
same time as the castle, the
palace was renovated two
centuries later, in magnificent
Renaissance style, by King
Mátyás Corvinus *(see pp24–5)*.
Destroyed in the 16th century
after the Turkish invasion, then
buried in a mud slide, the ruins
were not rediscovered until
1934, when the excavations
took place here.

Szentendre ③

25 km (16 miles) N of Budapest.
🏛 *20,000.* 🚆 *from Batthyány tér.*
🚆 *from Árpád híd.* 🚢 *from Vigadó
tér (summer only).* ℹ️ *Dumtsa Jenő
utca 22.* **Tel** *(0626) 31 79 66.*
Belgrade Cathedral *Pátriárka utca 5.*
Tel *(0626) 31 23 99.* ♿
Museum of Serbian Art *Pátriárka
utca 5.* **Tel** *(0626) 31 23 99.* ⬤ *May–
Sep: 10am–6pm Tue–Sun, Oct–Apr:
10am–4pm Tue–Sun (Jan & Feb Fri–
Sun).* 📷 📸 **Margit Kovács
Museum** *Vastag György út 1.* **Tel**
(0626) 31 07 90. ⬤ *Jun–Aug: 9am–
7pm Tue–Sun; Sep–May: 9am–5pm
Tue–Sun.* 📷 📸 📸 *by arrangement.*
Hungarian Open Air Museum
Sztaravodai u. Pf 63. **Tel** *(0626) 50
25 11.* ⬤ *Apr–Nov: 9am–5pm
Tue–Sun.* 📷 **www**.skanzen.hu

Only 25 km (16 miles) outside Budapest, Szentendre is
a town built and inhabited by a

**Blagovestenska church in Fő tér,
Szentendre's main square**

succession of Serbian refugees. Most of Szentendre's
older buildings date from the
18th-century.

Orthodox religious tradition
lies at the heart of the town,
which contains many
Orthodox churches. The western European façades hide
Slavic interiors filled with
incense, icons and candlelight.
Blagovestenska Church on
Fő tér, is just one example.
Look out for the magnificent
iconostasis that separates the
sanctuary from the nave. Also
of interest is Sunday mass at
Belgrade Cathedral.

Next door is a **Museum of
Serbian Art**, full of icons and
other religious artifacts.
Since the 1920s, Szentendre

has been home to an ever
increasing number of artists
and the town contains many
galleries exhibiting the work
of local artists.

Margit Kovács Museum
shows the work of one of
Hungary's best-known
ceramic artists. Margit Kovács
(1902–77) drew inspiration
from Hungarian mythology
and folk traditions.

To the west of town is the
Hungarian Open Air Museum,
an ethnographical museum,
illustrating the different
Hungarian regions and their
rural architecture and culture
across the social groups, from
the 18th to the 20th century.
The museum is set in a
pleasant park.

Vác ④

40 km (25 miles) N of Budapest.
🏛 *36,000.* 🚆 *from Nyugati pu.*
🚆 *from Árpád híd.* ℹ️ *Március 15
tér 17.* **Tel** *(0627) 31 61 60.*

Vác has stood on the eastern
bank of the Danube since
1000 AD. Destroyed by war
in the late 17th century, the
town was rebuilt and today
its centre, built around four
squares, dates from the early
18th century. At its heart is
Március 15 tér, where the
Town Hall and **Fehérek
Church** are located. At the
northernmost end of the old
town, on Köztársaság út, is
Hungary's only **Arc de Triomph**. This was built in 1764,
after a visit from the Habsburg
Empress, Maria Theresa.

*Arc de Triomph in Vác, built in
honour of Empress Maria Theresa*

Exterior of Fót's Church of the Immaculate Conception

Fót ❺

25 km (15 miles) NE of Budapest. 🚶 16,000. 🚆 Nyugati pu. 🚌 Árpád hid. 🚏 Vörösmarty tér 3. **Tel** (0627) 53 82 60. **Károlyi Palace and park** Vörösmarty tér 2. ⬜ by appt. **Tel** (0627) 35 80 22. ⬛ ♿ ground floor only. 📷 obligatory. **Church of the Immaculate Conception** Vörösmarty út 2. 📷

Just outside Budapest is the small town of Fót. Its main attraction is the **Károlyi Palace**, birthplace of the country's first president, Mihály Károlyi (*see p34*). The palace was built in the 1830s, with a pavilion added on each side a decade later. Also worth a visit is the town's attractive 19th-century **Church of the Immaculate Conception**, with its impressive many-columned nave.

Gödöllő ❻

30 km (18 miles) NE of Budapest. 🚆 Hév from Örs vezér tere. **Grassalkovich Mansion** ⬜ Apr–Oct: 10am–6pm daily; Nov–Mar: 10am–5pm Tue–Sun. ⬛ Jan. **Tel** (0628) 41 01 24. ⬛ ♿ 📷

Gödöllő is most famous for its restored Baroque palace, the **Grassalkovich Mansion**. Built in 1741, it was the favourite residence of Queen Elizabeth, wife of Franz Joseph. The permanent exhibition in the Royal Museum incorporates the Ceremonial Hall and royal suites, and details the life of the Austro-Hungarian monarchy.

Kecskemét ❼

86km (52 miles) SE of Budapest. 🚶 110,000. 🚆 Nyugati pu. 🚌 Népstadion. 🚏 Kossuth tér 1. **Tel** (0676) 48 10 65. **Town Hall** Kossuth tér 1. **Tel** (0676) 51 35 13. ⬜ 8am–4:30pm Mon–Thu, 8am–2pm Fri. 📷 by appointment. **Cifra Palace** Rákóczi utca 1. **Tel** (0676) 48 07 76. ⬜ 10am–5pm Tue–Sun. ⬛ ♿ 📷 www.kecskemet.hu

Spreading out in a vast sweep around Budapest is the Great Hungarian Plain, or *Alföld*, which covers nearly half of modern Hungary. For hundreds of years, Kecskemét has been the major market town of the central-southern plain. Distributing and processing the products of the surrounding rich farmland, Kecskemét grew affluent, particularly towards the end of the 19th century. As a result, the town today boasts many gracious squares and splendid 19th and early 20th century buildings. The most famous is Ödön Lechner's massive **Town Hall**. Built between 1893–6, the building is a combination of both Renaissance and Middle-Eastern influences. The flamboyant **Cifra Palace** (Ornamental Palace), built as a casino in 1902, is a uniquely Hungarian variation of the Secession style (*see pp54–7*).

Kecskemét Town Hall, designed by Ödön Lechner

Kiskunfélegyháza ❽

110 km (66 miles) SE of Budapest. 🚶 40,000. 🚏 Szent János tér 2. **Tel** (0676) 56 14 20. 🚆 Nyugati pu. 🚌 Népstadion. **House of Nature Visitor Centre** Liszt Ferenc u. 19, Kecskemét (for information on Kiskunsági Park). **Tel** (0676) 50 15 96. ⬜ 9am–4pm Tue–Fri, 10am–2pm Sat ⬛ **Kiskun Museum** Dr Holló Lajos utca 9. **Tel** (0676) 46 14 68. ⬜ late Mar–Oct: 9am–5pm Wed–Sun. ⬛ 📷

Much of the Great Hungarian Plain is now used to grow maize and vines. Small areas, however, have been preserved as national parks. About 15 km (9 miles) to the west of Kiskunfélegyháza is the **Kiskunsági National Park**. Many rare native animals and birds can

Detail of the ornate Town Hall façade at Kiskunfélegyháza

be seen here, as well as the traditional way of life of the plains herdsman. Visitors can also explore nature trails; information is available from the Visitors' Centre in Kecskemét.

The poet Sándor Petőfi was born in Kiskunfélegyháza, and his childhood home is now part of the **Kiskun Museum**. The **Town Hall** is a masterpiece, combining influences of the Secession style *(see pp54–7)* with motifs from folk art.

Ráckeve ❾

43 km (26 miles) SW of Budapest.
🏘 8,500. 🚊 Eötvös utca 11.
🚉 Stadion. ℹ Kossuth Lajos út 51. *Tel (0624) 42 97 47.*

The village of Ráckeve is built on Csepel Island, which extends 54 km (34 miles) south along the middle of the Danube from Budapest. Ráckeve (Rác means Serb in Hungarian) was founded in the 15th century by Serbs from Keve, who fled Serbia after the Turkish invasion *(see pp26–7)* .

The oldest building in the village is the **Orthodox church**, built by some of the first of the Serbian refugees. Dating back to 1487, this is the oldest Orthodox church in Hungary. Its walls are covered in well-preserved frescos, the first telling the story of the Nativity and the last showing the Resurrection. The church also boasts a beautiful iconostasis separating the sanctuary from the nave.

Ráckeve's peaceful and convenient situation made it the country home of one of Europe's greatest military strategists, Prince Eugene of Savoy *(see p26)*. Credited with the expulsion of the Turks from Hungary at the end of the 17th century, Prince Eugene built himself a country **mansion** on what is now Kossuth Lajos utca. Now used as a hotel, the interior of the house has been modernized, but the elegant façade has been preserved. The formal gardens can be seen from the river.

Well-preserved frescoes in the Orthodox church at Ráckeve

Martonvásár ❿

30 km (18 miles) SW of Budapest.
🏘 4,900. ℹ Buda út 13. *Tel (0622) 46 00 16.* 🚉 Déli pu.
Brunswick Palace Brunswick utca 2.
◯ 8am–dusk daily (park only). 📷
Beethoven Museum ◯ 10am–noon, 2–6pm Tue–Sun. In winter: 10am–noon, 2pm–4pm Tue–Sun. 📷
🖥 www.martonvasar.hu

The village of Martonvásár has existed here since medieval times, but its principal tourist attraction is now the **Brunswick Palace**. Towards the end of the 18th century the whole village was bought by the German Brunswick family, and the original palace was built for Anton Brunswick in grand Baroque style. A century later, in 1875, the palace was totally rebuilt, this time in the Neo-Gothic style. Little evidence of the original palace remains today, among the flamboyant turrets and pinnacles. The magnificent parklands, however, are open to the public and are much as they always have been. The estate's church, built in 1775, also remains largely unaltered. The interior of the church is decorated with well-preserved frescoes.

Ludwig van Beethoven was a regular visitor to the original palace. He gave music lessons to the daughters of the house, Thérèse and Josephine, with whom he is said to have fallen in love. Some of the palace rooms have been converted into a small **Beethoven Museum**. The Beethoven festival is held in the gardens during the summer months.

The Neo-Gothic Brunswick Palace at Martonvásár

THREE GUIDED WALKS

Anchor at Vasmacska restaurant, Óbuda

Budapest is a city made for exploring on foot. From Turkish bathhouses to Baroque palaces, evidence of the city's past is visible at every turn. These guided walks take you through three fascinating areas: Óbuda to the north of the city centre, once the site of a Roman garrison and now a residential district; Margaret Island, a park in the middle of the Danube; and the historic stretch that extends from Buda across Chain Bridge and into Pest. Óbuda has yielded some of the oldest archeological finds in Hungary. This walk takes in the ruins of a Roman amphitheatre, and more modern attractions. The walk around car-free Margaret Island includes an exotic landscaped garden. The third excursion encompasses the old buildings of Buda's Castle District, an underground labyrinth and Pest's lively Central Market.

A Three-Hour Walk Around Óbuda
(see pp170–71)

Wedding car parked outside Fő tér Palace *(see p171)*

A Two-Hour Walk Around Margaret Island
(see pp172–3)

A 90-Minute Walk from Buda to Pest
(see pp174–5)

Central Market, the largest in the city *(see p175)*

0 kilometres 2

0 miles 1

KEY

•••••• Walk route

◁ Statue of a young girl in Margaret Island's landscaped Japanese Garden *(see p173)*

A Three-Hour Walk Around Óbuda

At first glance Óbuda today seems little more than a concrete jungle of tower blocks and flyovers. Behind the grey façade, however, there is a strong local identity and clues to the area's long and colourful past abound. Arriving here in AD 89, the Romans built a garrison in this district shortly before founding the civilian town of Aquincum *(see pp162–3)* to the north. After the departure of Romans in the 5th century AD, successive waves of invaders, including the Magyars *(see pp22–3)* all left their mark on Óbuda (literally "Old Buda"). By the end of the 16th century, Óbuda was a thriving market town, eventually forming part of the city of Budapest in 1873.

A section of Óbuda's impressive Roman amphitheatre ①

The elegant, Neo-Baroque Fő tér Palace with its sentry box ⑪

From the Roman Amphitheatre to the Roman Camp Museum

Begin the walk at the corner of Bécsi utca and Pacsirtamező út, which is dominated by the remains of a very fine Roman amphitheatre ①. The Romans arrived in the region soon after the time of Christ, building this impressive amphitheatre in the middle of the 2nd century AD, by which time Aquincum was the thriving capital of the province of Lower Pannonia *(see pp20–21)*. Originally used by the Roman soldiers from the nearby garrison, it became a fortress in the 9th century for the invading Magyar army. Not much remains of its once huge walls, but the scale of the theatre, which

was designed to seat 14,000, is still awe inspiring. From the amphitheatre, continue along Pacsirtamező út to No. 63, the Roman Camp (Táborváros) Museum ②. In the 1950s, this modern residential district, built on top of a Roman military camp complex, was found to be enormously rich in Roman artifacts. The museum (open Sundays and public holidays) houses Roman finds from the area, including ceramics, glassware and household tools.

Old Óbuda Synagogue to Flórián Tér

Retrace your steps and turn left down Perc utca, up Mókus utca, then Jós utca, turning left into Lajos utca. At No. 163 is the former Óbuda Synagogue ③, now a television studio. Built in the early 1820s to serve the area's growing Jewish community, this is a Neo-Classical building with a six-columned portico. Also on Lajos utca, at No. 168, is Óbuda Parish Church ④. Constructed in 1744–9 on the site of the Roman military camp, the church has survived since then largely unchanged. The interior includes a magnificently

carved pulpit showing the Good Shepherd and Mary Magdalene. Turning left up Óbudai utca, you will pass the house where the popular novelist, bon viveur and local character, Gyula Krúdy once lived ⑤. Writing in the early 20th century, much of

The former home of novelist and colourful local figure, Gyula Krúdy ⑤

Krúdy's work looks back at an idealized rural Hungary and is extremely popular in his country. From here, turn right along Tanuló utca and pass the ruins of the 14th-century St Clare's Nunnery ⑥. Then turn left towards Flórián tér. As you

Zichy Palace, built in the 18th century for an aristocratic family ⑩

KEY

● ● ● Walk route

🚉 HÉV railway station

0 metres   400

0 yards   400

pass Kálvin köz, on the left at No. 2 is the 18th-century Óbuda Calvinist Church ⑦. Next door is the presbytery, built in 1909 to a design by Károly Kós, better known for his work on the Wekerle Estate *(see p157)*. No. 4 is home to a collection of folk crafts. Walk back up to busy Flórián tér, where in 1778 Roman thermal baths were discovered. Hidden in the underpasses beneath the square are the Roman Baths Museum and the Roman Settlement Museum ⑧.

Szentlélek Tér and Fő Tér

Tavasz utca, off to the right from north of Flórián tér, leads to Szentlélek tér. In the south wing of the Zichy Palace, on Szentlélek tér, is the Vasarely Museum ⑨. The 20th-century artist Victor Vasarely is remembered as the founder of the Op-Art movement,

producing work full of bright colours and optical illusions. The crumbling Zichy Palace ⑩ itself was built for the Zichy family in 1757.

Continue north up to Fő tér, one of the few areas of 18th- and 19th-century architecture remaining in Óbuda. On one side of the square stands the Neo-Baroque Fő tér Palace ⑪, its entrance still guarded by an 18th-century sentry box.

Imre Varga Gallery to the Hercules Villa

From Fő tér Palace walk up Laktanya utca, where there is a group of statues, *Women with Umbrellas*, by contemporary sculptor Imre Varga ⑫. At No. 7 Laktanya utca is the Imre Varga Gallery ⑬, where further examples of the sculptor's work can be seen. Finally, make your way up to Szentendrei út and cross it at an underpass. Turn right into Kerék ut (if you miss this, take the next right up Szél utca), then left into Herkules utca then onto Meggyfa utca to finish the walk at No. 21, the ruins of the Hercules Villa ⑭. Once a lavish Roman home, it takes its name from some stunning mosaics *(see p21)*. Near the villa are the remains of the *cella trichora*, an early Christian chapel dating from the fourth century AD.

One of several *Women with Umbrellas* by Imre Varga ⑫

TIPS FOR WALKERS

Starting point: Pacsirtamező út.
Getting there: Bus 60 or tram 17.
Length: 3 km (1.8 miles).
Stops: The Kéhli Restaurant (see p205) on Mókus utca, or the Régi Sipos Étterem on Lajos utca for the city's freshest fish.

A Two-Hour Walk Around Margaret Island

Historically inaccessible in the middle of the Danube, Margaret Island was a retreat for religious contemplation from at least the 11th century onwards. Relics of the island's past include the remains of two monastic churches and also the ruins of the convent home of Princess Margit, daughter of King Béla IV, who gave the island its name. Opened to the public in 1869, Margaret Island is today Budapest's most beautiful park, a car-free haven of greenery in the middle of the city and the ideal location for a peaceful stroll. On the western shore, the Palatinus Strand bathing complex makes use of the mineral-rich hot springs rising on the island.

The Water Tower ⑤

A relief of Archangel Michael on St Michael's Church ⑧

Centenary Monument to Palatinus Strand

The walk begins amid the peace and greenery of the southern tip of Margaret Island. Proceeding to the north, the first landmark is the Centenary Monument ① (see p62), which stands in front of a sizable fountain. Designed by István Kiss, the monument was made in 1973, to commemorate the centenary of the unification of the towns of Buda, Óbuda and Pest (see p32). At night the fountain is dramatically illuminated. You can also rent four-wheel family bikes here called *Bringóhintó*. Taking a left turn ahead, the Hajós Olympic Pool Complex (see p53) ② is soon reached. Built in 1930, the complex was designed by the multi-talented Alfréd Hajós. He won gold medals in swimming

events in the 1896 Olympic Games and was also a member of the Hungarian football team. Continuing northwards, there is a rose garden to the right before the ruins of the early 14th-century Franciscan Church ③ come into view. Constructed in the Gothic style of the time, the church was originally attached to a monastery. Visible in the west wall is the doorway which once led to the organ loft, as well as a spiral staircase and fine arched window. Further on is the busy Palatinus Strand ④ (see p53). In front of the entrance to its pools stands a statue by French sculptor Emile Guillaume.

Water Tower to St Michael's Church

Clearly visible to the northeast of Palatinus Strand, is the 57-m (187-ft) high Water Tower ⑤. Built in 1911 and now protected by UNESCO, this graceful tower is currently used as an exhibition space for a variety of previously unexhibited modern crafts and artworks, ranging from puppets to paintings. At the foot of the Water Tower is the Summer Theatre, a large modern amphi-theatre seating 3,500 people, which hosts a summer season of operatic performances. To the southeast of the Water Tower are the ruins of a 13th-century Dominican Church and Convent ⑥.

Ruins of the 14th-century Franciscan Church ③

HAJÓS ALFRÉD SÉTÁNY

Danube

Danube

Margit híd

🚇 Margit híd

250 metres / 300 yards

The latter was once home to Princess Margit, after whom the island is named. King Béla IV *(see p23)* swore that if he succeeded in repelling the Mongol invasion of 1241 that he would offer his daughter to God. He kept his oath, building the church and convent, to which the 9-year-old Princess Margit was sent in 1251. She led a godly and ascetic life and died here at the age of 29. Nearly 300 years later, in 1541, the nuns of the convent fled to Pozsony (now Bratislava, capital of the Slovak Republic) in the face of the Turkish invasion, *(see pp26–7)*, leaving the church and the convent to be destroyed. Severe floods in 1838 led to the discovery of the ruined church and its underground vaults. The tomb of the now-canonized Margit was also excavated here 20 years later. Just to the north of the Dominican Church and Convent, near to the Water Tower, is the beginning of Artists' Avenue ⑦. A collection of contemporary busts of Hungarian writers, painters and musicians lines this promenade leading up to the Grand Hotel Margitsziget. A little way before the hotel is

Bust of Zsigmond Móricz on Artists' Avenue ⑦

Stepped pathway through the lush foliage of the Japanese Garden ⑪

St Michael's Church ⑧. Originally built by members of the Premonstratensian Order, this is the oldest building on the island. In addition, the foundations of an 11th-century chapel have been excavated inside the 12th century church. Destroyed by the invading Turks in 1541, the church was eventually reconstructed in the 1930s, using materials from the original building. In the bell tower hangs a bell which, unusually, survived the Turkish invasion. Probably buried by the monks at the time of the invasion, the bell dates from the early 15th century. It was discovered in 1914 when its walnut-tree hiding place was uprooted during a violent storm.

Grand Hotel Margitsziget to Árpád Bridge

The Grand Hotel Margitsziget ⑨ *(see p185)* was designed in 1872 by Miklós Ybl *(see p119)*. For many years it was the most fashionable hotel in Budapest, known simply as "The Grand". After World War II, the hotel was modernized and called the Danubius Grand, and in the 1970s the luxurious Danubius Health Spa Resort Margitsziget ⑩ was built nearby. The two hotels are joined by an underground walkway and offer thermal baths and a variety of spa treatments *(see p52)*. Heading west from the latter hotel, the final stretch of the walk passes beside the Japanese Garden ⑪. A variety

of exotic plants, a rock garden, waterfalls and streams crossed on rustic bridges all add to the garden's atmosphere. The final stopping point on the walk is an unusual musical well, known as the Bodor Well ⑫. The original well was designed and constructed by Transylvanian Péter Bodor in 1820 and stood in the town of Marosvásárhely (modern-day Tirgu Mures, in Romania), which was then part of the Austro-Hungarian Empire. In 1936 this copy was built on Margaret Island. Continuing past the well, at the northern tip of Margaret Island the Árpád Bridge provides another link from the island to the city.

The musical Bodor Well ⑫

TIPS FOR WALKERS

Starting point: *Southern end of Margaret Island, reached from Margaret Bridge.*
Getting there: *Bus 26. Tram 4, 6.*
Length: *3.3 km (2 miles).*
Stops: *There are numerous take-away kiosks and cafés on the island, selling drinks, snacks and ice creams. The Danubius Grand Hotel and Danubius Health Spa Resort Margitsziget also have restaurants and cafés.*

KEY

• • • Walk route

⛴ River boat boarding point

🚉 HÉV railway station

0 metres	500
0 yards	500

A 90-Minute Walk from Buda to Pest

Buda and Pest were unified in 1873, an act made possible by the construction of the monumental Chain Bridge some 20 years earlier. Before that, the two areas had shared a relatively common history, but they always retained separate identities. Even today, Buda remains more regal and relaxed than commercial, dynamic Pest. This walk reveals such differences, while highlighting the bond that makes Budapest's whole greater even than the sum of its sublime parts.

views of the Royal Palace and the unmistakable Neo-Gothic silhouette of Mátyás Church.

Roosevelt tér to Váci utca
Facing the Pest side of the river there are rewarding vistas too: of Budapest's peerless Parliament building

The terrace and conical towers of Fishermen's Bastion ②

The Castle District
The walk begins at the 13th-century Mátyás Church ① *(see pp82–3)*, one of the oldest buildings in Buda, and coronation church of the Hungarian kings. Directly behind are the ramparts of Fishermen's Bastion ② *(see p80)*, from where there are famous views across the Danube to Pest. Return past the main portal of Mátyás Church and onto Tárnok utca, running the gauntlet of its myriad souvenir shops, before arriving at Dísz tér

(see p73) and the Honvéd Monument ③. The monument was raised in honour of those who died in the Hungarian revolution of 1848–9.

Head south out of the square, along stately Szinház utca to Sándor Palace ④ *(see p73)*, one of Buda's finest buildings and the residence of the Hungarian president. Past the terminus of the Sikló, the funicular that links the Royal Palace to the embankment below, an extravagantly ornamental gateway ⑤ *(see p70)* leads from the Habsurg Steps to the Royal Palace. A wide path meanders in front of the palace and offers more fine views of Pest.

Across the Danube into Pest
The path leads down through well-kept terraces to Clark Ádam tér, named after the Scottish engineer Adam Clark, who built the awe-inspiring Chain Bridge and the Neo-Classical Alagút tunnel ⑥, which channels traffic underneath the Royal Palace. In the centre of the square is the Kilometre 0 Stone ⑦, from which the official distance from Budapest to Vienna is measured. Walk to the centre of Chain Bridge ⑧ *(see p112)* and look back towards the Castle District. On a clear day there are glorious

(see p106); and of the city's grandest hotel, the Four Seasons Gresham Palace ⑨ *(see p114)*, on the far side of Roosevelt tér. The hotel's astonishingly opulent foyer is well worth a visit.

From Roosevelt tér, a walkway runs south alongside the tram lines on Belgrád Rakpart. After a short walk, the Budapest Marriott hotel ⑩, a modernist masterpiece, appears on the left. Nearby, on the right, perched on the railings next to the tram line, is László Marton's charming

TIPS FOR WALKERS

Starting point: Mátyás Church, Moszkva tér.
Getting there: Várbusz from Moszkva tér.
Length: 3.8 km (2 miles).
Stops: Gresham Palace Kávéház on Roosevelt tér, Corso Etterem at Vigadó tér 2, or 1000 Tea at Váci utca 65 (see p207).

View from Buda to the Parliament Building in Pest

The striking architecture of Vigadó Concert Hall on Vigadó tér ⑬

Turn left at the church, and, with the Danube at your back, head towards Váci utca to the point where it crosses the busy Szabadsajtó utca. Here, the Klotild Palaces ⑯ *(see p127)*, massive twin apartment blocks built on either side of the road, provide a splendid gateway to the bridge.

Cafés and the Central Market
The southern part of Váci utca ⑰ *(see p127)* is less charming and more commercial than its northern counterpart, but on summer afternoons it is thronged with people, many of whom stop to enjoy coffee or something

Street tram and the *Little Princess* by László Marton ⑪

stronger on its many terraces. Halfway along on the right is the hapless St Michael City Church ⑱, built around 1230, devastated by the Turks in 1541, rebuilt in 1701, and finally completely renovated from 1964-8. Its unimpressive exterior belies a rich interior.

From here, more cafés and bars lead along a widening street to Central Market Hall ⑲ *(see p211)*. The largest market in the city, its stalls sell fruit and vegetables, fish, meat and cheese, and Hungarian crafts.

sculpture of a little boy, oddly entitled *Little Princess* ⑪. Passing the small pier at Vigadó tér ⑫ *(see p126)*, you cannot miss the eclectic architecture of Vigadó Concert Hall ⑬ on the square's eastern side.

Continuing along the embankment, take a left turn just before Petőfi tér onto Régiposta utca. Next, a sharp right turn onto Apáczai utca leads to the Roman remains of Contra Aquincum ⑭ *(see p122)*, and the Inner City Parish Church ⑮ *(see pp124-5)*, now sadly hemmed in by the approach to the Elizabeth Bridge.

KEY

- • • Walk route
- Pedestrianized street
- Good viewing point
- Ⓜ Metro station

0 metres 400
0 yards 400

The shops and busy terrace cafés of Váci utca ⑰

TRAVELLERS'
NEEDS

WHERE TO STAY 178–189

RESTAURANTS, CAFES AND BARS 190–209

SHOPS AND MARKETS 210–213

ENTERTAINMENT IN BUDAPEST 214–219

WHERE TO STAY

B udapest has a broad range of accommodation from top-class hotels, some with spa facilities, and private apartments to campsites and hostels. The larger hotels often belong to well-known groups and meet international standards, but are more expensive. Cheaper accommodation can be found in hostels or bed and breakfasts, or outside the city centre.

Travel agents and tourist information offices (see p181) will provide information on these options. Of the 200 hotels and pensions we surveyed, over 80 have been selected from across the price categories and are, in our opinion, the best on offer. Each of these is listed, along with a short description, on pages 182–9 to help you choose the right hotel.

The exterior of the Kempinski Corvinus Hotel (see p186)

WHERE TO LOOK

When deciding on accommodation, first choose the general location: Buda or Pest, or maybe even the picturesque suburbs further afield. In low-lying Pest, many hotels are literally only a few steps away from most of the major tourist attractions, while visitors who choose to stay in hilly Buda can enjoy cool, fresh air and quiet surroundings.

Good value for money can be found by renting a room in one of the small pensions or private hotels in and around Budapest. The more exclusive hotels offer a luxurious stay, but at a much greater price – as much as 40,000 Hungarian forints and above per night.

Many luxury hotels, such as the Sofitel Atrium Budapest (see p184), are set along the eastern bank of the Danube. Others, such as the Marriott (see p185) or the Kempinski

Corvinus (see p186) are situated nearer to the centre of Pest, close to the theatres and shops. Those located further out of town are usually an easy journey from the city centre, particularly since hotels are often situated close to metro stations.

Tourinform (see p181) is a chain of tourist offices in Budapest that provide information (in Hungarian, English, French, German, Russian, Spanish and Italian) on accommodation and places to eat, as well as on tourist and cultural events. Maps can be found on sale here, as well as free booklets and pamphlets.

The offices are open daily, including during the winter months. Should visitors need information to supplement this guide, Tourinform offices can offer details on alternative accommodation – from hotels to campsites – car rental, sightseeing, and purchasing tickets to cultural and spectator sports events.

The Sofitel Atrium Budapest (see p184), with suspended model plane

Reception desk at the Hilton Hotel (see p182) in the Castle District

HOTEL AND PENSION CLASSIFICATION

Hotels are classified in five categories from one to five stars and there are two categories of pension.

At the luxury end of the scale – the five-star and four-star hotels – all rooms have a bathroom, a telephone, a TV, a radio and a refrigerator, and many will be air-conditioned. The majority of these hotels will also offer business and fitness facilities. Three-star hotels have at least one restaurant and one bar, and staff are expected to speak at least one foreign language. Two thirds of the rooms in two-star hotels have their own shower or bath, while rooms in one-star hotels simply have wash-basins with hot and cold running water.

Pensions have a standard minimum room size, and every room has a shower or a bath. The accommodation is clean and simple, and all the necessary services and amenities should be provided by friendly and helpful staff.

◁ Interior of Gresham Palace Hotel (see p114)

The Radisson SAS Béke Hotel *(see p184),* featuring a mosaic of György Szondi

HOTEL PRICES

Room tariffs reflect the hotel classification, but it is always wise to double check the price at the time of booking. A centrally located, higher category hotel will be much more expensive than in an out-of-town, lower category hotel. Relatively cheap rooms can be found in pensions and hostels. Hotel prices usually include breakfast, which in hotels with three stars or more typically means a self-service buffet. Pensions also offer good value, substantial meals.

Many luxury hotels, such as the Ramada Plaza *(see p189),* offer substantial weekend reductions in the low season (mid-September to mid-March). During this period a three-night stay would cost the same as one-night stay during the high season.

In spa hotels, such as the Danubius Hotel Gellért *(see p183),* which offer hydrotherapy, the fee for using the pools and sauna is included in the room price. However, any treatments, such as massage, will incur an extra charge. Check these details with the hotel in advance.

Prices in Budapest's hotels and pensions are invariably quoted in Euros.

HIDDEN EXTRAS

Both VAT and resort tax are included in the price of the room (resort tax is charged because Budapest is classed as a health resort), but there are often hidden surcharges that can greatly increase the overall cost of a stay. For example, a number of hotels have currency exchange desks, but these offer a poor rate of exchange. It is better to change money at a bank or *bureau de change* where rates tend to be much more favourable.

Telephone calls, particularly international calls, cost almost twice as much when made from hotel rooms as opposed to public telephones. There are plenty of these in Budapest, although it may be necessary to buy a phone card *(see p230).*

Most hotels have their own car parks. Some, such as the InterContinental *(see p186),* the Sofitel Atrium Budapest *(see p184)* or the Victoria *(see p183),* offer off-street or garage parking, for which a modest fee may be charged.

HOW TO BOOK

The Budapest tourist season starts in the middle of June and lasts until the end of September. During this period, as well as around New Year and the Hungarian Grand Prix weekend *(see p59),* hotels become fully booked very quickly.

It is advisable to book at least two weeks ahead. Most hotels accept bookings made by email or fax and reply in the same way. Guests should confirm their reservations with a follow-up phone call a few days before they arrive.

It is possible to find accommodation without booking in advance, but rooms may be harder to come by, especially in high season. Bookings can be made in the tourist offices at Ferihegy airport, Terminals 1 and 2 *(see p225 and p232)* and at Nyugati pu, the city's western railway station *(see pp234–5).*

Stained-glass window in the Danubius Hotel Gellért *(see p183)*

The Danubius Grand Hotel Margitsziget *(see p189)*, Margaret Island

SERVICE

The services and amenities offered by each hotel will vary according to price. As in most other countries, hotel rooms are cleaned regularly, and most higher category hotels offer 24-hour service, including meals that can be brought to the room. This usually incurs an extra charge, but tips are always welcome.

Most reception personnel will speak some foreign languages, most commonly English and German. They are happy to help make sightseeing suggestions.

TRAVELLING WITH CHILDREN

Most hotels welcome children and offer free accommodation to those up to the age of four travelling with their parents. Additional beds can often be provided for older children in the parents' room for a small extra charge. Many hotels also offer a child-minding service.

DISABLED TRAVELLERS

Budapest is trying to make up for the neglect that disabled travellers to the city have suffered. Specialist facilities are gradually being introduced throughout the city. For example, most hotels have facilities enabling disabled guests to have as pleasant and easy a stay as able-bodied people. Such hotels will display information about their facilities for disabled guests. Further information can be obtained from tourist information offices and travel agents.

SELF-CATERING

A few hotels in Budapest, especially those in the embassy district, such as the Radio Inn *(see p186)*, offer accommodation in suites with kitchenettes. This type of accommodation is particularly good for families as it gives them the option of eating "at home", rather than taking every meal at a restaurant. Another advantage is, of course, the extra space, which allows greater freedom of movement; often hotel suites are equal in size to an apartment.

There are also some specially converted buildings that consist solely of self-catering apartments. The **Charles Apartment Hotel** is a good example of this type of accommodation; the apartments are spacious and well equipped.

HOSTELS

Budapest has a few hostels that stay open all year. For visitors on a tight budget, these provide good, if basic, low-cost accommodation. **Marco Polo Hostel** and the **Citadella** *(see p182)*, which is situated in the Citadel *(see pp92–3)* on Gellért Hill, are just some examples. Hostels often provide guests with a choice of staying in a dormitory or a single or double room.

SEASONAL HOSTELS

The closest thing to youth hostels that Budapest has are the college halls of residence, which are only available during the summer vacation in July and August. Many students' halls of residence are turned into hostels, adding approximately 4,000 beds to Budapest's accommodation list and providing tourists with a convenient and inexpensive place to stay.

Given their popularity, it is advisable to book a room in advance. This is best done on the Internet via the **Mellow Mood Travel Agency**, or via tourist offices and travel bureaux. International Youth Hostels Organisation membership will enable guests to get a discount on room rates.

The interior of the Danubius Astoria Hotel *(see p185)*

STAYING IN PRIVATE ROOMS AND APARTMENTS

Some visitors choose to stay in a private home. Accommodation usually consists of a separate bedroom and use of a kitchen and bathroom. The price depends on the facilities and the area, and varies from 5,000–10,000 Hungarian forints (€20-€40) per day for a double room and upwards of 5,000 forints (€20) for a single. **TO-MA Tour** and **Ibusz** are reputable agencies through which this type of accommodation can be booked.

Renting an apartment is economical for longer stays. As well as using agencies to find private apartments, it is worth checking the *albérlet* (to rent) advertisements in newspapers such as *Expressz* and *Hirdetés*.

CAMPING

Camping is only permitted at designated campsites. There are several of these situated on the outskirts of Budapest. The biggest and most picturesque of them all is **Római Camping**, which is located on the road leading from Óbuda to Szentendre. Campsites are open, in general, from May until the end of October. Some operations, such as **Heller Camping**, are open only from May to September, while others are open throughout the year.

The restaurant of the Danubius Hotel Erzsébet *(see p185)*, in the city centre

DIRECTORY

INFORMATION

Hungarian National Tourist Office (UK)
Embassy of the Republic of Hungary, 46 Eaton Place, London SW1X 8AL.
Tel 020 7823 1055.
www.gotohungary.co.uk

Hungarian National Tourist Office (US)
350 Fifth Avenue, 71st Floor, Empire State Building, New York, NY 10118.
Tel 212 695 1221.
www.gotohungary.com

Tourinform Call Centre
24-hour Tel 438 80 80.
From abroad +36 14 38 80 80.
From Hungary 06 80 630 800.

Tourinform Buda Castle
1016 Budapest, Szentháromság tér.
Map 1 B4 (9 A2).
Tel 488 04 75.

Tourinform Ferihegy 2 Airport
1185 Budapest, Terminals 1 & 2.
Tel 438 80 80.

Tourinform Liszt Ferenc tér
1061 Budapest, Liszt Ferenc tér 11.
Map 7 A1.
Tel 322 40 98.

Tourinform Nyugati Pu
Left wing of main station.
Map 2 F2.
Tel 302 85 80.

AGENCIES

Express Utazási Iroda
1052 Budapest, Semmelweis utca 4.
Map 4 F1 (10 E4).
Tel 327 70 93.
www.expresstravel.hu

Hungarian Youth Hostels Federation
1086 Budapest, Könyves Kálmán körút 64.
Tel 210 08 16.
www.budapest
youthhostel.hu

IBUSZ Travel Agency
1053 Budapest, Ferenciek tere 10.
Map 4 F1 (10 E4).
Tel 485 27 65/6.
www.ibusz.hu

SELF-CATERING

Charles Apartment Hotel
1016 Budapest, Hegyalja út 23.
Map 3 B2 (9 B5).
Tel 212 91 69.
www.charleshotel.hu

HOSTELS

Citadella
1118 Budapest, Citadella sétány. **Map** 4 D3.
Tel 466 57 94.
www.citadella.hu

Marco Polo Hostel
1072 Budapest, Nyár utca 6.
Map 7 A3.
Tel 413 25 55.
www marcopolohostel.com

Red Bus Hostel
V. Semmelweis utca 14.
Map 4 F1. *Tel 266 01 36.*
www.redbusbudapest.hu

Boat Hostel Fortuna
1137 Szent István Park, Alsó rakpart. **Map** 2 D1.
Tel 288 81 00.
www.fortunahajo.hu

Back Pack Guesthouse
XI, Takás Menyhért utca 33.
Map 3 B5. *Tel 209 84 06.*

SEASONAL HOSTELS

Mellow Mood Travel Agency
1077 Budapest, Baross tér 15. **Map** 7 C2.
Tel 411 23 90.
www.mellowmood.hu

PRIVATE ROOMS AND APARTMENTS

TO-MA Tour
1051 Budapest, Oktober 6 utca 22.
Map 2 E4. *Tel 353 08 19.*
www.tomatour.hu

IBUSZ Travel
1053 Budapest, Ferenciek tere 10. **Map** 4 F1 (10 E4).
Tel 485 27 70.
www.ibusz.hu

CAMPING

Csillebérc Autós Camping
1121 Budapest, Konkoly Thege út 21.
Tel 395 65 27.

Haller Camping
1096 Budapest, Haller utca 27. *Tel 476 34 18.*

Római Camping
1031 Budapest, Szentendrei út 189.
Tel 388 71 67.

Choosing a Hotel

Hotels have been selected across a wide price range for good value, facilities and location. They are listed by area of the city, in the same order as the rest of the guide. Within each area, they are listed alphabetically within each price category, from the least to the most expensive. Where breakfast is an optional extra, this is indicated.

PRICE CATEGORIES
For a standard double room with bathroom per night, including breakfast, service charges:
under 15,000 HUF
15,000–25,000 HUF
25,000–35,000 HUF
35,000–50,000 HUF
over 50,000 HUF

CASTLE DISTRICT

Kulturinnov
Szentháromság tér 6, 1014 **Tel** *355 01 22* **Fax** *375 18 86* **Rooms** *6*   **Map** *1 B4*

At the heart of Budapest's Castle district, the Kulturinov is a reasonably priced, simple hotel where location is paramount. Guests are not overwhelmed by luxury here, the rooms are all large, have ensuite facilities and offer peace and quiet. For serious sightseers it's a great choice, and the hotel building itself is a Neo-Gothic treat. **www.mka.hu**

Burg
Szentháromság tér 7-8, 1014 **Tel** *212 02 69* **Fax** *212 39 70* **Rooms** *26*   **Map** *1 B4*

Located almost directly opposite the Mátyás Church in the heart of the Castle District, location is everything at the Burg. The rooms are comfortable, if a little spartan, and the bathrooms (all ensuite) are quite small. There is no extra charge for a room overlooking the church – ask for one when booking. **www.burghotelbudapest.com**

Carlton Hotel Budapest
Apor Péter utca 3, 1011 **Tel** *224 09 99* **Fax** *224 09 90* **Rooms** *95*   **Map** *1 C5*

Despite its rather bleak exterior, this is a very comfortable hotel, situated beneath the Royal Palace just off Fő utca, close to Clark Ádám tér and handy for the Chain Bridge and Pest. It has good-sized, if slightly basic, single, double and triple rooms, all with large, bright bathrooms. A hearty buffet breakfast is available. **www.carltonhotel.hu**

Hilton
Hess Andrástér 1–3, 1014 **Tel** *889 66 00* **Fax** *889 66 44* **Rooms** *322*   **Map** *1 B4*

The Hilton *(see p81)*, one of the most luxurious hotels in Budapest, is located in a remarkable old-new building in a great location. It offers three restaurants, serving Hungarian and international cuisine. With magnificent views over the Danube and the Pest cityscape, the high prices here are more than justified. **www.budapesthilton.hu**

GELLÉRT HILL AND TABÁN

Citadella
Citadella sétány, 1118 **Tel** *466 57 94* **Fax** *386 05 05* **Rooms** *13*   **Map** *4 D3*

This hostel-style hotel occupies the casements of the Citadel *(see p92)*. It offers relatively inexpensive, neat and clean double and multiple-occupancy rooms, and there's no curfew. Getting back here late at night can be a trek, however. A popular wine bar, restaurant and nightclub are nearby in the Citadella complex. **www.citadella.hu**

Danubius Hotel Flamenco
Tas Vezér utca 3–7, 1113 **Tel** *889 56 00* **Fax** *889 56 51* **Rooms** *355*   **Map** *3 C5*

This good value hotel is a little out of the centre but easily reached by the 47 or 49 tram. The rooms are smart and the Bolero restaurant serves great breakfasts. There is a well-equipped gym in the basement. Popular with business people. **www.danubiusgroup.com/flamenco**

Best Western Orion
Döbrentei utca 13, 1013 **Tel** *356 85 83* **Fax** *375 54 18* **Rooms** *30*   **Map** *4 D1*

Hidden in a secluded spot, this pleasant hotel offers clean, plainly decorated rooms with bathrooms, controlled air conditioning and colour TVs. A small restaurant serves a good range of inexpensive Hungarian and international cuisine. **www.bestwestern.hu/orion**

Astra
Vám utca 6, 1011 **Tel** *214 19 06* **Fax** *214 19 07* **Rooms** *9*   **Map** *1 C4*

A good-value hotel, set in a 300-year-old listed building, which is small and cozy. The larger rooms – all set around a courtyard – need to be booked well in advance in high summer. A very good buffet breakfast is included in the price. There's a cellar bar and games room, too. **www.ohb.hu/astra**

Key to Symbols *see back cover flap*

Rácz Hotel

Hadnagy utca 8-10, 1013 **Tel** *266 06 06* **Fax** *266 06 76* **Rooms** *67* **Map** *4 D2*

A luxury hotel incorporating the historic Rác thermal baths *(see p95)*. Rooms are spacious and well-appointed and guests can take advantage of the spa facilities, enjoy Italian cuisine in the restaurant or marvel at the spectacular views of the Royal Palace, thermal spa or surrounding park. **www.raczhotel.com**

Buda Gold

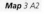

Hegyalja út 14, 1016 **Tel** *209 47 75* **Fax** *209 54 31* **Rooms** *30* **Map** *3 A2*

This wonderful, grand house in the Buda hills offers panoramic views – many including a view of the garden – and luxurious bathrooms. There's a very smart restaurant on site, and the buffet breakfast is hearty. Families should go for the good-value apartments, romantics for the tower rooms. **www.goldhotel.hu**

Danubius Hotel Gellért

Szent Gellért tér1, 1111 **Tel** *889 55 00* **Fax** *889 55 05* **Rooms** *234* **Map** *4 D2*

This legendary spa hotel *(see pp90–91)* has both indoor and outdoor pools. Treatments such as massages are available. Other facilities include a restaurant, a bar, a nightclub and banqueting halls. The guests' rooms, it should be said, have probably seen grander days. **www.danubiusgroup.com/gellert**

NORTH OF THE CASTLE

Mercure Budapest Buda

Krisztina körút 41–43, 1013 **Tel** *488 81 00* **Fax** *488 81 77* **Rooms** *399* **Map** *1 A5*

A good value hotel by the Vérmező (Blood Meadow) Park and conveniently close to Déli Railway Station. The comfortable rooms have views up towards the Castle District. Facilities include a swimming pool, restaurant and bar. Children and dogs are welcome. **www.mercure-buda.hu**

art'otel

Bem rakpart 16–19, 1011 **Tel** *487 94 87* **Fax** *487 94 88* **Rooms** *164* **Map** *1 C4*

Everything here – from the artwork decorating the walls, to the carpets and chinaware – is the work of American designer Donald Sultan. Rooms are individually styled with supreme taste. The Chelsea restaurant is worth a visit even if you don't stay. **www.artotels.com**

Papillon

Rózsahegy utca 3/B, 1024 **Tel** *212 47 50* **Fax** *212 40 03* **Rooms** *30* **Map** *1 B2*

Small, garishly decorated in pinks and purples but charming all the same, this is an unpretentious place where the family who own and run it make all guests feel very welcome. Rooms are small but acceptable, pets are allowed, and there's a garden with a paddling pool for children. Breakfast is included in the price. **www.hotelpapillon.hu**

Lánchíd 19

Lánchíd utca 19–21, 1013 **Tel** *419 19 00* **Fax** *419 19 19* **Rooms** *48* **Map** *1 C5*

At this four-star design hotel the emphasis is on style. Even the hotel staff wear uniforms created by award-winning local fashion designers. With well-appointed rooms and a superb location by the Chain Bridge *(Lánchíd)*, this is a good choice. **www.lanchid19hotel.hu**

Victoria

Bem rakpart 11, 1011 **Tel** *457 80 80* **Fax** *457 80 88* **Rooms** *27* **Map** *1 C4 (9 B2)*

On the western bank of the Danube, within easy reach of Buda's main tourist sights, this hotel provides big, comfortable air-conditioned rooms, many with views of the Chain Bridge, the Elizabeth Bridge and Pest. There is no restaurant, so breakfast is served in the bar. Facilities include a sauna and an in-house doctor. **www.victoria.hu**

AROUND PARLIAMENT

Medosz

Jókai tér 9, 1061 **Tel** *374 30 01* **Fax** *332 43 16* **Rooms** *67* **Map** *7 A1*

This former trade union hostel has been successfully converted into a basic hotel. Designed for communist comrades as opposed to courting couples, most of the modest rooms have beds arranged end-to-end. Such hardships are compensated for by its excellent location close to Liszt Ferenc tér and Oktogon tér. **www.medoszhotel.hu**

City Hotel Ring

Szent István körút 22, 1137 **Tel** *340 54 50* **Fax** *340 48 84* **Rooms** *39* **Map** *7 A1 (10 F1)*

The City Hotel is within easy reach of Parliament *(see pp108–9)*. All rooms are clean and subtly decorated in neutral shades. There are few facilities and services, and this is reflected in the reasonable prices. There is a cheerful breakfast room but no restaurant. There are, however, many places to eat nearby. **www.taverna.hu/ring**

Four Seasons Gresham Palace

Roosevelt tér 5–6, 1051 **Tel** *268 60 00* **Fax** *268 50 00* **Rooms** *179* **Map** *2 D5*

After decades of neglect this magnificent building was restored and is now one of the finest in Central Europe. The entrance hall and galleries should be visited on the way to the *Kávéház* (coffee house) for coffee and cakes. The staff are impeccable and this place is a real treat. **www.fourseasons.com**

K + K Opera

Révay utca 24, 1065 **Tel** *269 02 22* **Fax** *269 02 30* **Rooms** *205* **Map** *2 F4 (10 E2)*

This hotel belongs to the K + K group and is situated close to the State Opera House *(see pp118–19)*. Behind a splendid façade it offers guests comfortable accommodation in modern, clean and incredibly spacious rooms. There is also a café, a pub, a bar and secure car parking. Buffet breakfast included. **www.kkhotels.com**

Hilton Budapest WestEnd

Váci út 1–3 (inside WestEnd City Center), 1069 **Tel** *288 55 00* **Fax** *288 55 88* **Rooms** *230* **Map** *2 F2*

This is the second Hilton to open in the city. It is sited next to the hubbub of the WestEnd shopping centre, yet the contrast between the two places could not be greater. The hotel is an oasis of calm – especially in the charming rooftop garden – and offers the usual Hilton mix of modernity, efficiency and service. **www.hilton.com**

Radisson SAS Béke

Terézkörút 43, 1067 **Tel** *889 39 00* **Fax** *889 39 15* **Rooms** *247* **Map** *2 F3*

This old, magnificent hotel *(see p115)*, close to Nyugati pu metro station, has been restored and is now equipped with the latest facilities. The restaurants serve European and Hungarian delicacies, while the first-floor Zsolnay Café serves tea and coffee from Zsolnay porcelain *(see p56)*. **www.radissonblu.com/hotel-budapest**

Sofitel Atrium Budapest

Roosevelt tér 2, 1051 **Tel** *266 12 34* **Fax** *266 91 01* **Rooms** *350* **Map** *2 D5 (9 C3)*

Located close to the Danube, most of the Atrium's rooms have terrific views of the Castle District and Pest. There are stylish restaurants, serving international and Hungarian cuisine, terrace cafés and a cocktail bar. Souvenir boutiques and the Las Vegas Casino *(see p217)* are on the ground floor. **www.sofitel.com**

CENTRAL PEST

Marco Polo Hostel

Nyár utca 6, 1072 **Tel** *413 25 55* **Fax** *413 60 58* **Rooms** *47* **Map** *7 A3*

Excellent value backpacker hostel, right in the heart of the city and close to public transport, nightlife and sights. Dormitory rooms are partitioned into two-bed cubicles for a little extra privacy. There are also double, triple and quad rooms with en suite facilities, a lively bar and an Internet café. Breakfast is included. **www.marcopolohostel.com**

Anna

Gyulai Pál utca 14, 1085 **Tel** *327 20 00* **Fax** *327 20 01* **Rooms** *31* **Map** *7 A3*

A small, charming hotel in the centre of the city. Standard rooms are on the small side, but are stuffed full of amenities, while the two apartments come with classic wooden furniture, including enormous beds, original wooden floors and an antique table and chairs. A good buffet breakfast is included. Parking costs €15 per day. **www.annahotel.hu**

City Panzió Mátyás

Március 15 tér 8, 1056 **Tel** *338 47 11* **Fax** *327 90 86* **Rooms** *85* **Map** *4 E1*

This small, neat pension offers basic rooms, all with showers (but no baths). There's no restaurant, although a good buffet breakfast is offered and the pension sits above the *Mátyás Pince* (Matthew's Cellar), a restaurant popular with visitors. It's also in a great location for all the sights. **www.taverna.hu**

Club Hotel Ambra

Kisdiófa utca 13, 1077 **Tel** *321 15 33* **Fax** *321 15 40* **Rooms** *21* **Map** *7 A2*

The exterior is starkly modern, but the interior is a real joy, made all the more homely by the friendly staff. Rooms are actually apartments, all individually air conditioned, with satellite TV and comfy sofas. There's a small fitness centre with a sauna, and buffet breakfast is included in the price. **www.hotelambra.hu**

Ibis Budapest Emke

Akácfa utca 1–3, 1072 **Tel** *478 30 50* **Fax** *478 30 55* **Rooms** *84* **Map** *7 B3*

Situated in the city centre, in a quiet side street close to Blaha Lujza tér. One of the Ibis chain of low-price, good-quality hotels, the Emke offers pleasant accommodation, including non-smoking rooms, and rooms that have been adapted for the needs of disabled visitors. Service is very friendly and breakfast is good. **www.ibis-emke.hu**

King's Hotel Kosher

Nagy Diófa utca 25–27, 1072 **Tel** *352 76 75* **Fax** *352 76 17* **Rooms** *100* **Map** *7 A2 (10 F3)*

Right in the heart of the Jewish Quarter *(see p134)*, this beautifully restored 19th-century building has been a hotel since 1995. The rooms are modern and plain, but many have small balconies overlooking the quiet residential street outside. The hotel's restaurant offers a tasty range of strictly Kosher meals. **www.kingshotel.hu**

Key to Price Guide *see p182* **Key to Symbols** *see back cover flap*

Leo Panzio

Kossuth Lajos utca 2/A, 1053 **Tel** *266 90 41* **Fax** *66 90 42* **Rooms** *14* **Map** *4 F1*

In the very heart of Budapest, this is a superb little pension that offers good accommodation at a more than reasonable price. Rooms have private bathrooms (with shower and toilet), air conditioning and TVs. Some have great views of the lively streets below. A good buffet breakfast is included in the price. **www.leopanzio.hu**

Mercure Budapest Metropol

Rákóczi út 58, 1074 **Tel** *462 81 00* **Fax** *462 81 81* **Rooms** *130* **Map** *7 A3*

Located in the city centre, close to all amenities and transport links, the Mercure Budapest is housed in a refurbished 19th-century building. It offers every modern convenience, including sound-proofing – much needed in this location – and Internet access in all rooms. It is popular with business travellers. **www.mercure-metropol.hu**

Mercure Nemzeti

József körút 4, 1088 **Tel** *477 20 00* **Fax** *477 20 01* **Rooms** *74* **Map** *7 B3*

Built at the end of the 19th century, the Nemzeti's powder blue façade gazes out on one of Pest's busiest squares. The grand staircase and Secession restaurant add to the experience. Rooms are comfortable; the ones facing the courtyard are quieter. **www.mercure.com**

Buddha Bar Hotel Klotild Palace

Váci utca 34, 1052 **Tel** *70 455 0391* **Fax** *321 4851* **Rooms** *102* **Map** *4 E1*

In a restored historic building and almost overwhelming in its opulence, the Buddha Bar is the height of luxury. Buddha's presence is everywhere and gold, orange and red hues dominate. The Asian theme runs through every spacious, sumptuous room and staying here is certainly an experience. **www.buddhabarhotelbudapest.com**

Cotton House

Jókai utca 26, 1066 **Tel** *354 26 00* **Fax** *354 13 41* **Rooms** *18* **Map** *2 F3*

Upstairs at the Cotton Club bar is the Cotton House, offering some of the best decorated rooms in Hungary. Luxurious and classy, this is a great choice for couples or music fans – all the rooms are named and decorated in honour of a star of the stage or screen. This hotel offers incredible value for money. **www.cottonhouse.hu**

Danubius Astoria Hotel

Kossuth Lajos utca 19–21, 1053 **Tel** *889 60 00* **Fax** *889 60 91* **Rooms** *131* **Map** *4 F1 (10 E4)*

This old hotel, designed in the Secession style *(see pp54–5)* but with a Neo-Baroque breakfast room, has been refurbished in its original style. Non-guests should visit the café just to admire the interior. Guests can enjoy luxurious rooms that are now in tune with the rest of the building. **www.danubiusgroup.com/astoria**

Danubius Hotel Erzsébet

Károlyi Mihály utca 11–15, 1053 **Tel** *889 37 00* **Fax** *889 37 63* **Rooms** *123* **Map** *10 E5*

Despite the rather awful façade, this hotel almost in the very heart of Budapest is tremendous value. There's been a hotel on this site since 1873, though the current building went up in 1976. It offers comfortable rooms, all with large bathrooms, pay TV and sound-proofed windows. **www.danubiushotels.com**

Continental Hotel Zara

Dohány utca 42–44, 1074 **Tel** *815 50 00* **Fax** *815 50 01* **Rooms** *272* **Map** *7 A3*

It's great to see the once beautiful but decayed exterior of the old Hungária Fürdő resplendent again – as part of a spa and business hotel. Standard rooms can be a little cramped but the Art Deco inspired interiors mitigate in their favour, along with the hotel's spa and range of amenities. **www.continentalhotelzara.com**

Marriott

Apáczai Csere János utca 4, 1052 **Tel** *486 50 00* **Fax** *486 50 05* **Rooms** *362* **Map** *4 E1*

The Marriott's excellent facilities include banqueting rooms, three restaurants, a business centre, and a fitness centre. The rooms are of a high standard and the staff provide an exemplary level of service. It was here, in 1991, that the decision was taken to dissolve the Warsaw Pact. **www.marriott.com/budhu**

Mercure Budapest City Center

Váci utca 20, 1052 **Tel** *485 31 00* **Fax** *485 31 11* **Rooms** *227* **Map** *4 E1 (10 D4)*

This is the most centrally located hotel in Budapest, situated right on Váci utca, or Váci Street *(see p127)*. The sound-proofed, elegant rooms are oases of calm amid the noise and bustle of this busy commercial district. Suites come with jacuzzis and saunas. The Zsolnay Café on the ground floor is famous for its pastries. **www.mercure.hu**

Mercure Budapest Korona

Kecskeméti utca 14, 1053 **Tel** *486 88 00* **Fax** *318 38 67* **Rooms** *424* **Map** *4 F2*

Big, modern and sophisticated, the Mercure Korona is situated in a small street off Kálvin tér, close to cafés and restaurants. The hotel has a wide range of amenities, including its own swimming pool, gymnasium, sauna and solarium. Room rates are reasonable, but breakfast costs an extra 15 euros. **www.mercure-korona.hu**

Corinthia Grand Hotel Royal

Erzsébet körút 43–49, 1073 **Tel** *479 40 00* **Fax** *479 43 33* **Rooms** *414* **Map** *7 A2*

Behind its distinguished façade, what was the Grand Hotel Royal has been transformed into the modern and elegant Corinthia Grand Hotel Royal. The lobby is a joy in itself, setting a luxurious scene even before guests reach their rooms, which are equally stunning. All are classically furnished in mahogany. **www.corinthia.hu**

InterContinental

Apáczai Csere János utca 12–14, 1052 **Tel** *327 63 33* **Fax** *327 63 57* **Rooms** *398*   **Map** *2 D5 (9 C3).*

This luxury hotel, situated close to Pest's riverside promenade, offers a magnificent view across the Danube to Buda's Castle District. Rooms are enormous with wonderful bathrooms. The facilities include a cocktail bar and a buffet restaurant. The beautifully decorated Viennese Café is on the first floor. **www.budapest.intercontinental.com**

Kempinski Corvinus

Erzsébettér 7–8, 1051 **Tel** *429 37 77* **Fax** *429 47 77* **Rooms** *365*   **Map** *2 E5 (10 D5)*

This exclusive hotel – all glass and class – often welcomes heads of state and other notable personalities among its guests. The large and expensively furnished rooms are enormously relaxing, and perfectly mix luxury with modernity. The hotel has excellent fitness facilities, two good restaurants, bars and a pub. **www.kempinski-budapest.com**

Le Meridien Budapest

Erzsébet tér 9–10, 1050 **Tel** *429 55 00* **Fax** *429 55 55* **Rooms** *218*   **Map** *2 E5 (10 D5)*

Housed in the centrally-located and tastefully renovated Adria Palace, Le Meridien Budapest is an elegantly furnished hotel, where attention to detail is evident. Standard-size rooms are among the largest in Budapest. The fitness centre is one of the city's best, complete with an enchanting plunge-pool and jacuzzi. **www.budapest.lemeridien.com**

Marriott Millennium Court

Pesti Barnabás utca 4, 1052 **Tel** *235 18 00* **Fax** *235 19 00* **Rooms** *108*   **Map** *4 E1*

A luxury, centrally-located executive apartment block, with individual apartments available for the night or for longer. All apartments are serviced and impeccably tasteful. The price is not cheap but, for a family, taking space in one of these apartments can actually work out to be highly economical. **www.execapartments.com**

AROUND VÁROSLIGET

Best Western Hotel Hungaria

Rákóczi út 90, 1074 **Tel** *889 44 00* **Fax** *889 44 11* **Rooms** *499*   **Map** *7 C2*

Reputedly the largest hotel in the land, the Hungaria's corridors are full of life and colour. Located by Keleti Railway Station, providing easy access to all the major sights, this good-value hotel has small but comfortable rooms and all the expected facilities. **www.danubiushotels.com/bwhungaria**

Golden Park

Baross tér 10, 1087 **Tel** *477 47 77* **Fax** *477 47 70* **Rooms** *172*   **Map** *7 C2*

The Golden Park is situated very close to Keleti Railway Station – not the fanciest part of town but great for those who want to explore the countryside. It offers excellent buffet breakfasts and comfortable rooms at reasonable prices. Public transport to the main sights of the city is also excellent. **www.goldenparkhotel.hu**

Ibis Budapest Váci út

Dózsa György út 65, 1134 **Tel** *329 02 00* **Fax** *340 83 16* **Rooms** *322*   **Map** *5 A1*

Almost equidistant from Margaret Island and City Park, the Ibis Vaci út is a hotel that appeals to families looking for a good base away from the crowds. Rooms are far from large, but well furnished and equipped, and bathrooms are surprisingly spacious. As with all Ibis hotels, the buffet breakfast is very good. **www.ibis.hu**

MaMaison Hotel Andrássy Budapest

Andrássy út 111, 1063 **Tel** *462 21 00* **Fax** *322 94 45* **Rooms** *70*   **Map** *5 B4*

Elegance and charm meet in this hotel on Andrássy Avenue, Budapest's grandest boulevard. The rooms are tasteful with a chic French style, and the City Park is a short walk away. Baraka restaurant *(see p203)* on the ground floor is one of the best in town. **www.andrassyhotel.com**

Radio Inn

Benczúr utca 19, 1068 **Tel** *342 83 47* **Fax** *342 83 84* **Rooms** *34*   **Map** *5 C4*

This pension-style hotel is the official guesthouse of Hungarian National Radio and entertains many visiting personalities. Accommodation is in spacious suites with well-equipped kitchens. Facilities are quite basic, but the Inn is ideal for families as it is situated in the peaceful embassy quarter and there is a garden. **www.radioinn.hu**

Unio

Dob utca 73, 1077 **Tel** *479 04 00* **Fax** *479 04 01* **Rooms** *52*   **Map** *7 B1*

The rooms in this reasonably priced hotel are not spectacular, but they are nicely furnished with tasteful wooden beds, wardrobes and desks, and bright blue carpets (that might be a little garish for some). Bathrooms have a bath and a toilet. There is a good restaurant, and breakfast is included in the room rate. **www.uniohotel.hu**

Benczúr

Benczúr utca 35, 1068 **Tel** *479 56 50* **Fax** *342 15 58* **Rooms** *93*   **Map** *5 C4*

Situated in a quiet street close to Városliget *(see p142)*, this hotel offers small but comfortable rooms. In addition, there is a good restaurant, as well as a terrace and a garden. Guests are able to make use of the services of an in-house dentist. Prices are sometimes considerably reduced out of the high season. **www.hotelbenczur.hu**

Key to Price Guide *see p182* **Key to Symbols** *see back cover flap*

Hotel Ibis Heroes Square

Dózsa György út 106, 1068 **Tel** *269 53 00* **Fax** *269 53 29* **Rooms** *139* **Map** *5 C3*

Situated on the edge of the Hösök tere or Heroes' Square *(see pp142–3)*, close to the Museum of Fine Arts *(see pp146–9)*, this bright, modern hotel offers pleasant rooms, a sauna, a solarium, wireless Internet and a rent-a-bike scheme. The buffet breakfast (included in the price) is excellent. **www.ibis.hu**

New York Palace Hotel Boscolo

Erzsébet körút 9-11, 1073 **Tel** *413 14 00* **Fax** *413 1964* **Rooms** *112* **Map** *7 B2*

This is a magnificent hotel. Built in 1894, its coffee house played a significant role in Hungarian literary life. Writers and poets sat beneath the gilded domes and now visitors can do the same. Sensitively restored by the Italian Boscolo group, the main hall is something to marvel at and rooms are luxurious. **www.boscolohotels.com**

Residence Izabella

Izabella utca 61, 1064 **Tel** *475 59 00* **Fax** *475 59 02* **Rooms** *38* **Map** *5 A5*

An apartment hotel offering spacious, one-, two- and three-bedroom apartments just off Budapest's most exclusive street, Andrássy út. There's a 24-hour reception, security, parking, and a health club with sauna. Apartments have DVD and sound systems, and fitted kitchens. Rates exclude parking and breakfast. **www.residenceizabella.com**

FURTHER AFIELD

Agro

Normafa út 54, 1121 **Tel** *458 39 00* **Fax** *458 39 01* **Rooms** *145*

This out-of-town hotel, situated on Sváb Hill *(see p161)*, retains echoes of Budapest's communist past. However, relaxing surroundings and good food are matched by excellent sports and leisure facilities. There are also splendid views, and walking in the Buda Hills *(see p161)* is an enjoyable pastime. **www.hotelagropanorama.hu**

Charles Apartment Hotel

Hegyalja út 23, 1016 **Tel** *212 91 69* **Fax** *202 29 84* **Rooms** *66* **Map** *3 B2*

The studio apartments are a bit larger than hotel rooms and have a tiny kitchen. Standard rooms are unrenovated, business-class rooms have been given a makeover. Rooms on the quiet side of the building do not suffer from traffic noise in the morning. The hotel's restaurant is very good, and breakfast is a real treat. **www.charleshotel.hu**

Grand Hostel

Hüvösvölgyi út 69, 1021 **Tel** *274 11 11* **Fax** *200 20 48* **Rooms** *55*

The expression "cheap and cheerful" might have been invented to describe the Grand Hostel, a brightly coloured building, with free Wi-Fi access and no curfew. The friendly staff will welcome you with a complimentary drink of your choice on arrival. **www.grandhostel.hu**

Mohácsi Panzió

Bimbó út 25/A, 1022 **Tel** *326 77 41* **Fax** *326 7784* **Rooms** *9*

Small, pleasant and inexpensive, this pension is located just off Margit körút, in the Rózsadomb area of the Buda Hills *(see p161)*. Rooms are clean and have either a shower or a bath, and television. Those on the upper floor have marvellous views of Budapest. Underground parking costs €5. **www.hotelmohacsipanzio.hu**

Nordic

Gyopár utca 6, 1028 **Tel** *274 62 92* **Fax** *274 62 92* **Rooms** *12*

Simple but clean and bright rooms await guests at this miniature castle in the Buda Hills *(see p161)*. The tower at the front is striking. A good breakfast is available, though at a small extra cost, and there is a sauna and plunge pool for guests' use (also for a small fee). To get here, take Bus 56 from Moszkva tér. **www.nordichotel.hu**

Vadvirág Panzió

Nagybányai út 18., 1025 **Tel** *275 02 00* **Fax** *394 42 92* **Rooms** *16*

A homely, family owned and operated pension, located in a quiet, green district of the Buda Hills *(see p161)*. There are comfortable rooms with balconies, and a restaurant, terrace and sauna. To get there, take Bus 11 from Batthany tér to the end of the line. **www.hotelvadvirangpanzio.hu**

Villa Korda

Szikla utca 9, 1025 **Tel** *325 91 23* **Fax** *325 91 27* **Rooms** *21*

The popular Hungarian singer, György Korda, built this exclusive pension-style hotel in a smart residential district on the slopes of Mátyás Hill. It offers a high standard of service and exclusive company. There is no lift, and it is best reached by car due to its location and the steep road that leads to it. A genuine bargain. **www.villakorda.com**

Boat Hotel Fortuna

Szent István Park, Alsó rakpart, 1137 **Tel** *288 81 00* **Fax** *270 03 51* **Rooms** *60* **Map** *2 D1*

For something out of the ordinary, try this boat-hotel-cum-youth-hostel on the Danube, moored next to Margaret Bridge on the Pest side of the river. Some of the rooms are surprisingly large, though some are smaller than a cabin boy's quarters. There's a bar and restaurant, and a super lounge with classy leather sofas. **www.fortunahajo.hu**

Bobbio

Béla Király út 47, 1121 **Tel** *274 40 00* **Fax** *395 83 77* **Rooms** *22*

A bargain. One of the best kept secrets in Budapest. Find it by taking Bus 28 from Moszkva tér to the end of the line. Set in a small house, the rooms all have individual charms – from sloping ceilings to garden views from small balconies – and modern facilities such as wireless Internet access. The buffet breakfast is superb. **www.bobbio.hu**

Budapest

Szilágyi Erzsébet fasor 47, 1026 **Tel** *889 42 00* **Fax** *889 42 03* **Rooms** *289*

This establishment was built in the late 1960s and was the pride of the local hotel industry for many years. Its unique cylindrical shape makes it a landmark still. Its location in the Buda Hills *(see p161)*, and the magnificent view from the roof terrace remains unrivalled. There are two restaurants and a wine cellar. **www.danubiusgroup.com/budapest**

Classic

Zólyomi út 6, 1118 **Tel** *319 72 22* **Fax** *319 34 50* **Rooms** *32*   **Map** *3 A4*

A lovely, almost alpine villa in the Buda foothills, with basic but homely accommodation at a good price. Rooms are quite big, a little austere but very clean and well looked after. There's a restaurant and a sauna, as well as conference and meeting rooms. Classic is reached by Bus 139 from Deli station (Metro Line 3). **www.classichotel.hu**

Gerand Hotel Ventura

Fehérvári út 179, 1119 **Tel** *208 12 32* **Fax** *208 12 41* **Rooms** *149*

The façade is intended to be Neo-Classical but is in fact Neo-Socialist, but that shouldn't put anyone off this presentable and well-run hotel. Rooms (some are non-smoking) are a reasonable size and furnished in a modern style. There's a fitness centre, and a restaurant with a small terrace. Dogs are welcome. **www.gerandhotels.hu**

Gloria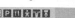

Bláthy Ottó utca 22, 1089 **Tel** *210 41 20* **Fax** *210 41 29* **Rooms** *28*

On the edge of Nepliget, the Gloria is a good hotel at a great price. Looking like a little cottage in the forest, it is not luxurious (the rooms are a bit stuffy), but there is enough here to keep most guests happy. Staff are very friendly and speak all major languages. Breakfast is included in the price. **www.hotelgloria.com**

Griff

Bartók Béla út 152, 1113 **Tel** *204 00 44* **Fax** *204 00 62* **Rooms** *108*

Hardly welcoming from the outside, nevertheless this three-star hotel offers more than adequate facilities, including colour television in small but bright rooms, and child-minding. There's an excellent fitness centre, including a sauna, jacuzzi, solarium and squash courts. The restaurant features live Hungarian music. **www.hunguesthotels.hu**

Hotel Panda

Pasaréti út 133, 1026 **Tel** *394 19 35* **Fax** *394 10 02* **Rooms** *29*

A bright and cheerful place to relax between sightseeing trips, and particularly well disposed towards disabled guests. Located in the Buda Hills (see p161), close to the forest of Pilis and Budapest Zoo. The staff can help visitors arrange everything from horse riding to dental services. **www.hotelpanda.hu**

Ibis Budapest Aero

Ferde utca 1–3, 1091 **Tel** *347 97 00* **Fax** *280 64 03* **Rooms** *139*

By virtue of its situation close to Ferihegy airport, this hotel is particularly convenient for those making only a short visit to Budapest. The rooms are cosy and tastefully decorated, and there are suites for families and rooms for non-smokers. All rooms have balconies, and some are adapted for the use of disabled guests. **www.ibis-aero.hu**

Mediterran

Budaörsi út 20/A, 1118 **Tel** *372 70 20* **Fax** *372 70 21* **Rooms** *40*   **Map** *3 A2*

This bright hotel is a good choice for people who don't mind being a bus ride away from the city centre. Rooms are well sized and have modern facilities including wireless Internet, and bathrooms with both a bath and a shower. Bus 112 from Ferenciek tér reaches Mediterran in about 10 minutes. Children welcome. **www.hotelmediterran.hu**

Molnár Panzió

Fodor utca 143, 1124 **Tel** *395 18 73* **Fax** *395 18 75* **Rooms** *23*

A mid-range pension in a residential district on the slopes of the Buda Hills *(see p161)*. Its green surroundings add to the homely atmosphere and offer guests complete peace. Family rooms are available. The amenities include a bar, fitness facilities and secure parking. There's also a restaurant with a bright, sunny terrace. **www.hotel-molnar.hu**

NH Budapest

Vigszínház utca 3, 1137 **Tel** *814 00 00* **Fax** *814 01 00* **Rooms** *160*

Smart and stylish hotel north of Nyugati station. Rooms are not large, but are well furnished, with many extras – including high-speed Internet access – and terrific bathrooms. A delicious breakfast is included in the price, and on-site dining is good. The bar is popular late in the evening. Fitness facilities include a sauna. **www.nh-hotels.com**

Normafa

Eötvösüt 52–54, 1121 **Tel** *395 65 05* **Fax** *395 65 04* **Rooms** *62*

Guests have the option of indulging in complete relaxation at the Normafa, or exploring the beautiful scenery on foot. All rooms have terraces, and there is a large swimming pool, a sauna, tennis courts, a restaurant, a café and a beer bar. Rooms are not the biggest in the world, but represent terrific value for money. **www.normafahotel.com**

Key to Price Guide *see p182* **Key to Symbols** *see back cover flap*

Platánus

Könyves Kálmán körút 44, 1087 **Tel** *333 65 05* **Fax** *210 43 86* **Rooms** *128*

A comfortable, inexpensive hotel situated on the edge of the People's Park and close to the Népliget metro station. From the outside it looks like a suburban block of flats, but inside it has clean, functional rooms, and offers good food. Other facilities available include a sauna, a solarium and an in-house doctor. **www.hunguesthotels.hu**

Veritas

Mogyoródi út 8, 1143 **Tel** *273 22 33* **Fax** *222 47 92* **Rooms** *54*

Yellow, orange and blue from the outside, the Veritas is no less garish inside. Rooms are well sized with large, comfortable beds and TV, though bathrooms are smallish – most have shower and toilet only. Breakfast is included in the room rate, and airport transfers are available at extra cost. **wwww.hotelveritas.hu**

Walzer Hotel

Németvölgyi út 110, 1124 **Tel** *319 12 12* **Fax** *329 29 64* **Rooms** *28*

A reproduction 19th-century mansion surrounded by greenery and original houses from that era. With spacious rooms, sparkling clean bathrooms, a restaurant and a touch of the boutique hotel in respect to service and design, it provides an alternative to the more typical, family-run establishment. **www.walzerhotel.hu**

Budai

Rácz Aladár út 45–47, 1121 **Tel** *249 02 08* **Fax** *249 21 86* **Rooms** *23*

Small but charming pension, well hidden from the city's bustle in the Buda Hills *(see p161)*. Some of the rooms have a great view, and some have balconies. (Not all do, so it is a good idea to ask when booking.) The best are loft rooms, with wooden beams and sloping ceilings. Tram 59 (from Moszkva tér) stops right outside. **www.hotelbudai.hu**

Danubius Grand Hotel Margitsziget

Margitsziget, 1138 **Tel** *889 47 00* **Fax** *889 49 39* **Rooms** *164*

This hotel on Margaret Island *(see pp172–3)* is linked by a tunnel to the Danubius Thermal Hotel, whose spa facilities guests at the Grand can use. Other attractions include shaded terrace cafés and restaurants, a swimming pool and tranquil walks. Bike hire is also available. **www.danubiusgroup.com/grandhotel**

Danubius Health Spa Resort Helia

Kárpát utca 62–64, 1133 **Tel** *889 58 00* **Fax** *889 58 01* **Rooms** *262*

One of the most modern spa hotels in Budapest. Light and airy, and located on the bank of the Danube with views of the boats on the river and Margaret Island *(see pp172–3)*. The Helia offers a full range of health and beauty facilities including massage, thermal waters and qualified medical advice. **www.danubiusgroup.com/helia**

Danubius Health Spa Resort Margitsziget

Margitsziget, 1138 **Tel** *889 47 00* **Fax** *889 49 88* **Rooms** *267*

The hotel hosts one of Europe's leading wellness centres, and sits on top of a natural spa that brings water to the surface at 70°C. It is then cooled to a range of temperatures and used for healing all sorts of ailments. The rooms offer comfort and luxury. Good restaurants. **www.danubiushotels.com/thermalhotel**.

Novotel Budapest Congress

Alkotásutca 63–67, 1123 **Tel** *372 54 00* **Fax** *466 56 36* **Rooms** *319*   **Map** *3 A2*

Situated in the immediate vicinity of the Congress and World Trade Centre *(see p160)*, the hotel offers modern rooms, swimming pool, sauna, bowling alley and cocktail bar. There is also a large car park. The reception rooms and banqueting halls can accommodate approximately 2,500 people. **www.novotel-bud-congress.hu**

Rubin Hotel & Business Center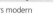

Dayka Gábor utca 3, 1118 **Tel** *505 36 00* **Fax** *505 36 01* **Rooms** *85*

There are various relaxation and sporting facilities at this modern hotel, including sauna, swimming pool, tennis courts and bowling alley. In a quiet location close to the M1 and M7 motorways, the accommodation includes some suites with kitchenettes and some larger maisonettes for families. **www.hotelrubin.com**

Sissi

Angyal utca 33, 1094 **Tel** *215 00 82* **Fax** *216 60 63* **Rooms** *44*

Sissi was the affectionate name by which Hungarians referred to Empress Elizabeth, wife of Emperor Franz Joseph. She certainly did not stay in this modern and rather odd-looking hotel, but she might have enjoyed the luxury of the rooms, some of which have small balconies. There is a nice garden and terrace, too. **www.hotelsissi.hu**

Ramada Plaza Budapest

Árpádfejedelem utca 94, 1036 **Tel** *436 41 00* **Fax** *436 41 56* **Rooms** *310*

This hotel offers everything guests need to relax or to improve their health. Facilities include a swimming pool, hot- and warm-water spas, a jacuzzi and sauna, massage and a gymnasium. There is a resident doctor, and some staff are dedicated to the needs of disabled guests. Some rooms have views of the Danube. **www.ramadaplazabudapest.com**

Adina Apartment Hotel Budapest

Hegedűs Gyula utca 52–54, 1133 **Tel** *236 88 88* **Tel** *236 88 99* **Rooms** *97*   **Map** *2 F1*

Total luxury. Modern, serviced apartments are set around an exclusive, leafy courtyard. There is an indoor swimming pool, jacuzzi, steam room, gym, parking and 24-hour security. The apartments and studios are huge, far bigger than any hotel room in the city. Prices are deservedly high. Long-term rentals are available. **www.adina.eu**

RESTAURANTS, CAFES AND BARS

Following a visit to Budapest, the Nobel Prize-winning Latin American writer Miguel Ángel Asturias said that "the exquisite taste of Hungarian cuisine is a language understood by all". The numerous restaurants, cafés and bars in Budapest give the visitor ample opportunity to sample the delights of this distinctive cuisine. The most typical examples of

Hungarian coffee

traditional Hungarian cooking can be seen on pages 192–3, while information on what to drink is given on pages 194–5. A detailed guide to the city's best restaurants, highlighting Hungarian specialities and covering a selection of price categories, is provided on pages 196–205. Cafés, wine bars, beer houses, pubs and clubs can be found on pages 206–9.

WHERE TO LOOK

There are a great many eating establishments in Budapest and the surrounding suburbs. Good traditional Hungarian dishes can be found within all price ranges in restaurants and inns. Budapest has also seen the arrival of cuisine from all over the world. Among the ethnic eating options now available are Italian, Greek, Chinese and Thai restaurants. American-style fast food chains are also appearing and are rapidly becoming popular.

The city's main tourist areas are well off for places to eat, but may not offer the best fare or prices. It is often worth looking off the main roads or away from popular areas to find establishments frequented by local Budapest residents. The restaurants, cafés and bars on Váci utca (Váci Street, *see p127*) are notorious for over-charging, especially at night.

Entrance to Ruszwurm Cukrászda (see p207), in the Castle District

TYPES OF RESTAURANTS, CAFES AND BARS

Budapest offers a variety of places to eat and a range of prices to suit most budgets. The differences between the types of establishments can be subtle, but they break down roughly into the following types. *Étterem* simply means restaurant – any type of cuisine may be served. A *csárda* comes in various forms. Most are folky restaurants typically offering interesting local specialities. A fisherman's *csárda*, known as a *halászcsárda*, will offer mainly fish dishes and soups. There are two types of inn, a *vendéglő*, which has an informal ambience, and a *kisvendéglő*, (literally a "small inn"), which is similar to a cosy pub. Cafés range from a *kávéház* (coffee house) to a *cukrászda* (patisserie), and types of bars include a *borozó*, a *söröző* and an *eszpresszó (see pp206–9)*.

WHAT TO ORDER

Ordering a Hungarian meal may not be as simple as it may first seem. There are many different varieties of Hungarian soups, some of which are a meal in themselves. *Bogrács*, which is often served in a kettle, and bean soups are the heartiest soups and would normally be followed by a light, hot pudding or pancakes. Hungarian fish soup is a particular speciality

Lantern outside the Gerbeaud Cukrászda

and owes its red colour to paprika. This should be followed by delicate homemade noodles served with crackling, cheese and cream. There are also many light soups, or small portions of the more substantial soups, which can be eaten as a starter, thus leaving room for the main course.

The archetypal Hungarian main dish is goulash soup (*gulyás leves*) and there are several versions of the basic thick meat stew. Another Hungarian speciality is *pörkölt* (a paprika stew very similar to goulash). This stew is made with lean meat such as veal, poultry or fish, with sour cream added at the end of cooking. Almost all meals are eaten with bread; the white wheat variety is particularly delicious.

Food served in bars or bought from street kiosks is a different matter. More akin to fast food, it is often eaten standing up or on the move. Spicy sausages, liberally seasoned with paprika and garlic are served grilled or boiled. Grilled chicken and various smoked meats are also widely available. Another alternative is the delicious *lángos* (pronounced "langosh"), which is sold at markets. This flat, savoury, yeast cake is served with cream or cheese.

For more detailed information see *What to Eat* in Budapest on pages 192–3.

VEGETARIAN FOOD

Vegetarian cuisine *per se* is not found in abundance in Budapest. There are very few vegetarian restaurants, of which one, Govinda, is recommended in this guide *(see p198)*. Ethnic restaurants may offer a wider vegetarian choice.

Nevertheless, meat-free dishes can be found on most Hungarian menus. *Főzelék*, a vegetable dish that normally accompanies steak, sausage or a hamburger, can be ordered on its own or with egg. *Lecsó* is another popular vegetable side dish that makes a substantial meal by itself. Other specialities include *túrós csusza*, a pasta dish served with cottage cheese, sour cream and bacon. There are also many sweet and savoury *palacsinta* (pancakes).

RESERVING A TABLE

In Hungary it is customary to join other guests at a table, especially during the busy lunch period. To secure a private table, it is advisable to book in advance. This applies equally to Budapest's exclusive restaurants and cheaper establishments.

MENUS AND PRICES

All Hungarian restaurants display a menu by the entrance, and, as a rule, this is translated into English or German. The name of the dish is followed by a brief description. The day's "specials" – a set meal consisting of a soup, a main course and a dessert –

A charming outdoor café on Margaret Island

are listed at the head of the menu. Set menus are often very good value and provide an ideal opportunity to sample several Hungarian specialities.

The prices should also be displayed. If they are not, it is wise to go elsewhere or at least see the prices, including any surcharges, before ordering the meal. The introduction of printed and itemized bills has made it more difficult for hidden "extras" to be added to the final bill.

In most Hungarian restaurants the waiters tend to round up the bill, particularly when serving foreign customers. This practice led to a minor scandal in 1997 when several embassies, including the American and British delegations, compiled a blacklist of dishonest restaurants, after receiving numerous complaints, and published it on the Internet. The government closed the offending establishments and the situation has

now improved. Visitors should still be cautious, however. By selecting a restaurant from those listed in this guide *(see pp196–205)*, this problem should be easily avoided.

TIPPING

In some restaurants a service charge is included in the final bill, in others it is customary to tip. If a service charge is added, this should be stated on either the menu or the bill; this could be up to 15 per cent. However, if there is any doubt, it is always courteous to leave a tip. In general, an acceptable tip is between 10–15 per cent of the cost of the meal.

CHILDREN

Children are welcomed in all restaurants without exception. If children's portions do not appear on the menu, the chef will prepare suitable dishes to order. These are usually charged at half price. The only exception is dessert, but this can often be shared. However, the desserts in Hungarian restaurants are so delicious that most children will happily eat a whole portion.

OUTDOOR EATING

Hungarian summers are long and dry, and eating *al fresco* has been popular throughout the country, and especially in the capital, since the early 1930s. Those who are looking for a quick lunch or to stop for coffee and watch the world go by during their city wanderings, should head for one of two redeveloped and fashionable locations on the Pest side of the Danube: Liszt Ferenc tér *(see p206)*, which runs off Andrássy út, not far from Oktogon metro station; or Ráday utca, which starts at Kálvin tér. Both areas are full of cosy restaurants, bars and cafés, and attract a youthful clientele. Every kind of restaurant can be found in these locations, too – from those serving traditional Hungarian food to Italian, Chinese and even Argentinian establishments.

The coffee shop at the Four Seasons Gresham Palace Hotel *(see p114)*

The Flavours of Budapest

The fusion of Magyar, Turkish, Balkan and even French influences has made Hungarian cuisine one of the most interesting and flavourful in central Europe. Hungary is a country where cooking know-how has always been a key aspect of the national culture. The improvised stews of nomadic Asiatic settlers survive as a delicacy to this day. Noted for its game, *foie gras* and rich meaty preparations, such as goulash and the legendary Debrecziner sausages, it is also a good place to enjoy freshwater fish and an array of delicious cakes and pastries.

Hungarian peppers

Sausages and cured meats on sale in the Central Market

MEAT

Beef is Hungary's favourite meat and, as a result, is produced in large quantities, usually to a very high standard. Cuts of beef are a regular feature on Hungarian tables and menus, especially in Budapest, and veal is becoming increasingly

popular too. Steak is widely dished up, often with a rich sauce as in *Budapest módra* (Budapest medallions). Beef is also used to make the many different types of goulash, although pork is another key ingredient in this dish, especially when it is prepared as *gulyásleves* (goulash soup). Pork is found in a wide range of other stews and sausages, and is eaten as bacon.

POULTRY & GAME

Geese are an important farmyard animal in Hungary, which is the world's second biggest producer of *foie gras* (after France). *Foie gras* is almost the national dish, usually cooked in its own fat and served warm. It is also found in pâtés and *confits*. Goose skin is widely enjoyed too, fried in its own fat and served with pickles.

Chestnut slice
Chocolate marzipan cake
Chocolate wafer cake
"Domino" cake
Apple slice
Poppy seed slice
Cheesecake

Selection of typical Hungarian cakes and pastries

LOCAL DISHES AND SPECIALITIES

White asparagus

Despite strong foreign influences, the classic dishes of Hungary dominate menus in the restaurants and cafés of Budapest. Many show their roots in one of the country's three historical regions. Goulash and its many variants, for example, is a dish of the Great Plain, the traditional method of cooking it in a kettle reflecting the nomadic past of the Plain's inhabitants. *Foie gras* may have been introduced into the country by the Austrian Habsburgs, but has become so popular that it is key to the cuisine of eastern Hungary, where most geese are now bred. The centre of the country, and the area around Budapest, has always had the sweetest tooth and nearly all the nation's favourite cakes and desserts originate from here.

Lángos *Crisp and golden, these deep-fried potato cakes make a popular, filling snack, served with soured cream.*

Market stall, laden with root vegetables and strings of dried peppers

Duck is another regular on Hungarian menus, frequently roasted with chestnuts or berries and served with red cabbage. Partridge may also be on offer, roasted with bacon and herbs. Rabbit, hare and venison are common as well, usually dished-up in spicy, goulash-style sauces.

FISH

Trout is probably the most widely eaten fish, although carp, perch, roach, zander and even eels can be found on most menus. A popular soup is *balászlé*, made with trout and carp and seasoned with a generous dash of paprika. Another favourite is *csuka tejfölös tormával* (pike in horseradish sauce). Many Budapest restaurants offer a variety of imported fish, but these are usually expensive.

VEGETABLES

Potatoes, parsnips and cabbage are usually the main vegetables. But from May to July, fine white asparagus appears on market stalls, with many restaurants

Roasting chestnuts, a common sight on Budapest's winter streets

serving *spárgaleves*, a rich creamy soup made from asparagus and veal stock.

Paprika peppers are a culinary staple. They are either cooked as part of a dish – *töltött paprika* (peppers stuffed with meat and rice) are served up everywhere – or dried and ground up to be used as a spice. There are hundreds of different types of ground paprika, which vary in flavour and strength, but they all fit into seven broad categories: "special" (sweet and very mild); "mild" (faintly spicy); "delicatesse" (slightly hot); "sweet" (mild but fairly aromatic); "semi-sweet" (medium hot); "rose" (hot); and "hot" (fiery).

BEST LOCAL SNACKS

Sausages Street vendors everywhere offer the lightly smoked Debercziner sausage, made from beef, pork, paprika and garlic. It is generally eaten with bread and mustard.

Chestnuts In winter, Budapest is crammed with stalls selling freshly roasted chestnuts.

Pancakes, fritters and doughnuts Snack bars all over the country serve tasty, fried, doughy snacks all day long. Try *alma pongyolában* (apple fritters).

Gingerbread Shops devoted to selling gingerbread are everywhere. At Christmas it is often highly decorated and given as a present.

Budapest Módra *Slices of fine sirloin steak are lightly cooked and served in a creamy, peppered sauce.*

Gulyásleves *A type of goulash, this pork, beef and vegetable soup is flavoured with garlic, caraway and paprika.*

Dobos torta *Fine slices of sponge cake are layered with chocolate cream and topped with chocolate icing.*

What to Drink in Budapest

American-style drinks cabinet

Hungary is famous for its excellent wines and, although it is not a big country, it has as many as 22 wine regions. These regions produce all the characteristic wine styles, from *pezsgő* (sparkling wine) and light whites that come from Mátra, near Lake Balaton, to dry reds from Villány or Eger, as well as Tokaji, a distinctive sweet dessert wine. Many wines from different vineyards are matured in a maze of underground cellars in Budafok. They are all widely available in Budapest's many restaurants, wine bars and wine shops. As well as being a prominent wine producer, Hungary also makes beer, *pálinka* (a drink distilled from different orchard fruits), several types of brandy and a bitter herb liqueur called Unicum.

Light Hungarian beers

PÁLINKA

Kecskemét is the largest region that produces the alcoholic drink *pálinka*, which is distilled from fruit grown in the orchards situated on the Great Hungarian Plain, some 100 km (60 miles) southeast of Budapest. *Pálinka* is a spirit native to Hungary and comes in a variety of flavours including *barack* (apricot) and *cseresznye* (cherry). The best of them, however, is *szilva* (plum) which comes from the Szatmár district and is much favoured by the Hungarians.

Pálinka is not the only spirit indigenous to Hungary. Other examples include Törköly, a spirit distilled from rape, which possesses a very delicate flavour, and Vilmos, a brandy made from Williams pears.

Barack pálinka

SPARKLING WINES

Sparkling wine, called *pezsgő* (the Hungarian word for "sparkling"), enjoys a good reputation in Hungary. The classic method of producing these wines was introduced to Hungary from France by József Törley, in 1881. It was Törley *(see p161)* who built

Pezsgő by Törley and Hungaria

the first production plant in Budafok, which continues to produce excellent sparkling wines over 100 years on. Today, Hungary has several other vineyards producing *pezsgő*, mainly concentrated around Budapest, in the Pannonia and Balatonboglár regions. As well as Törley, Hungaria is another good label to look out for.

HUNGARIAN BEERS

Hungarians are turning increasingly to beer as their chosen drink, as its thirst-quenching quality goes well with many traditional, paprika-flavoured Hungarian dishes, goulash among them. There are three remaining authentic Hungarian breweries. These are Arany Ászok, Kőbányai (which was established in the Kőbánya district of Budapest some 150 years ago) and the excellent Dreher. Unfortunately, many other formerly Hungarian breweries have now been taken over by large foreign corporations. However, many of these brands are also well known and all are widely available in Budapest.

HUNGARIAN WINES

The choice of good wine available in Hungary has increased dramatically over the past few years. This is thanks to the ever-improving wines being matured in private cellars. The styles currently

One of Budafok's cellars, where wines are aged in barrels

Egri Bikavér, "Bulls' Blood", a full-bodied red wine

A dry white wine from the Badacsony vineyards

SPRITZERS

On hot days, Hungarians enjoy drinking refreshing spritzers. The various types are differentiated by the proportion of white wine to soda water:

Quantity of wine	Quantity of water
Small spritzer *(Kisfröccs)*	
10 cl	10 cl
Large spritzer *(Nagyfröccs)*	
20 cl	10 cl
Long step *(Hosszúlépés)*	
10 cl	20 cl
Janitor *(Házmester)*	
30 cl	20 cl

favoured by the producers include dry white Chardonnay and Reisling, medium-dry Zödszilváni, Hárslevelű and Szürkebarát, medium-sweet Tramini and the aromatic Muskotály, which is produced in Badacsony, Balatonboglár, Csopak and Somló.

Among red wines, the dry Kékfrankos, Burgundi, Oportó, Cabernet and Pinot Noir are popular, as is the medium-dry Merlot, which is produced in Siklós, Sopron, Szekszárd, Tihány and Villány.

Another vine-growing district is Eger, which is famous for its aromatic, robust red Egri Leányka and the dry red Egri Bikavér, or "Bulls' Blood", which is produced from a combination of three grape varieties. Other Hungarian wines take their names from their place of origin or the variety of grape from which they are produced.

TOKAJI

The dessert wine Tokaji has a very different style. Its bouquet and flavour come from a mould that grows only in the fork of the Bodrog and Tisza rivers and the volcanic soil in which the vines grow.

Tokaji ranges from sweet to dry and is full-bodied and rich. Particularly worth sampling is Aszú, which is made with the addition of over-ripe grapes harvested after the first frost. The proportion of these grapes added to the must (grape juice) determines the wine's body and sweetness. The more of these grapes used, the sweeter and richer the Aszú.

Although cheap varieties of Tokaji do exist, they do not share the quality of the genuine article.

UNICUM

For over 150 years, a blend of 40 Hungarian herbs has been used to create Unicum. The herbs, which are gathered in three separate areas, are combined to produce this bitter liqueur. Unicum can be drunk either as an apéritif before a meal or afterwards as a digestif with coffee.

The recipe has been held by the Zwack family, and remained a secret, since the reign of King Franz I *(see p19)*. Originally, Unicum was prescribed as a remedy for the king by the court physician, who was himself a member of the Zwack family.

Unicum herb liqueur

Sweet Tokaji Szamorodni

Dry Tokaji Szamorodni

Tokaji Aszú, a renowned golden dessert wine

Pear-flavoured Vilmos liqueur

Sisi, an apricot liqueur

Choosing a Restaurant

The restaurants in this section have been selected for their good value and exceptional food. Within each area, entries are listed alphabetically within each price category, from the least to the most expensive. For details of Budapest's best cafés and bars, beer halls, pubs and clubs, refer to pp206–09.

CASTLE DISTRICT

Café Miró
Úri utca 30, 1014 **Tel** *375 54 58*   🔲🔲V   (HUF)
Map *1 B4*

This popular, hip hangout in the Castle District is a great place to grab a bite while seeing the sights. It's a Mediterranean-style venue with a great summer terrace, a sparse interior and a good range of salads and snacks. It's always buzzing with locals and tourists alike and the service is swift and charming.

Pierrot Café Restaurant
Fortuna utca 14, 1014 **Tel** *375 69 71*   🔲🎵V   (HUF)(HUF)(HUF)
Map *1 B4*

This popular place opened as a private café during socialist times when it was one of a kind. Though it now faces stiff competition, it still attracts a loyal crowd. The café has been redesigned but retains the original, elegant interior and a cosy café atmosphere. Live piano music in the evening, and all day at weekends.

21 a Magyar Vendéglő
Fortuna utca 21, 1014 **Tel** *202 21 13*   (HUF)(HUF)(HUF)
Map *1 B4*

A stylish restaurant that strives to recreate traditional Hungarian cuisine in a contemporary setting. Brick walls, wooden floors and subdued lighting create the perfect atmosphere to enjoy the excellent goose liver and other classic dishes. The wine list is particularly inspired.

Pest Buda Vendéglő
Fortuna utca. 3, 1014 **Tel** *212 58 80*   🔲🎵   (HUF)(HUF)(HUF)(HUF)
Map *1 B4*

Small, elegant restaurant with arcaded walls in a listed building. Part of an ancient system of underground caves, the restaurant provides space for a popular and extensive Hungarian and international wine cellar. The food menu itself is not all that extensive, but is interesting nevertheless, and everything is excellently prepared.

Rivalda Café & Restaurant
Színház utca. 5–9, 1014 **Tel** *489 02 36*   🔲🔲🎵V   (HUF)(HUF)(HUF)(HUF)
Map *1 C5*

Next to the Castle Theatre, with tasteful theatre-inspired decor. Contemporary international cuisine with a frequently changing menu reflects the seasons, and most dishes are based on local, fresh ingredients. Many dishes are inventive, and all are superbly presented. There's pleasant jazz piano music in the evenings.

Alabárdos Étterem
Országház utca 2, 1014 **Tel** *356 08 51*   🔲🎵V   (HUF)(HUF)(HUF)(HUF)(HUF)
Map *1 B4*

A truly exclusive place in an outstanding Gothic building. Hungarian specialities of pre-paprika times are made to please today's taste buds. Everything from the service to the atmosphere reeks of class, though the prices are as expensive as anywhere in the city. Guitar music adds to the candle-lit medieval atmosphere.

GELLÉRT & TABÁN

Siesta
Villányi út 4, 1114 **Tel** *466 24 05*   🔲V   (HUF)
Map *4 D5*

Siesta is a small, family-friendly air-conditioned restaurant in the heart of Buda. The menu has mainly Mediterranean dishes, although it does include Hungarian specialities and a variety of international cuisine. Goose is featured on the menu on Mondays.

Márványmenyasszony Étterem
Márvány utca 6, 1012 **Tel** *487 30 90*   🔲🔲🎵   (HUF)(HUF)
Map *3 A1*

An old-style Hungarian restaurant with a fine gypsy band every night. Although hidden away, tourists tend to make the effort to find it, as tales of fine food, great prices and a relaxed atmosphere are legendary. Its many different rooms make it a great choice for groups, families or those wanting peace and quiet.

Key to Symbols *see back cover flap*

Marcello

Bartók Béla út 40, 1111 **Tel** *466 6231*

Map *4 E4*

A super little treat where all sorts of tourists, locals, expatriates and businessmen meet and become equals. Housed in a cellar accessed by a low staircase, Marcello is famed for its pasta and its great salad bar – there is a wide range of choice for vegetarians. Make a reservation if you want to get a table in the evening.

Negy Musketas Etterem es Sorozzo

Tétényi út 18, 1115 **Tel** *203 14 01*

Relax at this faintly kitsch restaurant with its pleasantly leafy exterior and comfy wooden interior. The menu is quite extensive, comprising reasonably priced, heart-warming Hungarian fare. There are even a few tables outside, in season.

Szeged Étterem

Bartók Béla út 1, 114 **Tel** *209 16 68*

Map *4 E3*

Next to the Gellért Hotel *(see pp90–91)*, this is a traditional Hungarian restaurant offering a good selection of specialities including several river fish dishes. The *Szegedi halászlé* (Szeged fish soup) is particularly tasty. A lively gypsy band belts out local popular favourites every evening.

Citadella Étterem

Citadella sétány, 1118 **Tel** *386 48 02*

Map *4 D3*

The casements of the Citadel up above southern Buda have been turned into a restaurant of several rooms, all of which can suffer from disappearing wait staff. Once that problem is dealt with, the menu is a joy of traditional Hungarian food, though prices are steep. A gypsy band plays every night.

Hemingway

Kosztolányi Dezső tér 2, (on Feneketlen Lake), 1113 **Tel** *381 05 22 ext 103*

Map *3 C5*

Papa Hemingway sure knew how to live large. He would have appreciated the spread-out, island-resort feel of this restaurant, set on a small lake. The terrace is one of Budapest's more impressive al fresco dining venues. The menu's flexible, and offers plenty of choice. Weekend lunchtime "playhouse" for children.

Búsuló Juhász Étterem

Kelenhegyi út 58, 1118 **Tel** *209 16 49*

Map *3 C3*

Traditional Hungarian restaurant on the western slopes of Gellért Hill, offering spectacular views and pleasant gypsy music. A wide choice of Hungarian specialities have been made lighter in the spirit of international gastronomy, but the often astronomically priced bill can leave a nasty aftertaste.

NORTH OF THE CASTLE

Gusto

Frankel Leó út 12, 1027 **Tel** *316 3970*

Map *1 C2*

You'll need to get here early to get a seat in this tiny café that's always packed out. There are only a few places on the minuscule terrace but it's a lovely place to while away the evening. The genial Gusto is ever-present behind the bar, offering drinks and light snacks. The tiramisu is to die for.

À la carte Kisétterem

Iskola utca 29, 1011 **Tel** *202 05 80*

Map *1 C3*

A small and really rather charming restaurant conveniently situated near Batthyány tér (on the red metro line). There is an unusually wide choice of fish dishes on the respectably long menu, and everything is given a homely, home-cooked touch by two caring chefs. Reservation is recommended for both lunch and dinner.

Mandragóra

Kacsa utca 22, 1027 **Tel** *202 21 65*

Map *1 C2*

Small and friendly restaurant close to the Buda banks of the Danube, with a particularly atmospheric terrace under the shade of large trees. The portions are small for the price but the salads are well conceived. It's more of a place for a light bite than a big gastronomic feast but evenings here are always fun.

Csalogány Étterem és Kávézó

Csalogány utca 26, 1015 **Tel** *201 78 92*

Map *1 A3*

Popular and trendy restaurant/café with a modern, bright and breezy Mediterranean interior. Excellent poultry, fish and meat dishes are all grilled on lava stones for a real burst of flavour. For such a meat-orientated place, there's also a surprisingly good selection of vegetarian dishes and salads. A small selection of good wines.

Le Jardin de Paris

Fő utca 20, 1011 **Tel** *201 0047*

Map *1 C5*

This French restaurant is impressive in every aspect. The building is a national treasure, and protected as such, and the main dining room is a sparsely decorated, tasteful treat. The service is efficient and friendly without being pretentious, and live jazz softens the mood most evenings. The food is international-French, and there's a garden.

Arany Kaviár 🧍🎵Ⅴ ☺☺☺☺☺
Ostrom utca 19, 1015 **Tel** *201 67 37* **Map** *1 A3*

Superb Russian seafood restaurant where, provided you do not over-indulge in caviar, you need not spend a fortune. Most dishes are based around fish and seafood, but there are Russian specialities on the menu, too, such as *pelmenyi* (Russian ravioli). Also, a surprisingly good vegetarian selection.

Fekete Hollo 🧍 ☺☺☺☺☺
Országház utca 10, 1014 **Tel** *356 2367* **Map** *1 B4*

In a terrific location up on Castle Hill, this little gem is a traditional Hungarian restaurant where the kitsch medieval decor does little to detract from the excellent food. All Hungarian favourites are on the menu, though there is little for vegetarians. Service can be slow, but that's because the place is always full of happy diners.

Kacsa 🧍♿🎵Ⅴ ☺☺☺☺☺☺
Fő utca 75, 1027 **Tel** *201 99 92* **Map** *1 C2*

Kasca serves some of the finest food in the country. The service is as ostentatious as the food is splendid, with dishes presented under silver serving domes, whisked away with great ceremony. Though duck dominates the menu, there is far more on offer, including inventive vegetarian options. Outstanding, but dreadfully expensive.

AROUND PARLIAMENT

Govinda Ⅴ ☺
Vigyázó Ferenc utca 4, 1051 **Tel** *473 13 10* **Map** *2 D4*

Popular at lunchtimes. this fast food-style restaurant serves vegetarian meals and salads. Here, no meat doesn't mean no flavour. In fact, some of the dishes are hotter than many people will ever have tasted – choose carefully. There's a shop attached, selling Eastern-style gifts and Krishna literature, and a meditation room.

Stand Bistro Ⅴ ☺
Sas utca 3, 1051 **Tel** *411 09 09* **Map** *2 E4*

At Stand diners can enjoy expertly prepared dishes at reasonable prices in sophisticated surroundings. Talented chef Viktor Segal was in the kitchen at the masterly Baraka *(see p203)* and brings his expertise to every dish. The emphasis is on fresh, seasonal produce.

Via Luna 🧍♿ ☺
Nagysándor József utca 1, 1054 **Tel** *312 80 58* **Map** *2 E4*

A truly Italian place, owned and operated by Italians, with an extensive menu of trattoria favourites. Excellent pasta is made on the premises, which is a rarity in Budapest, and so word has got out and the restaurant is always crowded. It is best to reserve a table. Both Hungarian and Italian wines are available.

Belvárosi Lugas Étterem ♿Ⅴ ☺☺
Bajcsy-Zsilinszky út 15/A, 1065 **Tel** *302 53 93* **Map** *2 E4*

Well-made, hearty dishes are served in a simple, appealing atmosphere. It's a favourite with locals, informal and relaxed. The food is great value, especially the daily specials that are chalked up on a blackboard. Great soups. In the summer a terrace is set up on the pavement, although constant traffic noise may disturb any conversation.

Cotton Club 🧍🎵Ⅴ ☺☺
Jókai utca 26, 1066 **Tel** *354 08 86* **Map** *2 F3*

Part of a three-part project on the same premises – with Cotton Club bar *(see p209)* and Cotton House hotel *(see p185)* – the restaurant is classy and clean, and serves unusual dishes in a unique atmosphere. It's a great place for a long evening: eat, then head downstairs for the live music.

Dzsungel 🧍♿Ⅴ ☺☺
Jókai utca 30, 1065 **Tel** *302 40 03* **Map** *2 F3*

Children love Dzsungel (it means jungle), decorated as it is with parrots and monkeys and elephants, all making a vocal contribution at regular intervals. Most of the really rather original food is a little too fancy for some children, but there are more simple dishes on offer if you ask. A 10% service charge is imposed.

Regös Vendéglő 🎵Ⅴ ☺☺
Szófia u. 33, 1068. **Tel** *3271 19 21* **Map** *7 B1*

A small, authentic restaurant reminiscent of 1970s Hungary, offering traditional, delicious Hungarian food at extremely reasonable prices and in a warm and friendly atmosphere. There is a daily-changing menu and a popular lunchtime buffet.

Abszint ♿Ⅴ ☺☺☺
Andrássy út 34, 1061 **Tel** *332 49 93* **Map** *2 F4*

Abszint does serve a green absinthe, but without the wormwood. Still, it is the food that people flock here for: a French-inspired bistro menu that changes regularly, always features a good selection of game dishes, and never costs a great deal of money. A popular breakfast and lunchtime spot.

Cactus Juice Pub and Restaurant

Jokái utca tér 5, 1061 **Tel** *302 2116*　　　　　　　　　　**Map** *7 A1*

The Cactus Juice has a fun, Western-themed decor and a lively atmosphere. After dinner, you are encouraged to move on to the bar, where there are over 50 kinds of whiskies on offer and an exclusive cocktail list. There is a DJ and dancing and large groups are catered for.

Café Kör

Sas utca 17, 1051 **Tel** *311 00 53*　　　　　　　　　　**Map** *2 E4*

Popular bistro-style place, serving good salad plates and Hungarian/European-inspired dishes. None will win prizes, but all offer great value. Vegetarian food is made to order. A good selection of Hungarian wines offered by the glass betray the fact that this was once a wine bar. Reserving is recommended.

Dió Étterem

Sas utca 4, 1051 **Tel** *328 03 60*　　　　　　　　　　**Map** *2 E4*

Dió is the Hungarian word for "walnut" and here at this classy restaurant the warm wooden surroundings and stylish furnishings provide the ideal venue to enjoy modern versions of classic Hungarian dishes. This is a great venue for a romantic date or a lunch. The bar is gigantic so guests can round the meal off with a *pálinka (see p194)*.

Iguana

Zoltán utca 16, 1054 **Tel** *331 43 52*　　　　　　　　　　**Map** *2 D4*

Iguana is a perennial expatriate favourite. The food is standard Tex Mex fare, such as *chorizo*, *jalepeno* soup, *quesadillas* and *burritos*. On the menu a helpful green "Y" points the way to the many vegetarian choices, while a red chilli marks out the hot dishes. It is wise to reserve a table in the evening.

Magdalena Merlo Étterem

1072, Kiraly u.59/b **Tel** *322 3278*　　　　　　　　　　**Map** *7 A1*

Cuisine at this family-friendly restaurant is based on Italian recipes, and Hungarian traditional dishes. The atmosphere is ideal for getting together with friends, accompanied by excellent food and refreshing beer. The weekly specials always take the seasons into consideration and there are often a few surprises.

Marquis de Salade

Hajós utca 43, 1065 **Tel** *302 40 86*　　　　　　　　　　**Map** *2 F4*

This wonderfully named restaurant boasts an extensive menu featuring recipes from around the world, including interesting lamb dishes from Azerbaijan and Georgia. Basic Hungarian fare, such as *goulash*, is also on offer. Vegetarians have plenty to choose from, too. The reasonable prices are rare in this part of town.

Művész Vendéglő

Vígszínház utca 5, 1136 **Tel** *784 44 83*　　　　　　　　　　**Map** *2 E2*

Located behind the Vígszínház (Variety Theatre), this is an intimate, homely restaurant. The walls display photos of theatre personalities and, with its antique furniture, it looks like a grandmother's dining room. The cooking is also home-style and simple, but effortlessly tasty. A late breakfast is served.

Paris Budapest

Roosevelt tér 2, 1051 **Tel** *266 12 34*　　　　　　　　　　**Map** *2 D5 (9 C3)*

This establishment at the Sofitel Atrium Budapest has just about everything that is required in a fine restaurant: great food (French, Asian, Mediterranean and Hungarian), superb service and lovely views over the Danube. Diners are mostly regulars – locals and businessmen – who know their food. Exemplary wine list.

Sir Lancelot lovagi Étterem

Podmaniczky utca 14, 1065 **Tel** *302 44 56*　　　　　　　　　　**Map** *2 F3*

Excellent Renaissance-inspired dishes, brought to the table by waiters in period costume. Only knives and spoons are provided with the food, which is served in such substantial portions that diners rarely manage to finish. Renaissance music is played in the evenings. Reserving is advisable, especially at weekends.

Belcanto

Dalszínház utca 8, 1061 **Tel** *269 27 86*　　　　　　　　　　**Map** *2 F4*

A legendary Hungarian restaurant, as famous for its good-time atmosphere as for its excellent food. In the evenings, diners enjoy favourite international and Hungarian dishes while waiters sing well-known operatic arias. Customers and visiting professional singers join in, and an orchestra plays dance music.

Buena Vista Étterem

Liszt Ferenc tér 4–5, 1061. **Tel** *344 63 03*　　　　　　　　　　**Map** *7 A1*

This restaurant is an oasis of peace from the busy whirl of the street. The menu offers both Hungarian and international dishes, carefully prepared and beautifully served. There is an extensive wine list, making it easy to match your food to a wine.

Trattoria Pomo D'oro

Arany János utca. 9, 1051 **Tel** *302 64 73*　　　　　　　　　　**Map** *2 D4*

Far too big to be a genuine Italian restaurant, this place is recommended nonetheless for its superb atmosphere, created by different dining levels and excellent staff, who ensure that everyone has a good time. There's little besides the usual tourist fare on the menu, but the fresh mussel dishes are exceptional.

Articsoka   V   ⓤⓤⓤⓤⓤ

Zichy Jenő utca 17, 1062 **Tel** *302 77 57*

Map *2 F4*

This place has been around for ages but following refurbishment is now decorated black and gold, with eye-catching, contemporary chandeliers. This establishment can lay claim to being one of Budapest's best kept dining secrets, with its selection of well presented and usually very good continental fare.

Fausto's   ⓧⓖV   ⓤⓤⓤⓤⓤ

Székely Mihály Street 2, 1061. **Tel** *877 62 10*

Map *2 F5*

Opened in 1994, Fausto's offers sophisticated Mediterranean and international specialities. Choose from dishes such as wild salmon carpaccio with a caper sauce or homemade spaghetti with duck ragout, or from a selection of beautifully prepared meat dishes. There is also an excellent Italian wine list.

Gresham Kávéház   ⓧⓖV   ⓤⓤⓤⓤⓤ

Roosevelt Tér 5-6, 1051 **Tel** *268 51 10*

Map *2 D5*

The more informal of the two restaurants at the Gresham Palace Four Seasons hotel *(see p114)* is the perfect place for a light lunch or early evening dinner. The stand-out choice on the menu is the exquisite "Three Foie Gras", the dessert menu is a real treat, and there is a wicked selection of freshly made cakes.

CENTRAL PEST

Alföldi Étterem   ⓖ   ⓤ

Kecskeméti utca 4, 1053 **Tel** *267 02 24*

Map *4 F2*

Popular, cheap and simple restaurant serving tasty Hungarian food in enormous portions. *Pogácsa* (savoury, heavy scones) are always fresh and on the table. It's tremendously crowded at lunchtime. The menu has been extended to include a choice of salads, though it must be said that this is not a great place for vegetarians.

BohémTanya   ⓧⓖ♫   ⓤ

Paulay Ede utca 6, 1061 **Tel** *267 35 04*

Map *2 F5*

Reasonably priced, hearty Hungarian food in plain surroundings. (Bohém Tanya means Bohemian Farm.) Customers are allocated places in wooden cubicles big enough for eight, but when the place is busy they are often required to share the cubicle with other diners.

Bangkok House   ⓧⓖV   ⓤⓤ

Só utca 3, 1056 **Tel** *266 05 84*

Map *4 F2*

The food served here may not be convincingly Thai, but it is certainly a good imitation, and about as authentic as you will find in this part of the world. The decor is great – all statuettes and funky South East Asian artwork – and the staff are extremely helpful. Prices aren't too bad, though portions can be a little small.

Carmel Étterem   ⓧⓖV   ⓤⓤ

Kazinczy utca 31, 1074 **Tel** *322 18 34*

Map *10 F3*

Legendary, non-kosher, Hungarian-Jewish cellar restaurant, always crowded with locals and tourists enjoying its famed *sólet (cholent)* with smoked goose. The food may not be entirely kosher but there are some super kosher wines available. Reservations recommended, especially at the weekend.

Central Kávéház és Étterem   ⓖ   ⓤⓤ

Károlyi Mihály utca 9, 1053 **Tel** *266 21 10*

Map *4 F1*

The Central holds a special place in locals' hearts. It was one of the great literary cafés at the start of the 20th century, when Budapest was a city of 500 cafés. Open for a coffee and divine pastry at breakfast until late at night for a post-theatre dinner, the ambience never disappoints with its old-world charm and style.

Dupla   ⓖ♫V   ⓤⓤ

Kertész utca 48, 1073 **Tel** *321 91 19*

Map *7 A2*

This split-level restaurant has something of a pleasantly cluttered Bohemian feel, where the ensemble becomes more than the individual pieces. Enormous portions of less than original but tasty Hungarian food are on offer at terrific prices, and there's good live music most nights of the week, though not at weekends.

Fészek Klub   ▤ⓧⓖV   ⓤⓤ

Kertész utca 36, 1073 **Tel** *322 60 43*

Map *7 A2*

People come here for two things: the sublime courtyard in summer, and the reasonable prices. The food is nothing special, but at these prices nobody complains. The staff are polite, professional and accommodating, and the menu even says that if you don't find your favourite dish, the house will make it for you.

Hanna Ortodoxkóser Étterem   ⓧⓖV   ⓤⓤ

Dob utca 35, 1074 **Tel** *342 10 72*

Map *7 A2*

A simple, Orthodox, kosher eating place in the courtyard of the Orthodox Synagogue on Kazinczy utca. Traditional Jewish dishes and kosher wines are served. Note that it is open from 8am–3:30pm, except on Friday and the Sabbath, when it opens in the evenings too. For Sabbath meals, customers pay the day before or after.

Key to Price Guide *see p196* **Key to Symbols** *see back cover flap*

Kaltenberg Étterem

Kinizsi utca 30–36, 1092 **Tel** *215 97 92*

Map *7 A5*

Attractively furnished beer cellar close to the Museum of Applied Arts. Huge portions of simple Hungarian and Bavarian specialities (plenty of sausage and cabbage) are served by friendly staff and eaten by a friendly patronage. Beer is brewed in the restaurant's own, on-site brewery and several good wines are available.

Repetasarok Étterem

Curia utca 2, 1054 **Tel** *266 11 65*

Map *4 F1*

The word "repeta" means second helping in Hungarian. This interesting restaurant/concert venue serves great food and drinks and hosts a wide variety of events. Particularly recommended are the English language comedy nights and parties; check the website calendar for more details.

Soul Café and Restaurant

Ráday utca 11–13, 1092 **Tel** *217 69 86*

Map *7 A5*

Ráday utca has been semi-pedestrianized and is now a food lover's paradise. It is lined with restaurants, cafés and bars for its entire length. Leading the way is the Soul Café with its young and friendly atmosphere. There's a good mix of standard Magyar fare and international favourites in a relaxing setting.

Vista Café and Restaurant

Paulay Ede utca 7, 1063 **Tel** *268 08 88*

Map *2 F5*

Connected to the pioneering travel agency of the same name, situated just down the road, Vista Café brightens up this gloomy crumbling street with its wide range of international dishes and great cakes. There are Internet facilities, travel advice and often live jazz evenings. The decor is simple and understated.

Club Verne

Váci utca 60, 1056 **Tel** *202 46 88*

Map *4 F2*

Rapidly becoming something of a Budapest legend, Club Verne is both a restaurant and a night-time venue for the city's hip crowd. Its dead-central location also makes it popular with visitors. The menu is based around American seafood favourites, though there is plenty for vegetarians too. The submarine decor may be too much for some.

Columbus Pub

Vigadó tér, Port No. 4, 1051 **Tel** *266 75 14*

Map *4 D1*

All aboard for superb food and good times on probably the most kitsch theme boat in Europe. Nobody complains, however, as the views are superb and the jazz mellow. Once on board, most people don't want to get off, and stay here long into the night. Reservations are essential for the restaurant.

Costes

Ráday utca 4, 1092 **Tel** *219 06 96*

Map *7 A4*

Now considered to be one of the best restaurants in Budapest, Costes continues to shine with skilfully executed cuisine and an international flair. The Portuguese chef worked at the world famous El Bulli restaurant in Catalonia, Spain, and it shows. A meal here will certainly be an event. Excellent wine list.

Cyrano

Kristóf tér 7, 1052 **Tel** *266 47 47*

Map *10 D4*

The central location of this chic eaterie keeps prices higher than they should be, but the food is never less than outstanding, and the ambience is hard to beat in this city. The fusion menu is inventive to the point of being extraordinary, but that's how most of the patrons like things to be. It is advisable to reserve a table for the evening.

Dionysos Taverna

Belgrád rakpart 16, 1056 **Tel** *318 12 22*

Map *4 F3*

Designed not entirely without success to recreate the atmosphere of a traditional Greek village, Dionysos is a good place for groups. The *meze* (of which there are at least 30), are great, and the main dishes authentic. The management deserves full marks for serving Italian not Greek olive oil, too. Reservations essential in the evenings.

Fatál

Váci utca 67, 1056 **Tel** *266 26 07*

Map *4 F2*

Often crowded, cellar restaurant serving enormous portions of standard Hungarian fare as made at home, with a huge quantity of beef and pork. It's a no-frills, all-comers-welcome type of place, although the service can be a little slow. There is little English spoken.

Jazz Garden

Veres Pálné utca 44/A, 1053 **Tel** *266 73 64*

Map *4 F2*

A cellar, but it looks and feels like a garden, so the name is not entirely misleading. It's very popular among jazz fans, not only for the daily changing music, but also for its fine international cuisine featuring vegetarian options. Booking is recommended for the evening. Jazz usually kicks off around 9:30pm.

Károlyi Étterem és Kávéház

Károlyi Mihály utca 16, 1053 **Tel** *328 02 40*

Map *4 F2*

An elegant restaurant in the lovely courtyard of the Károlyi Palace. Worth trying is the *borjúpaprikás lángosban* (veal paprika stew in potato pancake). The attractive gardens are uncommon in the city centre and therefore often booked for weddings. At weekends, it is worth phoning to check it is open.

Két Szerecsen   V   ⓦⓦⓦ

Nagymező utca 14, 1065 **Tel** *343 19 84*

Map 2 F4

A bright, friendly place with a pleasant atmosphere on Pest's "Broadway". It offers a good range of tasty salads, and Hungarian and French main courses. Most wines are available by the glass, keeping prices down. Booking is recommended, especially in the evening.

Kispipa Étterem   🎵   ⓦⓦⓦ

Akácfa utca 38, 1073 **Tel** *342 25 87*

Map 7 A2

An establishment that hasn't changed in essence in 25 years that serves a wide choice of international and Hungarian dishes. Rezső Seres, composer of "Gloomy Sunday", no longer sits at the piano, but many of his songs are still played. Both the food and the service are as good now as they were in his day.

Kulacs   🏃♿🎵   ⓦⓦⓦ

Osvát utca 11, 1073 **Tel** *322 3611*

Map 7 B2

This restaurant serves a very good selection of tasty Hungarian specialities, including some delicious and devilishly hot *goulash* soup. A gypsy band serenades the diners, many of whom don't appear to like being serenaded. Though entertaining for a while, the attention can become wearing. To encourage the band to ignore your table, tip them well.

Maharaja   🏃 V   ⓦⓦⓦ

Csengery utca 24, 1074 **Tel** *351 12 89*

Map 7 A1

Run by a Punjabi family, Maharaja serves the best North Indian food in Budapest. Vegetarians in particular will be pleased by the wide vegetable selection. Decor is simple and stylish and the staff friendly and cheerful. There is a terrace as well as a private dining room.

Matyas Pince   🏃🎵♿   ⓦⓦⓦ

Március 15. tér 7, 1056 **Tel** *318 1693*

Map 10 D5

This place is unquestionably touristy, and tour groups make getting a table a challenge, but it's great. The food is super – huge portions of Hungarian classics are served up by friendly waiters – and there's usually a gypsy band on hand to create a rollicking atmosphere.

Pata Negra   ♿🏃🛡V   ⓦⓦⓦ

Kálvin tér 8, 1091 **Tel** *215 56 16*

Map 7 A4

Pata Negra was one of the first Spanish-themed restaurants to open in Budapest and still remains one of the most authentic. The Serrano ham and Manchego cheese are traditionally prepared, and it's all served in a typically Iberian setting. The decor is simple and classic and the extensive Spanish wine list ensures a good evening for all.

Aranybárány   🎵   ⓦⓦⓦⓦ

Harmincad utca 4, 1051 **Tel** *317 27 03*

Map 2 E5

A legendary, traditional Transylvanian restaurant, where fine stews are served up in enormous portions. There is plenty of lamb on the menu (the title of the restaurant translates as "The Golden Lamb"), though lamb is certainly not a Hungarian speciality. Famous the world over, prices are high.

Bistro Jardin   🏃♿V   ⓦⓦⓦⓦ

Erzsébet tér 7–8, 1051 **Tel** *429 39 90*

Map 2 F2

The flagship restaurant of the Kempinski Corvinus hotel. The hotel management has every right to be proud. From the jazz brunch on Sundays, which has become an expatriate institution, to the many theme weeks during which the menu is given over to a country or region, the food is never less than sensational.

Comme Chez Soi   🏃♿   ⓦⓦⓦⓦ

Aranykéz utca 2, 1052 **Tel** *318 39 43*

Map 4 E1

Not to be confused with the three-Michelin-starred Brussels establishment of the same name, nevertheless this Budapest restaurant does offer Belgian food, including the usual number of dishes cooked in beer, and mussels galore. Though some of the prices are high, there are less expensive choices on the menu.

Il Terzo Cerchio   🏃♿V   ⓦⓦⓦⓦ

Dohány utca 40, 1072 **Tel** *354 07 88*

Map 7 A3

The Third Circle of the title is the third circle of Dante's Hell, but here it alludes not to the acid rain with which gluttons were punished in the original, but to the gluttonous portions of fantastic Italian food that are served in this restaurant. Prices are good if you avoid the Italian wines.

Osteria   ♿🎵V   ⓦⓦⓦⓦ

Dohány utca 5, 1072 **Tel** *269 68 06*

Map 10 F4

Probably the best Italian restaurant in Budapest, indeed the country. It is popular with power-diners who like to impress clients, while well-to-do couples also enjoy its understated atmosphere. Try the duck *carpaccio*, followed by the black ravioli with cottage cheese. There isn't a pizza in sight.

Empire   V   ⓦⓦⓦⓦ

Kossuth Lajos utca 19–21, 1053 **Tel** *889 6022*

Map 10 E4

The Astoria hotel is the home of the Empire, which has fortunately retained its imperial charms, being all marble columns and fine-liveried, classically designed chairs. Male staff in immaculate attire serve traditional dishes to business people and travellers. Breakfast is served until 10am.

Key to Price Guide *see p196* **Key to Symbols** *see back cover flap*

RESTAURANTS, CAFES AND BARS

Kárpátia Étterem és Söröz

Ferenciek tere 7–8, 1053 **Tel** *317 35 96* **Map** *4 F1*

First opened in 1877, this is Hungarian cuisine, hospitality and imperial elegance at its best, set in an understated, beautifully ornamented interior. The beer hall on the premises serves the same dishes, but at cheaper prices and in a less formal atmosphere. Gypsy music is played in the evenings. Reservation recommended.

Múzeum Kávéház és Étterem

Múzeum körút 12, 1088 **Tel** *338 42 21* **Map** *10 F5*

Next to the National Museum, this is a distinguished restaurant and café, established in 1855. It serves Hungarian specialities, though visitors should always be aware of what they are ordering, and how much it costs. Ostensibly friendly waiters often try to tempt the undecided with expensive items on the menu.

Százéves Étterem

Pesti Barnabás utca 2, 1052 **Tel** *266 52 40* **Map** *4 E1*

This is apparently the oldest restaurant in Budapest. First opened in 1831, it is housed in a beautiful Baroque building furnished with antique pieces. It offers Hungarian and international cuisine, and gypsy music is played in the background. Desserts are outstanding. Expensive, but justifiably so.

AROUND VÁROSLIGET

Himalaya Nepalese

Csengery utca 24, 1074 **Tel** *351 12 89* **Map** *7 B1*

Located in the heart of Budapest, this Nepalese restaurant stands out with its exotic and spicy cuisine. The chefs are from Kathmandu and prepare a range of dishes to suit all palettes and budgets. The surroundings are modest but the welcome is genuine and heart-warming.

Bagolyvár Étterem

Állatkerti út 2, 1141 **Tel** *468 31 10* **Map** *5 C3*

The "Owl Castle", as the name translates, is an enchanting restaurant found next to the City Park. It's the little sister of the grand Gundel *(see p204)* and offers homely Hungarian cooking at more reasonable prices. There's gypsy music in the evenings and also cookery courses for those who want to learn more.

HanKukGuan

Ilka utca 22, 1143 **Tel** *460 08 38* **Map** *6 F4*

The food of Korea has never been as celebrated as that of its Chinese or Japanese neighbours, but a few more restaurants like HanKukGuan might change that. The menu is short, but everything on it is authentic, and some ingredients are clearly imported at great cost. It is astonishing then that prices are so reasonable.

Platán Étterem

Városligeti fasor 46, 1068 **Tel** *322 66 15* **Map** *5 C5*

At the base of a huge, 250-year-old sycamore tree and tucked away on a side street is this large dining hall which serves à la carte dishes as well as fast food options. Open around the clock, and only a stone's throw from busy Andrássy, it somehow feels like an escape from city living.

Shalimar Indian Restaurant

Dob utca 50, 1072 **Tel** *352 03 05* **Map** *7 A2*

This well-regarded North Indian restaurant offers Muglai cooking and friendly service at reasonable prices. All dishes are made fresh to order and can be spiced to your tastes. There are excellent luxurious seafood dishes, plenty of vegetarian choice and a selection of eight freshly baked Indian breads.

Baraka Restaurant and Lounge

Andrássy út 111, 1063 **Tel** *483 13 44* **Map** *5 C4*

On the ground floor of the Bauhaus Andrássy Hotel, Baraka offers an exclusive, gourmet dining experience. Guests sit at one long table or outside in the garden. The fusion menu respects fresh ingredients with a blend of Asian and European tastes. The service is personal and welcoming. Save room for the magnificent desserts.

Haxen Kiraly

Király utca 100, 1068 **Tel** *351 67 93* **Map** *7 B1*

This place serves up the classic Germanic experience of leather-trouser-wearing gentlemen playing accordion music as pretty waitresses serve up *bratwurst*, *sauerkraut* and huge mugs of beer – all to Budapest's friendliest patrons. It's raucous and not for the faint-hearted, but for an all-round good time it's hard to beat.

Anonymus

1146 Vajdahunyad sétány (in the Vajdahunyad castle) **Tel** *363 59 05* **Map** *6 D4*

The magical Vajdahunyad Castle is the home to this exclusive restaurant located next to the Városliget Lake. You can enjoy a romantic dinner while listening to live music from Hungarian stars. Excellent Hungarian cuisine and warm hospitality makes your stay unforgettable.

1894 BorVendéglő

Állatkerti út 2, 1146 **Tel** *468 40 44*   **Map** *5 C3*

There is a stunning choice of over a hundred Hungarian wines in this cellar restaurant at the Gundel Palace in Vrosliget (City Park). Dishes are prepared by the kitchen that serves Gundel Étterem, but are less expensive. As with Gundel, the emphasis is on quality and Hungarian specialities.

Gundel Étterem

Állatkerti út 2, 1146 **Tel** *468 40 40*   **Map** *5 C3*

Probably Hungary's most famous restaurant. Not cheap, but no longer the most expensive. It features innovative Hungarian and international cuisine, including goose liver prepared in many different ways – warm, confit or paté. Gypsy music livens up the atmosphere and Sunday brunch is excellent value. Lovely gardens.

Robinson

Városligeti-tó, 1146 **Tel** *422 02 22*   **Map** *5 C3*

This award-winning and stylish restaurant has an unbeatable location – on its own island on City Lake. There is an outdoor terrace for summer dining and a fireplace in winter, and live guitar music in the evenings. The menu ranges from traditional classics to exotic seafood and vegetarian dishes.

FURTHER AFIELD

Fenyőgyöngye Vendéglő

Szépvölgyi út 155, 1025 **Tel** *325 97 83*

Small, incredibly popular restaurant up in the Buda Hills, offering traditional Hungarian fare made in a lighter, healthier way. The garden area is perfect for families, and popular with Buda's middle classes on Sunday afternoons. Reserving a table is a good idea. Bus 65 runs to the door from Szépvölgyi út HEV station.

Firkász Étterem

Tátra ú. 18, 1136 **Tel** *450 11 18*   **Map** *2 E1*

The name means "scribbler", and this restaurant has a literary, quiet atmosphere, ideal for a sedate dinner after a long day sightseeing. The menu is traditional Hungarian, with a wide selection of excellent wines. There is also live piano music. Booking is recommended.

Kerék Vendéglő

Bécsi út 103, 1034 **Tel** *250 42 61*

An authentic Old Buda restaurant from the 1960s, offering Hungarian cuisine to the music of an accordion player. It's not the most exclusive place in the city, nor will it win any design contests, but the garden is lovely and the food is great – both hearty and cheap. Tram 17 from Margaret Bridge gets you there. Booking is advised at weekends.

Nefrit Chinese Restaurant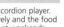

Apor Vilmos tér 4k, 1124 **Tel** *213 90 39*

Cantonese and Sechaun specialities in a pleasant restaurant in an old villa. Tasty *dim sum* are on offer, and prices are remarkably reasonable. Finding Chinese food in Budapest is easy; finding good Chinese food is tricky, so make your way here. You can do so on Bus 105 from Erszebet tér.

Bajai Halászcsárda

Hollós út 2, 1121 **Tel** *275 52 45*

Located next to the Svábhegy cog-wheel stop. Traditional Hungarian dishes specializing in fresh river fish. A real treat is the Bajai fish soup with a huge portion of carp fillets served on the side. There is also *goulash*, and for dessert the fried doughnuts are worth trying. If you don't fancy the cog-rail, Bus 21 from Moskva tér runs close by.

Chez Daniel

Szív utca 32, 1063 **Tel** *302 40 39*

Choose from the daily specials chalked up on the blackboard, then kick back and enjoy great food in one of Budapest's most relaxed restaurants. The food is mainly French, unfussy and accessible. The wine list is very good, and evenings here tend to be long. The small terrace-cum-courtyard is lovely. You'll need a reservation.

Gotti Restaurant

Ráday utca 29, 1092 **Tel** *212 62 25*   **Map** *7 A5*

Popular modern bar and restaurant in the buzzy café district of the city. There is a heated outdoor patio, weekend music performances and concerts and an excellent cocktail list. The food on offer ranges from traditional Hungarian to international cuisine. The desserts in particular are recommended.

Jardinette

Németvölgyi út 136, 1112 **Tel** *248 16 52*

During the summer there are a number of tables in the garden, where chestnut trees provide shade from the sun, and the whole ambience is warm and Mediterranean. Sitting inside in winter, however, can feel a little like sitting in a greenhouse. Food is contemporary European – not fancy, but good.

Key to Price Guide *see p196* **Key to Symbols** *see back cover flap*

Jókai Étterem

Hollós út 5, 1121 **Tel** *395 36 58*

Relaxed restaurant in a lovely 19th-century villa in the hills near the Svábhegy cog-wheel station. Attentive service and well-prepared classic Hungarian dishes at incredibly good prices. The terrace is pleasant in the summer. For those who don't fancy the journey on the cog-wheel railway, Bus 21 from Moszkva tér runs close by.

Kéhli Vendéglő

Mókus utca 22, 1036 **Tel** *250 42 41*

Excellent, long-forgotten tastes of Pest and Buda are served here in large portions. Established more than a century ago in Old Buda, this was the favourite eating place of Gyula Krúdy, the great Hungarian gourmet writer. Standards have not dropped a notch since he dined here. Reservations recommended.

Külvárosi Kávéház

István út 26, 1041 **Tel** *379 15 68*

A gem in the district of Újpest. International cuisine with excellent Hungarian dishes, including a three-course *betyárleves* (bone marrow on toast, golden soup with noodles and vegetables, beef cooked in soup). This is one of Budapest's most popular restaurants so reserve a table. Take metro M3 to Újpest-Központ.

Náncsi Néni Vendéglője

Ördögárok út 80, 1029 **Tel** *398 71 27*

Customers are offered a wide choice of interesting, home-style interpretations of traditional Hungarian dishes. Giant *túrógombóc* (curd cheese dumplings) is a favourite dessert – with those who have remembered to save room. Booking is essential, especially for the popular garden area in summer.

Öreghalász Étterem

Árpád út 20–22, 1042 **Tel** *231 08 00*

There's a homely atmosphere in this restaurant, where fresh river fish is the speciality. The decor is nautical but not over-the-top, and it enhances enjoyment of the super food. It is worth trying any fish soup from the wide range on offer, though non-fish dishes are also available. Booking recommended.

Voros Postakocsi

Ráday utca 15, 1092 **Tel** *217 67 56*

It's worth eating here simply to gaze out of the enormous windows at the super-trendy people passing by on up-and-coming Ráday utca. The main dining room is large, but charmingly decorated. The food is good – mainly Hungarian but with an international and contemporary twist. The name means Red Post Wagon.

Arcade Bistro

Kiss János Altáb utca 38, 1126 **Tel** *225 19 69*   **Map** *3 A1*

Few restaurants in Budapest can match the outstanding patio that attracts the Budapest jet set to Arcade during the summer. The food here is excellent, too, contemporary and inventive, and beautifully presented. Prices are a little high but represent real value for money.

Kisbuda Gyöngye Étterem

Kenyeres utca 34, 1043 **Tel** *368 64 02*

This restaurant has a natural, old-time drawing room atmosphere, where guests relax and enjoy excellent dishes from international and Hungarian cuisines to the soft music of a piano. A lunch here, where nothing should be hurried, usually turns into a long afternoon as the wine continues to flow.

Ristorante Krizia

Mozsár utca 12, 1066 **Tel** *331 87 11*

Krizia is a celebration of Mediterranean food and atmosphere. Elegance is balanced by hints of rusticity, from the terracotta pots to the overcrowded shelves of wine. The food is mainly Italian, and the pasta is made on the premises. There is a super wine list. Take the Millennium Metro to Oktagon to get here.

Fuji Japan

Csatárka utca 54, 1025 **Tel** *325 71 11*

In a pagoda-style interior, Japanese food enthusiasts can watch the chef at work while enjoying dishes such as a beautifully presented selection of *sashimi*. There is more than raw fish on the menu, however. This is a real Japanese restaurant, with the high prices to prove it.

Rosenstein Restaurant

Mosonyi utca 3, 1087. **Tel** *333 34 92*

Situated near Keleti railway station, in an area not known for fine dining, is Rosenstein Restaurant. The wide menu features both international and Hungarian cuisine as well as traditional Jewish food. Meat-eaters are well-catered for, but vegetarian options are limited.

Vadrózsa Étterem

Pentelei Molnár utca 15, 1025 **Tel** *326 58 17*

Exclusive restaurant set in a beautiful Neo-Baroque villa and run by one family for 30 years. Soft piano music plays in the evenings. The gardens are lovely in summer. A taxi is required to get here, but the house will tell you when, at the end of the meal, it's time for carriages. The food? Outstanding, adventurous and expensive.

Cafés and Wine Bars

To sample the true atmosphere of Hungary, it is essential to visit the smaller eating and drinking establishments that are scattered across the city and into the suburbs. Behind even the most ordinary of buildings, there could be hiding a timeless pocket of old Hungarian culture. Elsewhere, bright neon and loud music reflect the contemporary cultural interests of Budapest's youth. And between these extremes, visitors can still find a taste of 19th-century opulence in the old coffee houses and patisseries that once sat comfortably at the heart of the city's life.

CAFÉS & COFFEE HOUSES

Hungary has one of the oldest coffee-drinking traditions in Europe. Introduced by the Turks in the mid-16th century during their occupation (see pp26–7), the coffee culture blossomed towards the end of the Habsburg era (see pp32–3), when there were almost 600 kávéház (cafés) in the city.

The 19th-century café scene was a hotbed of intellectual activity dominated by literary and artistic circles. **New York Café** (see p129), which opened in 1894, was for many years the centre of this creative scene; its walls adorned with frescoes painted by the leading artists of the day. **Centrál Kávéház** café saw a revival in the 1990s and gives an open and cheerful picture of past and present traditions.

Today's café scene is continually changing. Eszpresszó bars first appeared in the 1930s but were most popular in the 1960s. Much cheaper than their pre-decessors, they catered for teenagers with a taste for Western culture. These have subsequently been replaced by more modern cafés, such as **Moyo Café**, **Menza**, **Barokko**, **Paris Texas** and **Leroy**.

Almost every luxurious traditional cukrászda (cake shop) and kávéház closed down when eszpresszó bars became popular, but many have now reopened again. A couple of old gems never closed: **Gerbeaud Cukrászda** serves the best coffee and cakes in the land, as it has done for well over a hundred years, while the **Gellért Eszpresszó** is a sublime recreation of a Habsburg-era coffee house, situated on the ground floor of the Gellért Hotel (see p183). Both of these places offer the genuine Budapest coffee-house experience, complete with immaculately liveried wait-resses in pinafore dresses and a lady who insists on taking your coat. They are sublime reminders of a bygone age.

There are many styles of coffee in Budapest. A kávé is an espresso with milk and sugar, and a dupla is a double espresso. French-style milky coffee is called a tejeskávé, while cappuccinos are often served with whipped cream or in the Viennese-style – without either chocolate or cinnamon. For decaffeinated coffee, ask for koffeinmentes.

Tea houses are also popular now. **Big Ben** and **1000 Tea** are great choices in the downtown area.

WINE BARS

Wine and wine bars occupy a different position in the social hierarchy in Hungary than they do in, say, Britain or the United States. Whereas in these countries wine drinking is regarded as a somewhat middle-class pursuit, in Hungary it has traditionally been considered a workers' pastime. Despite the fact that young men are now starting to adopt beer as their drink of choice, the old ways of drinking wine are still to be found underground, in the borozók of Budapest.

A traditional borozó is an unglamorous, cheap wine cellar, where wine is served straight from the barrel and sold by the decilitre. The best example is **6:3 Borozó** or **Vidocq Borozó**. Few places have tables and chairs. In the city centre, besides the tradi-tional borozós, like **Villányi-Siklósi** or **Grinzingi**, there is the more stylish **Rondella Borozó**, where wine is drawn from barrels and served in curious jugs with a tap at the bottom.

Várfok Borozó, at No. 10 Várfok utca in the Castle District, is of the simple but authentic kind. At the other end of the spectrum, there are places like the **House of Hungarian Wines** (see p180), where you can taste wines from each wine region in Hungary, or the **Hilton Hotel** (see p182), which houses a stylish wine bar in a medieval cellar. Such establishments tend to serve expensive wines in bottles, rather than straight from the barrel.

The popular, full-bodied range of dessert wines called Tokaji (see p195) also has a number of wine bars dedicated to it. The best is **Tokaji Borozó**, in central Pest, where most customers drink standing up.

Other good choices are the **Bor La Bor Pince** or the **Borpiac étterem**, which operate as wine bars and restaurants in one.

COCKTAIL BARS

Budapest is currently alive with trendy cocktail bars that buzz from the early evening onwards with a young crowd, enjoying after-work drinks in the Italian fashion (aperitivo).

There are cocktail bars all over the city, but the trendiest establishments tend to be found on "the tér" (Liszt Ferenc tér). Indeed, Liszt Ferenc tér is quite simply the social heart and soul of Budapest during the spring and summer months. Favourite places nearby include **Incognito** and **Karma**.

On the other side of the Danube, a hip crowd meets every evening at **Oscar's American Bar**, famous for its selection of more than 200 cocktails. The lucky few for whom money is no object head for the **Four Seasons Bar**, in the Gresham Palace hotel. Visitors to the city may like to follow suit, not least to enjoy the hotel's splendid interiors.

FOOD AND CUSTOMS

Wine bars, where people can pop in for a glass of wine or a spritzer *(see p195)* at any time of day, do not generally serve food. Occasionally, however, light snacks are available. Typically, these consist of a slice of bread and dripping garnished with raw onion and sprinkled with paprika; or *pogácsa*, a yeast pan-bread, served with crackling, cheese, caraway seeds or paprika. Wine bars with tables sometimes serve frankfurters or knuckle.

Visitors should take note of the following warning. In Hungary, unlike most other Europeans countries, it is not done to clink beer glasses together with fellow drinkers. This apparently innocent gesture was adopted by the Austrians as they executed Hungarian generals after the uprising of 1848–9, and can still cause great offence.

DIRECTORY

CAFÉS

Alkoholos Filc Kávézó
Várfok utca 15/B. **Map 1** A3. *Tel 213 51 55.* **Open** 9am–10pm Mon–Sat. *Closed* Sun.

Anna Café
Váci utca 7. **Map 4** E1. *Tel 266 90 80.* **Open** 8:30am–midnight daily.

Auguszt Cukrászda
Kossuth Lajos utca 14–16. **Map 4** F1. *Tel 337 63 79.* **Open** Mon–Sun daily.

Barokko Club and Lounge
Liszt Ferenc tér 5. **Map 7** A1. *Tel 322 07 00.* **Open** 11am–1am Sun–Tue, 11am–2am Wed–Sat.

Big Ben Teaház
Veres Pálné utca 10. **Map 4** F2. *Tel 344 43 81.* **Open** 10am–10pm daily.

Café Firenze
Szalay utca 5a. **Map 2** E3. *Tel 331 83 99.* **Open** 9am–6pm daily.

Centrál Kávéház and Restaurant
Károlyi Mihály u.9. **Map 4** F1. *Tel 266 21 10.* **Open** 7am–midnight Mon–Fri, 8am–midnight Sat–Sun.

Gerbeaud Cukrászda
Vörösmarty tér 7. **Map 2** E5. *Tel 429 90 00.* **Open** 9am–9pm daily.

Hattyú Kávézó
Hattyú utca 14. Map 1 A3. *Tel 202 77 77.* **Open** 24 hours daily.

Leroy Café
Ráday utca 11. **Map 10** F5. *Tel 219 54 51.* **Open** noon–midnight daily.

Lukács Café
Andrássy út 70. **Map 5** A5. *Tel 373 04 07.* **Open** 8:30am–7pm Mon–Fri, 9:30am–7pm Sat & Sun.

Menza
Liszt Ferenc tér 2. **Map 7** A1. *Tel 413 14 83.* **Open** 11am–midnight daily.

Moyo Café
Liszt Ferenc tér 10. **Map 7** A1. *Tel 342 44 57.* **Open** 11am–midnight.

Mozart Café
Erzsébet körút 36. **Map 7** B2. *Tel 352 06 64.* **Open** 9am–11pm daily.

Müvész Café
Andrássy út 29. **Map 2** F4 (10 E2). *Tel 352 13 37.* **Open** 9am–midnight daily.

New York Café
Erzsébet körút 9–11. **Map 7** B2. *Tel 886 61 67.* **Open** 10am–midnight daily.

1000 Tea
Váci utca 65. **Map 4** F2. *Tel 337 82 17.* **Open** noon–9pm Mon–Sat.

Paris Texas
Ráday utca 22. **Map 10** F5. *Tel 218 05 70.* **Open** 10am–2am Mon–Fri, 1pm–2am Sat, 4pm–2am Sun.

"R" Café
Károlyi Mihály utca 19. **Map 4** F2 (10 E5). *Tel 328 01 17.* **Open** 11am– midnight daily.

Ruszwurm Cukrászda
Szentháromság utca 7. **Map B4** (9 A2). *Tel 375 52 84.* **Open** 10am–7pm daily.

WINE BARS

6:3 Borozó
Lónyai utca 60. **Map 4** F2. *Tel 217 07 48.* **Open** 8am–midnight Mon–Sat.

Borpiac Étterem
Török utca 1. **Map 1** B1. *Tel 212 45 08.* **Open** 4:30–11pm Tue–Sat.

Bor La Bor Pince
Veres Pálné utca 7. **Map 4** F2 (10 ES). *Tel 328 03 82.* **Open** noon–midnight daily.

Grinzingi Borozó
Veres Pálné utca 10. **Map 4** F2 (10 E5). *Tel 317 46 24.* **Open** 9am–1am Mon–Sat, 3pm–11pm Sun.

House of Hungarian Wines
Szentháromság tér 6. **Map 1** B4. *Tel 212 10 31.* **Open** 12pm–8pm daily.

Móri Borozó
Fiáth János utca 16. **Map 1** A3. *Tel 214 92 16.* **Open** 2–11pm Mon–Sat, 4–9pm Sat & Sun.

Rondella Borozó
Régiposta utca 4. **Map 4** E1. *Tel 483 08 30.* **Open** 5pm–2am Tue–Sun.

Tokaji Borozó
Falk Miksa utca 32. **Map 2** D2. *Tel 269 31 43.* **Open** noon–9pm Mon–Fri.

Várfok Borozó
Várfok u.10. **Map 1** A3. *Tel 214 30 77.* **Open** 11am–8pm Mon–Fri, 10am–6pm Sat, Sun.

Vidocq Borozó
Lajos utca 98. *Tel 240 39 37.* **Open** noon–11pm Mon–Sun.

Villányi-Siklósi Borozó
Gerlóczy utca 13. **Map 4** F1 (10 E4). *Tel 267 02 41.* **Open** 8am–11pm Mon–Fri, 9am–10pm Sat & Sun.

Vincellér Borszaküzlet
Erd utca 10. **Map 1** B3. *Tel 201 15 61.* **Open** 10am–6pm Tue–Fri, 8pm–midnight Sat & Sun.

COCKTAIL BARS

Four Seasons Bar
Four Seasons Gresham Palace Hotel. Roosevelt tér 5–6. **Map 2** D5. *Tel 268 60 00* **Open** 11am–1am daily

Incognito
Liszt Ferenc tér 3. **Map 7** A1. *Tel 342 14 71.* **Open** 2pm–midnight daily.

Karma
Liszt Ferenc tér 11. **Map 7** A1. *Tel 413 67 64* **Open** 11am–1am daily.

Oscar's American Bar
Ostrom utca 14. **Map 1** A3. *Tel 212 80 17.* **Open** 5pm–2am Sun–Thu, 5pm–4am Fri–Sat.

Beer Halls, Pubs and Clubs

There are drinking establishments in Budapest to suit practically every taste, from traditional Hungarian beer halls to high-tech nightclubs, and many stay open late. Themed Irish, English or sports bars tend to cater to crowds of English ruffians who visit the city on "stag" weekends. It is still possible, however, simply to stroll around the city and drop into the places frequented by locals. You will find Budapest a very friendly and informal place to drink; if you sit at an empty table, others will probably join you. Note that in traditional pubs a waiter will automatically bring more beer as soon as you appear to be close to finishing your glass, unless you indicate otherwise.

TRADITIONAL BEER HALLS

Beer has now started to take over from wine as Hungary's favourite drink. Driven by this fashion, in Budapest many wine bars have been turned into *sörözs* (beer halls), and several new establishments modelled on the German *bierstube* and the English pub have opened. As a result, beer-drinking has become an aspirational pastime, and prices in the *sörözs* and pubs are much higher than in the *borozós* (traditional wine bars, *see p206*). This price difference is particularly noticeable in the popular tourist areas.

The cost of drinking beer is, however, reflected in the relative sophistication of the pastime; it is possible to buy almost all the major brands in the city, as well as Hungarian *világos* (light) and *barna* (dark) beers (*see p194*).

Beer is measured by the *korsó*, the equivalent of a pint, and the *pohár*, a smaller glass. A variety of good and moderately priced snacks and hot dishes, including smoked knuckle, is available in *sörözs*, as, indeed, is wine. By contrast, the *borozós* rarely offer food, and never beer.

The best of the old-style beer halls is probably historic **Fortuna Mátyás**, located in the Castle District. A more mainstream drinking experience can be had in the **Jam Pub** in the Mammut Shopping Centre, which even has live music most nights of the week, at 9pm.

IRISH PUBS & THEME BARS

Like many Eastern European cities, Budapest has been invaded by theme bars and pubs, notably Irish pubs. Some are friendlier than others, some are more Irish than others, but all have Guinness at the usual, extortionate prices. **Becketts** was the first Irish pub in Budapest and it remains popular with tourists, locals and expatriates. There's great pub food on offer, and good music at weekends. Equally celebrated is **Fregatt**, a hybrid Irish-English-Hungarian pub decked out in bizarre naval style. **Janis' Pub** is named after Janis Joplin and is a gem – with a bright blue exterior and live music at weekends. The small but enjoyable **Zappa Café** pays homage to another great legend of rock, Frank Zappa.

Budapest also has many easy-going venues where the music is less important than the atmosphere. For example, the **Cotton Club**, where sultry female singers croon to a trendy, upmarket crowd; and the **Old Man's Music Pub**, where a range of performers from Irish fiddlers to Hungarian punk bands entertain happy, drunk crowds from 9–11pm daily.

For Hungarian "oompah" music, complete with floor show, head for the peerless **Kalamajka Dance House**. It is touristy and expensive, but great. **Alcatraz**, where clients sit behind bars in their own private cells and staff wear prison warden's costumes, takes the theme pub concept perhaps too far; but it is still around after years on the scene, is more popular than ever, and has good live music most nights.

BOHEMIAN HANGOUTS

Though not in the same league as Prague, Budapest has nevertheless long been a haven for individualists looking for something a little different. Many are attracted by its glut of unusual places to eat and drink, such as the **Red Lion Tea House**, an Eastern-style retreat from modern life, where the serving of tea is an art form. Another favourite hangout is **Piaf**, a superbly decadent dive reminiscent of a speakeasy.

NIGHTCLUBS & DISCOS

Nightlife in Budapest is on its way to competing with that of other European capitals and new clubs open daily. Among the most recent arrivals on the scene is **Trafo Bar Tango**, a cultural centre for young, alternative artists housed in a renovated power station. It's also the setting for numerous exhibitions and literary events, and music styles range from reggae to classical Indian music.

The biggest and probably the most popular club in the city is **Bahnhof**, which is found, predictably enough, behind Nyugati train station and is frequented by a terrific mix of locals, expatriates and tourists, attracted by the relatively cheap drinks and mainstream dance music. It's open on Thursday, Friday and Saturday. Also popular is the disco boat **A38 Ship**, moored just past Petőfi bridge on the Buda side of the river. It is a cultural centre with a restaurant, bars and a concert hall, and hosts numerous national and international cultural events, exhibitions and festivals.

Older clubs are often centered around student venues. **Petőfi Csarnok**, a cavernous youth entertainment centre built in 1984 during the

Communist era, is a stage and disco complex that hosts local and international rock bands. **E-Klub** is open on Fridays and Saturdays and is always crowded with Technical University students. **Közgáz Pince Klub** is a really vibrant student club held in the huge hall of the University of Corvinus (*see p138*).

GAY VENUES

Among Budapest's gay bars is **Habrolo Bisztro Belvaros**, a small, friendly place with a neighbourhood atmosphere. It may not be the most hip and happening bar on the scene but it's a good place to start the night. Also good is **Upside Down**, which attracts

all sorts to its celebrated karaoke nights on Mondays and Wednesdays. Weekends are for hardcore techno fans and almost exclusively male. **Coxx**, a massive men-only complex with bar, disco, restaurant, internet café and gallery is famous for its theme nights – anything from fancy dress to no dress at all.

DIRECTORY

BEER HALLS

Astoria Café Mirror
Kossuth Lajos utca 19.
Map 4 F1.
Tel 889 60 22.
Open 7am–11pm daily.

Fortuna Mátyás
Fortuna Spaten, Hess András tér 4. **Map** 1 B5.
Tel 375 61 75.
Open 11am–midnight daily.

Gerbeaud Pub
Vörösmarty tér 7. **Map** 10 D3. *Tel* 429 90 22.
Open 12am–11pm daily.

Gösser Söröző
Régiposta utca 4.
Map 4 E1 (10 D4).
Tel 318 26 08. *Open* 10am–midnight daily.

Jam Pub
Lövöhaz utca 1–3, Mammut II. **Map** 1 A3.
Open 9am–4am Sun–Wed, 9am–6am Thu–Sat.

Kaltenberg Royal Bavarian Brasserie
Kinizsi utca 30–36. **Map** 7 A5. *Tel* 215 9792. *Open* noon–11pm daily.

Tóth Kocsma
Falk Miksa utca 17.
Map 2 D2.
Tel 302 64 43.
Open 3pm–midnight Mon–Fri, 5pm–midnight Sat & Sun.

IRISH PUBS & THEME BARS

Alcatraz
Nyár utca 1. **Map** 7 A3.
Tel 478 60 10. *Open* 4pm–2am Sun–Thu, 4pm–2am Fri & Sat.
www.alcatraz.hu

Becketts Irish Pub
Bajcsy Zsilinszky út 72.
Map 2 E3 (10 E1).
Tel 311 10 35. *Open* noon–1am Mon–Thu, noon–3am Fri, Sat.

Cotton Club
Jókai utca 26.
Map 2 F3.
Tel 354 08 86.
Open noon–1am daily.
www.cottonclub.hu

Fregatt
Molnár utca 26.
Map 4 E2 (10 D5).
Tel 318 99 97.
Open 5pm–2am daily.

Janis' Pub
Királyi Pál utca 8.
Map 4 F2.
Tel 266 26 19.
Open 4pm–2am Mon–Sat, 6pm–midnight Sun.

John Bull Pub
Apáczai Csere János utca 17. **Map** 2 D5.
Tel 338 21 68.
Open 11am–1am daily.

Kalamajka Dance House
Arany Idnos utca 10, Budapest V. **Map** 4 E2.
Tel 266 78 66.
Open 5pm–2am Sat.

Morrison's Music Pub
Révay utca 25. **Map** 2 F4.
Tel 269 40 60.
Open 7pm–4am Mon–Wed. www.morrisons.hu

Old Man's Music Pub
Akácfa utca 13.
Map 7 A2.
Tel 322 76 45.
Open 3pm–4am daily.

Zappa Café
Mikszáth Kálmán tér 2
Map 7 A4.
Tel 0620 972 17 11.
Open 10am–2am Mon–Fri, noon–4am Sat & Sun.

BOHEMIAN HANGOUTS

Piaf
Nagymezö utca 25.
Map 2 F3.
Tel 312 38 23. *Open* 10pm–5am Sun–Thu, 10pm–7am Fri–Sat.

Red Lion Tea House
Jókai tér 8. **Map** 10 F1.
Tel 269 05 79.
Open 11am–11pm Mon–Sat, 3pm–11pm Sun.

NIGHTCLUBS & DISCOS

A38 Ship
Pázmány Pétér sétány, Petöfi híd.
Tel 464 39 40.
Open 11am–4am on programme days.
www.a38.hu

Bahnhof
Váci út 1. **Map** 2 F2.
Tel 302 47 51.
Open 9pm–4am Thu–Sat.

D3 Music Club
Kossuth Lajos utca 20.
Map 4 F1. *Tel* 317 51 80.
Open 4pm–2am Tue–Fri, 8pm–4am Sat.

E–Klub
Népliget út 2.
Tel 263 16 14.
Open 10pm–5am Fri & Sat.

Fat Mo's Music Club
Nyári Pál utca 11.
Map 4 F2.
Tel 267 31 99.
Open 6pm–2am Sun–Wed, 6pm–4am Thu–Sat.

Közgáz Pince Klub
Fvám tér 8. **Map** 4 F3.
Tel 215 43 59. *Open* 10pm–5am Tue–Sat.
Closed Sun & Mon.

Petőfi Csarnok
Zichy Mihály utca 14.
Map 6 E4. *Tel* 363 37 30.
Open Times vary with events.

Trafo Bar Tango
Liliom utca 41, IX District, Ferencváros.
Tel 456 20 53.
Open 6pm–4am daily.
www.trafo.hu

GAY VENUES

Coxx
Dohány utca 38.
Map 7 A3.
Tel 344 48 84.
Open 9pm–4am daily.
www.coxx.hu

Habrolo Bisztro Belvaros
Szép utca 1B. **Map** 4 F1.
Tel 0620 211 67 01.
Open 7pm–5am daily.

Upside Down
Podmaniczky Tér 1.
Map 2 F3.
Tel 0670 367 96 22.
Open 10pm–5am daily.

SHOPS AND MARKETS

Shopping in Budapest has changed dramatically since the more spartan days of Communism. A huge variety of consumer goods, both foreign and home produced, are now available here. Major shopping streets include the pedestrianized and fashionable Váci utca (Váci Street, *see p127*) good for folk art and Zsolnay porcelain, and the less fashionable, but much cheaper

String of paprika peppers

Nagykörút, where locals come to do their shopping. For a more traditional shopping experience, don't miss a visit to some of Budapest's many markets. These range from stunning 19th-century food halls such as the Great Market Hall (Nagy Vásárcsarnok), to flea markets such as the huge and lively Ecseri Flea Market, for everything from bric-a-brac to furniture and antiques.

OPENING HOURS

Most shops in Budapest open from 9am to 5:30 or 6pm Monday to Friday, and from 9am to 1pm on Saturday. Greengrocers, bakeries and supermarkets are open from 7am until 8pm. Shopping centres, department stores and plazas open at 10am and close at 9pm except Sundays, when they close at 6pm. Indoor markets are open on Sunday, and most cafés sell milk and bread on Sunday morning. One result of the increase in private enterprise since 1989 is a large number of small shops which open 24 hours a day and sell groceries, cigarettes and alcohol.

Westend City Center shopping mall

HOW TO PAY

Credit cards and Euro-cheques can be used to pay for goods and services in many of the more touristy parts

of Budapest. Outside these areas it is best to carry plenty of cash in Hungarian forints.

VAT EXEMPTION

The price of all goods in Hungary includes a value-added tax of 20% (ÁFA). With the exception of works of art and antiques, it is possible for non-EU citizens to claim back the value-added tax on anything costing more than 50,000 forints. First, present your goods at customs within 90 days of purchase to receive your customs certification and a refund claim form. You will need your sales receipt and currency exchange or credit card receipt, plus the customs certification, to apply for your refund within 183 days of your return home.

DEPARTMENT STORES AND MALLS

There are a number of department stores in the city, many housed in spectacular old buildings.

Traditional folk crafts, on sale around Váci utca

More of a mall than a department store, the **Duna Plaza** on Váci út is smart but not centrally located. A store worth a look is **Skála Metro** on Nyugati tér opposite the railway station in Pest.

Many large stores are clustered in the old buildings of Váci utca, such as C&A and Zara, but most of these brands can be found in one place in the modern shopping centres.

Over the past decade more than 10 major shopping malls have opened and have proved popular with both locals and visitors. The most centrally-located mall is **Westend City Center**. Central Europe's largest, it has over 350 stores, including Armani, Benetton and Marks & Spencer, in addition to a 14-screen cinema and a food court.

The huge and stylish **Mammut** on Moszkva tér is frequented by the better off inhabitants of Buda, and is easily accessible for those who do not have the good fortune to live nearby.

Recently opened is the modern **Arena Plaza**, with more than 200 shops.

Delicate lace, an example of traditional Hungarian folk art

MARKETS

Markets of all sorts are an essential part of life in Budapest, and offer a delightfully traditional shopping experience to visitors. Perhaps the most spectacular are the five cavernous market halls which dot the city. All were built in the late 19th

Fruit and vegetable stalls at Central Market Hall

century and several are still used as markets. The three-level Great Market Hall (Nagy Vásárcsarnok) known officially as the **Central Market Hall** (Központi Vásárcsarnok) on Fővám tér is the largest of all. More than 180 stalls display a huge variety of vegetables, fruit, meat and cheese, under a gleaming roof of brightly-coloured Zsolnay tiles. The market opens from 6am–5pm Mon–Fri and 6am–2pm Sat (*see p138*).

In addition to the covered market halls, there are open-air food markets in every Budapest neighbourhood. In many you will see country women in traditional costumes selling fruit and vegetables, as well as local cheeses, honey and sausages. Some of the best markets are at Lehel tér (district XIII), Bosnyák tér (XIV) and Fehérvári út (IX). Delicious hot sausages with mustard and fresh bread, or *lángos,* a flat bread served with cream or grated cheese, are traditional and widely available market snacks.

Beginning at 156 Nagykőrösi út in district XIX, is the **Ecseri Flea Market**, open on

weekends. Outside, a maze of wooden tables is covered in Communist artifacts, second-hand clothes and all sorts of bric-a-brac, while from tiny cubicles inside the market, serious antique dealers sell porcelain, icons, silverware, jewellery and much more. It is necessary to obtain permission from the Museum of Applied Arts *(see pp136–7)* before you can take antiques out of the country.

Another market well worth a visit is the extremely busy **Józsefvárosi Market**, situated close to Józsefváros pu on Kőbányai út and open 7am–6pm daily. Many of the traders here are Chinese, using the Trans-Siberian railway to transport a huge variety of new goods from China, southeast Asia, the former Soviet Union and eastern Europe, all sold at knock-down prices. Look out for all sorts of entertaining and obvious southeast Asian fashion fakes, as well as electronic goods, Chinese silks, Russian caviar and vodka, and Stalinist memorabilia.

Marks & Spencer, a branch of the British department store

What to Buy in Budapest

Despite price rises since the return to a free-market economy, many Hungarian goods are still great bargains. Embroidered peasant blouses and wooden carvings make unique souvenirs, as does the distinctive porcelain produced at the world-famous Zsolnay and Herend factories. Cheap, good quality CDs and records are widely available, and Hungarian wines, salamis and other foodstuffs can be bought in the city's many lively markets. Clothes and shoes made to your specifications represent one of the city's most luxurious bargains.

from the Tokaji region, Muscats from Kiskunhalas on the central plain, and Chardonnays from Mátraalja. Also popular are the herbal liqueur Unicum, and the strong, fiery *pálinka*, which is made from plums, cherries or apricots. Wines and spirits are available in supermarkets and in specialist shops such as the **House of Hungarian Wines**, **Borház** and **House of Pálinka**.

FOLK ART

Hungarian folk culture is still alive and well in many parts of rural Hungary. You can buy textiles, ceramics and woodwork from flea markets *(see p211)* and from street vendors around Moszkva tér and Parliament *(see pp108–9)*. Folk art shops such as **Folkart Centrum**, sell machine-made products, and, for genuine Transylvanian textiles there is the **Judit Kézműves** hand-made shop. For the cheapest authentic folk costumes, head for the **Central Market Hall** (Nagy Vásárcsarnok).

ANTIQUES

Dominated by 18th- and 19th-century pieces in the Habsburg style, the Budapest antiques scene is concentrated in the Castle District, around Falk Miksa utca and on Váci utca (Váci Street, *see p127*). **Moró Antik** is a tiny shop specializing in 18th-century weapons, while the huge **Nagyházi Gallery** sells everything from jewellery to furniture. The **Ecseri Flea Market** *(see p211)* is also a good place for antiques.

PORCELAIN

There are two major porcelain manufacturors in Hungary, **Herend** and **Zsolnay**. Herend enjoys a reputation as the producer of the country's finest porcelain, while Zsolnay's brightly glazed tiles can be seen on many of the city's notable buildings. Second-hand porcelain can be bought in antiques shops and markets. Both companies have shops selling new pieces.

CLOTHES AND SHOES

Made-to-measure clothes and shoes, and ready-made designer clothes offer some of the best deals to be had by visitors to Budapest. Many people have clothes made up in their choice of fabric by a local designer – who is likely to be happy to oblige for a fairly modest fee. At the smart end of the market, there is **Naray Tamás Boutique**, the showcase for one of the most famous designers in Hungary. **Dáriusz Ekszerstudió** is now one of the country's most exclusive jewellers. Shoemakers in Budapest tend to make only men's shoes. **Vass** will make a one-off pair of dress shoes in about a month for around 130,000 Hungarian forints.

FOOD AND WINE

Food and wine in Hungary are great value and make excellent souvenirs for you to take home after your stay. Sausage is a national passion and can be bought in shops and markets all over the city. Some of the most popular types include spicy sausages from Debrecen, smoked sausages from Gyulai and a whole range of world-famous salamis. Also worth bringing home are dried mushrooms, *paté de foie gras*, a string of paprika or some fresh sheep's cheese. All these can be bought in Budapest's markets and in delicatessens like **Stonewell Gourmet**. Hungary's national beverage is wine *(see pp194–5)* and there are various top-quality bottles to look out for. These include fine dessert wines

MUSIC

Hungary's rich folk and classical music traditions make low-priced CDs, tapes and vinyl a tempting purchase in Budapest. For Hungarian folk music, from traditional Roma (Gypsy) music to recordings of village folk music, the old-style **Rózsavölgyi Zeneműbolt** is a good choice. In nearby Dob utca, **Concerto Records** offers a selection of new and second-hand vinyl and CDs, specializing in classical and opera, with some jazz, folk and funk. The state label, **Hungaroton**, has a shop in Rottenbiller utca that sells a wide range of classical music as well as some pop.

BOOKS

For illustrated books and English-language guide-books, try the **Litea Bookstore and Café**, where you can browse while enjoying coffee and cakes at tables set among the shelves. The large **Studium Libri** stocks many books in English. A range of English-language newspapers, magazines and novels are available at **Bestsellers**. **Írók Boltja** sells art books and some English-language books, while **Pendragon** stocks a varied assortment of fiction in English. For maps and English-language guide books try **Párizsi Udvar**. **Librotrade-Kodex** stocks books in English, French and German. For antique books, etchings and maps a good place to try is **Központi Antikvárium**. **Treehugger Dan's** is packed with secondhand books. They're mainly in English but there is a small selection of French and German ones, too.

DIRECTORY

DEPARTMENT STORES

Arena Plaza
Kerepesi út.
Map 8 E2. *Open*
10am–9pm Mon–Sat,
10am–7pm Sun.
Tel 061 880 70 00.
www.arenaplaza.hu

Duna Plaza
Váci út 178.
Tel 465 16 66.
www.dunaplaza.hu

Mammut I–II Mall
Lövőház út 3. **Map** 1 A2.
Open 10am–9pm
Mon–Sat, 10am–6pm Sun.
Tel 345 80 20.
www.mammut.hu

Westend City Center
Váci út 1–3. **Map** 2 F2.
Tel 238 77 77.
www.westendcity
center.hu

MARKETS

Central Market Hall (Központi Vásárcsarnok)
Vámház Körút 1–3
(Fővám tér).
Map 4 F3.
Open 6am–5pm Mon,
6am–6pm Tue–Fri,
6am–2pm Sat.
Tel 217 60 67.

Ecseri Flea Market
Nagykőrösi út 156.
Open Sat & Sun.
Tel 282 95 63.

Fehérvári út Market
Fehérvári út 20.
Map 4 D5.

Fény utca Market
Near Moszkva tér.
Map 1 A3.

Józsefvárosi Market
Kőbányai út.
Map 8 F4.

Lehel tér Market
Lehel tér.
Map 2 F1.

FOLK ART

Folkart Centrum
Váci utca 58.
Map 4 E1 (10 D3).
Open 10am–7pm daily.
Tel 318 58 40.
www.folkartcentrum.hu

Judit Kézműves
Szentháromság utca 5.
Map 1 B4.
Tel 212 76 40.

ANTIQUES

Moró Antik
Falk Miksa utca 5.
Map 2 D2. *Tel 311 08 14.*

Nagyházi Gallery
Balaton utca 8. **Map** 2 D2.
Tel 475 60 00.

PORCELAIN

Herend Shops
József Nádor tér 11.
Map 2 E5 (10 D3).
Tel 317 26 22.
Szentháromság utca 5.
Tel 225 10 50.
Andrássy út 16.
Map 2 F4.
Tel 374 00 06.
Váci útca 19-21.
Map 4 E1. *Tel 266 63 05.*

Zsolnay Shops
Kossuth Lajos u.10.
Map 4 F1. *Tel 328 08 44.*
József krt. 59–61.
Map 7 B4. *Tel 318 70 93.*
Kecskeméti u.14.
Map 4 F2. *Tel 318 26 43.*
Bajcsy Zs.u.23.
Map 2 F3. *Tel 311 40 94.*
www.porcelan.hu

CLOTHES AND ACCESSORIES

Dáriusz Ekszerstúdió
Wesselényi utca 36.
Map 7 B2.
Tel 328 05 98.
www.brilians.hu

Naray Tamás Boutique
Károlyi Mihály utca 12.
Map 10 E5.
Tel 266 24 73.

Vass Cipőbolt
Haris köz 2.
Map 4 E1.
Tel 318 23
75.www.vasshoe.hu

FOOD AND DRINK

Borház
Jókai tér 7.
Map 2 F3 (10 F1).
Tel 353 48 49.

La Boutique des Vins
József Attila utca 12.
Map 2 E5 (10 D3).
Tel 317 59 19.

House of Hungarian Wines
Szentháromság tér 6.
Map 9 A2.
Open noon–8pm.
Tel 212 10 32.
www.winehouse.hu

House of Pálinka
Rákóczi út 17.
Map 7 A3. *Open*
9am–7pm Mon–Sat.
Free tasting: Fri. www.
magyarpalinkaha za.hu

Stonewall Gourmet
Sütő utca 2. **Map** 2 E5.
Tel 0670 368 35 23.
www.stonewallgourmet.
hu

MUSIC

Concerto Records
Dob utca 33.
Map 2 F5 (10 F3).
Open noon–7pm
Mon–Fri.
Tel 268 96 31.

Hungaroton Records
Rottenbiller utca 47.
Map 7 C1. *Open 8am–*
3pm Mon–Fri.
Tel 322 88 39.

Liszt Ferenc Zeneműboltja
Andrássy út 45.
Map 2 F5 (10 E2).
Tel 352 7314.

Rózsavölgyi Zeneműbolt
Szervita tér 5.
Map 4 E1 (10 D4).
Open 9:30am–7pm
Mon–Fri, 10am–5pm Sat.
Tel 318 35 00.

BOOKS

Bestsellers
Október 6 utca 11.
Map 2 E4 (10 D2).
Tel 312 12 95.
www.bestsellers.hu

Írók Boltja
Andrássy út 45.
Map 2 F4 (10 E2).
Tel 322 16 45.

Központi Antikvárium
Múzeum Körút 13–15.
Map 4 F1 (10 E4).
Tel 317 35 14.

Librotrade-Kodex
Honvéd utca 5.
Map 7 C3.
Tel 428 10 10.

Litea Bookstore and Café
Hess András tér 4.
Map 1 B4 (9 A2).
Open 10am–6pm.
Tel 375 69 87.

Párizsi Udvar
Petőfi Sándor utca 2.
Map 4 E1 (10 E4).
Tel 235 03 79.
www.parisiudvar.hu

Pendragon
Pozsonyi út 21–23.
Map 2 F1.
Open 10am–6pm
Mon–Fri, 10am–2pm Sat.
Closed Sun.
Tel 340 44 26.

Pendragon at CEU
Zrínyi utca 12. **Map** 2 D4.
Tel 327 30 96.
Open 10am–6pm Mon–
Fri, 10am–2pm Sat.

Studium Libri
Váci utca 22 (main
pedestrian precinct).
Map 4 E1 (10 D4).
Tel 318 56 80.
www.libri.hu

Treehugger Dan's
VI, Csengery utca 48.
Tel 322 07 74.
www.treehugger.hu

ENTERTAINMENT IN BUDAPEST

Budapest has been known as a city of entertainment since the late 19th century, when people would travel here from Vienna in search of a good time. Its buzzing nightclubs were frequented for their electric atmosphere and the beautiful girls that danced the spirited *csárdás* and the cancan. Nowhere else did fiddlers play such heartrending music or were the gambling casinos wit-

Street performer

ness to such staggering losses as in Budapest. Between the wars the city was as famous for its glittering society balls as for its libertine delights. The half-century of Communist rule dampened the revelry, but since 1990 the music scene has flourished and theatres, cabarets, festivals, cinemas and discotheques are all buzzing. Above all, renowned nightclubs have risen convincingly from their ashes.

ENTERTAINMENT HIGHLIGHTS

Budapest has two opera houses, an orchestral concert hall at the **Franz Liszt Academy of Music** (*see p208*), several other concert halls including the **National Concert Hall** at the Palace of Arts (*see p156*), an operetta theatre, numerous cabarets and more than 50 theatres, including the fringe. Among them is the **Merlin Theatre** (*see p217*), which performs only in English.

The greatest concentration of theatres is in district V, in Nagymezö utca, which has been nicknamed "Budapest's Broadway". Along this 100-m (328-ft) stretch there are two theatres, the **Operetta Theatre** (*see p216*), the satirical cabaret **Mikroszkóp Színpad** (*see p217*), reputed to be the best in Hungary, and the **Moulin Rouge** (*see p217*) revue theatre. Film-lovers are

spoilt for choice, as Budapest boasts many **cinemas**.

Városliget (*see pp142–3*) offers a permanent circus, funfair and zoo, with bars and beer tents in the summer.

The youth entertainment centre, **Petőfi Csarnok** (*see p217*), hosts rock concerts and the largest disco in town. **A38 Ship** is a music club in a converted ship and **Millenáris** is a concert venue and cultural centre with a varied programme. The **Budapest Arena** holds 12,000 spectators, and stages a range of cultural events. Casinos and striptease clubs are the latest addition to the city's nightlife.

FREE ENTERTAINMENT

It is not difficult to find excellent, free entertainment in Budapest. During the summer, there always seem to be street entertainers and musicians wandering around the **Castle District**, often in elaborate period costume, playing instruments or acting out scenes from Hungarian history. During the **Budapesti Búcsú** in June (*see page 59*), all entertainments, from singing and dancing to theatre, are staged by the city council for free. In July, the **Danube Water Carnival** offers most of its thrills without charge, and the **Summer on the Chain Bridge**, Budapest's largest summer festival, offers a series of events every weekend, from mid-July to September. Hungarian culture, handicrafts, music and folklore are celebrated. Guided tours of Budapest's leading

sight, **Parliament**, are now free for citizens of the EU.

Unfortunately, entry to Budapest's museums is not free, although permanent exhibitions are usually cheaper than temporary ones.

BUYING TICKETS

Tickets for all plays and concerts can be purchased in advance, either at a booking office or by telephoning the venue direct. Addresses and telephone

Lavishly staged opera at the State Opera House (*see p216*)

numbers are listed in the directory on pages 216–17. The most difficult to obtain are tickets to the **Franz Liszt Academy of Music** concerts, as these tend to be sold many days in advance. Similarly, seats at opera and operetta performances sell out quickly. The best way of securing a seat, particularly for summer performances, is via **Rózsavölgyi Fegyirodá** or **Ticket Express**, which are

Actors in satirical cabaret at Mikroszkóp Színpad (*see p217*)

located right in the centre of town, close to Vörösmarty tér. In Budapest, like anywhere else, you can risk it and try buying returned tickets at the last minute. A cheap alternative, but not for the weary, is to buy a standing-room pass.

LATE NIGHT TRANSPORT

Budapest's metro *(see p238)* runs until just after 11pm. Buses marked with black numbers and the letter "E" provide the night transport on busy routes. There are also night trams running on some routes, though their frequency varies from between one and three an hour. Night buses should be boarded through the front door, and tickets shown to the driver. The stop-request button is situated above the exit door.

The HÉV train *(see p239)* that connects Budapest with its suburbs stops running at about 11:30pm.

DISABLED ACCESS

Much work has been done since Hungary joined the European Union to make the country's venues accessible to as wide a range of people as possible. However, a lot of Budapest's older venues are far from wheelchair-friendly. Places which are equipped for

Poster pillar

disabled visitors include the **Mátyás Church** *(see pp82–3)*, the **State Opera House** *(see pp118–19)* and the **Franz Liszt Academy** *(see p1129)*. The pedestrianized **Liszt Ferenc tér**, with its preponderance of outdoor cafés and terraces is also perfect for disabled travellers. The bars and pubs of Central Pest, many of which are located in basements, are not. Note that many venues (including the State Opera House) offer small reductions for disabled visitors.

The Hungarian Disabled Association
San Marco utca 76. **Tel** 250 90 13.
www.meosz.hu

LISTINGS MAGAZINES

The best Budapest listings publication is the free weekly *Pesti Est*, which, though published almost entirely in Hungarian, is comprehensible to most people. It is available in bars, restaurants, hotels and shops. Visitors should also try the *Budapest Times* and the *Budapest Sun*, English-language free weekly newspapers that list the best current events as well as comprehensive English-language cinema screening times, theatre, opera and classical music listings. Both newspapers, and *Pesti Est*, are also available online.

The dramatic entrance to the Moulin Rouge theatre *(see p217)*

A monthly edition of *Time Out* includes a useful events calendar. Other cultural bulletins include *Exit* and *Programme*, in English and German, and *Budapest Panorama*, in English, German, Russian, Italian and French.

LATE-NIGHT SCAMS

Budapest is generally a very safe city, but it is not without its dangers, especially late at night. Tourists are seen as easy prey by fraudsters, and it is important to stay alert at all times. Attractive peroxide-blondes promenading Váci utca and introducing themselves to single men may appear friendly and genuine at first sight, but, alas, they are not. It they insist you join them for a drink in a bar of their choice, you should refrain from doing so. They are not prostitutes, but "consumption girls", employed by bars to bring in foreign men to buy them drinks – which, as will become apparent only after the bill arrives, cost thousands of Hungarian forints.

Although a number of bars that carry out this practice have been closed by the authorities, it still goes on. Always check how much you are paying for a drink and be wary of instant female friends.

Late nights are also the delight of unscrupulous taxi drivers, eager to make a killing from tipsy tourists. Never get into a taxi that does not clearly state it belongs to a reputable taxi company, or which does not display its tariffs on the side of the driver's door. Always ask for a rough estimate of the cost before getting in.

The elegant interior of the Franz Liszt Music Academy *(see p216)*

Music

Thanks to great composers such as Liszt, Bartók and Kodály (see p144), and the wealth of its folk tradition, Hungary is famous for its music. Hungarians have always been a nation of music lovers; in addition to performances by national artists, Budapest is frequently visited by revered musicians from around the world.

OPERA AND OPERETTA

The standard of opera in Budapest is high. Performances are at either the **State Opera House** (see pp118–9) or the **Erkel Theatre** (see p151). At both there is a mainly classical repertoire, sung in Italian. The secondary focus is on Hungarian works. The **Operetta Theatre** (see p115) stages Hungarian operettas.

CLASSICAL MUSIC

The **Franz Liszt Academy of Music** (see p129) is the leading venue for classical music. The city's largest venue is the new **National Concert Hall** (see p156). Concerts are sometimes held in the domed hall of **Parliament** (see pp108–9), which has excellent acoustics, and at the **Congress Centre** (see p160). Budapest also has a strong tradition of music festivals, (see pp58–61).

SACRED MUSIC

Concerts of organ music are held between March and December in the magnificent setting of the **Mátyás Church** (see pp82–3). Among the composers whose works are featured, Bach is the most popular. **St Stephen's Basilica** (see pp116–7) serves sporadically as the venue for concerts of choral music. Between March and October the Musica Sacra Agency organizes concerts in the **Great Synagogue** (see p134).

FOLK & GYPSY MUSIC

Performances of folk and gypsy music are held at the **Duna Palota** and **Hungarian Heritage House**. Watch out for shows by the Hungarian State Song and Dance Ensemble and a Gypsy band that is part of the ensemble but also stages independent concerts.

During July and August the city is visited by folk troupes from all over the country.

From October to May, the city's dance houses rock to the sounds of fiddles and flutes. One of the most renowned is **Fonó Budai Zeneház**, which stages peasant and gypsy bands from Transylvania. The popular **Marcibányi téri** cultural centre stages folk and gypsy music events, and house music, as well as playing host to various other arts events and shows.

JAZZ

Jazz was very late in reaching Hungary. The best known and revered Hungarian jazz band is the Benkó Dixieland Band, which during Spring Festivals (see p58) plays in various theatres and large halls. The best place for jazz-lovers to congregate is **Columbus Jazz Club**, where Hungary's best players perform from 8:30pm every evening. The club boasts views of the Danube and it is a good idea to reserve a table. The **Cotton Club** (see p198) is also very popular.

DIRECTORY

TICKETS

Rózsavölgyi Jegyiroda
Szervita tér 5. Map 4 E1. Tel 266 83 37.

Ticket Express
Andrássy út 18. Map 10 E2. Tel 312 00 00. Deák Ferenc út 19. Map 4 E1. Tel 266 70 70. www.tex.hu

OPERA AND OPERETTA

Erkel Theatre
Köztársaság tér 30. Map 7 C3. Tel 333 05 40.

Operetta Theatre
Nagymező utca 17. Map 2 F3. Tel 472 20 30.

State Opera House
Andrássy út 22. Map 2 F4. Tel 331 25 50. www.opera.hu

CLASSICAL MUSIC

Congress Centre
Jagelló út 1–3. Tel 372 57 00.

Franz Liszt Academy of Music
Liszt Ferenc tér 8. Map 7 A1. Tel 462 46 79.

National Concert Hall
Palace of Arts Komor Marcell utca 1. Tel 555 30 00.

Parliament
Kossuth Lajos tér. Map 2 D3 (9 C1). Tel 441 49 04.

SACRED MUSIC

Great Synagogue
Dohány utca 2–8. Map 7 A3. Tel 342 89 49.

Mátyás Church
Szentháromság tér 2. Map 1 B4 (9 A2). Tel 355 56 57.

St Stephen's Basilica
Szent István tér. Map 2 E4 (10 D2). Tel 403 53 70.

FOLK AND GYPSY MUSIC

Hungarian Heritage House
Corvin tér 8. Map 1 C4 (9 A2). Tel 225 60 49.

Duna Palota
Zrínyi utca 5. Map 2 E5 (10 D2). Tel 317 13 77.

Fonó Budai Zeneház
Sztregova utca 3. Map 2 E5 (10 D3). Tel 206 53 00.

Marczibányi téri
Művelődési Központ Marczibányi tér 5/A. Tel 212 28 20.

JAZZ

Columbus Jazz Club
Vigadó tér, Dock 4. Map 4 D1. Tel 223 53 95.

Cotton Club
Jókai utca 26. Map 2 F3. Tel 354 08 86.

Theatre, Cinema and Casinos

Budapest has many theatres, which are worth visiting not only for their impressive repertoires, but also because they are invariably located in beautiful, historic buildings. Cinemas show the latest films, although few retain the original soundtrack. For late-night dancing, the city has a wealth of popular clubs to choose from.

THEATRE

The first theatre to stage plays in Hungary was the **National Dance Theatre** *(see p73)*. Other established theatres include the **Madách Theatre, Nemzeti Theatre, Pesti Theatre** and **Laser Theatre**. The **Merlin Theatre** performs in English. **Trafó** is an exciting showcase for all the contemporary arts.

Budapest has over 30 drama and cabaret theatres including **Mikroszkóp Színpad**, which hosts satirical cabaret shows *(see p214),* and the **Moulin Rouge**. The most prestigious is the **József Katona Theatre**, which became famous following performances in Paris and London. The **Vígszínház**, meaning "comedy theatre", specializes in musicals (as does the Madách Theatre). In summer rock-operas are staged on Margaret Island. These shows are remarkable both for the quality of the production and the magnificent island setting.

CINEMA

Many of Budapest's cinemas were built during the 1920s and 1930s and, despite renovations, have been superceded by modern multiplexes such as those in the shopping malls **Duna Plaza, Westend City Center,** and **Corvin Filmpalota.**

Most foreign films in Hungary are now both dubbed and subtitled into Hungarian, leaving cinemagoers free to choose which version they prefer. Those who do not understand Hungarian should choose the *angyol nelvű* (English soundtrack) version of the film. For films in English with no subtitles at all, look out for the words, *angol nyelvű, felirat nélkül.*

Apart from foreign films, the cinemas also show native Hungarian films. The range covers both the latest releases and vintage films from a time of Hungarian cinematic glory, notably when Miklós Jancsó and István Szabó received international awards for directing. The renovated, Moorish style **Uránia Filmszínház** film palace dates from this time.

All cinema tickets can be bought a few hours in advance. Some cinemas will sell tickets for showings the next day.

CASINOS

Budapest has several casinos. Most occupy historical buildings next to smart hotels.

Casino Várkert, for example, occupies one of the city's finest Secession-era buildings, built to a design by Miklós Ybl *(see p119)*. It originally functioned as the engine room of the water supply system of the Royal Palace. For the past 40 years it has operated as an elegant restaurant and, since 1992, as both a casino and a restaurant.

At any of the casinos listed below, players can try their hand at roulette, Black Jack, poker and the wheel of fortune. All are open 24 hours a day and, with the exception of the **Las Vegas Casino**, require evening dress. Passports are also universally required.

DIRECTORY

THEATRE

National Dance Theatre
Színház 1-3. **Map** 9 A3.
Tel 356 40 85.

József Katona Theatre
Petőfi Sándor utca 6.
Map 4 E1 (10 D4).
Tel 318 37 25.

Laser Theatre
Népliget, Planetárium.
Tel 263 08 71.

Madách Theatre
Erzsébet körút 29–33.
Map 7 A2. *Tel 478 20 41.*

Merlin Theatre
Gerlóczy utca 4.
Map 4 F1 (10 E4).
Tel 317 93 38.

Mikroszkóp Színpad
Nagymező utca 22–24.
Map 2 F3 (10 E1).
Tel 332 53 22.

Moulin Rouge
Nagymező utca 17.
Map 2 F3. (10 E1.)
Tel 434 99 95.
www.moulinrouge.hu

Nemzeti Theatre
Bajor Gizi Park 1.
Map 7 B1. **Tel** 476 68 68.

Pesti Theatre
Váci utca 9. **Map** 4 E1 (10 D4). *Tel* 266 52 45.

Trafó
Lilom utca 41.
Map 7 B5.
Tel 215 16 00.

Vígszínház
Pannónia utca 1.
Map 2 E1. *Tel 340 46 50.*

CINEMA

Corvin Filmpalota
Corvin köz 1.
Tel 459 50 50.

Palace Duna Plaza
Váci út 178.
Tel 999 61 61.

Palace West End
Váci út 1–3.
Map 2 F2. *Tel 999 61 61.*

Uránia Nemzeti Filmszínház
Rákóczi út 21
Map 7 A3.
Tel 486 34 13.

CASINOS

Casino Tropicana
Vigadó utca 2.
Map 4 D1.
Tel 327 72 50.

Casino Várkert
Ybl Miklós tér 9.
Map 9 C4.
Tel 202 42 44.

Grand Casino Budapest
Deak Ferenc tér 13.
Map 2 E5.
Tel 483 01 70.

Las Vegas Casino
Roosevelt tér 2
(Sofitel Atrium Hotel).
Map 2 D5.
Tel 317 60 22.

Sports

Hungarians are fine athletes, as is testified by their consistently outstanding performances at competitive events, such as the Olympic Games. Budapest's world-class sports facilities serve as venues for many of these international events, including European and World championships. Sporting opportunities for visitors to the city are both varied and accessible.

SPECTATOR SPORTS

Most competitive sporting events are held either in the magnificent **Ferenc Puskás Stadium** *(see p155)*, which seats 80,000 spectators, or in the modern, indoor **Budapest Aréna**.

Soccer remains the most popular spectator sport, although Hungarian fans can only look wistfully back to the time when their national side was highly successful. In the 1950s, for instance, Hungary beat England 6:3 at Wembley. League matches in Budapest attract big crowds. The atmosphere is particularly electric when local favourites Ferencváros, FTC, take to the pitch.

Two of the three great events regularly held in Budapest are the Welcom Marathon Hungary and the Budapest Marathon. These are run on the last Sundays of April and September, respectively. The third big sporting event of the year is the Hungarian Grand Prix *(see p59)*, which takes place during August at the Mogyoród racing circuit.

Hungarians achieve impressive results in boxing, canoeing, swimming, water polo and fencing, which are all widely supported.

HORSE RACING AND RIDING

As a nation of former nomads, the Hungarians have retained a great love of horses. In Budapest this passion finds its expression in horse racing, which is enormously popular. A few hours spent at a racetrack can be a cheap and fun way of soaking up the local atmosphere. Near the Albertirsai út *(see p234)* is the Trotters' Racecourse, at the **Kincsem Park**.

Those wishing to be rather more energetic and ride instead of watch horses, should contact the **National Riding School**, the **Petneházy School**, the **Kincsem Horsepark** or the **Budapest Riding Club**.

SPORTING ACTIVITIES

Practising sport for fitness and pleasure is both cheap and popular in Budapest.

Strolling through the city's parks, particularly on Margaret Island, you will encounter scores of eager joggers, both young and not so young. The indoor and outdoor swimming pools are also full of regular visitors, who come here for an hour or so of healthy exercise. Particularly popular is the **Hajós Olympic Pool** on Margaret Island, which is named after Hungary's first Olympic gold winner for swimming, who was also the pool's architect. Busy open-air swimming options include **Komjádi Pool** *(see p52)* and the neighbouring **Lukács Baths** *(see p101)*, both of which can be enjoyed even in winter as the hot spring water creates a steamy atmosphere over the water's surface. For the hottest spa water in the city, head to the **Széchenyi Baths** *(see p151)*, which is the largest bathing complex in Europe. However, the most atmospheric and beautiful baths are undoubtedly the 16th-century Turkish **Rudas Baths** *(see p93)*.

Cycling is also gaining in popularity, particularly since the introduction of cycling lanes to the city's roads *(see p229)*. If you want to play tennis, there are numerous courts available, but these tend to be monopolized by local Hungarians. Your best bet for a game is to befriend a local tennis player, or find a hotel that has its own court.

Despite the moderate climate, it is also possible to undertake winter sports in Budapest. From December until March the **Városliget Lake** *(see pp142–3)* is turned into a skating ring and many people take to the ice. **Sváb Hill** *(see p161)* is generally snow-covered from December to March and has several ski runs and ski lifts.

DIRECTORY

STADIA

Papp László Budapest Aréna
Stefánia út 2.
Map 8 F1. **Tel** 422 26 00.
www.budapestarena.hu

Ferenc Puskás Stadium
Istvánmezei út 3–5.
Map 8 F1.
Tel 471 41 00.

HORSE RACING AND RIDING

Budapest Riding Club
Albertirsai út 4.
Tel 0630 92 12 36.

Kincsem Horsepark
Sóregi út 1.
Tel 0629 423 056.

National Riding School
Kerepesi út 7. **Tel** 0630 301 83 44.

Petneházy School
Feketefej utca 2–4.
Tel 397 50 48.

Kincsem Park
Albertirsai út 2–4.

SWIMMING POOLS

Császár Komjádi Uszoda
Frankel Leó út 55.
Map 1 B1. **Tel** 212 27 50.

Lukács Baths
Frankel Leó utca 25–29.
Map 1 C1. **Tel** 326 16 95.

Hajós Olympic Pool
Margitsziget. **Tel** 450 42 20.

Rudas Baths
Döbrentei tér 9. **Map** 4 D2.
Tel 356 13 22.

Széchenyi Baths
Allatkerti körút 11.
Map 6 D3. **Tel** 363 32 10.

Children's Budapest

Visiting Budapest can be made great fun for children. There are several choices of energetic outdoor pursuits, including a funfair, a terrific zoo and, of course, a range of glorious of swimming venues. If the weather is poor, the city's historic buildings, museums and art galleries will entertain and inform. In addition, a handful of puppet theatres cater specifically for younger audiences.

youngsters occupied. Shows, which often star international artists, take place daily.

At **Vidám Park Funfair** *(see p151)* in Városliget, there are merry-go-rounds, a railway, shooting galleries and games machines.

SIGHTSEEING FOR KIDS

Busy Pest is a difficult area in which to entertain kids, but the **Postal Museum**, set in an opulent 19th-century mansion, is well worth a morning's visit.

In Buda's **Royal Palace** *(see pp70–71)* and **Castle District** *(see pp68–85)*, the city's long history can be understood instinctively just by wandering round the ancient and lovely buildings. The **Hungarian National Gallery** *(see pp74–7)* feeds young imaginations, as does the fabulous *turul*, the statue of a mythical giant bird that stands in the Palace Courtyard. The magnificently carved **Mátyás Fountain** *(see pp72–3)* is also worth a look.

In the Old Town, the **Labyrinth of Buda Castle** *(see p85)* on Lords' Street is a bizarre underground exhibition that fascinates kids, and there are displays of armour and weapons in the **Museum of Military History** *(see p85)*. A final "must" is a ride on the **Budavári Sikló** funicular railway *(see p239)*.

SWIMMING

The most suitable complex for young families is the seasonal **Palatinus Strand** *(see p53)* on Margaret Island, where there are pools of varying temperatures, water slides and artificial waves. Numerous kiosks sell snacks, ice cream and fruit.

During the winter season, the **Gellért Hotel and Baths Complex** *(see pp90–91)* is a better alternative. Here, the large swimming pool has artificial waves, and the paddling pool's warm water is wonderful for toddlers. **Széchneyi Baths** *(see p151)* also welcome children.

CIRCUS, FUNFAIR & ZOO

People of all ages love the Budapest **Zoo** *(see pp150-51)*, which is one of the best in Europe. Attractions include a large sea-water aquarium, a terrarium with splendid snakes, and an impressive aviary.

A visit to the **Great Capital Circus** is an easy way to keep

INDOOR ATTRACTIONS

Budapest Bábszínház and **Kolibri Színház** are two of several puppet theatres that stage international favourites, such as *The Jungle Book, Cinderella* and *Snow White,* as well as Hungarian classics.

In People's Park, the **Planetárium** is known for its special entertainment shows – remarkable compositions of laser effects, pictorial projections and music, staged under an impressively large dome.

SCENIC RAILWAYS

Children love the trip up into the **Buda Hills** *(see p161)*. The first stage is a ride on the cogwheel railway that runs up Széchényi Hill. At the top, there is a playground and the start of the Children's Railway, which follows the ridge of the hills to the Hvös Valley. The way back down is on the Libeg chair-lift that runs from the top of János Hill to Zugliget (linked by bus 158 to Moszkva tér). Young railway enthusiasts also enjoy the **Railway History Park** *(see p156)*.

DIRECTORY

SIGHTSEEING

Budavári Sikló
Clark Ádám tér,
Szent György tér.
Map 1 C5 (9 B3).

Hungarian National Gallery
Szent György tér 2.
Map 3 C5. **Tel** 375 55 67.

Labyrinth of Buda Castle
Úri utca 9.
Map 1 A4 (9 A2).
Tel 212 02 07.

Postal Museum
Andrássy út 3.
Map 2 F4 (10 E2).
Tel 268 19 97.

Mátyás Fountain
Royal Palace.
Map 1 C5 (9 B3).

Museum of Military History
Tóth Árpád Sétány 40.
Map 1 A4. **Tel** 356 95 22.

Railway History Park
Tatai út 95. **Tel** 450 14 97.

Royal Palace
Map 1 5C (9 4B).

SWIMMING

Gellért Hotel and Baths Complex
Kelenhegyi út 4. **Map** 3 C3. **Tel** 466 61 66.

Palatinus Strand
Margitsziget.
Tel 340 45 05.

Széchneyi Baths
Állatkerti körút 11.
Map 6 D3.
Tel 363 32 10.

RECREATION

Great Capital Circus
Állatkerti körút 7.
Map 5 C3.
Tel 344 60 08.

Vidám Park Funfair
Állatkerti körut 14–16.
Map 5 C3.
Tel 363 83 10.

Zoo
Állatkerti körút 6–12.
Tel 363 37 10.
Map 5 C3.

INDOOR ATTRACTIONS

Budapest Bábszínház
Andrássy út 69.
Map 5 A5 (10 E2).
Tel 321 52 00.

Kolibri Színház
Jókai tér 10.
Map 2 F3 (10 F1).
Tel 311 08 70.

Planetárium
Népliget.
Tel 263 18 11.

SURVIVAL
GUIDE

PRACTICAL INFORMATION 222–231
GETTING TO BUDAPEST 232–235
GETTING AROUND BUDAPEST 236–241
STREET FINDER 242–256

PRACTICAL INFORMATION

Budapest was always famous for its hospitality, and the Hungarians have been increasingly emphasizing tourism as an important part of the national economy. The biggest problem in its development has been the formidable barrier posed by the Hungarian language, which hinders access to information. Familiarizing yourself with a

TOURIST

i

SERVICE

Tourist information sign

few Hungarian words and phrases is a good idea *(see pp271–2)*. However, English and German are spoken in all tourist offices and bigger hotels, and tourist brochures and pamphlets are now published in several languages. Sights in the city centre are easy to reach on foot, while more distant monuments are accessible by public transport *(see pp236–41)*.

WHEN TO GO

The best time to visit Budapest is between March and the end of June, and from the middle of August until October. July and early August are generally very hot, while the winter months can be extremely cold.

Various festivals and cultural programmes take place throughout the year, the biggest events being the Spring and Autumn Festivals and the Sziget Festival (August). The end of the year is an enjoyable time, when visitors can experience the Christmas Fair and the New Year's Eve street party *(see pp58–61)*.

VISAS AND PASSPORTS

Citizens of the UK, Ireland, the US, Canada, Australia and New Zealand need only a valid passport to visit Hungary for up to 90 days. Visitors from any of the 24 European states which are signed up to the Schengen Agreement on border controls can enter with just an ID card for a stay of up to 90 days.

All other visitors should check their visa requirements

– and, if necessary, apply for a visa at their local Hungarian embassy before travelling. Note that visas for other Schengen countries are also valid for Hungary. For more information, see the **Hungarian Ministry of Foreign Affairs** website.

TOURIST INFORMATION

Prior to your arrival in Budapest it is worth getting in touch with your nearest **Hungarian National Tourist Office**, which can supply useful information and put you in touch with reputable tour operators.

Many agencies specialize in organizing individual trips and tours to Hungary, including **Great Escapes**, **Kirker Holidays** and **Page & Moy**. They can all provide you with detailed information on itineraries and accommodation and help you to make reservations. Official tourist information centres in Budapest, **Tourinform**, can be found at a number of locations in the city, including at Liszt Ferenc tér, Sütő utca at Deák tér, Buda Castle and Ferihegy airport terminals.

General tourist information in a variety of languages is provided by these centres. They also sell the Budapest Card *(see below)* as well as souvenirs, guide books and maps.

Brown tourist signs can be found at all the important points of the city to help visitors find their way around.

Budapest Card

BUDAPEST CARD

The Budapest Card is designed for tourists visiting the city for two or three days. It entitles a visitor, together with one child under the age of 14, to use most city transport – metro, bus, tram, trolley bus and HÉV – free of charge, as well as providing discounted or free entry to 60 museums. It also entitles you to a 50 per cent discount on guided tours of the city, a 10–20 per cent discount on tickets to selected spas and cultural events, and a 10–20 per cent discount in selected restaurants.

The card costs 6,300 forints for 48 hours and 7,500 forints for 72 hours. Cards can be purchased at tourist offices, hotels, museums and most large metro stations. Enclosed with the card is an information pamphlet, in four languages, which lists its benefits.

One of several tourist information offices in Budapest

◁ River Danube cruise ship, overlooked by the Royal Palace and Erszébet bridge

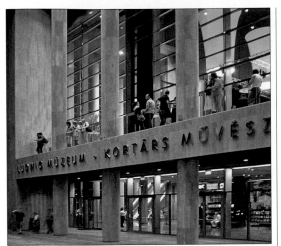

Ludwig Museum of Contemporary Art, Palace of Arts *(see p156)*

OPENING HOURS

Museums and galleries are generally open year round. Most museums are closed on Monday; one exception is the Jewish Museum *(see p134)*, which is closed on Saturday. Opening times for specific venues are given under their individual entries.

During winter (November to March) most museums have shorter opening hours. In summer, from April until October, they tend to stay open a couple of hours longer, typically from 10am until 6pm. Most museums charge an entrance fee, though it is worth checking to see if there are any discounts.

Shopping centres in Budapest are open daily until 8 or 9pm; grocery stores are open from 7am to 6pm and other shops from 10am until 6pm Monday to Friday. On Saturdays many shops close at 1pm. Further information on the opening hours of shops and markets in Budapest can be found on pages 210–13.

ADMISSION PRICES

Tickets to museums and historical monuments can be purchased at the sight. Some may also be bought in advance at museum websites. Average prices vary from 700 to 1,500 forints per person,

but some can be as much as 4,000 forints. Students, schoolchildren and seniors are often entitled to reductions. Opera, concert and other tickets can be bought at ticket agencies *(see pp214–17)*. Theatre and opera tickets are also sold at individual box offices, either for shows on the same day or in advance. Ticket prices can vary from 1,500 to 10,000 forints, depending on the show.

SOCIAL CUSTOMS AND ETIQUETTE

Casual clothes are often worn to the theatre, particularly during summer. By comparison, classical music concerts and operas are much smarter affairs and even tourists will feel more comfortable wearing evening dress. Traditionally, Hungarians attach great importance to being properly dressed when going to an opera or concert hall.

In Hungary, when introduced to someone it is customary to shake hands and say your name. Hungarians also shake hands when meeting people with whom they are already acquainted, though between friends kissing on both cheeks is the norm, for men as well as women. Some older men still bow to kiss a woman's hand *(see also Senior Travellers, p224)*.

TIPPING

It is standard practice to tip when paying for taxis, meals and drinks (though not for drinks at a bar counter); 10 per cent of the total or thereabouts is acceptable. In restaurants, check to see whether between 10 and 12 per cent has been added to the bill – in which case you don't have to leave more. The usual practice is to include the tip when you pay – just indicate the amount you want to pay and you will be given change accordingly. If you expect change back, don't say *köszönöm* (thank you) when handing over payment, as it will be assumed that you want the change to be kept.

Note that when visiting baths and pools in Hungary it is customary to tip the attendant who unlocks your cubicle (100–200 forints is usual). Even medical staff in hospitals expect to be tipped.

TRAVELLERS WITH SPECIAL NEEDS

Budapest is gradually becoming more accessible for disabled visitors. However, it is best to call ahead to the sights or obtain specialist information prior to your visit to ensure it is as hassle-free as possible. Newer buses are now equipped for easier boarding and some metro stations have special lifts.

For advice and help, contact the **Hungarian Disabled Association**. Many museums and monuments present difficulties for the disabled, although increasingly they are being renovated to be wheelchair-friendly.

The State Opera House *(see pp118–19)*, a venue with disabled access

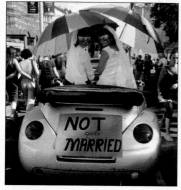

A Europride parade on the streets of Budapest

GAY AND LESBIAN TRAVELLERS

While Hungarian society is largely conservative, Budapest is a cosmopolitan city and its gay scene is thriving, with overtly gay clubs now replacing the old covert meeting places.

This greater prominence is also reflected in Hungarian law – the age of consent is 14 for homosexuals and heterosexuals alike. The Budapest gay scene is male-dominated, however. The **Gay Guide Network** has information on gay-friendly accommodation, bars, clubs, restaurants and baths. The free monthly magazine Na Végre, which can be picked up at most gay venues, has listings for gay establishments and events in English.

It is worth noting that in the past, extreme right-wing groups, such as Magyar Garda, have attacked Gay Pride marches (Europride) – so caution is always advised at this annual summer event.

International Student Identity Card

SENIOR TRAVELLERS

The older generation in Hungary is accorded great respect. You shouldn't be surprised if people allow older ladies to cut ahead in shop and post office queues, for instance. Senior travellers to Hungary are also afforded some special

courtesies. Many museums offer discounts of up to 50 per cent for EU citizens between the ages of 62 and 70, and free admission for those aged 70 and over. On the public transport system, seniors are also entitled to reductions on ticket prices of 50 per cent, and more for monthly and quarterly passes. For EU residents over the age of 65, travel on the metro, buses and trolley buses is free.

TRAVELLING ON A BUDGET

The days when you could live like a prince on a pauper's budget in Hungary are long gone – today the top hotels and restaurants charge international rates. However, there are still plenty of places in the city where you can sleep and eat well for a modest cost.

For cheap accommodation try the **Top Hostels** chain of student hostels, which has an office by the platforms in Keleti station. For cheap places to eat, look for an *önkiszolgáló étterem* (a self-service restaurant), *étkezde* (lunchtime diner), or a *főzelék* bar (*főzelék* is dish of creamed vegetables). More restaurants are now offering a lunchtime *menu* – an inexpensive two-course lunch. There are also many Turkish kebab restaurants in the city centre, as well as a number of cheap Chinese restaurants.

Student cards (ISICs) are widely accepted in Budapest. They are useful for obtaining discounts at many museums and monuments throughout the city. If you don't already have an ISIC card, go to the Vista Travel Office at Andrássy út 1 – they should be able to issue you with one. If you are travelling as a family, renting

an apartment can help keep costs down – try the Internet-based **Budapest Lets** *(see also pp178–81)*.

BUDAPEST TIME

Budapest uses Central European time, in keeping with the rest of mainland Europe, which means it is 2 hours ahead of Greenwich Mean Time (GMT) in the summer and 1 hour ahead in the winter.

Examples of the summer time differences between Budapest and other major cities are as follows: London: -1 hour; New York: -6 hours; Dallas: -7 hours; Los Angeles: -9 hours; Perth: +6 hours; Sydney: +8 hours; Auckland: +10 hours; Tokyo: +7 hours.

ELECTRICAL APPLIANCES

Hungarian electricity supply is 220 V and the plugs needed are the standard Continental 2 pin type. Adapters can be purchased in most countries. Since sockets are generally earthed, the most commonly used plugs are the flat type.

PUBLIC TOILETS

There are few public toilets in Budapest, and most require a small fee for their use. It is worth carrying some small change for this eventuality.

Cubicles can be found in some squares and parks and these are usually free. In cafés and restaurants there are toilet attendants and the price for using the facility is usually clearly displayed.

There are no public toilets in metro stations, except for Batthyány tér. Apart from the generally understood picture symbols, the toilets are signed in Hungarian: *Hölgyek* (ladies) and *Urak* (gentlemen), or *Nők* (women) and *Férfiak* (men).

Sign for a ladies' toilet

Sign for a gentlemen's toilet

RESPONSIBLE TOURISM

Environmental awareness has been slowly gathering strength in Hungary. As far back as the 1980s there were protests against the hydroelectric scheme on the Slovakian border which diverted the Danube. Today, however, environmental issues are a low priority for most households struggling to meet daily costs. Nevertheless, some attention is paid to green matters.

There are recycling centres in every district of the city for paper, glass and cardboard, and many bottles can be returned to shops on a deposit basis.

There are several organic food outlets in the city. The largest organic market is the Bio-piac, which takes place on Saturday mornings from 6am to noon on Csörsz utca, not far from Déli station. Another option is the Biritmus Csarnok, located inside Cédrus Piac market Hall on Ferhér út.

To ease the city's air pollution, Budapest has become more pedestrian-friendly, with greater areas of downtown Pest in particular being blocked off to traffic.

A useful organization which has a website packed with green facilities in Budapest is **Green Map**. You can pick up a green guide to the city, "Go Green", at Treehugger Dan's, the second-hand bookshop that also hosts environmental events *(see p212)*.

DIRECTORY

TOURIST OFFICES ABROAD

Hungarian National Tourist Office
46 Eaton Place, London
SW1X 8AL,
United Kingdom.
Tel 020 7823 1055.
www.gotohungary.co.uk

350 Fifth Ave, Suite 7107,
New York, NY 10118,
United States.
Tel 212 695 12 21.
www.gotohungary.com

TOURIST OFFICES IN BUDAPEST

Tourinform Buda Castle
Szentháromság tér.
Map 1 B4 (9 A2).
Tel 488 04 75.

Tourinform Call Centre
24-hour Tel 438 80 80.

Tourinform Ferihegy Airport
Ferihegy 1.
Tel 296 57 94.
Ferihegy 2,
Terminal A.
Tel 296 54 94.
Ferihegy 2,
Terminal B.
Tel 296 54 95.

Tourinform Hotline
Tel from abroad
+36 30 30 30 600.
Tel from Hungary
06 80 660 044.

Tourinform Liszt Ferenc tér
Liszt Ferenc tér 11.
Map 7 A1.
Tel 322 40 98.

Tourinform Sütő utca
Sütő utca 2 (Deák Ferenc tér). **Map** 2 E5 (10 D3).
Tel 438 80 80.

TRAVEL AGENTS ABROAD

Great Escapes
Cutter House 1560
Parkway, Solent Business Park, Fareham,
Hampshire, PO15 7AG,
United Kingdom.
Tel 0845 330 2084.
www.greatescapes.co.uk

Kirker Holidays
4 Waterloo Court,
10 Theed St, London
SE1 8ST, United Kingdom.
Tel 020 7593 1899.
www.kirkerholidays.com

Page & Moy
Compass House,
Rockingham Road,
Market Harborough,
Leicestershire LE16 7QD,
United Kingdom.
Tel 0116 217 8005.
www.pageandmoy.com

HUNGARIAN EMBASSIES

United Kingdom
35 Eaton Place, London
SW1X 8BY.
Tel 020 7201 3440.

United States
3910 Shoemakers
Street NW,
Washington D.C.
20008.
Tel 202 362 6730.
www.huembwas.org

FOREIGN EMBASSIES AND CONSULATES IN BUDAPEST

Australia
Királyhágó tér 8–9.
Tel 457 9777.
Fax 201 97 92.
www.ausembbp.hu

Canada
Ganz ú. 12–14.
Map 1 B2.
Tel 392 33 60.
Fax 392 33 90.

New Zealand
Nagymező utca 47.
Map 1 2 F3.
Tel 302 24 84.
Fax 311 80 92.

South Africa
Gárdonyi Géza
utca 17.
Tel 392 09 99.
Tel 200 72 77.
www.sa-embassy.hu

United Kingdom
Harmincad utca 6.
Map 2 E5.
Tel 266 28 88.
Fax 266 09 07.
www.britishembassy.hu

United States
Szabadság tér 12.
Map 2 E4.
Tel 475 44 00.
Fax 475 47 64.
www.usembassy.hu

TRAVELLERS WITH SPECIAL NEEDS

Hungarian Disabled Association
San Marco utca 76.
Tel 250 9013.
Fax 454 1144.
www.meosz.hu

USEFUL WEBSITES

Budapest Lets
www.budapestlets.com

Budapest Tourism Office/Tourinform
www.budapestinfo.hu

Gay Guide Network
www.gayguide.net

Green Map
www.zoldterkep.hu

Hungarian Ministry of Foreign Affairs
www.mfa.gov.hu

Hungarian National Tourist Office
www.hungarytourism.hu
www.gotohungary.com
www.gotohungary.co.uk

Top Hostels
www.mellowmood.hu

Personal Security and Health

Police Symbol

Budapest is safe for visitors as long as common-sense precautions are taken to guard your personal safety and possessions. Emergency services are reliable, and hospitals and medical clinics are clean and efficient. Nevertheless, as in any large city, social problems can have an impact. Petty crime rates are on the rise, with an increase of pickpocketing in particular. Sadly, any visitors to Budapest will also be aware of the growing numbers of homeless people living on the city's streets.

Police car

Ambulance

Road policeman on a motorbike

POLICE

Budapest is a pleasant city, with most neighbourhoods still safe to walk around at night. However, as with any large city, it has its share of crime.

The Hungarian police (*rendőrség*) are frequently seen patrolling the streets on motorbikes, on foot or in cars. Every district has its own police station, some of which offer 24-hour tourist assistance. In the event of loss or theft, a report should be made immediately to the police. For lost passports, *see Lost and Stolen Property*.

IN AN EMERGENCY

The number to call in an emergency is the **International Emergency Number** – 112. However, if you do not get an English-speaking operator, call the **Police Tourism Hotline**, which is open 24 hours a day. If you are involved in a police case as a witness or injured party, you should ask for consular assistance. For other emergency numbers see the Directory *(opposite)*.

WHAT TO BE AWARE OF

Documents and money should be carried in a secure inside pocket or in a money belt. Money should be exchanged at a bank, your hotel or an exchange bureau, never on the black market. There is generally no need to carry your passport with you, although it is advisable to have some form of ID – such as a driving licence.

Do not leave valuables in your car. If taking a taxi, use registered vehicles, which offer more security and are less likely to overcharge than unmarked ones *(see p239)*.

Pickpockets operate during rush hours, targeting people in crowded metro stations, buses and shopping centres. They also operate at all the main tourist sights, and on nearby public transport. When working as a group, they may surround unsuspecting tourists and jostle or distract them. For this reason, it is a good idea to have a photocopy of your passport and your travel insurance documents.

It is also worth noting that the rise of extreme nationalist and right-wing groups has created pockets of violence, which it is wise to avoid. In the past, violent clashes have taken place on major national holidays such as 15 March (Spring Uprising) and 23 October (Remembrance Day), and at Gay Pride marches, so it is wise to keep an eye out for trouble.

Women should not walk unaccompanied late at night in poorly lit areas and should avoid deserted streets. Rákóczi tér and Mátyás tér, in district VIII, have been infamous for their brothels since the 19th century and have a long-standing tradition as hangouts for prostitutes, although legislation has now made prostitution much less visible on the streets.

When eating in restaurants make sure that your menu includes prices, as some restaurants may try to take advantage of tourists. Single men should also beware of predatory females inviting them to a bar for a drink or meal, which then results in a disproportionately huge bill. Such scams are most often found in the less appealing places in the centre of Pest.

LOST AND STOLEN PROPERTY

The loss or theft of a passport should be reported to the local police station and then the appropriate embassy immediately *(see p225)*.

Any items left on public transport may be traced at the Lost Property Office, at No. 18 Akácfa utca, or by calling **BKV Lost Property**.

HOSPITALS AND PHARMACIES

First aid and ambulance services in Hungary are free for citizens of the UK and most other European countries. Before travelling to Hungary you should obtain a European Health Insurance Card (EHIC), which allows you to access state-provided healthcare at a significantly reduced cost. In the case of an accident or emergency, the largest state hospital in central Budapest is the Szent János Kórház in the XII district (or call an ambulance).

There are also a number of international clinics, such as the **First Med Centre** and **Fönix-Med Medical Service**, with English-speaking staff and a high standard of care, although these are expensive.

The shop front of a pharmacy in Budapest

Hungary has a well-deserved reputation for good dentistry at very reasonable prices. One popular, centrally located dental care specialist is **Dental Care Budapest**.

Budapest's pharmacies (*gyógyszertár or patika*) are well stocked and, in the case of a minor ailment, the chemist will be able to recommend a suitable treatment. Some drugs require a prescription, while others can be sold over the counter in pharmacies such as **Déli Gyógyszertár**. If your nearest pharmacy is closed, there should be a list displayed, on the door or in the window, of all the local chemists – it will indicate which ones are on 24-hour emergency duty, one of which is **Teréz Patika**.

Pharmacy sign

TRAVEL INSURANCE AND MEDICAL MATTERS

When travelling to Hungary it is highly recommended that visitors take out travel insurance before leaving home. Foreign nationals are only entitled to free medical help in emergencies, such as accidents or a sudden illness requiring immediate medical intervention. Any other medical care, including hospitalization, must be paid for. The cost depends on the type of insurance policy held and the relevant agreement between Hungary and the visitor's home country. Most insurance companies expect policy holders to pay for their treatment as they receive it and then apply for a refund on their return home. All the relevant bills and police reports must be submitted with any insurance claim. Remember that a report must be made to the police within seven days of any incident.

No special vaccinations are required for Hungary and the general standard of hygiene in the country is reasonably good. That said, allergy sufferers and people with breathing difficulties should take account of the air pollution during the summer months, which is particularly acute in the crowded streets of Pest. Those susceptible should consider staying in the Castle District, from which cars are banned, or retreating to the wooded Buda Hills or the greenery of Margaret Island *(see pp187–9)*.

The water in Budapest is of good quality. It is generally considered safe to drink water straight from the tap. The city's numerous thermal baths *(see pp50–53)* are an excellent way to relax.

DIRECTORY

POLICE AND EMERGENCY SERVICES

Ambulance
Tel 104.

Fire
Tel 105.

International Emergency Number
Tel 112.

Police
Tel 107.

Police Tourism Hotline
Tel 438 80 80.

Police Stations with 24-hour Assistance

I district: Pauler utca 13.
V district: Szalay utca 11–13.
XI district: Bocskai út 90.
XIII district: Szabolcs utca 36.

LOST PROPERTY

BKV Lost Property
Tel 461 66 88, choose option 3 on the menu.

HOSPITALS AND PHARMACIES

Szent János Kórház
Diós árok utca 1-3.
Tel 458 4500.

Déli Gyógyszertár
Alkotás u.1/b.
Tel 355 46 91.
Open 8am–8pm Mon–Fri, 8am–2pm Sat.

Teréz Patika
Teréz krt. 41.
Map 10 F1.
Tel 311 44 39.
Open 24 hours daily.

INTERNATIONAL CLINICS

Avicenna Medical and Dental
Podmaniczky utca 33, 3rd floor, 8. **Map** 2 F3.
Tel 302 5005.

Dental Care

SOS Dent Nonstop Clinic, Király utca 14.
Map 2 F5.
Tel 269 60 10 (24 hours).
www.dentalcarebudapest. com

First Med Center
Hattyúház 14, 5th floor Hattyú utca. **Map** 1 A5.
Tel 224 9090.
www.firstmedcenters. com

Fönix-Med Medical Service
Diós árok utca 1–3.
Tel 2000 100.
www.fonixmed.com

Local Currency and Banking

Bureau de change sign

The Hungarian banking system is rapidly approaching European standards. Budapest now boasts many modern banks, both Hungarian and foreign, which are located in smart and spacious buildings. The service is efficient and courteous. There are numerous automatic cash dispensers and bureaux de change in the town centre and around the railway stations. An increasing number of shops and restaurants now accept credit cards, but it is still more common in Budapest to pay for goods and services in cash. Most banks will now also advance money on a credit card.

An ATM (cash machine) outside a Budapest bank

BANKS AND BUREAUX DE CHANGE

For the best rate of exchange, take foreign currency to a bureau de change such as **Ibusz** or **M and M Exclusive Change**; these generally give better rates than Hungarian banks. Before changing money, check the rates of exchange, as they tend to vary quite widely. The rates quoted by some exchange offices can be misleading as they could apply only to sums in excess of 200,000 forints, which may be stated only in very small print.

The least favourable rates are in hotels and at the airport, while the best are offered by the bureaux de change near the railway stations and in the city centre, in Petőfi Sándor utca. A reasonable, average rate can usually be found at Hungarian banks.

Branches of the **Budapest Bank** are open Monday to Friday, from 10:30am until 2pm. **K & H Bank** are

Entrance to a branch of the Budapest Bank, on Váci utca

open Monday to Thursday, between 8am and 3pm, and on Friday between 8am and 1pm. Most banks are closed on Saturdays and Sundays, but the bureaux de change and ATMs remain open. Exchanging money is only permitted in licensed, designated places. Transactions on the street are illegal, and often involve counterfeit money.

ATMS

The easiest way of getting money is from cash machines (ATMs), which have instructions in various languages (including English). These can be found all over the city. Don't be put off if a bank machine rejects your card; try at another bank and it is likely to work. There are also exchange machines, which change foreign notes.

CREDIT CARDS AND TRAVELLER'S CHEQUES

Most hotels, shops and restaurants accept credit cards, but older establishments and some of the more inexpensive restaurants do not. It is therefore wise to carry some cash with you.

The most widely accepted cards are VISA, American Express, MasterCard and Diners Club. The logos of accepted credit cards are usually on display – it is always worth checking before you order, however. Traveller's cheques can be changed at most banks, as well as at some hotels, restaurants and shops.

WIRING MONEY

As a significant proportion of Hungarians don't have bank accounts, wiring is an effective way for them to receive and transfer money abroad. Western Union has branches all over Budapest. Look for their logo at foreign exchange bureaux, or the Intercash symbol (www.intercash.hu), the Western Union agent in Hungary. Western Union offices can also exchange foreign currency, though generally they do not offer the best rates.

DIRECTORY

BANKS

Budapest Bank
Váci út 188. **Map** 2 F1.
Tel 450 60 00.

K & H Bank
Vigadó tér 1. **Map** 4 D1.
Tel 335 33 55.

Magyar Külkereskedelmi Bank Rt
Váci utca 38. **Map** 4 E1.
Tel 0640 333 666.

BUREAUX DE CHANGE

Ibusz
Oktogon 3. **Map** 7 A1.
Tel 342 05 83.

M and M Exclusive Change
Bajcsy-Zsilinszky út 20. **Map** 2 E4.
Tel 235 84 84.

Hungarian currency

The Hungarian currency unit is the forint (HUF or Ft). Banknotes are issued in denominations of 500, 1,000, 2,000, 5,000, 10,000 and 20,000 forints. Both an old and a new style of some notes are currently legal tender, but an older version of the 5,000 forint note than the one shown here is no longer accepted.

1,000 HUF

500 HUF

5,000 HUF

2,000 HUF

10,000 HUF

20,000 HUF

Coins

The forint has coin denominations of 5, 10, 20, 50, 100 and 200 forints currently in circulation. As with Hungarian banknotes, new coins are gradually being phased in – the 200 forint coin with a nickel disc inside a brass ring is now the only legal version.

10 HUF

5 HUF

20 HUF

50 HUF

100 HUF

200 HUF

Media and Communications

Post office logo

The prevalence of mobile phones has transformed communications in Hungary, giving reliable access to the phone network for many who had struggled with the relatively inefficient landline telephone operating system. There remain many telephone boxes throughout the city, although card-operated telephones are much more widespread than coin-operated ones. Wi-Fi access is also available at many places around the city.

INTERNATIONAL AND LOCAL PHONE CALLS

Telephone cards are the best option for making landline calls, and can be obtained in denominations of 800, 1,800 or 5,000 forints. They are widely available from tobacconist shops, post offices, street vendors and some newspaper kiosks. Alternatively, coin phone boxes accept 10, 20 50 and 100 forint coins and also €1 and €2 coins.

The minimum rate for a local call is 20 forints, and 100 forints for an international call. To make an international call dial 00, wait for the dialling signal and then dial the country code, followed by the rest of the number. You can also phone abroad using a pre-paid international phonecard such as the Barangoló, available at post offices, which offers good rates to countries around the world.

Budapest telephone numbers consist of seven digits (when combined with the city dialling code 06-1 there are 10 digits). Hungarian mobile phone numbers consist of 11 digits: they start with 06-20, 06-30, 06-60 or 06-70, followed by seven digits. If you are calling any of these numbers from abroad the initial 06 is replaced by the country code, 36. To call the operator dial 198, or 199 for the international operator. There is little advantage in using the services of a hotel operator, and this only makes the call more expensive.

MOBILE PHONES

If you plan to bring your mobile phone when travelling, check with your provider about whether you have a roaming facility, and bring an adaptor and transformer with you to recharge your phone. US cell phones need to be tri-band to work in Hungary.

Alternatively, you can buy a Hungarian SIM card to use in your phone. You'll find providers such as **T-Mobile**, **Telenor**, **Vodaphone** and others in all big shopping malls.

INTERNET AND EMAIL

Cafés and bars offering a wireless connection are now common in Budapest. It is

Telephone box

easy to find Wi-Fi hotspots, too: go to www.hotspotter.hu. Budapest also has several Internet cafés offering coffee and snacks while you check your emails, search the Internet or play online games.

It is worth noting that connection speeds can vary. In some cafés the keyboards are laid out according to the Hungarian template, with extra letters.

ADDRESSES

Budapest is divided into 23 districts, identified by Roman numerals. A Budapest address is usually written with the district number placed first; in addition, the street number comes after the street name – for example, V Kossuth Lajos utca 4. However, in correspondence a four-digit postal code is used in place of the district number, the middle two digits indicating the district (so that 1054 refers to an address in the fifth district).

After the street number, an additional combination of numerals denotes the floor, and the number of individual apartments (eg Kossuth utca 14.III.24). Confusingly, some old buildings in Pest are designated as having a half-

Internet café in Vaci utca, a pedestrianized street in Pest

floor (*félemelet*) or upper ground floor (*magas földszint*) between the ground (*földszint*) and first floor (*elsőemelet*) proper. So what the British would call the second floor, and Americans the third, Hungarians might describe as the first floor.

POSTAL SERVICES

Postage stamps cost between 70 and 190 Hungarian forints for sending a postcard. Apart from ordinary stamps, all post offices sell various special issues. It costs 270 forints to send an airmail letter, and 250 forints for an airmail postcard. Care should be taken when sending valuable items, as packages often go missing.

On weekdays, most post offices are open from 8am until 6pm, and from 8am to 2pm on Saturday. They are closed on Sunday. The branch at Keleti station is open till

Red post box for national and international mail

9pm on weekdays. If you know the values of the stamps you require, it is easier to buy them from a *trafik* (a tobacconist shop) or a newspaper kiosk, as often there are long queues at post offices. Public fax machines can also be found at most post offices.

International couriers such as **DHL** operate in Budapest, but if you need to courier something within the city, local couriers such as **Hajtas Pajtas Bicycle Messengers** are faster and cheaper.

NEWSPAPERS, MAGAZINES AND LISTINGS

In Budapest all the world's top newspapers and magazines are easily accessible at hotels. A number of the larger newsstands maintain a constant stock of international newspapers and magazines. The largest number of these can be found at the underpasses near Nyugati and Keleti stations. There are also various shops around town which specialize in English-language newspapers, books and maps (*see pp212–13*).

Bear in mind that the foreign daily newspapers on sale tend to be yesterday's editions, but even so they often sell out by lunchtime. For English-speaking visitors there are also quite a few

A kiosk selling newspapers on a Budapest street

magazines, including *Time Out Budapest*, *The Budapest Times*, *Budapest Funzine* and *Where Budapest* (the last two are free). These provide the most comprehensive information on local events and full entertainment guides.

Two useful websites for news and events in the city are www.xpatloop.com and www.caboodle.hu.

TV AND RADIO

The city's larger hotels are geared up for the needs of the international traveller and, in addition to the state and independent Hungarian television channels, most offer tens of satellite TV and radio channels in English and other European languages.

DIRECTORY

MOBILE PHONE OUTLETS

Telenor
Károly körút 3/A.
Map 10 E3.
Tel 464 60 60.

T-Mobile
Petőfi Sándor utca 12.
Map 4 E1.
Tel 266 57 23.

Vodaphone
Váci út 1.
Map 2 F1.
Tel 0670 288 32 88.

INTERNET CAFES

Internet Galéria & Café
VI Szondi utca 79.
Map 5 A5.
Tel 269 00 73.
Open 8am–midnight daily.

Kávészünet Internet Café
XIII Tátra utca 12/b.
Map 2 E3.
Tel 236 08 53.
Open 8am–10pm Mon–Fri, 10am–8pm Sat–Sun.

Siesta Netcafé
VI Izabella utca 85.
Map 7 B1.
Tel 312 32 59.
Open 10am–2am Mon–Fri, noon–2am Sat, noon–midnight Sun.

POST OFFICES

Bajcsy-Zsilinszky út 16
Map 10 E1.
Open 8am–8pm Mon–Fri.

Krisztina körút
Map 3 C1.
Open 7am–8pm Mon–Fri, 7am–2pm Sat.

Teréz körút 51
Map 10 F1.
Open 7am–8pm Mon–Fri, 8am–6pm Sat.

Városház utca 18
Map 10 E4.
Open 8am–8pm Mon–Fri, 8am–2pm Sat.

COURIERS

DHL
Szabadság tér 7.
Map 2 E4. **Tel** 374 07 17.

Hajtas Pajtas Bicycle Messengers
Vörösmarty utca 20.
Map 5 A5. **Tel** 411 03 34.

GETTING TO BUDAPEST

Hungarians like to boast that Budapest is the heart of central Europe – a claim with some justification, as the city acts as a major crossroads linking north to south and west to east. It has excellent rail links with the whole of Europe and its two largest railway stations, Keleti and Nyugati *(see pp234–5)* are conveniently situated in the centre of town. The country's motorway network has undergone improvements, making up for decades of neglect. Budapest can

A plane owned by the Hungarian airline, Malév

now be reached by motorway from all directions but the north. Travelling by car from Slovakia and Poland, via Vác, is not recommended. The poorly maintained, narrow road makes for a very tedious journey. For convenience, it is better to make use of the air links Budapest has with major cities throughout Europe. The journey from London to Budapest, for example, takes just 2 ½ hours. Transfers from the airport by taxi or on public transport are quick and efficient.

ARRIVING BY AIR

Airlines from around 60 towns and cities, in 30 different countries, now fly to Budapest. The city's Ferihegy airport receives flights from major international airlines that include **Air France**, **British Airways**, **Northwest (KLM)**, the Hungarian national carrier **Malév**, and the larger low-cost airlines. Between them, British Airways, Malév and the low-cost airlines operate over a dozen flights daily between Budapest and London's international airports.

In the UK, it is also possible to fly to Budapest from Nottingham/East Midlands, Bristol and Manchester, and there are indirect connections via other European cities,

such as Brussels or Frankfurt, from a large number of cities.

Delta Airlines fly direct from New York, and several airlines fly from the US and Canada via other European cities, including Frankfurt, London and Zurich. Direct flights from New York take around 8 ½ hours. A direct service even operates between Beijing and Budapest.

FERIHEGY AIRPORT

Budapest's international airport terminals, Ferihegy 1, 2A and 2B, are 16–20 km (10–12 miles) from

Malév
stewardess

the city centre. Ferihegy 1, the oldest terminal, has been modernized and now mainly handles low-cost airlines. Terminals 2A and 2B are a 10-minute drive further out from the city centre: Terminal 2A handles arrivals and departures for countries covered by the Schengen Agreement on border controls, while Terminal 2B handles all other flights.

All terminals offer good amenities and services. Catering facilities include bars, cafés and restaurants. There are numerous boutiques and shops, as well as tourist offices and currency exchange facilities. All the major car rental firms, such as Avis and Hertz, have desks in the arrivals halls of all three terminals.

For departing travellers, there are several duty-free shops selling all kinds of international products – not only Hungarian goods.

PACKAGE DEALS AND BARGAINS

Low-cost airlines, such as **Easyjet**, make getting to Budapest much more affordable than in the past. Good deals are available year round, and the further in advance you book, the better chance of a bargain.

Check-in desks at Ferihegy Airport

Promotional offers from British Airways and Malév frequently stipulate that journeys include a Saturday night, and will often include stays at top hotels in the city centre. These kinds of deals are more plentiful during the low season, between September and March.

There are also specialist tour operators, such as Leisure To Taste, which offer reasonably priced, all-inclusive itineraries and special-interest holidays.

If you are booking accom-modation separately from your flights, travel websites such as Expedia (www. expedia.com) advertise some reasonable room rates year round, although there are more bargains in low season.

Malév airlines' logo

Airport shuttle company logo

Airport taxi company logo

GETTING TO THE CENTRE

From Ferihegy Terminal 1 the cheapest and quickest way to get into the city centre is to catch the mainline train to Nyugati railway station. You will need to walk 300 m with your luggage from Terminal 1 to Ferihegy station, but the fare is reasonable at 300 forints. The trains run as often as three times an hour, but

Shuttle buses waiting outside Ferihegy airport

only once an hour between midnight and 6am.

Alternatively, bus No. 200E runs from all three terminals to Kőbánya-Kispest metro station. Tickets cost 320 forints if bought at the Tourinform desk in the term-inals or 400 forints on the bus. From Kőbánya-Kispest station, take the blue M3 metro line into the centre (320 forints).

The airport taxi, **Zóna Taxi**, charges 4,800–5,400 forints, depending on which zone in Budapest you are travelling to. The drive into the centre is usually fairly brisk and a plea-sant introduction to the city.

For around 2,900 forints (4,900 forints return) the Airport Minibus Shuttle takes passengers from all three terminals to any address in the city centre (prices are lower if booked on the Internet). Minibuses have wheelchair access and can pick up returning passengers – they advise calling 24 hours before departure to book.

DIRECTORY

AIRPORT AND AIRLINES

Ferihegy Airport
Tel 296 96 96 (general information).
Tel 296 70 00 (flight information).

Air France
Tel 483 88 00.
www.airfrance.com

British Airways
Tel 777 47 47.
www.britishairways.com

Easyjet
www.easyjet.com

Malév Airlines
Tel 235 32 22.
www.malev.com

Northwest (KLM)
Tel 373 77 37.
www.klm.com

TOUR OPERATOR

Leisure To Taste
Ribáry utca 1, 1022 Budapest.
Tel 0800 686 0619 (UK);
+36 1 336 1917 (Hungary).
www.leisuretotaste.com

AIRPORT MINIBUS

Airport Minibus Shuttle
Tel 296 85 55.
www.airportshuttle.hu
(Phone booking 6am–10pm daily.)

AIRPORT TAXI

Zóna Taxi
Tel 365 55 55.

A Malév aircraft parked outside Ferihegy 2

Ticket offices at Nyugati Railway Station in Budapest

TRAVELLING BY RAIL

Budapest has direct rail links with 25 other capital cities. Every day, more than 50 international trains, many of them express services, arrive and depart from the city's three railway stations. The modern Hungarian trains used on the mainline services are generally considered to be an efficient means of transport, although some international services suffer occasional delays.

Trains from Budapest to Vienna, the main communication hub for western Europe, depart approximately every hour or two from Keleti station. The fastest trains run at top speeds of 140–160 km/h (85–100 mph). The travelling time is an efficient 2 hours 50 minutes.

Detailed information on all domestic and international rail services running to and from Budapest can be obtained from either Keleti station or on the **MÁV** (Hungarian Railways) website.

It is worth knowing that there are several concessionary fares available. Foreign visitors to Hungary can buy a season ticket that is valid for between seven and ten days and offers unlimited travel throughout the country. There are also a number of Europe-wide passes that allow you to travel cheaply on trains in Hungary.

Local trains (*személyvonat*) are slow and make frequent stops. The best option if time is tight is to take modern Intercity trains, which go to Pécs, Miskolc, Debrecen, Szeged and all the larger cities in Hungary in around 1–3 hours. Seat reservations required on these trains.

Reserve in advance and expect to pay a small fee.

RAILWAY STATIONS

There are three main railway stations in Budapest – Keleti (East), Nyugati (West) and Déli (South) – which take their names from the direction the trains serve (*see p235*).

The Hungarian for station is *pályaudvar*, often shortened in writing to *pu*. Most international trains run from Keleti station. Some trains to Vienna and one of the express trains to Croatia ("Maestral") leave from Déli station, as do trains to the Lake Balaton resorts, which go almost hourly in high season. Both Keleti pu and Déli pu are on the red M2 metro. For Nyugati pu take the blue M3 metro line, or trams 4 or 6.

TRAVELLING BY BOAT

Between April and October hydrofoils cruise the Danube from Vienna to Budapest, via Bratislava. It is also possible to take a hydrofoil or pleasure boat along to the Danube bend, to towns such as Esztergom and Visegrád (*see pp164–5*). See the

timetable at the departure point at Vigadó tér for details, or contact cruise companies such as **AMA Waterways**, **Legenda** or **Mahart Passnave**.

TRAVELLING BY CAR

Eight main roads lead out of Budapest, four of them motorways, which are marked "M". The M1 stretches from Budapest to the Hegyeshalom border crossing, where it joins the Austrian motorway network. The M3 links Budapest with Miskolc and Nyiregyháza to the northeast, the M5 leads south to Kecskemét (*see p166*) and Szeged, and the M7 links to the Balaton resorts. The M0 is being built as a ring motorway around Budapest, with only the west section still to be done. Drivers must purchase an electronic motorway sticker for all motorways except the M0; these can be bought at petrol stations near or on the motorway.

Traffic regulations include driving with the headlights on, day and night. All car occupants, in the front and back seats, are required by law to wear seat belts. Motorcycle drivers and passengers must wear helmets at all times.

The speed limits are 50 km/h (30 mph) in built-up areas, 90 km/h (60 mph) outside built-up areas, 110 km/h (68 mph) on main roads and 130 km/h (80 mph) on motorways.

In Hungary it is strictly forbidden to drive following any alcohol consumption. If any trace of alcohol is found in the bloodstream, the fine for drink-driving can be as high as 50,000 Hungarian

The imposing exterior of the Nyugati Railway Station

A luxury air-conditioned tourist coach

forints (approximately US $220) and is only payable in forints.

Visitors coming to Budapest by car are obliged to have the green insurance card, while those hiring a car need only present their driving licences. Hitchhiking, while not against the law, is not recommended.

Regulations permit the use of mobile phones by drivers only when the car is fitted with a hands-free system. Otherwise, it is advisable to pull over and stop if you wish to make or receive a call.

TRAVELLING BY COACH

Budapest's international coach station, Népliget (Üllői út 131) lies 5 km (3 miles)

southeast of the centre, and is on the blue M3 metro line.

There are three national coach stations: Népliget (with buses to western Hungary), Stadionok (to eastern Hungary) and Árpád Bridge (to northern Hungary and the Danube bend). Stadionok station can be reached by the M2 metro line, while Árpád Bridge is served by the M3 line. International routes are served by luxury coaches, which have all the usual facilities such as air-conditioning and toilets. The domestic and main international traffic is served by Volánbusz coaches (Eurolines), which operate on routes to the major towns in Hungary.

DIRECTORY

RAIL INFORMATION

MÁV (Hungarian Railways)
Tel 06 (40) 49 49 49 (domestic);
+ 36 (1) 444 44 99 (international).
www.mav-start.hu

CRUISE COMPANIES

AMA Waterways
Tel +44 (0) 808 223 5009 (UK).
www.amawaterways.co.uk
800 626 0126 (US toll free).
www.amawaterways.com

Legenda
Tel 317 22 03.
www.legenda.hu

Mahart Passnave
Tel 484 40 13.
www.mahartpassnave.hu

TRAVELLING BY CAR

Motorway Information
Tel 345 27 77.
www.motorway.hu

Vehicle Assistance
Tel 188 (for breakdowns).

COACH INFORMATION

Tel 382 08 88 or 219 80 86
(English not always spoken).

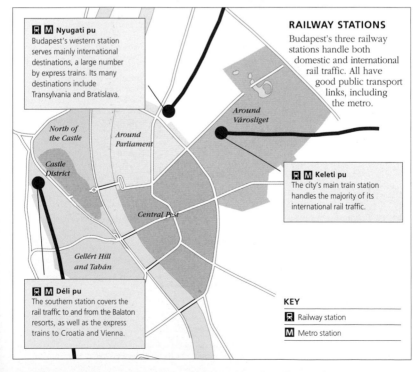

Nyugati pu
Budapest's western station serves mainly international destinations, a large number by express trains. Its many destinations include Transylvania and Bratislava.

North of the Castle

Around Parliament

Around Városliget

Castle District

Central Pest

Gellért Hill and Tabán

Keleti pu
The city's main train station handles the majority of its international rail traffic.

Déli pu
The southern station covers the rail traffic to and from the Balaton resorts, as well as the express trains to Croatia and Vienna.

RAILWAY STATIONS

Budapest's three railway stations handle both domestic and international rail traffic. All have good public transport links, including the metro.

KEY

🚉 Railway station

Ⓜ Metro station

GETTING AROUND BUDAPEST

Budapest is a sprawling city with many suburban districts. However, most of its main tourist attractions are centrally located and can be easily reached by the city's public transport system, or on foot. The many choices of transport by rail, road and even water provide visitors to Budapest with ample opportunity to travel through and around the city to reach their chosen destinations.

One of Budapest's buses

The infrastructure of Budapest is chiefly determined by the *körúts* (ring roads) and the boulevards that radiate out from the city centre and into the city's suburbs. The metro system mainly operates in Pest, while efficient tram and bus networks are easy to use and extend to all parts of the city. The overland HÉV train provides a service from the city centre to the suburbs.

GREEN TRAVEL

Budapest has long suffered from air pollution, and the proliferation of cars has made the problem worse. Moreover, the difficulties of parking in the city make it highly advisable to leave your car outside the centre.

A much better option is to use the excellent public transport system, which covers the whole city very well. The preservation of trolley buses and the extension of the tram network *(see pp240–41)* is good news for environmentalists. An increase in the number of cycle routes has also resulted in the growing use of bicycles in Budapest.

PUBLIC TRANSPORT IN BUDAPEST

Budapest has an excellent public transport system, which makes it easy to get around the city. Run by the **BKV** (Budapest Transport Company), it covers the metro,

Pedestrian zone

Pedestrian crossing

trams, buses, trolley buses, cog-wheel railway and suburban HÉV lines up to the city boundaries *(see pp238–41)*. Daytime services run from about 4:30am to 11pm, with a good range of night buses operating across the city every 15–60 minutes. Timetables for buses, trams and trolley buses are displayed at each stop. It is worth knowing that *az utolsó indul* means "the last service leaves at".

BUDAPEST ON FOOT

Budapest is a city in which every pedestrian will find something of interest. Those who like to stroll through picturesque alleyways should make a point of visiting the cobbled streets of Buda's Castle District. Another option might be to wander around the backstreets of central Pest. Here, there are plenty of opportunities to peer into historic courtyards and admire the wrought-iron balconies and exterior decorative details of Secession apartment blocks *(see pp54–7)*. Váci utca *(see p127)* is fully pedestrianized and has seats

Walk signal at a pedestrian crossing

V. Kerület, Lipótváros
Báthori utca
2 —— 2

New street name plate

OKTÓBER 6. UTCA

Old street name plate

Pedestrians beside the Danube

where weary walkers can rest and watch the bustle.
The promenade along the Danube is also a pleasant place to walk in Budapest. Visitors who enjoy rambling along leafy trails should take the railway or bus Nos 90 or 90A from Moszkva tér to the Buda Hills *(see p161)*.

When walking in the city it is worth remembering that you need to keep an eye on the traffic. Drivers in Budapest expect pedestrians to get out of their way – they will often swerve around you rather than stop if you venture onto a zebra crossing.

DRIVING IN BUDAPEST

The large number of one-way streets in Budapest makes it a very difficult city for visitors to navigate by car. The many changes of direction often result in drivers unfamiliar with the city becoming lost. Any confusion brought about by the complex system of roads is further aggravated by the heavy rush-hour traffic. There are also few places to park in the city, so it is much better to sightsee on foot or by public transport. Most road signs follow the European pattern, and people drive on the right-hand side of the road. In towns the use of the horn is legally restricted to cases of imminent danger. Despite this, Hungarian drivers often hoot at both pedestrians and other drivers.

HIRING A CAR

Cars can be hired from the airport on arrival in Budapest, or from one of several car hire offices in the city, such as **Avis**, **Budget Hungary**, **Europcar** or **Hertz**. Be prepared to leave a credit card deposit ranging between 100,000 forints and 800,000 forints, and to pay US$100–240 per day for unlimited mileage.

PARKING

There are several multi-storey car parks in the city centre, including at Nos. 4–6 Aranykéz utca, No. 20 Nyár utca, and Szervita tér. There are underground car parks at Szabadság tér and Sas utca. A lot of the larger hotels also have an underground garage. There are attended and unattended car parks situated in other busy parts of the city as well. In addition, hotels with car parks may offer spare parking spaces to non-guests, all of which helps to ease the problem of on-street parking.

When parking on the street, you must get a ticket from the nearest ticket machine to display in the car, specifying how long you will stay. Parking charges vary from 150 to 600 Hungarian forints per hour. Parking without a valid ticket or overstaying the allocated time can lead to either a parking fine or wheel-clamping.

Parking at the main tourist attractions, for example, near Hősök

Stopping and parking prohibited

Parking of cars allowed in this zone for a maximum of 2 hours

tere (Heroes' Square, *see pp142–3*) or the Citadel (*see pp92–3*), is free for the duration of the visit. Note that these car parks are only for the use of people visiting the particular sight. Cars parked improperly may be clamped or towed away to a car park outside the centre. Fines of up to 30,000 forints can also be imposed for parking offences.

CLAMPING AND TOWING

Wheel-clamping is growing in Budapest; all illegally parked vehicles are subject to clamping. As well as paying a fine, it costs around 7,000 forints (US $32) to release a car from a clamp, and around 9,300 forints (US $42) if a car has been towed away – usually to a car park outside the city. Parking meters often display the telephone number to contact in the event of wheel-clamping. It is also worth asking a car park attendant for advice. If the car has been towed away, call the Removed Cars Information line (tel 383 07 00) to find out where it has been taken.

CYCLING

Cycling in Budapest is often difficult and fairly dangerous. Cyclists have to be careful of the tram rails and the uneven, cobble-stoned surfaces of some roads. The poor air quality is an additional disadvantage. Budapest's

Using one of Budapest's cycle routes

main roads are closed to cyclists, and designated cycle lanes continue to be in short supply. However, the provision of other cycle routes in Budapest has made cycling an increasingly popular pastime. Bike-hire shops such as **Bikebase**, **Budapest Bike** and **Yellow Zebra** are also a good source of information about bicycle routes in the city.

An enjoyable way to spend time in Budapest is to take a cycling trip around Margaret Island (*see pp172–3*). There are several bike-hire stalls on the island, and they also rent out children's bikes, thus enabling family groups to explore the paths. The Danube riverbank also has dedicated cycle lanes.

DIRECTORY

PUBLIC TRANSPORT

BKV (Budapest Transport Company)
Akácfa utca 18. **Map** 7 A2.
Tel 258 46 36.
www.bkv.hu

CAR HIRE

Avis
Szervita tér 8. **Map** 10 D4.
Tel 318 42 40. www.avis.com

Budget Hungary
Hotel Mercure Buda, Krisztina körút 41–43. **Map** 3 C1.
Tel 214 04 20.
www.budget.hu

Europcar
Erzsébet tér 9-10. **Tel** 505 44 00.
www.europcar.hu

Hertz
Váci utca 19-21. **Tel** 296 09 99.
www.hertz.hu

BIKE HIRE

Bikebase
Podmaniczky utca 19 (moves to No.15 in winter). **Tel** 269 59 83.
www.bikebase.hu

Budapest Bike
Szóda bar, Wesselényi utca 18.
Tel 944 55 33.
www.budapestbike.hu

Yellow Zebra
Sütő utca 2. **Tel** 266 87 77.
www.yellowzebrabikes.com

Getting Around by Metro

Budapest has three metro lines *(see inside back cover)*, most easily distinguished by their colours: yellow, red and blue. The three lines intersect at Deák tér station, where passengers can change trains (stamping a new ticket for travelling on the new line), by following the clearly marked passageways. A fourth metro line, linking Kelenföldi station in the southwest of the city and Bosnyák tér in the northeast, is under construction. The oldest line, the yellow M1 line, runs just beneath the surface of the city. Built in 1894, it is known as the Millennium Line after the celebrations that took place two years later *(see p142)*, but its more common name is the *Földalatti* (Underground). Two more lines – the red M2 and blue M3 lines – were added after 1970.

Single ticket for all public transport

One-day travel card valid for all forms of public transport

One-week travel card valid for all forms of public transport

Signs for the M2 and M3 lines

THE METRO SYSTEM

A journey on the Millennium Line (M1) is an event in itself, with some beautifully tiled late-19th century stations.

Three words to remember when using the metro system are: *bejárat*, meaning entrance; *kijárat*, meaning exit (both are always clearly marked); and *felé*, meaning towards (the direction of trains is indicated by the name of the station at the end of the line). Remember to validate your ticket. Validation machines are located at the station entrances.

To plan a journey, consult the map at the back of this guide. Note that the M1, M2 and M3 lines only intersect at Deák Ferenc tér station. Most metro stations display maps of the local area. A recorded voice message announces

when the door is closing and gives the name of the next station. Smoking and eating are not permitted on the trains, and you must use head-phones to listen to music. Dogs are allowed to travel on the metro, but only when muzzled.

Sign over the entrance to the M1 metro line at Oktogen tér station

TICKETS

The same types of ticket and pass cover all forms of BKV transport. Single tickets must be validated in a machine at the start of your journey: on the metro they must be validated at the station before boarding; on buses, trams, trolley buses and the cog-wheel railway they must be validated on board.

Tickets are checked frequently, and there is a fine of 6,000 forints to be paid on the spot for travelling without a valid ticket. If you change metro lines or get on a new bus or tram you must validate a new ticket.

Tickets *(jegy)* can be pur-chased separately or, more economically, in booklets of 10 for 2,800 forints. Individual tickets cost 320 forints if you buy them in advance at metro stations, tobacconist shops

(trafiks) and newspaper kiosks; on night buses and certain daytime buses (such as the 200E running from the airport) you can buy tickets on board for 400 forints *(see p241)*. You can also buy transfer tickets *(Átszállójegy)* costing 490 forints, which are valid for two immediately consecutive journeys on any form of BKV transport. On the metro you can also get cheaper tickets for metro journeys of three stops *(Metrószakaszjegy)*, with no transfers.

TRAVELCARDS AND SEASON TICKETS

Travelcards are available for 24 hours, 72 hours or one week. Season tickets for 14 or 30 days, or an entire year, are also available. There are discounts for students, seniors, the disabled and parents with small children, but these only apply for periods of at least two weeks. Make sure you bring photographic ID with you when buying your pass, which can be purchased on the spot. The Budapest Card *(see p222)* entitles the holder to free city transport, as well as a range of discounts at some museums and restaurants, for periods of two or three days.

A typical station on the original M1 metro line

Travelling on the HÉV

The suburban railway logo

The overland HÉV railway is an essential means of transport connecting Budapest with its suburban districts. It carries residents to and from work and tourists to attractions located 20–30 km (12–20 miles) away from the city centre. The standard tickets used on other forms of transport (see p238) can be used to travel to central destinations and other places within the city limits, such as the Roman town of Aquincum, but additional fares are payable for more distant destinations. Tickets can be bought either at the station before travelling or from the conductor on the train.

A standard HÉV train carriage

SUBURBAN RAIL LINES

The HÉV line most commonly used by tourists runs north from Batthyány tér (see p100) towards Szentendre (see p165), taking in such sights as Aquincum (see pp162–3) along the way. Many of the trains on this line terminate at Békásmegyer rather than running on to Szentendre. You should check the destination on the front of the train before boarding.

Another line runs from Örs vezér tere (at the eastern terminus of the M2 metro line) to Gödöllő, passing the Hungaroring Grand Prix race track (see p59) near Mogyoród en route. Gödöllő, a small

Baroque town, was once the summer residence of the Habsburgs and has a beautifully restored Baroque palace, the Grassalkovich Mansion (see p166).

A third HÉV line begins at Közvágóhíd and terminates at Ráckeve (see p167). Tourists who make this long journey can enjoy a visit to the palace of Prince Eugene of Savoy.

The fourth HÉV service between Boráros tér and Csepel Island is the longest, extending approximately 50 km (30 miles).

HÉV trains run regularly between 4am and 11.30pm. BKV tickets are valid up to the city boundary; a supplementary ticket is required to go further.

OTHER TOWN TRANSPORT

Several modes of transport operate in the Buda Hills west of the city (see p161). A cog-wheel railway connects Szilágyi Erszébet fasor with Széchenyi Hill, with its picturesque walking trails – BKV tickets and passes are valid right along the line.

The Children's Railway runs from Széchenyi Hill to the Hűvös Valley (see p11). A chair lift, or libegő, descends from the top of János Hill down on to Zugligeti út.

In the centre of the city the Budavári Sikló is an old funicular railway which runs between the Buda end of the Chain Bridge and the top of Castle Hill.

Buy tickets for all three modes of transport at the ticket offices before boarding.

Getting Around by Taxi

Taxi sign

It has always been easy to find a taxi in Budapest, and now, with over 15,000 registered cabs, the competition for passengers is fierce. Nevertheless, not all taxi drivers read the meter correctly and they have been known to exploit foreign visitors, especially those unfamiliar with Budapest who are travelling to the city centre from airports or railway stations. To reduce this risk, choose a taxi whose tariffs and meter are clearly displayed.

A busy taxi rank

USING TAXIS

Taxi ranks can be found throughout Budapest and are seldom empty. Taxis can also be hailed on the street but to avoid problems it is often better to book one from your hotel or by phone. All of the companies listed in the Directory are likely to have

English-speaking operators on duty. The total fare you will be asked to pay is made up of three parts; a basic charge, a per-kilometre charge, and a waiting charge. On getting into the taxi, ensure that the meter is set at the beginning of the journey and ask for an estimate of what the fare will be.

DIRECTORY

TAXI COMPANIES

Budapest Taxi *Tel* 433 33 33.

Budataxi *Tel* 233 33 33.

City Taxi *Tel* 211 11 11.

www.citytaxi.hu

Fötaxi *Tel* 222 22 22.

Rádiótaxi *Tel* 777 77 77.

www.radiotaxi.hu

Taxi 2000 *Tel* 200 00 00.

Getting Around by Tram

There are more than 30 tram lines in Budapest, which extend to practically every part of the city except the hilly parts of Buda. Trams are yellow in colour and are a good way of travelling for sightseeing in the centre. They are easy to use and an efficient and speedy means of getting around Budapest, as they avoid traffic and run very frequently. Services start early in the morning, from about 4:30am, and run regularly throughout the day until 11pm or midnight, depending on the route. Night trams operate only on certain routes, at an average of four trams per route. Timetables are displayed at each stop.

One of the city's yellow trams, on route No. 2

THE TRAM SYSTEM

Tickets *(see p238)* for trams can be bought at metro stations, tobacconist shops *(trafiks)* and some newspaper kiosks. You can also get them from vending machines on some tram platforms. Validate your ticket in the machine inside the tram.

When a tram line is closed for maintenance, replacement buses *(potlóbusz)* are provided. These display the tram number, preceded by the letter "V".

TRAVELLING WITH LUGGAGE

Every passenger on all forms of public transport is entitled to carry two small pieces of luggage. You can also carry one pair of ice skates and one pair of skis, providing they are clean, as well as a child's buggy. For transporting a bicycle or a larger item of luggage, the rack railway or the designated carriages of the HÉV trains should be used.

TRAM STOP

Every tram stop displays the relevant tram numbers and the timetable.

Tram stop symbol

Name of the stop

Destination

Timetable

Map of the route

USEFUL BUS AND TRAM ROUTES

This map shows the best bus and tram routes for sightseeing in Budapest. The locations of major sights are marked, as well as the nearest useful stop. Sights should then only be a short walk away.

KEY

- ■ Major sight
- ▬ Tram No. 2
- ▬ Tram No. 4
- ▬ Tram No. 6
- ▬ Tram No. 49
- ▬ Tram No. 61
- ▬ Bus No. 16
- O Stop *(selected stops only)*

Getting Around by Bus

Budapest has about 200 different bus routes, covering the whole city. They are a recommended mode of transport for visitors, except during rush hour. Daytime services run from about 4:30am to 11pm, with departures on most routes every 10–20 minutes. There is a good range of night buses operating across the city every 15–60 minutes. Departure times and a list of destinations are on display at each stop. All buses are blue – ordinary buses are indicated by black numbers and halt at every stop. Buses with red numbers follow express routes and omit a number of stops.

BUS STOP

The layout of information at bus stops is very similar to that at tram and trolley bus stops.

- Bus stop symbol
- Name of the stop
- Destination
- Timetable

THE BUS SYSTEM

Budapest's bus system is extremely efficient and makes exploring the city easy, even for first-time visitors. Tickets must be punched upon entering the bus. The driver – or the dot matrix display on newer buses – always announces the next stop, often informing passengers about any interchanges. To ensure that the bus stops, you should press the button located by the door before your required stop. Remember that Budapest's bus drivers tend to drive fast and that the streets, particularly in Buda, can be steep. This combination makes it advisable to hang on tightly to the hand grips when standing on a bus.

It is worth noting that buses sometimes get caught in heavy traffic congestion in the

One of Budapest's modern buses

centre of the city during rush hours, and their progress at these times can be slow. If you are in a hurry it might be better to take a tram or the metro, or even to walk.

Getting Around by Trolley Bus

Trolley buses, which are red, operate only in Pest. They mainly serve the suburbs, so are used less often by tourists. It is advisable to hold on tight if you are standing, as they can accelerate very suddenly. Timetables are displayed at each stop.

THE TROLLEY BUS SYSTEM

The same rules apply for travelling on a trolley bus as when travelling on a bus. Remember to signal to the driver by pressing the button located above the door when approaching your stop.

Otherwise, if there are no passengers waiting at the stop, the driver will not automatically come to a halt.

Trolley buses are numbered from 70 upwards and there are about 15 different routes in Budapest. Tickets must be punched upon boarding. A particularly pleasant and useful route is taken by trolley bus No. 70, which runs from Parliament on Kossuth Lajos tér, past the City Park to Erzsébet királyné útja.

TICKET VENDING MACHINE

Tickets are sold at tobacconist shops (trafiks), metro stations and the vending machines at major transport junctions and HÉV railway stations (though these are often out of order).

- Insert 5, 10, 20, 50 or 100 HUF coins
- Press button to receive ticket
- Check the amount paid
- Collect the ticket and change

A red trolley bus in Budapest

STREET FINDER

The map references for all the sights, hotels, bars, restaurants, shops and entertainment venues described in this book refer to the maps in this section. A complete index of street names marked on the maps appears on pages 254–6. The map below shows the area of Budapest covered by the *Street Finder* and is colour-coded by area. The *Street Finder* also includes bus and tram routes, major sights and places of interest together with other useful information listed in the key below. As an aid to navigation, all street names, both on the *Street Finder* and in the index, are in Hungarian. Slightly confusing are the terms *utca* (often abbreviated to *u*), which means street, and út meaning avenue, a term mainly applied to wide, busy roads. Other commonly used terms are *körút* (ring road), *tér* (square), *köz* (lane), *körtér* (circus) and *hid* (bridge).

KEY TO STREET FINDER

- Major sight
- Place of interest
- Other building
- **M** Metro station
- HÉV station
- Train station
- River boat boarding point
- Main bus stop
- Tram route
- **P** Car park
- Tourist information point
- Hospital with casualty unit
- Police station
- Church
- Synagogue
- ⊠ Post office
- Railway line
- Pedestrianized street

SCALE OF MAPS 1–8:
0 metres 200
0 yards 200
1:12,000

SCALE OF MAPS 9–10:
0 metres 200
0 yards 200
1:10,500

House in the leafy Tabán district *(see p94)*

Deák Ferenc tér *(see p121)*, named after politician Ferenc Deák and home to the city's first ever public toilet

Flag-lined avenue in the Castle District *(see pp 78–9)*

0 kilometres 2

0 miles 1

Statue of King Ludwig I, part of the colossal Millennium Monument on Heroes' Square *(see p145)*, which was completed in 1929

Street Finder Index

A

Aba utca 5 B2
Abonyi utca 6 E5, 8 E1
Ady Endre utca 1 A1
Aga utca 3 A5
Ajtósi Dürer sor 6 E5
Akácfa utca 7 A2
Akadémia utca 2 D4 (9 C2)
Aladár utca 3 B2
Alagút utca 1 B5 (9 A3)
Alföldi utca 8 D3
Alkotás utca 1 A5, 3 A2
Alkotmány utca 2 E3
(10 D1)
Almássy tér 7 B2
Almássy utca 7 B2
Alpár utca 8 D1
Alsó utca 7 C2
Alsóhegy utca 3 A4
Ambrus utca 6 D1
Amerikai út 6 F2
Andrássy út 2 F4
5 A5, 7 A1 (10 E2)
Angyalföldi út 5 A2
Anker köz 2 F5 (10 E3)
Antal utca 3 C2
Apáczai utca 2 D5, 4 E2
(9 C3)
Apály utca 5 A1
Apostol utca 1 B1
Arany János utca 2 D4
(9 C2) (10 D2)
Aranykéz utca
4 E1 (10 D4)
Asbóth utca 2 F5 (10 E3)
Attila út 1 A4, 3 C1
(9 A4) (10 D3)
Aulich utca 2 E3 (10 D1)
Auróra utca 7 C1
Avar utca 3 A2
Avar út 3 A1

Á

Ábel Jenő utca 3 B4
Ág utca 3 A1
Áldás utca 1 A1
Állatkerti körút 6 D3
Állatkerti út 5 C3
Árpád fejedelem útja 1 C1

B

Babits Mihály sétany 1 B4
Bacsó Béla utca 7 B3
Badacsonyi utca 3 B5
Bajcsy-Zsilinszky út 2 E4
(10 E1)
Bajmóci utca 3 A4
Bajnok utca 5 A4
Bajza utca 5 B4
Bakator utca 3 B3
Balassa utca 8 D5
Balassi Bálint utca 2 D2
Balaton utca 2 D2
Balogh Tihamér lejtő 3 C4
Balogh Tihamér utca 3 C4
Balzac utca 2 E1
Bán utca 3 A2
Bank utca 2 E4 (10 D2)
Barát utca 7 B2
Barcsay utca 7 B2
Bárczy István utca 2 E5
4 E1 (10 D4)

Baross utca 7 A4 (10 F5)
Barsi utca 1 A1
Bartók Béla út 4 E4
Bástya utca 4 F2
Báthory utca 2 E3
(10 D1)
Batthyány tér 1 C3 (9 B1)
Batthyány utca 1 A3 (9 A1)
Bécsi kapu tér 1 B4
Bécsi utca 2 E5 (10 D3)
Békési utca 7 B4
Belgrád rakpart 2 D5
4 E1 (10 D4)
Bem J. utca 1 C2
Benczúr utca 5 B5
Beniczky L. utca 7 C5
Bérc utca 3 C3
Bercsényi utca 4 E5
Berényi utca 3 B2
Bérkocsis utca 7 B3
Bertalan Lajos utca 4 E4
Berzsenyi utca 7 C2
Bethesda utca 6 E3
Bethlen Gábor tér 7 C1
Bethlen Gábor utca 7 C1
Bezerédi utca 7 B3
Bicskei utca 4 E5
Bihari János utca 2 E3
Bimbó utca 1 A2
Blaha Lujza tér 7 B3
Bocskai út 3 C5
Bókay János utca 7 C5
Bólyai utca 1 A1
Botond utca 5 A2
Bródy Sándor utca 7 A4
(10 F5)
Budafoki út 4 E4
Budai Nagy
Antal utca 2 D1
Budaörsi út 3 A4
Buday László utca 1 B2
Bugát utca 1 A4
Bulcsú utca 5 A3

C

Cházár András utca 6 E5
8 E1
Citadella sétany 4 D3
Clark Ádám tér 1 C5 (9 B3)
Corvin tér 1 C4 (9 A2)
Csalogány utca 1 A3
Csanády utca 2 F1
Csángó utca 5 A1
Csányi utca 7 A2
Csarnok tér 4 F3
Csata utca 5 C1
Csengery utca 2 F2
5 A5, 7 A1
Csepreghy utca 7 B5
Cserhát utca 8 D1
Csetneki utca 3 B4
Csobánc utca 8 E5
Csokonai utca 7 B3
Csörsz utca 3 A2
Csukló utca 3 A3
Cukor utca 4 F2 (10 E5)
Czakó utca 3 B2 (9 A5)
Czuczor utca 7 A5

D

Dalszínház utca 2 F4 (10 E2)
Damjanich utca 5 C5, 7 C1

Dankó utca 8 D4
Dárda utca 1 B4
Daróci út 3 B5
Dávid Ferenc utca 3 B5
Deák Ferenc utca 4 E1
(10 D4)
Deák tér 2 E5 (10 D3)
Delej utca 8 F5
Délibáb utca 5 C4
Dembinszky utca 6 D5
7 C1
Derék utca 3 B2 (9 A5)
Déri Miksa utca 7 C4
Dessewffy utca 2 F4
(10 E1)
Dévai utca 5 A2
Dévényi út 6 D2
Dezső utca 3 B1 (9 A5)
Dinnye utca 3 B5
Diószeghy
Sámuel utca 8 E5
Dioszegi út 3 B4
Dob utca 2 F5, 7 A2
(10 F3)
Dobozi utca 8 D4
Döbrentei tér 4 D2 (9 C5)
Döbrentei utca 4 D1
(9 C4)
Dohány utca 7 A3 (10 F4)
Dologház utca 8 D3
Donáti utca 1 B4 (9 A1)
Dorottya utca 2 E5
Dorozsmai köz 6 F2
Dorozsmai út 6 F2
Dózsa György út 5 C4
8 E1
Dózsa tér 3 C1 (9 A4)
Dugonics utca 8 E5
Duna utca 4 E2 (10 D5)

E

Edison köz 6 F3
Edömér utca 3 C5
Egry József utca 4 F5
Egyetem tér 4 F2 (10 E5)
Elek utca 3 B4
Eötvös tér 2 D5 (9 C3)
Eötvös utca 2 F3
5 A5, 7 A1
Erdélyi utca 8 D4
Erkel utca 4 F3, 7 A5
Erőd utca 1 B2
Erzsébet királyné útja 6 E3
Erzsébet körút 7 A2
Erzsébet tér 2 E5 (10 D3)
Eszék utca 4 D5
Eszter utca 1 A1

F

Fadrusz utca 4 D5
Falk Miksa utca 2 D2
Farkas Bíró utca 1 C5
(9 B2)
Fazekas utca 1 B3
Fecske utca 7 C3
Fehér Hajó utca 4 E1
(10 D4)
Fehérló utca 3 A4
Fehérvári út. 4 D5
Fejér G. utca 4 F2 (10 E5)
Fekete Sas utca 1 C2
Felka utca 2 E1

Felső erdősor 5 B5
Fém utca 3 B1 (9 A4)
Fény utca 1 A3
Fényes E. utca 1 B2
Fenyő utca 3 B1
Ferdinánd híd 2 F1, 5 A4
Ferenciek tere 4 F1
(10 E4)
Ferenczy I. utca 4 F1
(10 E5)
Feszty Á. utca 1 A5
Fiáth János utca 1 A3
Fiumei út. 8 D2
Fő utca 1 C5 (9 B3)
Fortuna köz 1 B4
Fortuna utca 1 B4
Fővám tér 4 F3
Francia út 6 F3
Frankel Leó utca 1 B1
Franklin utca 1 B4 (9 A1)
Füge utca 1 A1
Futó utca 7 C5
Füvészkert utca 8 D5

G

Galamb utca 4 E1 (10 D4)
Galeotti utca 3 B2 (9 A5)
Ganz utca 1 C2
Garay utca 8 D1
Garibaldi utca 2 D4 (9 C1)
Gázláng utca 8 D3
Gellérthegy utca 3 B1
(9 A4)
Gergely G. utca 2 E1
Gerlóczy utca 4 F1
(10 E4)
Gidófalvy L. utca 5 B1
Gimnázium utca 1 B4
(9 A1)
Gizella út 6 F5
Goldman György tér 4 F5
Golgota tér 8 F5
Golgota út 8 F5
Gömb utca 5 C1
Gombocz
Zoltán utca 3 B3
Gönczy utca 4 F3
Groza Péter rkp. 1 C5
4 D1 (9 B4)
Gül Baba utca 1 B1
Gutenberg tér 7 B3
Gyarmat utca 6 F4
Gyöngyház utca 2 F1
György utca 8 D2
Győri utca 3 A1
Györök utca 3 B5
Gyorskocsi utca 1 C3
Győző utca 3 A1
Gyula utca 2 E1, 3 B3
Gyulai Pál utca 7 A3

H

Hajós utca 2 F4
Halász utca 1 C4 (9 B2)
Haris köz 4 E1 (10 D4)
Harkos utca 3 A5
Harmincad utca 2 E5
(10 D3)
Hársfa utca 7 A1
Hattyú utca 1 A3
Havas utca 4 F2
Hegedű utca 7 A1

Hegyalja út 3 B2 (9 B5)
Henger utca 1 C2
Henszlmann utca 4 F2 (10 E5)
Hercegprímás 2 E4 (10 D2)
Hermina út 6 F4
Hernád utca 5 C5, 8 B1
Hevesi S. tér 7 B1
Himfy utca 4 D4
Hock J. utca 7 C5
Högyes E. utca 7 B1
Hold utca 2 E3 (10 D1)
Holdvilág utca 3 A4
Hollán Ernö utca 2 E3
Holló utca 2 F5 (10 F3)
Hollókö utca 3 B5
Homok utca 7 C3
Honvéd tér 2 E2
Honvéd utca 2 E3 (10 D1)
Horánszky utca 7 B4
Horvát Boldizsár utca 6 F2
Horvát utca 1 B2
Horváth Mihály tér 7 C4
Hösök tere 5 C4
Huba utca 5 A1
Hufalvy utca 1 B3
Hun utca 5 B1
Hungária körút 6 F4
Hunyadi János út 1 B4 (9 A2)
Hunyadi tér 7 A1
Huszár utca 7 C2
Hutyra F. utca 7 C1

I

Ibrahim utca 3 A5
Ida utca 6 F4
Iglói utca 3 C3
Ilka utca 6 F4
Illés utca 8 D5
Illés köz 8 D5
Imre utca 4 F3
Irányi utca 4 E2 (10 D5)
Irinyi József utca 4 F5
Iskola utca 1 C3 (9 A1)
István út 7 C1
Istvánmezei út 8 E1
Izabella utca 5 A5, 7 B1
Izsó utca 6 E5

J

Jász utca 6 D1
Jászóvár utca 3 A5
Jávor utca 6 F5
Jázmin utca 8 D5
Jégverem utca 1 C5 (9 B3)
Jobbágy utca 8 E1
Jókai tér 2 F3, 7 A1 (10 F1)
Jókai utca 2 F3 (10 F1)
Jósika utca 7 B1
József Attila utca 2 E5
József körút 7 B3
József Nádor tér 2 E5 (10 D3)
József utca 7 B4
Jurányi utca 1 B2

K

Kacsa utca 1 C2

Kadar utca 2 E2
Kagyló utca 1 B3 (9 A1)
Káldy Gyula utca 2 F5 (10 E2)
Kálmán Imre utca 2 E3
Kálvária tér 8 D5
Kálvária utca 8 E5
Kálvin tér 7 A4 (10 F5)
Kapás utca 1 B2
Kapisztrán tér 1 A4
Karácsony Sándor utca 8 D4
Kard utca 1 B4
Karinthy Frigyes út 4 E5
Kármán utca 2 f3
Karolina út 3 B4
Károly körút 2 F5, 4 F1 (10 E3)
Károlyi M. utca 4 F2 (10 E5)
Kartács utca 5 C1
Kassai tér 6 F2
Kassák Lajos utca 5 A2
Kászony utca 3 A5
Katona József utca 2 E1
Kazinczy utca 2 F5, 7 A3 (10 F3)
Kecskeméti utca 4 F2 (10 F5)
Kelenhegyi út 3 C3
Keleti Károly utca 1 A2
Kemenes utca 4 E3
Kende utca 4 E4
Kenese utca 3 B5
Kenyérmezö utca 7 C2
Képíró utca 4 F2 (10 F5)
Kerekes utca 6 D1
Kerepesi út 8 D2
Kereszt utca 3 C2 (9 B5)
Kertész utca 7 A2
Késmárki utca 3 B3
Kígyó utca 4 E1 (10 D4)
Kinizsi utca 7 A5
Király utca 2 F5, 7 A1 (10 E3)
Királyi Pál utca 4 F2 (10 E5)
Kis Diófa utca 7 A2
Kis Fuvaros utca 7 C3
Kis Stáció utca 7 B4
Kisfaludy utca 7 B5
Kisgömb utca 6 D1
Kisrókus utca 1 A2
Kiss E. utca 2 E4 (10 D1)
Kiss János Altáb. utca 3 A1
Kiss József utca 7 C3
Kitaibel Pál utca 1 A2
Klapka utca 5 A1
Klauzál tér 7 A2
Klauzál utca 7 A2
Kmetty György utca 5 B4
Knázits utca 7 A5
Köbányai út 8 F5
Köbölkút utca 3 B3
Kocsány utca 3 C3
Kodály körönd 5 B5
Köfaragó utca 7 A3
Kökörcsin utca 3 B5
Kölcsey utca 7 B4
Kolumbusz utca 6 F3
Korányi Sándor utca 8 E5
Köris utca 8 D5
Korlát utca 1 A4
Körönd 5 B5
Korong utca 6 F4
Körösy József utca 4 D5

Kós Károly sétány 6 D3
Kosciuszko Tádé utca 1 A5
Kossuth L. utca 4 F1 (10 E4)
Kossuth Lajos tér 2 D3 (9 C1)
Koszorú utca 7 C4
Kosztolányi Dezsö tér 3 C5
Kozma F. utca 2 E3 (10 D1)
Közraktár utca 4 F3
Köztársaság tér 7 C3
Köztelek utca 7 A5
Kresz Géza utca 2 F2
Krisztina körút 1 A4, 3 C1
Krisztina tér 1 A5
Krúdy utca 7 B4
Krusper utca 4 E5
Kun utca 8 D3
Kuny D. utca 1 A5
Kúria utca 4 F1 (10 E5)
Kürt utca 7 A1
Kút utca 1 B1

L

Lágymányosi utca 4 E5
Laky Adolf köz 6 F2
Laky Adolf utca 6 F2
Lánchíd utca 1 C5, 4 D1 (9 B4)
Lapály utca 6 F2
Laufenauer utca 3 A5
Lázár utca 2 F4 (10 E2)
Légszesz utca 7 C2
Lehel tér 2 F1
Lehel utca 5 A3
Lendvay utca 5 B4
Leonardo da Vinci utca 7 C5
Lépcsö 4 D4
Levél utca 1 A1
Lippa utca 8 D5
Lipthay utca 1 C1
Lisznyai utca 3 B1 (9 A4)
Liszt F. tér 7 A1
Logodi utca 1 A4
Lónyay utca 4 F2, 7 A5
Lóportár utca 5 A2
Losonci utca 8 D5
Lósy I. utca 8 D5
Lovag utca 2 F3 (10 E1)
Lovas út 1 A4
Lóvásár utca 8 D2
Lovassy I. utca 7 C4
Lövöház utca 1 A2
Lövölde tér 5 B5
Lujza utca 8 D4
Luther utca 7 C2

M

Madách tér 2 F5 (10 E3)
Madách utca 2 F5 (10 E3)
Magdolna utca 7 C4
Magyar utca 4 F1 (10 F4)
Málna utca 1 B3 (9 A1)
Mányoki út 4 E4
Március 15 tér 4 E1 (10 D5)
Marek József utca 6 D5, 8 D1
Margit körút 1 A3
Margit tér 1 B1
Mari tér 2 D2

Mária tér 1 B3 (9 A1)
Mária utca 7 B5
Markó utca 2 E3
Markovits utca 1 C3
Márkus E. utca 7 B3
Markusovszky tér 7 A5
Márvány utca 3 A1
Mátray utca 1 A3
Mátyás tér 7 C4
Mátyás utca 4 F3, 7 A5
Mecset utca 1 B1
Medve utca 1 B3
Ménesi utca 3 B3
Menta utca 3 A3
Mérleg utca 2 E5 (10 D3)
Mészáros utca 3 A1
Mészöly utca 4 E4
Mexikói út 6 F3
Mihály utca 3 B2
Mikó utca 1 B5
Mikszáth K. tér 7 A4
Mimóza utca 6 E4
Minerva utca 4 D4
Mohács utca 5 C1
Molnár F. tér 8 D5
Molnár utca 4 E2 (10 D5)
Mór utca 6 D1
Móricz Zsigmond körtér 4 D5
Mosonyi utca 8 D2
Moszkva tér 1 A3
Mozsár utca 2 F4
Müegyetem rakpart 4 F4
Munkás utca 7 C2
Munkácsy Mihály utca 5 B4
Murányi utca 6 D5, 8 D1
Muskotály utca 3 A3
Múzeum körút 4 F1 (10 F4)
Múzeum utca 7 A4 (10 F5)

N

Nádor utca 2 D4 (9 C1) (10 D2)
Nagy Diófa utca 7 A2
Nagyfuvaros utca 7 C4
Nagy Ignác utca 2 E3
Nagy Imre tér 1 C3
Nagy Lajos Király út 6 F2
Nagy Templom utca 7 C5
Nagymezö utca 2 F3
Nagy Sándor J. utca 2 E4 (10 D1)
Nagyszölös utca 3 A5
Nap utca 7 B5
Naphegy tér 3 B1
Naphegy utca 3 B1 (9 A4)
Nedecvár utca 3 A4
Nefelejcs utca 5 C5, 7 C1
Német utca 7 B4
Népszínház utca 7 B3
Nyár utca 7 A2
Nyárs utca 3 B1
Nyáry Pál utca 4 E2 (10 E5)
Nyugati tér 2 F2

O

Október 6 utca 2 E4 (10 D2)
Orczy tér 8 D2
Orczy út 8 E5

Orgona utca — 1 B1
Orlay utca — 4 E4
Orom utca — 3 C2
Országház utca — 1 B4
Orvos utca — 3 B1 (9 A4)
Ostrom utca — 1 A3
Osvát utca — 7 B2
Otthon utca — 3 A3

Ó

Ó utca — 2 F4 (10 E2)

Ő/Ö

Őr utca — 7 C4
Ötpacsirta utca — 7 A4

P

Pál utca — 7 B5
Pala utca — 1 C5
Pálma utca — 6 E3
Palóc utca — 6 D1
Palota út — 1 B5, 3 C1
(9 A3)
Pálya utca — 3 A1
Pannónia utca — 2 E1
Papnövelde utca — 4 F2
(10 E5)
Párizsi utca — 4 E1 (10 D4)
Paulay Ede utca — 2 F5
7 A1 (10 E2)
Pauler utca — 1 B5
Pesti B. utca — 4 E1
Peterdy utca — 6 D5
Péterfy Sándor utca — 7 C2
Petőfi Sándor utca — 4 E1
Pilvax köz — 4 E1 (10 E4)
Pipa utca — 4 F3
Pipacs utca — 4 D3
Piroska utca — 3 B2 (9 A5)
Podmaniczky tér — 2 E4
(10 D2)
Podmanieczky utca — 2 F3
5 A4
Pollack M. tér — 7 A4
Ponty utca — 1 C4 (9 A2)
Pozsonyi utca — 2 F1
Práter utca — 7 B5
Purczel M. utca — 2 E4
Puskin utca — 7 A3

R

Ráday utca — 7 A5
Radnóti Miklós utca — 2 E1
Radványi utca — 3 A4
Rákóczi tér — 7 B4
Rákóczi út — 7 A3 (10 F4)
Reáltanoda utca — 4 F1
(10 E4)
Régiposta utca — 4 E1
(10 D4)
Reitter Ferenc utca — 6 D1
Retek utca — 1 A3
Révay utca — 2 F4 (10 E2)
Révész utca — 5 A1
Reviczky utca — 7 A4
Rezeda utca — 4 D3
Rigó utca — 7 B4
Rippl-Rónai utca — 5 B3
Róbert Károly körút — 5 C1
Rőf utca — 3 A5
Roham utca — 1 B5
Róka utca — 3 A1
Rökk Szilárd utca — 7 B4

Rómer Flóris utca — 1 A1
Róna utca — 6 F3
Roosevelt tér — 2 D5 (9 C3)
Rottenbiller utca — 7 C1
Rózsa utca — 5 A5
Rózsa utca — 7 B1
Rózsafa utca — 5 B1
Rózsák tere — 7 C2
Rumbach S. utca — 2 F5
(10 E3)

S

Sajó utca — 8 D1
Salétrom utca — 7 B4
Sánc út. — 3 C2 (9 A5)
Sárkány utca — 8 E5
Sarló utca — 3 B1 (9 A4)
Saru utca — 4 E5
Sas utca — 2 E4 (10 D2)
Schweidel utca — 3 A3
Semmelweis utca — 4 F1
(10 E4)
Semsey Andor utca — 6 F5
Serleg utca — 3 C3
Síp utca — 2 F5, 7 A3
(10 F3)
Siroki utca — 4 D5
Só utca — 4 F2
Sóház utca — 4 F3
Somló Lépcső — 4 D4
Somlói köz — 3 C3
Somlói út — 3 B3
Somogyi Béla utca — 7 B3
Sörház utca — 4 E2 (10 E5)
Stáhly utca — 7 B3
Stefánia út — 6 F5, 8 F1
Steindl I. utca — 2 D4 (9 C2)
Stollár B. utca — 2 E2
Sütő utca — 2 E5 (10 D3)
Szabadság tér — 2 E4 (10 D1)
Szabadsajtó út — 4 E1
(10 D5)
Szabó Ilonka utca — 1 B3
(9 A1)
Szabó J. utca — 6 E5, 8 F1
Szabolcs utca — 5 A3
Szabolcska M. utca — 4 D5
Szalag utca — 1 C4 (9 A2)
Szalay utca — 2 E3
Számadó utca — 3 C3
Szarka utca — 4 F2
Szász Károly utca — 1 B2
Százház utca — 8 E1
Széchenyi rakpart — 2 D4
(9 C2)
Széchenyi utca — 2 D4 (9 C2)
Szegedi út — 6 D1
Székely Bartalan utca — 5 B4
Székely M. utca — 2 F4
(10 E2)
Szemere utca — 2 E3
Szemlőhegy utca — 1 A1
Széna tér — 1 A3
Szende Pál utca — 2 D5
(10 D3)
Szent István körút — 2 E2
Szent István tér — 2 E5
(10 D2)
Szent László utca — 6 D2
Szentháromság tér — 1 B4
(9 A2)
Szentkirályi utca — 7 A3
Szép utca — 4 F1 (10 E4)
Szerb utca — 4 F2 (10 E5)
Szerdahelyi utca — 8 D4
Szervita tér — 4 E1 (10 D4)

Szeszgyár utca — 8 E5
Szigetvár utca — 8 D4
Szigony utca — 7 C5
Szilágyi tér — 1 C4
(9 B2)
Szilágyi utca — 7 C3
Szinva utca — 8 E1
Szinyei Merse utca — 5 A4
Szirom utca — 3 C2
Szirtes utca — 3 B2
Szittya utca — 3 A2
Szív utca — 5 A5
Szobi utca — 2 F3
Szófia utca — 7 A1
Szondi utca — 2 F3
5 A5
Szőnyi út — 6 F2
Szövetség utca — 7 B2, 7 C2
Szt. György tér — 1 C5
(9 A3)
Sztoczek utca — 4 F5
Szüret utca — 3 C4
Szűz utca — 7 C4

T

Táltos utca — 3 A2
Takács M. utca — 3 B5
Taksony utca — 5 A2
Táncsics M. utca — 1 B4
Tar utca — 5 C1
Tarcali utca — 3 B4
Tardoskedd utca — 3 A5
Tárnok utca — 1 B5 (9 A2)
Társ utca — 3 A2
Tas Vezér utca — 3 C5
Tatai utca — 6 E1
Tátra utca — 2 E2
Tavaszmező utca — 7 C4
Teleki Blanka utca — 6 E1
Teleki tér — 8 D3
Tengerszem utca — 6 F1
Teréz körút — 2 F3 (10 F1)
Thököly út — 6 F5, 8 D2
Tibavár utca — 3 A5
Tibor utca — 3 B1
Tigris utca — 3 B1 (9 A5)
Tisza utca — 5 A2
Töhötöm utca — 3 A5
Toldy Ferenc utca — 1 B3
(9 A1)
Tölgyfa utca — 1 B2
Tolnai Lajos utca — 7 C3
Tömő utca — 7 C5
Tornavár utca — 3 A5
Török P. utca — 7 A5
Török utca — 1 B1
Trefort utca — 7 A3
Tüköry utca — 2 D4 (9 C2)
Turbán utca — 1 B1
Türbe tér — 1 B1
Türr utca — 4 E1
(10 D4)
Tüzér utca — 5 B1

U

Ulászló utca — 3 C5
Ungvár utca — 6 F2
Uzsoki utca — 6 F3

Ú

Újpesti rakpart — 2 D1
Újpesti utca — 2 D1
Úljaki rakpart — 1 C1
Úri utca — 1 A4 (9 A2)

Ü

Üllői út — 7 A5
Üstökös — 1 C1
Üteg utca — 5 C1

V

Váci utca — 4 E1 (10 D4)
Váci út — 2 F1, 5 A2
Vadász utca — 2 E3 (10 D1)
Vág utca — 5 A2
Vágány utca — 5 C3
Vágfarkasd utca — 3 A5
Vajda Péter utca — 8 C5
Vajdahunyad utca — 7 B5
Vajkay utca — 2 E3
Váli utca — 4 D5
Valkói utca — 3 A5
Vám utca — 1 C4 (9 A1)
Vámház körút — 4 F3
Varannó utca — 6 D2
Várfok utca — 1 A3
Vármegye utca — 4 F1 (10 E4)
Városház utca — 4 E1
(10 E4)
Városligeti fasor — 5 C5
Varsányi Irén utca — 1 B3
Vas utca — 7 A3
Vásár utca — 7 A4
Vasvári P. utca — 4 D5, 2 F4
(10 F2)
Vay Á. utca — 7 C3
Vécsey utca — 2 E3 (10 D1)
Veres Pálné utca — 4 F2
(10 E5)
Vérmező út — 1 A3
Verseny utca — 8 E2
Vértanúk tere — 2 D3 (9 C1)
Véső utca — 5 A1
Victor Hugó utca — 2 F1
Víg utca — 7 B3
Vigadó utca — 2 E5, 4 D1
(10 D4)
Vigadó tér — 4 D1 (10 D4)
Vigyázó F.utca — 2 D4 (9 C2)
Villányi út — 3 B4
Vincellér utca — 3 B5
Visegrádi utca — 2 E2, 5 A1
Vitéz utca — 1 B3
Vörösmarty tér — 2 E5
(10 D3)
Vörösmarty utca — 5 A5

W

Wallenberg utca — 2 E1
Weiner Leó utca — 2 F3
(10 E1)
Wesselényi utca — 7 A3

Y

Ybl Miklós tér — 4 D1 (9 C4)

Z

Zenta utca — 4 E4
Zichy Mihály utca — 6 E5
Zichy Jenő utca — 2 F4
(10 E2)
Zivatar utca — 1 B1
Zólyomi köz — 3 A4
Zólyomi út — 3 A4
Zoltán utca — 2 D4 (9 C1)
Zrínyi utca — 2 E5 (10 D2)
Zsolt utca — 3 B2
Zsombolyai utca — 3 C5

Index

Page numbers in **bold** type refer to
main entries.

A

Ábrahám, Pál 115
Adami, Carlo 80
Addresses 230
The Advance of the Hussars (Than) 30
Ady, Endre 139
  grave of 155
Aids Helpline 227
Air France 233
Air travel **232–3**
Airport Minibus Shuttle 233
Akadémia utca
  Street-by-Street map 112
Alabardos 10
Alagút tunnel 174
Albert of Austria 18
Alcohol
  drink-driving 234
  What to Drink in Budapest 194–5
All Saints' Day 61
Allio, Donato 44
Alpár, Ignác 107, 110, 150
Aman, Johann 73
Ambulances 226–7
American Embassy **111**
Amerling 149
Andokides 148
András II, King 90
András III, King 18, 23
András Hess Square **81**
Andrássy, Count György 30
Andrássy family 29
Angevin dynasty 17, 18, 24, 131
Anne, Queen 137
Antal, Károly 111, 125
Antall, József 35
Antiques shops 212, 213
Apartments 181
Aquincum 20–21, 41, **162–3**
Arany, János 91
  monument 132
Architecture
  Budapest's Best: Churches and
    Synagogues **42–3**
  Budapest's Best: Palaces and
    Historic Buildings **46–7**
  Budapest's Best: the Secession **54–7**
Árkay, Aladár 45, 57, 144
Árpád, Prince 17, 22
  Millennium Monument 145
  Parliament 109
Árpád dynasty 18, **22–3**, 32
  Hungarian National Museum 132
Artists' Avenue 173
ATMs 228
Attila the Hun 17, 21
Australian Embassy 225
Austro-Hungarian Empire 17, 33
Autumn Festival 60
Autumn in Budapest 60
Avars 17, 20, 21

B

Bajor, Gizi 160
Balassi, Bálint 26
Baldung Grien, Hans 148
Ballet
  Budapest Summer Opera and
    Ballet Festival 59
Bandholtz, General Harry Hill 111
Banknotes 229
Banks 228

Barabás, Miklós
  Placing the Cornerstone 130
Baroque style
  churches 44
  palaces and historic buildings **48**
Barry, Charles 108
Bars 190
  late-night scams 215, 226
  theme bars 208, 209
Bartók, Béla 41, 81, 157
Bartók Béla utca apartments
  Budapest's Best: the Secession 55
Baths (general)
  Budapest's Best: Baths and Pools
    50–53
  tipping 223
Baths (individual)
  Aquincum 162
  Corinthia Aquincum 53
  Danubius Grand Hotel
    Margitsziget 52, 173
  Danubius Thermal Hotel
    Margitsziget 52–3, 173
  Gellért Hotel and Baths Complex
    51, 52, 54, 57, 64, 89, **90–91**
  Király Baths 27, 50, 52, **101**
  Komjády Pool 52
  Lukács Baths 50, 52, **101**
  Rác Baths 50, 52, **95**
  Rudas Baths 27, 51, 52, 89, **93**
  Széchenyi Baths 10, 51, 52, 53,
    141, 143, **151**, 218, 219
  Thermal Hotel Helia 53
Batthyány, Count Lajos
  assassination 31
Batthyány Square 100
  Lajos Batthyány Eternal Flame 31
  Liberty Square 110
  tomb of 155
Batthyány family 73
Batthyány Palace 48, 73
Batthyány Square **100**
  Street-by-Street map 98
Baumgarten, Alájos 135
Baumgarten, Sándor 139
Beatrice (wife of Mátyás Corvinus)
  24, 76
Bebó, Károly 44, 102, 103
Beers
  beer halls 208, 209
  What to Drink in Budapest 194
Beethoven, Ludwig van
  Beethoven Museum
    (Martonvásár) 167
  Brunswick Palace
    (Martonvásár) 167
  Castle Theatre 73
  Franz Liszt Museum 144
  Mihály Táncsics Street 81
Béla III, King
  crusade 23
  Hungarian National Museum 133
  sculpture of 76
  tomb of 83
Béla IV, King 17, 18
  castle 23
  Church of St John the Evangelist 73
  Dominican Church and Convent 173
  "Golden Bull" 23
  Inner City Parish Church 44
  Jewish Quarter 134
  Mátyás Church 44, 82, 83
  Royal Palace 70
  Visegrád Castle 165
  Visegrád Palace 165

Belgrade, Battle of (1456) 25
Belgrade Cathedral (Szentendre)
  165
Bem, General József
  József Bem Monument 101
  No. 1 Akadémia utca 112
Benczúr, Gyula
  The Christening of Vajka 17
  Hungarian National Gallery 77
  The Liberation of Buda in 1686
  26
  The Recapture of Buda 77
  Lutheran Church 145
  St Stephen's Basilica 117
Berény, Robert 77
Bergl, Johan 44, 139
Bicycles 218, 237
Bike hire 237
BKV (Budapest Transport Company)
  237, 238
BKV Lost Property 227
Blagovestenska Church
  (Szentendre) 165
Blaha, Lujza
  tomb of 155
Blumenthal, Ben 115
Boat travel 234
Bodor, Péter 173
Bodor Well 173
Bogdány, Jakab 76
Bohemian hangouts 208, 209
Böhm, Henrik 128
Boltraffio, Giovanni
  Madonna and Child 149
Bonnard, Pierre 149
Bookshops 212, 213
Borozók (wine-cellar bars) 190
Borsos, Miklós 95
Bösinger, Ferenc Ignác 80
Boxing Day 61
Brestyánszky, Béla 129
Bridges
  Chain Bridge 10, 31, 32, 48, 62,
    63, 112, 174
  Elizabeth Bridge 35, 63, 64
  Lágymányosi Bridge 65
  Liberty Bridge 65
  Margaret Bridge 63
British Airways 233
Bruegel, Pieter the Elder
  St John the Baptist's Sermon 147, 148
Brunswick, Anton 167
Brunswick Palace (Martonvásár)
  167
Buda Hills 11, **161**
Buda Lutheran Church **84**
Budapest Aréna 218
Budapest Bank 228
Budapest Card 222
Budapest Christmas Fair 60, 61
Budapest History Museum 25, 41,
  72
  Budapest's Best: Museums and
    Galleries 38
Budapest International Book
  Festival 58
Budapest Marriott hotel 174, 185
Budapest Operetta Theatre **115**
Budapest Riding Club 218
Budapest Summer Music Festival 59
Budapest Taxi 239
Budapest Wine Festival 60
Budapesti Búcsú 59
Budataxi 239
Budget travel 224

Bufakeszi Wildlife Park 11
Bukovics, Gyula 110
Budapest Bábszínház 219
Bureaux de change 228
Buses 241
  airport buses 233
  night buses 215

C

Cafés 190, 206, 207
Calvinist Church (Central Pest) 44, 45, **135**
Calvinist Church (North of the Castle) 14, 97, **100**
  Street-by-Street map 99
Camping 181
Canadian Embassy 225
Capuchin Church **100**
  Budapest's Best: Churches and Synagogues 42
  Street-by-Street map 99
Carmelite order 73
Cars 234–5, **236–7**
  clamping and towing 237
  driving to Budapest 234–5
  hiring 237
  parking 237
Casanova, Giacomo Girolamo 98
Cash machines 228
Casino Tropicana 217
Casino Vakert 217
Casinos 217
Castle District 10, **69–85**
  area map 69
  hotels 182
  Hungarian National Gallery **74–7**
  Mátyás Church **82–3**
  restaurants 196
  Street-by-Street: the Royal Palace 70–71
  Street-by-Street map: the Old Town 78–9
  Tunnel 32
Castle Museum *see* Budapest History Museum
Castles
  Esztergom 164
  Visegrád 165
Cathedrals
  Belgrade Cathedral (Szentendre) 165
  Esztergom 153, 164
  see also Churches
Caves
  Labyrinth **85**
  Pál-völgy Cave **154**
  Szemlő-hegy Cave **154**
Çelebi, Evliya 90
Celts 20, 87, 94
Cemeteries
  Jewish Cemetery **156–7**
  Kerepesi Cemetery **155**
  Municipal Cemetery **158–9**
Centenary Monument 172
  River View of Budapest 62
Central European University 111
Central Market Hall 11, 138, 175, 211
Central Pest 121–39
  area map 121
  hotels 184–6
  Hungarian National Museum **130–33**
  Inner City Parish Church **124–5**
  Museum of Applied Arts **136–7**
  restaurants 200–203
  Street-by-Street map: Around Váci Street 122–3

Ceresola, Venerio 73, 80
Cézanne, Paul
  Credenza 149
Chain Bridge 10, 31, 48, 174
  Chain Bridge Festival 59
  River View of Budapest 62, 63
  Street-by-Street map 112
  Unification of Budapest 32
Chapel of St Roch **135**
Charles, Prince of Wales 65
Charles I Robert of Anjou 18, 83
Charles II of Durazzo 18
Charles III, Emperor 19, 128
Charles IV, Emperor 19, 33
Charles of Lorraine 26
Charles Apartment Hotel 181
Châtillon, Anne de
  tomb of 83
Chekhov, Anton 127
Chemists 227
Children
  entertainment **219**
  in hotels 180
  in restaurants 191
Children's Railway 11, 239
The Christening of Vajka (Benczúr) 17
Christianity 22
Christmas 61
Christmas (Rippl-Rónai) 77
Christmas Fair 60, 61
Chronica Hungarorum 25
Churches (general)
  Budapest's Best: Churches and Synagogues **42–3**
  music in 216
  spires and domes 44–5
Churches (individual) **42–5**
  Blagovestenska Church (Szentendre) 165
  Buda Lutheran Church **84**
  Calvinist Church (Central Pest) 44, 45, **135**
  Calvinist Church (North of the Castle) 14, 97, 99, **100**
  Capuchin Church 42, 99, **100**
  Chapel of St Roch **135**
  Church of St Mary Magdalene 44, **84**
  Cistercian Church of St Imre **157**
  Dominican Church 172–3
  Fehérek Church (Vác) 165
  Franciscan Church 43, 44, **139**, 172
  Inner City Parish Church 11, 43, 44, 64, 123, **124–5**, 175
  Ják Chapel 143
  Józsefváros Parish Church **155**
  Kőbánya Parish Church 45, **156**
  Lutheran Church 43, 45, **128**
  Mátyás Church 10, 25, 27, 42, 44, 62, 79, **82–3**, 174, 216
  Óbuda Calvinist Church 171
  Óbuda Parish Church 170
  Rock Church 42, 89, **92**
  St Anne's Church 29, 42, 44, 62, 99, **102–3**
  St Francis's Wounds Church 62, 98, **101**
  St John the Evangelist 73
  St Michael's Church 44, 173, 175
  St Stephen's Basilica 33, 43, 44, 45, 59, 63, 113, **116–17**, 216
  Serbian Church **138**
  Servite Church 44, 122, **128**
  Tabán Parish Church **95**
  Újlaki Parish Church **154**
  University Church 44, **139**

Churches (individual) (cont)
  Városliget Calvinist Church 45, 57, 144–5
  Churning Woman (Munkácsy) 75
  CIB Bank 228
  Cifra Palace (Kecskemét) 166
  Cinema *see* Film
  Circus 219
  Cistercian Church of St Imre **157**
  Citadel **92–3**
    Street-by-Street map 88
  Citadella 181
  Citizens' Party 35
  City Council Chamber 37, **138**
  City Taxi 239
  Clark, Adam 174
    Chain Bridge 31, 62
    Tunnel 32, 100
  Claude Lorrain 149
  Climate 222
  Clothes
    etiquette 223
    shops 212, 213
  Coach travel 235
  Cocktail bars 206, 207
  Coffee houses 206
  Coins 229
  Columbus Jazz Club 216
  Communism 17, 34
    Park of Monuments **160**
  Compromise of 1867 32, 114
  Congress and World Trade Centre **160**, 216
  Constantine IX Monomachus, Emperor 132
  Contra Aquincum 21, 175
  Convent, Dominican 172–3
  Correggio, Antonio 40, 149
  Corvin Filmpalota 217
  Cotton Club 216
  Courbet, Gustave 149
  Couriers 231
  Cranach, Lucas 148
  Credenza (Cézanne) 149
  Credit cards 210, 228
  Cresola, Venerio 154
  Crime 226
  Cruise companies 235
  Csárda (restaurants) 190
  Császár Komjádi Uszoda 218
  Csepel Island 22
  Csillaghegyi Strand 53
  Csillebérc Autós Camping 181
  Csontváry, Tivadar Kosztka 77
  Cukrászda (patisseries) 190
  Currency 228–9
  Currency exchange 179, 228
  Curtis, Tony 134
  Cycling 218, 237
  Czettrich, Ulrik 24
  Cziegler, Győző 151
  Czóbel, Béla 77

D

Dagály Strand 53
  Budapest's Best: Baths and Pools 51
Damkó, József 81, 161
Dance
  Budapest Summer Opera and Ballet Festival 59
  National Dance Theatre 73
Danube,
  River 17
  boat travel 234
  River View of Budapest **62–5**

Danube Carnival International
  Cultural Festival 59
Danube Fountain 129
Danubius Grand Hotel Margitsziget
  52, 173, 189
Danubius Astoria Hotel 53, 185
Danubius Health Spa Resort Helia 53,
  189
Danubius Health Spa Resort
  Margitsziget 52–3, 173, 189
David, Gerard 148
Dávid, Károlyi 155
De Prati, Fortunato 70
Deák, Ferenc 32
  monument 114
  tomb of 155
Delacroix, Eugène 149
Dembiński, General Henryk 30
Democratic Hungarian Forum 35
Dental Care Budapest 227
Dentists 227
Department stores 210–11, 213
Derkovits, Gyula 77
Descartes, René 114
Dialling codes 230
Diescher, József 128
Disabled travellers 223, 225
  entertainment 215
  in hotels 180
Discos 208–9
The Discovery of Louis II's Body
  (Székely) 24–5
Doctors 227
Domes, churches 44–5
Dominican Church and Convent 172–3
Dominican order 81
Donner, Georg Raphael 76
Dorfmeister, Joseph 76
Dózsa, György 25
Drechsler Palace 49, 115
Drentwett, Philip Jacob 136
Drinks see Food and drink
Dual Monarchy 32
Duna Palota 216
Dürer, Albrecht
  Hungarian National Museum 133
  Museum of Fine Art 149
  Portrait of a Young Man 148
Dvorzsák, Ede 151

E

Eagle Hill Nature Reserve 160
Easter 58, 61
Eberhardt, Antal 103
Ébner, Lajos Deák 150
The Eight 77
Electrical appliances 225
Eleöd, Ákos 160
Elizabeth, Empress 166
  Queen Elizabeth Monument 88, 93
Elizabeth, Queen 100
Elizabeth Bridge 35
  River View of Budapest 63, 64
Elizabeth Sisters 101
ELTE Kollegium 181
Email 230
Embassies 225
  American Embassy 111
Embellishment Commission 30,
  48, 127
Emergency services 226–7
Engels, Friedrich
  statue of 160
Entertainment 214–19
  casinos 217

Entertainment (cont)
  children's Budapest 219
  film 217
  music 216
  sport 218
  theatre 217
Eötvös, Baron József
  statue of 114
Eötvös, Lóránd 139
Eravi 20, 87, 94
Erdődy Palace 48, 49, 81
Erkel, Ferenc 118, 144
Erkel Theatre 151, 216
Erste Bank 228
Erszébet Look-Out Tower 11, 161
Ervin Szabó Library 135
  Budapest's Best: Palaces and
  Historic Buildings 47
Esterházy, Prince 135
Esterházy family 146, 149
Esterházy Madonna (Raphael) 146,
  149
Eszpresszó (bars) 190
Esztergom 22, 153, 164
Esztergom, Battle of (1594) 26
Eszterházy Palace 135
Ethnographical Museum 41, 110
  Budapest's Best: Museums and
  Galleries 39
  Street-by-Street map 106
Etiquette 223
Étterem (restaurants) 190
Eucharistic Congress 34
Eugene of Savoy, Prince
  Municipal Council Offices 128
  Ráckeve 167
  statue of 71
Eurocheques 210
European Union 35
Euzebiusz of Esztergom, Canon 92, 139
Excursions 164–7
Exekias 148
Express Központi Iroda 181

F

Fadrusz, János 70
Falkoner, Francis 154
Farkas, István 77
Fehérek Church (Vác) 165
Feketéhazy, János 65
Fellner 115
Ferdinand I, King 18
Ferdinand II, King 18
Ferdinand III, King 18
Ferdinand V, King 19
Ferenc, Béli 92
Ferenc II Rákóczi, Prince
  chair 29
  Hungarian National Museum
  130–33
  monument 107
  portrait of 28
  Turkish Bank 128
  uprising 28
Ferenc Hopp Museum of Far
  Eastern Art 41, 145
Ferenc Puska's Stadium 155, 218
Ferenczy, Béni 77
Ferenczy, István 40
Ferenczy, Károly 77
  The Paintress 77
Feretti, Bernard 154
Festetics, Prince Antal 111, 135
Festetics family 155

Festetics Palace 135
Festivals 58–61
Festival Celebrating the Day of Dance
  58
Feszl, Frigyes
  Great Synagogue 134
  Vidagó concert hall 49, 126
Feszler, Leó 43, 116, 117, 129
Film 217
  Hungarian Film Festival 61
Finta, József 126, 127, 160
Fire Brigade 227
Fischer von Erlach, Johann Bernard
  150
Fishermen's Bastion 10, 49, 80, 174
  Street-by-Street map 79
Fö tér Palace 170, 171
Fodor, Gyula 157
Folk art shops 212, 213
Folk music 216
Fönix SOS Medical Service 227
Fonó Budai Zeneház 216
Food and drink
  Flavours of Budapest 192–3
shops 212, 213
  What to Drink in Budapest
  194–5
  wine bars 206
  see also Restaurants
Foreigners' Registry Office 227
Förster, Ludwig 45, 134
Fót 166
Fötaxi 239
The Founding of the Academy
  (Holló) 30–31
Fountains
  Danube Fountain 129
  Mátyás Fountain 70, 72–3
Four Seasons Gresham Palace 114,
  174
Franciscan Church 44, 139, 172
  Budapest's Best: Churches and
  Synagogues 43
Franciscan order
  Church of St Mary Magdalene 84
  Mátyás Church 82–3
  St Elizabeth's Church 98, 101
François I, King of France 148
Francsek, Imre 93
Franz I, King 19, 29
Franz Joseph, Emperor 19
  coronation 133
  death of 33
  Dual Monarchy 32
  Liberty Bridge 65
  Museum of Applied Arts 136
  Roosevelt Square 112
  Springtime Revolutions 17
Franz Liszt Academy of Music 32,
  56, 129
  concerts 216
Franz Liszt Museum 41, 144
Frederick Barbarossa 23
Funfair 151, 219
Funicular railways 239

G

Gábor Bethlen, Prince of
  Transylvania 131
Gainsborough, Thomas 149
Galleries see Museums and galleries
Gardens see Parks and gardens
Gauguin, Paul 77, 149
Gay and lesbian travellers 224
Gay venues 209

Gellért, Bishop
  Inner City Parish Church 124
  martyrdom 22, 87
  St Stephen's Basilica 117
  Statue of St Gellért 87, 88, **93**
Gellért Hill and Tabán **87–95**
  area map 87
  hotels 182–3
  restaurants 196–7
  Street-by-Street map: Gellért Hill
    88–9
Gellért Hotel and Baths Complex
  52, 57, **90–91**
  Budapest's Best: Baths and Pools
    51
  Budapest's Best: the Secession 54
  children in 219
  River View of Budapest 64
  Street-by-Street map 89
Geology Institute **154–5**
Gerbeaud, Emil 126
Gerbeaud Cukrászda 10
Géza, Prince 22
Géza I, King 22
Gfall, Johann 161
Giergl, Kálmán
  Franz Liszt Academy of Music
    129
  Klotild Palaces 127
  Luxus department store 126
Giessl, József 73
Giorgione 149
Gizi Bajor Theatre Museum **160**
Gödöllő **166**
Goldberger's textile factory 29
"Golden Bull" 23
Golden Eagle Pharmacy Museum
  41, **80**
  Street-by-Street map 79
Golden Stag House **95**
Göncz, Árpád 19, 35
Gothic Buda **24–5**
Goths 17, 20
Gouin, Ernest 63
Goya, Francisco de 40
  The Water Carrier 146, 149
Grand Casino Budapest 217
Grand Hotel Margitsziget *see*
  Danubius Grand Hotel Margitsziget
Grassalkovich, Antal 44
Grassalkovich Mansion (Gödöllő)
  166
Great Capital Circus 219
Great Fire of Buda (1723) 28
Great Flood (1838) 30, 31
Great Market Hall *see* Central
  Market Hall
Great Synagogue 11, 44, 45, **134**
  Budapest's Best: Churches and
    Synagogues 43
  music 216
El Greco 40, 149
  *The Penance of St Mary
  Magdalene* 149
Green card 235
Green travel 236
Gresham, Sir Thomas 114
Gresham Kávéház 11
Gresham Palace **114**
  Budapest's Best: Palaces and
    Historic Buildings 47
  Budapest's Best: the Secession
    54, 57
  Street-by-Street map 112
Gresham Palace hotel 11, **114**, 184

Gross Palace 48
Guilleaume, Emile 172
Gül Baba 97
  tomb of **101**
Gulácsy, Lajos 56
Gundel 10
György I Rákóczi 27
Győri, Deszó 129
Gypsy music 216

H

Habsburg dynasty 17, 19
  Citadel 92
  Compromise of 1867 32
  Habsburg Budapest **28–9**
  Royal Palace 70
  sieges of Buda 26
  "Springtime of Revolutions" 30
Habsburg Steps 174
Hajós, Alfréd 50, 172
Hajós Olympic Pool 53, 172, 218
  Budapest's Best: Baths and Pools 50
Halászcsárda (fisherman's
  restaurant) 190
Halbig, Johann 126
Haller Camping 181
Hals, Frans 148
Hámon, Kristóf 44, 102, 154
Haranghy, Jenő 115
Hauszmann, Alajos
  Ethnographical Museum 110
  New York Palace 49, 129
  Royal Palace 71
  Széchenyi National Library 72
  tomb of 155
Havel, Václav 35
Health 227
Hebenstreit, József 139
Hegedűs, Ármin 90, 128
Helmer 115
Hercules Villa 21, 171
Hermina Amália 151
Hermina Chapel 151
Hermina Street **151**
Heroes' Monument (Jovánovics) 159
Heroes' Square 11
  Street-by-Street map 142–3
Herzog, Fülöp
  Lóránd Eötvös University 139
  Műcsarnok Palace of Art 150
  Museum of Fine Arts 146
Hess, András 25, 81
HÉV railway **239**
Hikisch House 100
  Street-by-Street map 98
Hild, János 31
  Embellishment Commission 48
  Inner City Parish Church 124
Hild, József 43, 112
  Calvinist Church 135
  Gross Palace 48
  Hermina Chapel 151
  József Nádor Square 126
  Józsefváros Parish Church 155
  Lutheran Church 45, 128
  Roosevelt Square 114
  St Stephen's Basilica 45, 116–17
  Váci Street 127
Hillebrandt, Franz Anton 84
Hilton Hotel 48, **81**, 182
Hiring cars 237
Historicism 49
History **17–35**
  museums **41**
Hitchhiking 235

Hofrichter, József 127, 135
Hogarth, William 149
Holbein, Hans 148
Hölbling, János 70, 128
Holidays, public 61
Holló, Barnabás 30
  The Founding of the Academy
    30–31
Hollywood Multiplex Duna Plaza 217
Holocaust Memorial 11, **134**
Holocaust Memorial Center **156**
Holy Trinity Column 79, 80
Holy Trinity Square **80**
  Street-by-Street map 79
Honvéd Monument 73, 174
Hopp, Ferenc 145
Hörger, Anton 80
Horse racing 58, 218
Horse riding 218
Horthy, István 92
Horthy, Admiral Miklós 19, 34
Hospitals 227
Hostels 180, 181
Hotels **178–89**
  Around Parliament 183–4
  Castle District 182
  Central Pest 184–6
  children in 180
  disabled travellers 180
  Further afield 187–9
  Gellért Hill and Tabán 182–3
  Gellért Hotel and Baths Complex
    90–91
  hidden extras 179
  hotel and pension classification 178
  how to book 179
  North of the Castle 183
  prices 179
  Radisson SAS Béke Hotel **115**
  self-catering accommodation 180,
    181
  service 180
  Városliget 186–7
  where to look 178
House of Hungarian Wines **80**, 206
  Street-by-Street map 79
House of Terror Museum **144**
Hungarian Academy of Sciences
  30–31, 33, **114**
  Budapest's Best: Palaces and
    Historic Buildings 47
  Street-by-Street map 112
  Zoo 150
Hungarian Disabled Association 223,
  225
Hungarian Film Festival 61
Hungarian Grand Prix 59
Hungarian Heritage House 216
Hungarian National Bank 49, 57, 110
Hungarian National Gallery 40,**74–7**
  Budapest's Best: Museums and
    Galleries 38
  children in 219
  floorplan 74–5
  Gothic works 76
  Lapidarium 76
  late-Gothic altarpieces 76–7
  19th-century works 77
  Renaissance and Baroque works 76
  Secession Budapest 56
  Street-by-Street map 71
  20th-century works 77
  Visitors' Checklist 75
Hungarian National Museum 11,
  30, 31, 40, 41, 48, **130–33**

Hungarian National Gallery (cont)
 archaeological exhibition 132
 Budapest's Best: Museums and
  Galleries 39
 Coronation Mantle 132
 11th-17th-century exhibition
  132–3
 18th-19th-century exhibition 133
 floorplan 130–31
 museum building 132
 20th-century exhibition 133
 Visitors' Checklist 131
Hungarian National Style 45, 56
Hungarian National Tourist Office
 181, 225
Hungarian Open Air Museum 165
Hungarian Socialist Workers' Party
 34, 35
Hungarian TV headquarters 110
 Street-by-Street map 107
Hungarian Youth Hostels
 Federation 181
Huns 20, 21
Hunyadi, János 24, 133
Hunyadi, László 77
Hurnagel, Georgius 26

I
IBUSZ Travel Agency 181
Ilonka 70, 73
Imre, St 157
Imre Varga Gallery 171
Ingres, Jean-Auguste-Dominique 75
Inner City Parish Church 11, 44,
 124–5, 175
 Budapest's Best: Churches and
  Synagogues 43
 River View of Budapest 64
 Street-by-Street map 123
Innocent XI, Pope
 statue of 81
Insurance 227
Internet 230
Internet cafés 231
Interoperett 216
Irish pubs 208, 209
Iron Age 20
Istók, János 33, 128
István I, King (St Stephen) 17, 22
 coins 23
 Esztergom 164
 Hungarian National Museum 130,
  132
 Inner City Parish Church 124–5
 Millennium Monument 145
 relics 117
 St István's Day 59
 St Stephen's Basilica **116–17**
 statues of 79, 80, 92, 117
István V, King 18
Izsó, Miklós 47, 112, 114

J
Jadwiga, Queen of Poland 24
 Jagiełło dynasty 18, 133
Ják 23
Ják Church 23
 Street-by-Street map 143
Jakab, Dezső 151
Jakab, Hans 101
Janich, Miahai 138
Jankovits, Gyula 93
János I Zápolyai, King 18, 26
Japanese Garden (Margaret Island)
 169, 173

Jazz 216
Jesuits 28, 81
 Mátyás Church 44
 St Anne's Church 102
Jews
 Central Pest 121
 Great Synagogue **134**
 Holocaust Memorial **134**
 Jewish Cemetery **156–7**
 Jewish Museum 11, 39, 41
 Jewish Old People's Home 57
 Jewish Quarter 11, **134**
 Jewish Summer Cultural Festival
  60
 Mihály Táncsics Street 78, 81
 Óbuda Synagogue 170
 Raoul Wallenberg Monument
  154
Johannus Corvinus 24
John Paul II, Pope 35
Jókai, Mór 139
Jordaens, Jacob 148
Joseph (József), Archduke 17, 76
 death of 31
 Embellishment Commission 30
 József Nádor Square 126
 sarcophagus of 76
 statue of 126
 Váci Street 127
Joseph (József) I, King 19
Joseph (József) II, King 19, 84
 Castle Theatre 73
 churches 45
 dissolves Pauline order 92
 Lóránd Eötvös University 138
 Lords' Street 85
 St Anne's Church 102
 St Elizabeth's Church 101
 White Cross Inn 98
Jovánovics, György
 Heroes' Monument 159
József, Atilla 139
 grave of 155
 statue of 106
József Attila utca
 Street-by-Street map 113
József Bem Monument 101
József Katona Theatre 217
József Nádor Square 48, **126**
Józsefváros Parish Church **155**
Jungfer, Gyula 135

K
K & H Bank 228
Kádár, János 19, 34
Kálmán, Aladár 111
Kálmán, Imre 115
Kamermayer, Károly
 monument 127
Kapisztory, Joseph 99
Kapisztory House
 Street-by-Street map 99
Károlyi, György 31
Károlyi, Count Lajós 135
Károlyi, Mihály 19
 Károlyi Palace 139
 presidency 34, 166
Károlyi Palace 48, 49, 135, **139**
Karolyi Palace (Fót) 166
Kasselik, Fidél 155
Kauser, József 45, 116
Kávéház (coffee houses) 190
Kecskemét **166**
Kempelen, Farkas 73
Kerepesi Cemetery **155**

Kernstok, Károly 77
Kertész, Imre 35
Kilometre 0 Stone 100, 174
Kincsem Horsepark 218
Kings and queens 18–19
Király, József 160
Király Baths 27, 52, **101**
 Budapest's Best: Baths and Pools
  50
Kisfaludi Stróbl, Zsigmond 40
 Liberation Monument 14, 92
 statue of Saint George 73
Kiskun Museum (Kiskunfélegyháza)
 167
Kiskunfélegyháza **166–7**
Kiskunsági National Park 167
Kiss, György 109
Kiss, István 172
Kisvendéglő(inn) 190
Klemperer, Otto 118
Klotild, Archduchess 127
Klotild Palaces 11, 49, **127**, 175
 Street-by-Street map 123
Kőbánya Parish Church 45, **156**
Koch, Henrik 139
Kodály, Zoltán 157
 Kodály Memorial Museum 41, **144**
Kolbe, St 92
Kölcsey, Ferenc
 monument to 98
Kolibri Színház 219
Kollina, Mór 84
Komjádi Pool 52
Komor, Marcell 151
Korb, Flóris 126, 127, 129
Körösföi-Kriesch, Aladár 56, 129
Körössényi, Tamás 73
Kós, Károly 57, 171
 School on Rose Hill 54
 Zoo 151
Kossuth, Lajos 19, **106**
 death of 33
 portrait of 106, 114
 tomb of 155
 Turkish Bank 128
Kossuth Square
 Street-by-Street map 106–7
Kovács, Margit
 Margit Kovács Museum
  (Szentendre) 165
Kozma, Lajos 127
Kremer, Victor Tardos 139
Krúdy, Gyula 170–71
Kugler, Henrik 126
Kun, Béla
 statue of 160
Kupelwieser, Leopold 155
Kupetzky, Jan 76
Kurszán 22

L
Labyrinth of Buda Castle 10, **85**, 219
 Street-by-Street map 78
Ladislas IV "the Cuman", King 18
Ladislas V "Posthumous", King 18
Lágymányosi Bridge
 River View of Budapest 65
Lajta, Béla 57, 129, 157
Lang, Adolf 144
Language Act (1840) 31
Lantai, Lajos 82
Las Vegas Casino 217
Late-night scams 215, 226
Late-night transport 215
Lechner, Ödön 41, **56**

Lechner, Ödön (cont)
 Bartók Béla Utca apartments 55
 Drechsler Palace 115
 Geology Institute 154–5
 Hermina Street 151
 Jewish Cemetery 157
 Kőbánya Parish Church 45, 156
 Museum of Applied Arts 136
 portrait of 56
 Post Office Savings Bank 55, 111
 Sipecky Balazs Villa 55
 Thonet House 122
 tomb of 155
 Town Hall (Kecskemét) 166
 Wekerle Estate 157
Lehár, Ferenc 115
Leibl, Wilhelm 149
Lenbach 149
Lendvay, Márton
 statue of 84
Lenin, VI
 statue of 160
Leonardo da Vinci 149
 figure of François I 148
Leopold I, Emperor 19, 141
Leopold II, Emperor 19
Lessenyei, Márta 89
Lézerszínház 217
The Liberation of Buda in 1686
 (Benczúr) 26
Liberation Monument 14, **92**
 Street-by-Street map 88
Liberty Bridge
 River View of Budapest 65
Liberty Square **110–11**
Libraries
 Ervin Szabó Library 47, **135**
 Széchenyi National Library 30, **72**
 University Library **139**
Ligeti, Antal
 Trading on the Pest Embankment
 32–3
Ligeti, Miklós
 Statue of Anonymous 143
Listings magazines 215, 231
Liszt, Franz
 Franz Liszt Academy of Music 32,
 56, **129**
 Franz Liszt Museum 41, **144**
 Inn of the Seven Electors 127
 State Opera House 118
 statue of 129
Liszt Ferenc tér 11
Little Princess (Marton) 65, 126,
 174–5
Lochbihler, Franz Sales 128
Longobards 17, 20
Lóránd Eötvös University **138–9**
Lords' Street 10, **85**
 Street-by-Street map 78
Lost property 226
Lotz, Károly
 City Council Chamber 138
 Ethnographic Museum 110
 Franciscan Church 43, 139
 Hungarian Academy of Sciences
 112
 Hungarian National Gallery 77
 Hungarian National Museum
 39, 132
 Mátyás Church 83
 New York Palace 129
 Parliament 109
 St Stephen's Basilica 113, 117
 State Opera House 118–19

Lotz, Károly (cont)
 University of Fine Art 144
 University Library 139
 Woman Bathing 75
Louis I (Lajos) "the Great", King 18,
 24, 70
Louis II, King 18, 24–5
Ludovika Academy **155**
Ludwig Museum Budapest-Museum
 of Contemporary Art 40, 156
Lufthansa 233
Luggage, on public transport 240
Luischen (Stróbl) 75
Lukács Baths 52, **101**, 218
 Budapest's Best: Baths and Pools
 50
Luther, Martin 41, 128
Lutheran Church 45, **128**
 Budapest's Best: Churches and
 Synagogues 43
Lutheran Museum 41
Lux, Kálmán 92

M

Macellum 20–21
Madách Theatre 217
Madarász, Viktor 77
Mader, Johann Christoph 29, 128
Mádl, Ferenc 19
Madonna and Child (Boltraffio)
 149
Magazines, listings 215, 231
Magyar Külkereskedelmi Bank Rt
 228
Magyars 17, 20, 21
 Árpád dynasty 22–3
Mahler, Gustav 118
Majtényi family 29
Malév Airline 233
Malmai, Béla 115
Máltás, Hugó 126
Manet, Edouard 75, 149
Mann, Thomas 34, 84
Mannheimer, Gusztav 129
Mantl, György 39
Mányoki, Ádám 76
 Ferenc II Rákóczi 28
Maps
 Around Parliament 105
 Árpád dynasty 22
 Budapest and environs 13
 Budapest's Best: Baths and Pools
 50–51
 Budapest's Best: Churches and
 Synagogues 42–3
 Budapest's Best: Museums and
 Galleries 38–9
 Budapest's Best: Palaces and
 Historic Buildings 46–7
 Budapest's Best: the Secession
 54–5
 Bus routes 240
 Castle District 69
 Central Budapest 14–15
 Central Pest 121
 Europe 12
 Excursions from Budapest 164
 Four-Hour Walk around Óbuda
 170–71
 Further afield 153
 Gellért Hill 88–9
 Gellért Hill and Tabán 87
 Gothic and Renaissance Buda
 24
 Habsburg Budapest 28

Maps (cont)
 Heroes' Square 142–3
 Kossuth Square 106–7
 90-Minute Walk from Buda to
 Pest 174–5
 North of the Castle 97
 Old Town 78–9
 railway stations 235
 River View of Budapest 62–5
 Roosevelt Square 112–13
 Royal Palace 70–71
 Tabán 94
 tram routes 240
 Turkish occupation 26
 Two-Hour Walk Around Margaret
 Island 172–3
 Unification of Budapest 32
 Váci Street 122–3
 Városliget 141
 Víziváros 98–9
Marathons 60
Marcibányi téri 216
Marffy, Ödön 77
Margaret Bridge
 River View of Budapest 63
Margaret Island 169
 Two-Hour Walk Around Margaret
 Island **172–3**
Margit, Princess 172, 173
Margit Kovács Museum
 (Szentendre) 165
Maria, Queen 18, 24, 133
Maria Theresa, Empress 17, 19
 Arc de Triomph (Vác) 165
 Lóránd Eötvös University 138
 Municipal County Offices 48
 Royal Palace 70
 Városliget 141
 "Vitam et Sanguinem" 28–9
Markets 211, 213, 225
 Central Market 11, 175
Márkus, Géza 151
Marschalkó, János 63
Martinelli, Anton Erhard 48, 128
Martinovics, Ignác 85
Marton, László
 Little Princess 65, 126, 174–5
 statue of Attila József 106
Martonvásár **167**
Marx, Karl
 statues of 138, 160
Masked-Ball Season 61
Master MS
 The Visitation 74
Mátyás II, King 18
Mátyás Church 10, 25, 44, **82–3**,
 174
 Budapest's Best: Churches and
 Synagogues 42
 music 216
 River View of Budapest 62
 Street-by-Street map 79
 Turkish occupation 27
Mátyás Corvinus, King 17, 18, 24, 25
 Hilton Hotel 81
 Hungarian National Gallery 76
 Hungarian National Museum 133
 Mátyás Church 25, **82–3**
 Mátyás Fountain 70, 72–3
 portrait of 24
 Royal Palace 70
 Széchenyi National Library 72
 Visegrád Palace 165
Mátyás Fountain 10, **72–3**
 Street-by-Street map 70

Mátyás Museum (Visegrád) 165
Maulbertsch, Franz Anton 76, 148
Maximilian I, Emperor 18
May Day 58, 61
Mayer, Ede
  statue of Miklós Ybl 94
Medgyaszay, István 57
Medgyessy, Ferenc 77
Medicine 227
  Golden Eagle Pharmacy Museum 41, 79, 80
  Semmelweiss Museum of Medical History 41, 95
Medieval Budapest 22–3
Meining, Artur 113, 135
Melocco, Miklós 73
Memento Park 160
Menus 191
Menzel 149
Merlin Theatre 217
Merse, Pál Szinyei
  Picnic in May 75, 77
Metro 238
Meyerhoffer, András 44
  Károlyi Palace 139
  Péterffy Palace 122
  Serbian Church 138
  University Church 139
Mihály Pollack Square 49, 135
Mihály Táncsics Street 81
  Street-by-Street map 78
Mihály Vörösmarty Square 126–7
  Street-by-Street map 122
Miklós Ybl Square 95
Mikroszkóp Színpad 217
Mikszáth, Kálmán 155
Mikulás 61
Millenaris Cultural Centre 216
Millennium Celebrations (1896) 142
  Millennium Monument 145
  Vajdahunyad Castle 150
  Városliget 141
Millennium Line 10, 238
Millennium Monument 11, 145
  Street-by-Street map 142
Mindszenty, Cardinal Joseph 34, 111
Ministry of Agriculture 110
  Street-by-Street map 107
Mithraic cult 20
Moblile phones 230
Mohács, Battle of (1526) 25, 26, 27
Molnár, Ferenc 155
Molnar, Pál C 125
Monasteries
  Rock Church 92
  Trinitarian Monastery 48
Monet, Claude 75, 149
Money 228–9
  currency exchange 179
Mongols 22, 23
Monuments
  Centenary Monument 62, 172
  Count István Széchenyi 114
  Ferenc Deák 114
  Ferenc Kölcsey 98
  Ferenc Rákóczi II 107
  Fishermen's Bastion 10, 49, 79, 80, 174
  Holocaust Memorial 134
  Holy Trinity Column 79, 80
  Honvéd Monument 73, 174
  Imre Nagy 107

Monuments (cont)
  János Arany 132
  József Bem 101
  Károly Kamermayer 127
  Liberation Monument 14, 88, 92
  Mihály Téncsics 84
  Mihály Vörösmarty 122, 126
  Millennium Monument 142, 145
  Queen Elizabeth 88, 93
  Raoul Wallenberg 154
  Samu Pecz 99
  Statue Park 160
  World War I 33
  see also Statues
Móricz, Zsigmond 155, 173
Mother and Child (Picasso) 147, 149
Motor racing 59
Motorways 234, 235
Műcsarnok Palace of Art 150
  Street-by-Street map 142
Municipal Cemetery 158–9
Municipal Council Offices 48, 128
Munkácsy, Mihály 40, 77
  Churning Woman 75
  The Yawning Journeyman 38, 77
Murillo, Bartolomé Estebán 40, 149
Museums and galleries 38–41
  Budapest's Best: Museums and Galleries 38–9
  opening hours 223
  Aquincum 41, 162–3
  Beethoven Museum (Martonvásár) 167
  Budapest History Museum 25, 38, 41, 72
  Ethnographical Museum 39, 41, 106, 110
  Ferenc Hopp Museum of Far Eastern Art 41, 145
  Franz Liszt Museum 41, 144
  Geology Institute 154–5
  Gizi Bajor Theatre Museum 160
  Golden Eagle Pharmacy Museum 41, 79, 80
  House of Terror Museum 144
  Hungarian National Gallery 10, 38, 40, 56, 71, 74–7, 219
  Hungarian National Museum 11, 30, 31, 39, 40, 41, 48, 130–33
  Hungarian Open Air Museum 165
  Imre Varga Gallery 171
  Jewish Museum 11, 39, 41
  Kiskun Museum (Kiskunfélegyháza) 167
  Ludwig Museum Budapest-Museum of Contemporary Art 40, 156
  Lutheran Museum 41
  Margit Kovács Museum (Szentendre) 165
  Mátyás Museum (Visegrád) 165
  Mucsarnok Art Gallery 142, 150
  Museum of Agriculture 150
  Museum of Applied Arts 39, 41, 56, 57, 136–7
  Museum of Ecclesiastical Art 82
  Museum of Fine Arts 10–11, 39, 40, 142, 146–9
  Museum of Military History 38, 41, 85, 219
  Museum of Musical History 41, 81
  Museum of Serbian Church Art (Szentendre) 165
  Nagytétény Palace Museum 57, 161

Museums and galleries (cont)
  National Lutheran Museum 128
  Palace of Arts 156
  Petőfi Exhibition 139
  Postal Museum 219
  Railway History Park 156, 219
  Ráth György Museum 41, 145
  Roman Baths Museum 171
  Roman Camp Museum 41, 170
  Roman Settlement Museum 171
  Semmelweiss Museum of Medical History 38, 41, 95
  State Archive of Historic Documents 78
  Telephone Museum 85
  Transport Museum 41, 151
  University of Fine Art 144
  Vajdahunyad Castle 150
  Vasarely Museum 40, 171
  Water Tower 172
  Zoltán Kodály Museum 41, 144
Music
  Beethoven Museum (Martonvásár) 167
  Budapest Operetta Theatre 115
  Budapest Summer Opera and Ballet Festival 59
  classical music 216
  Erkel Theatre 151
  folk music 216
  Franz Liszt Academy of Music 129
  Franz Liszt Museum 144
  jazz 216
  Museum of Musical History 81
  museums 41
  New Year's Gala Concert 61
  opera and operetta 216
  organ concerts in St Stephen's Basilica 59
  sacred music 216
  shops 212, 213
  State Opera House 118–19
  tickets 223
  Zoltán Kodály Museum 144
Musketeer (Picasso) 40

N
Nádor Hotel 127
Nádor utca
  Street-by-Street map 113
Nagy, Imre
  death of 34, 35
  monument 107
  Municipal Cemetery 159
  Remembrance Day 60
Nagytétényi Palace Museum 161
  Secession Budapest 57
Napoleon I, Emperor 30
Napoleonic Wars 30
National Concert Hall 216
National Dance Theatre 69, 73, 217
National Gallery 10
National Lutheran Museum 128
National Park, Kiskunsági 167
National Riding School 218
National Theatre 69, 73
Nature Reserve, Eagle Hill 160
Nazis 116, 134, 144
Nemzeti Theatre 217
Neo-Classical palaces and buildings 48
Neolithic era 21
Nepauer, Mátyás 44, 80, 81, 95, 102, 154

Neuschloss-Knüsli, Kornél 55, 151
New Theatre **129**
New Year's Day 61
New Year's Gala Concert 61
New York Palace 49, 57, **129**
New Zealand Embassy 225
Newspapers 231
Newton, Isaac 114
Nightlife 215
Nightclubs 208–9
North of the Castle **97–103**
    area map 97
    hotels 183
    restaurants 197–8
    St Anne's Church **102–3**
    Street-by-Street map: Víziváros
    98–9
Northwest (KLM) 233

O

Obergruber, Keresztély 95
Óbuda 22
    Four-Hour Walk around Óbuda
    170–71
Óbuda Calvinist Church 171
Óbuda Parish Church 170
Óbuda Synagogue 170
Old Town *see* Castle District
Old Town Hall 80
Open-Air Theatre Festival 59, 60
Opening hours 223
    shops 210
Opera 216
    Budapest Summer Music Festival 59
    Erkel Theatre **151**
    State Opera House 11, 34, 49,
    118–19
    Summer Theatre 172
Operetta Theatre 216
Oriental crafts museums **41**
Orthodox Synagogue 45
Ostade, Adrien van 148
OTP Bank 228
Otto Wittelsbach of Bavaria 18
Ottoman Empire 18, **26–7**

P

Paál, László 40, 77
Package deals 232–3
The Painter (Ferenczy) 77
Pál-völgy Cave **154**
Palace of Arts **156**
Palace West End 217
Palaces **46–9**
    Budapest's Best: Palaces and
    Historic Buildings **46–7**
    Batthyány Palace 48, 73
    Brunswick Palace (Martonvásár)
    167
    Cifra Palace (Kecskemét) 166
    Drechsler Palace 49, **115**
    Erdődy Palace 48, 49, 81
    Esterházy Palace 135
    Festetics Palace 135
    Fő tér Palace 170, 171
    Gresham Palace 47, 54, 57, 112, **114**
    Gross Palace 48
    Károlyi Palace 48, 49, 135, **139**
    Karolyi Palace (Fót) 166
    Klotild Palaces 49, 123, **127**, 175
    Nagytétény Palace Museum 57, **161**
    New York Palace 49, 57, **129**
    Pallavicini Palace 47
    Péterffy Palace 47, 48, 122

Palaces (cont)
    Royal Palace 10, 14, 29, 46, 49,
    64, **70–71**, 174
    Sándor Palace 46, 48, **73**, 174
    Visegrád Palace 165
    Wenckheim Palace 47, 135
    Zichy Palace 29, 48, 49, 171
Palatinus Strand 53, 172
    Budapest's Best: Baths and Pools 50
    children in 219
Pálinka
    What to Drink in Budapest 194
Pallavicini Palace
    Budapest's Best: Palaces and
    Historic Buildings 47
Pannonia 20, 21, 22
Parade Square **73**
Párizsi Udvar
    Street-by-Street map 123
Parking 237
    in hotels 179
Parking meters 237
Parks and gardens
    Brunswick Palace (Martonvásár)
    167
    Eagle Hill Nature Reserve **160**
    Japanese Garden 173
    Statue Park **160**
    Tabán **94**
    University Botanical Gardens **155**
Parliament 10, 15, 49, 105, **108–9**,
    174
    grand opening of 33
    River View of Budapest 63
    Street-by-Street map 106
Parliament area **105–19**
    area map 105
    hotels 183–4
    restaurants 198–9
    St Stephen's Basilica **116–17**
    State Opera House **118–19**
    Street-by-Street map: Kossuth
    Square 106–7
    Street-by-Street map: Roosevelt
    Square 112–13
Parliament Street **84**
Pártos, Gyula 115, 122, 136
Paskievicz, General Ivan 31
Passports 222
Pásztor, János 107
Pauer, György 124, 128
Pauline order
    Rock Church 42, 89, 92
    University Church 139
Pázmány, Cardinal Péter 138
Pecz, Samu 84
    Calvinist Church 100
    Lutheran Church 145
    monument to 99
The Penance of St Mary Magdalene
    (El Greco) 149
Pensions 178
Pest 22, 23
Pest County Hall 29, **127**
Pest Theatre 127, 217
Péterffy Palace 48
    Budapest's Best: Palaces and
    Historic Buildings 47
    Street-by-Street map 122
Petneházy School 218
Petőfi, Sándor 11
    Kiskunfélegyháza 167
    Petőfi Exhibition 139
    portrait of 31
    spring uprising 31, 58, 132

Petri, Lajos 144
Petschacher, Gustáv 47
Pharmacies 227
Philanthia Florists
    Budapest's Best: The Secession
    55, 57
Philostratus Codex 24
Picasso, Pablo 77
    Mother and Child 147, 149
    Musketeer 40
Pichler House
    Street-by-Street map 113
Pickpockets 226
Picnic in May (Merse) 75, 77
Pintér, Béla 81
Pisano, Andrea 148
Pisk, Battle of 101
Pissarro, Camille 149
Placing the Cornerstone (Barabás)
    130
Planetárium 219
Plus Budapest International
    Marathon and Running Festival
    60
Pogány, Móric 31
Police 226, 227
Pollack, Mihály
    Central European University 111
    Hungarian National Museum 48,
    130–33
    Ludovika Academy 156
    Lutheran Church 43, 45, 128
    Mihály Pollack Square 135
    Sándor Palace 73
    University Botanical Gardens 155
Polnay, Konrád
    tomb of 156–7
Ponti, Raffael 132
Pools *see* Swimming pools
Poor Clares 84
Porcelain shops 212, 213
Portrait of a Man (Veronese) 39
Portrait of a Young Man (Dürer)
    148
Post Office Savings Bank **111**
    Budapest's Best: the Secession
    55, 57
Post Offices 231
Postal Museum 219
Postal services 231
Poussin, Nicolas 149
Praxiteles 85
Premonstratensian Order 173
Private homes, staying in 181
Prostitutes 226
Public holidays 61
Pubs, Irish 208, 209
Puska, Ferenc 155

Q

Queen Elizabeth Monument **93**
    Street-by-Street map 88
Quittner, Zsigmond 47, 54, 114

R

Rác Baths 52, **95**
    Budapest's Best: Baths and Pools
    50
Racing
    horse racing 58, 218
    Hungarian Grand Prix 59
Ráckeve **167**
Radio 231
Radio Budapest 34

Rádiótaxi 239
Radisson SAS Béke Hotel **115**
Railway History Park **156**, 219
Railways *see* Trains
Rainfall 60
Rajk, László 34
 tomb of 155
Rákóczi, Ferenc *see* Ferenc II
 Rákóczi
Rákosi, Mátyás 19, 34
Ramada Plaza Budapest 53, 189
Raoul Wallenberg Monument **154**
Raphael 128, 149
 Esterházy Madonna 146, 149
 Museum of Fine Art 40, 146
Ráth György Museum 41, 145
Rauscher, Lajos 144
Ray, Rezső Vilmos 161
Reitter, Ferenc 100
Rembrandt 148, 149
Remeda Cave 20
Remembrance Day 60, 61
Removed Cars Information 237
Renaissance Buda **24–5**
Renoir, Pierre 149
Reservoir, Gellért Hill 89
Resort tax 179
Responsible tourism 225
Restaurants **190–205**
 Around Parliament 198–200
 Castle District 196
 Central Pest 200–203
 children in 191
 Flavours of Budapest **192–3**
 Further afield 204–5
 Gellért Hill and Tabán 196–7
 menus and prices 191
 North of the Castle 197–8
 outdoor eating 191
 reserving a table 191
 tipping 191
 types of restaurants, cafés and
 bars 190
 Városliget 203–4
 vegetarian food 191
 What to Drink in Budapest
 194–5
 what to order 190
 where to look 190
 see also Food and drink
Révay, Miklós 114
Reynolds, Joshua 149
Ribera, Jusepe de 149
Riding 218
Riegl, Anton 139
Rippl-Rónai, József 77
 Christmas 77
 Woman in White-Spotted Dress 56
 Woman with a Birdcage 54
Rivalda 10
River View of Budapest
 Elizabeth Bridge to Lágymányosi
 Bridge **64–5**
 Margaret Bridge to Elizabeth
 Bridge **62–3**
Rock Church **92**
 Budapest's Best: Churches and
 Synagogues 42
 Street-by-Street map 89
Római Camping 181
Római Strand 53
Romans 17, 20–21
 Amphitheatre 170
 Aquincum 41, **162–3**
 Contra Aquincum 175

Romans (cont.)
 Hercules Villa 171
 Roman Baths Museum 171
 Roman Camp Museum 41, 170
 Roman Settlement Museum 171
 Tabán 94
Róna, József
 statue of Eugene of Savoy 71
Ronni family 148
Roosevelt Square **114**
 Street-by-Street map **112–13**
Rosavolgyi 216
Róth, Miksa
 Calvinist Church 135
 Gresham Palace 114
 Kőbánya Parish Church 156
 Turkish Bank 128
Royal Palace 10, 14, 29, 49, **70–71**,
 174
 Budapest's Best: Palaces and
 Historic Buildings 46
 River View of Budapest 64
 Street-by-Street map 70–71
 Széchenyi National Library 72
Rózsavölgyi Building 57
Rubens, Peter Paul 148
Rubik, Ernő 157
Rudas Baths 27, 52, **93**, 218
 Budapest's Best: Baths and Pools
 51
 Street-by-Street map 89
Rudnyánszky, József 161
Rudolf I, Emperor 18
Ruisdael, Jacob van 148
 View of Amsterdam 147
Rulers **18–19**
Russworm, General Herman 26

S
Sacred music 216
Ságvári, Endre 110
St Anne's Church 29, 44, **102–3**
 Budapest's Best: Churches and
 Synagogues 42
 River View of Budapest 62
 Street-by-Street map 99
St Clare's Nunnery 171
St Francis's Wounds Church **101**
 River View of Budapest 62
 Street-by-Street map 98
St Gellért and St Emeryka (Stróbl)
 117
St István's Day 59, 61
St James Conquers the Moors
 (Tiepolo) 146, 149
St John the Baptist's Sermon
 (Bruegel) 147, 148
St Mary Magdalene 10
St Michael's Church 44, 173, 175
St Stephen's Basilica 33, 44, 45,
 116–17
 Budapest's Best: Churches and
 Synagogues 43
 music 59, 216
 River View of Budapest 63
 Street-by-Street map 113
Sándor, Count Vincent 73
Sándor Palace 48, **73**, 174
 Budapest's Best: Palaces and
 Historic Buildings 46
Sárffy, Ferenc 24
Satyr and Peasants (Jordaens) 146,
 149
Sávolya, Pál 63
Scams, late-night 215, 226

Schaffer, Károly 135
Schickedanz, Albert
 Lajos Batthyány tomb 155
 Millennium Monument 145
 Műcsarnok Palace of Art 150
 Museum of Fine Arts 146
Schmidl family 157
Scholtz, Robert 144
School on Rose Hill
 Budapest's Best: the Secession
 54
Schulek, Frigyes
 Erszébet Look-Out Tower 161
 Fishermen's Bastion 49, 79, 80
 Mátyás Church 82, 83
Scythians 20
Seasonal hostels 180, 181
Sebestyén, Artúr 90
Secession **54–7**
Security 226–7
Self-catering accommodation 180,
 181
Semmelweis, Dr Ignáz 95
Semmelweis Museum of Medical
 History 41, **95**
 Budapest's Best: Museums and
 Galleries 38
Senior travellers 224
Senyei, Károly 110, 129
Serbian Church **138**
Servite Church 44, **128**
 Street-by-Street map 122
Shoe shops 212, 213
Shopping **210–13**
 antiques 212, 213
 books 212, 213
 clothes and shoes 212, 213
 department stores and malls
 210–11, 213
 folk art 212, 213
 food and wine 212, 213
 how to pay 210
 markets 211, 213
 music 212, 213
 opening hours 210, 223
 porcelain 212, 213
 VAT exemption 210
Sigismund of Luxembourg 18, 24
 Hungarian National Museum
 133
 Mátyás Church 82, 83
 Old Town 78
 Parliament Street 84
 Royal Palace 70
Sikló 10
Sikot, Győző 92
Silver and Gold Sunday 61
Singer-Somossy, Károly 115
Sipeky Balázs Villa 55
Skála Metro (agency) 181
Skating 218
Skiing 218
Smallholders' Party 34
Social customs 223
Sofitel Atrium Budapest 184
Sokoli Mustafa 93
Sólyom, László 19
Sommer, Auguste 65, 138
Somogyi, Árpád 110
Soros, George 111
Söröző (bars) 190
South African Embassy 225
Sovának, István 56
Spa hotels 52–3
Spas *see* Baths

Speed limits 234
Spires, churches 44–5
Sport **218**
　Ferenc Puska's Stadium **155**
Spring Festival 58
Spring in Budapest 58
Spring Uprising 58, 61
"Springtime of Revolutions" (1848)
　17, **30–31**
Spritzers
　What to Drink in Budapest 195
Squares
　András Hess Square **81**
　Batthyány Square **100**
　Heroes' Square **142–3**
　Holy Trinity Square 79, **80**
　József Nádor Square **126**
　Kossuth Square 106–7
　Liberty Square **110–11**
　Mihály Pollack Square 49, **135**
　Mihály Vörösmarty Square **126–7**
　Miklós Ybl Square **95**
　Parade Square **73**
　Roosevelt Square **112–13**, **114**
　Vienna Gate Square 48, **84**
　Vigadó Square **126**
Stadia 218
Staffenberg House 49
Stalinism 34
Stamps 231
Stanisits, Bózó 91
State Archive of Historic
　Documents
　Street-by-Street map 78
State Opera House 11, 34, 49,
　118–19, 216
Statue Park see Memento Park
Statues
　Archduke József 126
　Attila József 106
　Baron József Eötvös 114
　Eugene of Savoy 71
　Franz Liszt 129
　Imre Varga 40
　Innocent XI 81
　Karl Marx 138, 160
　Little Princess (Marton) 65, 126,
　174–5
　Márton Lendvay 84
　Miklós Ybl 94, 95
　St Gellért 86, 87, 88, **93**
　St István 79, 80, 92
　St Luke 101
　Statue of Anonymous 143
　see also Monuments
Steen, Jan 148
Steindl, Imre
　City Council Chamber 138
　Parliament 49, 108
　Technical University 157
Stephen, St see István I, King
Sterio, Károly 138
Sterk, Izidor 90
Stock Exchange 110
Stone Age 20
Strands **53**
　Csillaghegy Strand 53
　Dagály Strand 53
　Palatinus Strand 53, 172, 219
　Római Strand 53
Straub, Philip Jakob 76
Stróbl, Alajos
　Franz Liszt Academy of Music 129
　János Arany monument 132

Stróbl, Alajos (cont)
　Lajos Kossuth tomb 155
　Luischen 75
　Mátyás Fountain 70, 72
　St Gellért and St Emericus 117
　St Stephen's Basilica 113
　State Opera House 118
　statue of St István 117
　tomb of 155
Stüler, Friedrich August 114
Süleyman "the Magnificent" 18, 26
Summer in Budapest 59
Summer Theatre 172
Sunshine 59
Swimming pools **53**, 218, 219
　Budapest's Best: Baths and Pools
　50–51
　Gellért Hotel and Baths Complex
　219
　Hajós Olympic Pool 50, 53, 172
　Komjádi Béla Swimming Stadium 53
　Rudas Baths **93**
　strands 53
Synagogues **42–5**
　Budapest's Best: Churches and
　Synagogues **42–3**
　Great Synagogue 11, 43, 44, 45,
　134, 216
　Óbuda Synagogue 170
　Orthodox Synagogue 45
Szabados, Béla 127
Szabó, Ervin 135
Szabo, István 35
Szakasits, Árpád 19
Száraz, György 161
Széchenyi, Count Ferenc 72
Széchenyi, Count István
　Chain Bridge 62
　Hungarian Academy of Sciences
　30–31
　Hungarian National Museum 130
　monument 114
　On Credit 31
　Turkish Bank 128
Széchényi Baths 10, 52, 53, 141,
　151, 218, 219
　Budapest's Best: Baths and Pools
　51
　Street-by-Street map 143
Széchényi National Library 30, **72**
Székely, Bertalan
　Buda Lutheran Church 84
　The Discovery of Louis II's Body
　24–5
　Matthias Church 83
　State Opera House 118
　Women of Eger 77
Székesfehérvár 22
Szemlő-hegy Cave **154**
Szentendre **165**
Szentpetery, Joseph
　"Vitam et Sanguinem" 28–9
Sziget Festival 59
Szilveszter 61
Szinyei-Merse, Pál 40
Szkalniczyky, Antal 139
Szondi, György 115
Sztéhló, Gábor 84

T

Tabán 34, **94**
　map 94
　see also Gellért Hill and Tabán
Tabán Parish Church **95**

Táncsics, Mihály 81
　monument to 84
Tápióbicske, Battle of (1849) 30
Tar, István 155
Taxes
　hotels 179
　VAT 210
Taxi 2000 239
Taxis **239**
　late-night scams 215
Technical University **157**
　River View of Budapest 64
Telcs, Ede
　Franz Liszt Academy of Music 129
　Gresham Palace 114
　Vörösmarty monument 122, 126
Telephones 230
　dialling codes 230
　in hotels 179
　Telephone Museum 85
Television 231
Temperatures 61
Tennis 218
Thabart, Adolphe 63
Than, Mór
　The Advance of the Hussars 30
　Hungarian National Museum 39, 132
　State Opera House 118
　University Library 139
Theatre 217
　Budapest Operetta Theatre **115**
　Castle Theatre **73**
　Erkel Theatre **151**
　Gizi Bajor Theatre Museum **160**
　New Theatre **129**
　Open-Air Theatre Festival 59, 60
　State Opera House **118–19**
　Summer Theatre 172
　tickets 223
Theme bars 208, 209
Thermal baths see Baths
Thermal Hotel Helia see Danubius
　Health Spa Resort Helia
Thermal Hotel Margitsziget see
　Danubius Health Spa Resort
　Margitsziget
These Women in the Refectory
　(Toulouse-Lautrec) 147, 149
Thonet House 127
　Street-by-Street map 122
Ticket Express 216
Tickets
　air travel 232–3
　Budapest Card 222
　for concerts 216
　for entertainments 214–17, 223
　HÉV railway 239
　Metro 238
　to museums 223
　trolley buses 241
Tiepolo, Giambattista 40
　St James Conquers the Moors 146,
　149
Tierney Clark, William 62
Tildy, Zoltán 19
Time zones 224
Tintoretto, Jacopo 40, 149
Tipping 191, 223
Titian 40, 149
Toilets, public 224
Tokaji
　What to Drink in Budapest
　195
Tomb of Gül Baba **101**
Törley, József 161

Törley Mausoleum **161**
Török, Richárd 73
Toulouse-Lautrec, Henri de 77
These Women in the Refectory 147, 149
Tourinform 178, 181, 222, 225
Tourist information 222, 225
Tourist Offices 223, 225
Trading on the Pest Embankment (Ligeti) 32–3
Trafó 217
Trains **234–5**
  Buda Hills 11, 161
  funicular railways 239
  HÉV railway **239**
  Railway History Park **156**
  railway stations 234, 235
  scenic railways 219
Trams **240**
  night trams 215
Transport Museum 41, 151
Travel **232–41**
  air travel **232–3**
  Around Parliament 105
  boats 234
  budget 224
  buses **241**
  cars 234–5, 236–7
  Castle Hill and the Old Town 69
  Central Pest 121
  coach travel 235
  cycling 218, 237
  driving in Budapest **236–7**
  Gellért Hill and Tabán 87
  HÉV railway **239**
  insurance 227
  late-night transport 215
  Metro **238**
  North of the Castle 97
  railways **234–5**
  taxis 215, **239**
  trams **240**
  trolley buses **241**
  Városliget 141
  walking 236
Travel agents 222
Travel cards 238
Traveller's cheques 228
Trinitarian Monastery 48
Trolley buses **241**
Tunnel 32, **100**
Turkish Bank **128**
Turkish baths *see* Baths
Turkish occupation 26–7

U

Ügetőpálya 218
Újlak Parish Church **154**
Ullmann, Gyula 111
UNESCO 35, 172
Ungleich, Philipp 80
Ungradt, Fülöp 124
Unicum
  What to Drink in Budapest 195
United Kingdom Embassy 225
United Kingdom tourist office 225
United States Embassy 225
United States tourist office 225
Universities
  Central European University **111**
  Lóránd Eötvös University **138–9**
  Technical University 64, **157**
  University of Corvinus 65, **138**
  University of Fine Art **144**

Universities (cont)
  University of Nagyszombat 28, 29
University Botanical Gardens **155**
University Church 44, **139**
University Library **139**
Universum Hostel Rózsa 181
Uprising (1956) 34, 35
  Municipal Cemetery 158
  Museum of Military History 85
  Remembrance Day 60
Uránia Nemzeti Filmszínház 217

V

Vác **165**
Vaccinations 227
Váci Street 11, 15, **127**
  Street-by-Street map 122–3
Vágó, József 54, 114
Vágó, László 54, 114, 129
Vajda, Zsigmond 108
Vajdahunyad Castle 141, **150**
  Street-by-Street map 143
Van Dyck, Anthony 148
Varga, Imre 40
  Ferenc Puska's Stadium 155
  Holocaust Memorial 134
  Imre Varga Gallery 171
  Raoul Wallenberg Monument 154
  sculpture of King István I 22
  Women with Umbrellas 171
Várkert Casino
  Budapest's Best: Palaces and Historic Buildings 46
Varna, Battle of (1444) 25
Városliget 32, **141–51**
  area map 141
  hotels 186–7
  Museum of Fine Arts **146–9**
  restaurants 203–4
  Street-by-Street map: Around Heroes' Square 142–3
Városliget Calvinist Church 45, 57, 144–5
Városligeti Avenue **144–5**
Vasarely, Victor 40, 171
Vasarely Museum 40, 171
Vaszary, János 56
VAT (value-added tax) 210
  in hotels 179
Vata, Prince 88
Vegetarian food 191
Vehicle Assistance and Breakdown Emergency Service 227, 235
Velázquez, Diego 149
Vendéglő (inn) 190
Vermeer, Jan 148
Veronese, Bonifazio 149
Veronese, Paolo 40
  Portrait of a Man 39
Vezekény, Battle of 136
Vidám Park Funfair 219
Vienna, Treaty of (1624) 27
Vienna–Budapest Super Marathon Running Competition 60
Vienna Gate Square 48, **84**
  Budapest's Best: Palaces and Historic Buildings 46
View of Amsterdam (Ruisdael) 147
Vigadó Concert Hall 49, 175
Vigadó Square **126**
Vígszínház 217
Visas 222
Visegrád **165**
The Visitation (Master MS) 74

"Vitam et Sanguinem" (Szentpetery) 28–9
Víziváros 97
  Street-by-Street map 98–9
Vogl, Gergely 103
Vörösmarty, Mihály 72–3
  monument 122, 126

W

Wagenschön, Franz 103
Wagner, Otto 45
  Orthodox Synagogue 45
Wagner, Richard 115
Waldmüller 149
Walesa, Lech 35
Walks **169–75**, 236
  Four-Hour Walk around Óbuda **170–71**
  90-Minute Walk from Buda to Pest **174–5**
  Two-Hour Walk Around Margaret Island **172–3**
Wallenberg, Raoul
  Raoul Wallenberg Monument **154**
Warsaw Pact 35
Warsch, Jakab 135
Water, drinking 227
The Water Carrier (Goya) 146, 149
Water Tower 172
Weather 58–61, 222
Websites 231
Wekerle, Sándor 157
Wekerle Estate 57, **157**
Wellisch, Arthur 156
Wellisch family 156
Wenceslas II of Bohemia 18
Wenckheim family 135
Wenckheim Palace 135
  Budapest's Best: Palaces and Historic Buildings 47
Wesselényi, Count Miklós 30
Wheelchair access *see* Disabled travellers
Whit Monday 61
White Cross Inn 100
  Street-by-Street map 98
"White Terror" 34
Wieser, Ferenc 113
Wi-Fi 230
Wines
  Budapest Wine Festival 60
  House of Hungarian Wines 79, **80**
  shops 212, 213
  What to Drink in Budapest 194–5
  wine bars 206, 207
Winter sports 218
Wiring money 228
Władysław (Ulászló) I, King 18, 25
Władysław (Ulászló) II, King 18, 25
Wolff, Emil 47, 114
Woman Bathing (Lotz) 75
Woman in White-Spotted Dress (Rippl-Rónai) 56
Woman with a Birdcage (Rippl-Rónai) 54
Women of Eger (Székely) 77
Women with Umbrellas (Varga) 171
World War I 17, 34
  Hungarian National Museum 133
  Monument 33
World War II 17, 34
  Hungarian National Museum 133
  Jewish Quarter 134
  Liberation Monument 92
  Raoul Wallenberg Monument **154**

Woroniecki, Brigadier M. 107, 110
Woroszyłow, Marshal Klimient 92

Y

Yalta Agreement (1945) 34
The Yawning Apprentice (Munkácsy)
   38, 77
Ybl, Miklós **119**
   Danube Fountain 129
   Festetics Palace 135
   Grand Hotel Margitsziget 173
   Károlyi Palace 135
   Miklós Ybl Square **95**
   Rác Baths 95
   Royal Palace 70
   St Stephen's Basilica 45, 116
   State Opera House 49, 118
   statue of 94, 95
   Széchenyi National Library 72
   Tabán 94

Ybl, Miklós (cont)
   University of Corvinus 138
   Várkert Kiosk 46

Z

Zala, György 73
   Millennium Monument 142, 145
   Queen Elizabeth Monument 93
Zenta, Battle of (1697) 71
Zero Kilometre Stone 100, 174
Zichy family 171
Zichy Palace 29, 48, 49, 171
Zitterbarth, Mátyás the younger 112, 127
Zoo 57, **150–51**, 219
   Budapest's Best: the Secession 55
Zrumeczky, Dezső 54, 151
Zsigmond, Vilmos 151
Zsolnay, Vilmos 56
Zsumrák, Pál 100
Zurbarán, Francisco de 40

Acknowledgments

Dorling Kindersley would like to thank the following people whose contributions and assistance have made this book possible:

Main Contributor

Tadeusz Olszanski was born in 1929 in Poland. During World War II, he fled with his parents to Hungary, where he attended a Polish school in Balatonboglar. He has since visited Hungary many times as a journalist and is the author of five books about the country. These include a volume of articles, Budapesztanskíe ABC. In addition, he has translated over 30 Hungarian novels and dramas into Polish. From 1986 to 1994, he lived in Hungary, working both as the manager of the Institute of Polish Culture and as a correspondent for Polish Radio and TV. In recognition of his activities in promoting Hungarian literature and culture, he was awarded the Pro-Hungarian Culture Award and the Tibor Derye Literary Prize.

Additional Contributors

Sławomir Fangrat, Mariusz Jarymowicz, Iza Mo cicka, Barbara Olszanska, Ágnes Ördög, Ewa Roguska, Craig Turp.

Editorial and Design

SENIOR MANAGING EDITOR Vivien Crump DEPUTY ART DIRECTOR Gillian Allan PRODUCTION Jo Blackmore, David Proffit DTP DESIGNERS Lee Redmond, Ingrid Vienings MAPS Maria Wojciechowska, Dariusz Osuch (D Osuch i Spółka), Elizabeth Atherton, Lydia Halliday, Claire Baranowski, Arwen Burnett, Lucinda Cooke, Mariana Evmolpidou, Fay Franklin, Anna Freiberger, Rhiannon Furbear, Vicki Ingle, Maite Lantaron, Catherine Palmi, Helen Partington, Rebecca Milner, Amir Reuveni, Ellen Root, Rachel Symons, Anna Streiffert, Andrew Szudek, Julie Thompson, Ros Walford, Sophie Warne, Scott Alexander Young.

Researchers

Julia Bennett, Javier Espinosa de los Monteros

Indexer

Hilary Bird.

Additional Photography

Demetrio Carrasco, Ian O'Leary, Scott Alexander Young.

Special Assistance

The Publisher would like to thank the staff at shops, museums, hotels, restaurants and other organizations in Budapest for their invaluable help. Particular thanks go to: the Ambassador for the Republic of Hungary in Warsaw; the Ambassador for the Republic of Poland in Budapest; Gábor Bányai; Katalin Bara and the rest of the staff at the Hungarian airline, Malév; Beatrix Basics, Tibor Kovács, Izabella Bósze and Péter Gaál at the Hungarian National Museum; Éva Benkő and Judit Füredi Hamvasné at the Museum of Fine Arts; Zoltan Fejős and Endre Stefana Szemkeő at the Ethnographical Museum; Béla Juszel and Éva Orosz at the Hungarian National Bank; the staff of the Kiscelli Museum; Imre Kiss, Zsuzsa Mátyus and Tivadar Mihalkovics at the State Opera House; Konrad Adenauer Stifung; the staff of the Franz Liszt Museum; Zsuzsa Lovag at the Museum of Applied Arts; the Meteorological Office of the Republic of Hungary; the staff at the Hungarian Post Office; Katalin Neray at the Ludwig Museum; Anita Obrotfa at the Budapesti Turisztikai Hivatal; Csilla Pataky at Cartographia Ltd; Géza Szabó; Mária Vida at the Semmelweis Museum of Medical History; Annamária Vigh at the Budapest History Museum. Ágnes Ördög and Judit Mihalcsik at the Tourism Office of Budapest, 1056 Március 15 tér 7, for sourcing pictures and providing new information.

Photography Permissions

Dorling Kindersley would like to thank the following for their kind permission to photograph at their establishments: Ágnes Bakos, Margit Bakos and Bence Tihanyi at the Budapest History Museum; the staff of the Budapesti Turisztikai Hivatal; Eszter Gordon; István Gordon at the Kurir Archive; Astoria Hotel; Dénes Józsa at the Museum of Fine Arts; Ágnes Kolozs at the Museum of Applied Arts; the Ludwig Museum; the Hungarian National Museum; the Hungarian Academy of Sciences; Tibor Mester at the Hungarian National Gallery; Béla Mezey; the Imre Varga Gallery; András Rázsó at the Museum of Fine Arts; the Semmelweis Museum of Medical History; Judit Szalatnyay at the Kiscelli Museum; Ágnes Szél; Ferenc Tobias and Erzsébet Winter at the Ethnographical Museum; Richard Wagner at the Museum of Applied Arts; the Hungarian airline, Malév.

Dorling Kindersley would also like to thank all the shops, restaurants, cafés, hotels, churches and public services who aided us with our photography. These are too numerous to mention individually.

Particular thanks are due to Marta Zámbó at the Gundel Étterem, who provided the Hungarian cuisine photographed for this guidebook.

Picture Credits

t=top; tc=top centre; tr=top right; tl=top left; cla=centre left above; ca=centre above; cra=centre right above; cl=centre left; c=centre; cr=centre right; clb=centre left below; cb=centre below; crb=centre right below; bl=bottom left; bc=bottom centre; br=bottom right; b=bottom.

The publisher is grateful to the following individuals, companies and picture libraries for permission to reproduce their photographs:

AIRPORTSHUTTLE.HU.ZRT: 233cl; ALAMY IMAGES: Tibor Bognar 175tl; Kevin Foy 10cla; 47tr; Peter Horree 126br; Michael Jenner 190tc; INSADCO Photography/ Martin Bobrovski 193c; Jon Arnold Images/Doug Pearson 192cl; nagelestock.com 80cr; PBstock 230bl; Sergio Pitamitz 41bc, 79c; Jean-Yves Roure 231tr; Travelog Picture Library 11br; Westend61/Johannes Simon 174cla; ASTORIA HOTEL: 180b.

BUDAPESTI KÖZLEKÉDSI ZRT. BKV: 238cl, 238cra, 241c; WWW.BRIDGEMAN.CO.UK: Bibliotheque Polonaise, Paris, Aleksander Lesser (1814-84) *Grand Duke of Lithuania* (engraving) 25br; Magyar Nemzeti Galeria,

Budapest 77tr; BUDAPEST FESTIVAL CENTRE: 58ca; BUDAPEST HISTORY MUSEUM: 32c, 33c, 38cb, 38b, 72t; BUDAPEST SPA LLC: 51tc, 53tr, 143tc; BUDAPESTI TURISZTIKAI HIVATAL: 50cr, 50clb, 50br, 51b, 58t, 59b, 60b, 156b.

CORBIS: Jon Hicks 175cr, Barry Lewis 91tl, 193tl.

DANUBIUS HOTEL GROUP: 180b.

EUROPRESS FOTOUGYNOKSEG: 11tr, 25crb, 27crb, 51crb, 83cr, 95cl, 122bl, 140, 152, 156cl, 166tl, 166tr, 214bl; Darnay Katalin 93tr, Szabu Tibor 123crb.

GETTY IMAGES: AFP/Attila Kisbenedek 224tl; Getty Images Sport/Paul Gilham 226cl; Eszter Gordon: 35ca.

ROBERT HARDING PICTURE LIBRARY: Gavin Hellier 174bl; HOUSE OF TERROR: 144tl; HUNGARIAN NATIONAL GALLERY: 16, 23b, 24cb, 26ca, 38ca, 54cla, 56cl, 74tl, 74tr, 75ca, 75cr, 75cra, 75b, 76t, 76c, 76b, 77t, 77c, 77b; HUNGARIAN NATIONAL MUSEUM: 8, 20t, 20ca, 20cr, 20cb, 20b, 21t, 21cra, 21c, 21crb, 22t, 22c, 22cl, 22br, 23t, 23c, 23cra, 23crb, 23b, 24cl, 24c, 25t, 25c, 26t, 26b, 27t, 27cra, 27crb, 27cla, 28t, 28ca, 28c, 28cb, 29t, 29c, 29cra, 29crb, 30cl, 31tr, 32t, 32cra, 32cl, 32crb, 33cr, 37cl, 40tl, 130tr, 130tl, 130ca, 130cb, 131t, 131ca, 131cb, 131bc, 133t, 133c, 133b; HUNGARIAN NATIONAL TOURIST OFFICE: 226t.

JEWISH MUSEUM: 39cr.

KURIR ARCHIVE: 34tr, 34br, 35br.

LEONARDO MEDIA BANK: 180tl; LUDWIG MUSEUM: 40b, 73b.

Béla Mezey 34ca; MUSEUM OF APPLIED ARTS: Ágnes Kolozs 5br, 56tr, 57bl, 136tr, 136tl, 136c, 137tl, 137cra, 137cr, 137crb, 137b; MUSEUM OF FINE ARTS: 39tr, 146tl, 146tr, 146c, 146clb, 146b, 147t, 147ca, 147cb, 147b, 148tl, 148tr, 148c, 148bl, 149t, 149c, 149b.

OFFICE OF THE PRESIDENT OF THE REPUBLIC: 19tr.

RED DOT, BUDAPEST: 50t, 85tr; Serenc Isza 51cra, 190cla, 190br, 190t, 191cb, 191bl, 222bl, 216bl; Reuters:STR 59cr.

STA TRAVEL GROUP: 224c; Széchenyi National Gallery: 39tl, 126tr, 110t; SZÉCHENYI NATIONAL LIBRARY: 24c, 25c, 26c, 27c, 72b; Ágnes Szél: 34tl, 37br, 41c, 78bc, 84b, 160b.

TOURISM OFFICE OF BUDAPEST: 10tc, 10br, 45tr, 50br, 65tl, 78clb, 114tl, 127bc, 151tr, 175br, 215tr, 222bl, 222cr, 223tl, 226cla, 232bl, 233tr, 236cra, 237bc, 239crb, 240cla, 241bl.

WESTEND CITY CENTER: 210cra.

ZONA TAXI: 233c.

Front Endpaper: Europress Fotougynokseg: crb.
Map cover
AWL IMAGES: Doug Pearson.
Jacket
Front – AWL IMAGES: Doug Pearson. Back – AWL IMAGES: Doug Pearson cla; DORLING KINDERSLEY: Rough Guides/Eddie Gerald bl, clb. Spine – AWL IMAGES: Doug Pearson t.

All other images © Dorling Kindersley. For further information see: www.dkimages.com

Phrase Book

Pronunciation

When reading the literal pronunciation given in the right-hand
column of this phrase book, pronounce each syllable as if it
formed part of an English word. Remember the points below,
and your pronunciation will be even closer to correct Hungarian.
The first syllable of each word should be stressed (and is shown
in bold). When asking a question the pitch should be raised on
the penultimate syllable. "R"s in Hungarian words are rolled.

a	as the long 'a' in father
ay	as in 'pay'
e	as in 'Ted'
ew	similar to the sound in 'hew'
g	always as in 'goat'
i	as in 'bit'
o	as in the 'ou' in 'ought'
u	as in 'tuck'
y	always as in 'yes' (except as in ay above)
yuh	as the 'yo' in 'canyon'
zh	like the 's' in leisure

In Emergency

Help!	Segítség!	shegeetshayg
Stop!	Stop!	shtop
Look out!	Tessék vigyázni	teshayk vidyahzni
Call a doctor	Hívjon orvost!	heevyon orvosht
Call an ambulance	Hívjon mentőt!	heevyon menturt
Call the police	Hívja a rendőrséget	heevya a rendur shayget
Call the fire department	Hívja a tűzoltókat!	heevya a tewzoltowkot
Where is the nearest telephone?	Hol van a legközelebbi telefon?	hol von a legkurzelebbi telefon
Where is the nearest hospital?	Hol van a legközelebbi kórház?	hol von a legkurze lebbi koorhahz

Communications Essentials

Yes/No	Igen/Nem	igen/nem
Please (offering)	Tessék	teshayk
Please (asking)	Kérem	kayrem
Thank you	Köszönöm	kurssurnurm
No, thank you	Köszönöm nem	kurssurnurm nem
Excuse me, please	Bocsánatot kérek	bochanutot kayrek
Hello	Jó napot	yow nopot
Goodbye	Viszontlátásra	vissontlatashruh
Good night	Jó éjszakát/jó éjt	yaw-aysssukat/yaw-ayt
morning (4-9 am)	reggel	reggel
morning (9am-noon)	délelőtt	daylelurt
morning (midnight-4am)	éjjel	ay-ye l
afternoon	délután	daylootan
evening	este	eshteh
yesterday	tegnap	tegnup
today	ma	muh
tomorrow	holnap	holnup
here	itt	it
there	ott	ot
What?	mi	mi
When?	mikor	mikor
Why?	miért	miayrt
Where?	hol	hol

Useful Phrases

How are you?	Hogy van?	hod-yuh vun
Very well, thank you	köszönöm nagyon jól	kurssurnurm nojjon yowl
Pleased to meet you	Örülök hogy megismerhettem	ur-rewlurk hod-yuh megishmerhettem
See you soon	Szia!	seeyuh
Excellent!	Nagyszerű!	nud-yusserew
Is there ... here?	Van itt ... ?	vun itt
Where can I get ...?	Hol kaphatok ...-t?	hol kuphutok ...-t
How do you get to?	Hogy lehet ...-ba eljutni?	hod-yuh lehet ...-buh el-yootni
How far is ...?	milyen messze van ...	meeyen messeh van ...
Do you speak English?	Beszél angolul?	bessayl ungolool
I can't speak Hungarian	Nem beszélek magyarul	nem bessaylek mud-yarool
I don't understand	Nem értem	nem ayrtem
Can you help me?	Kérhetem a segítségét?	kayrhetem uh shegeechaygayt
Please speak slowly	Tessék lassabban beszélni	teshayk lushubbun bessaylni
Sorry!	Elnézést!	elnayzaysht

Useful Words

big	nagy	noj
small	kicsi	kichi
hot	forró	meleg
cold	hideg	hideg
good	jó	yow
bad	rossz	ross
enough	elég	elayg
well	jól	yowl
open	nyitva	nyitva
closed	zárva	zarva
left	bal	bol
right	jobb	yob
straight on	egyenesen	ejeneshen
near	közel	kurzel
far	messze	messeh
up	fel	fel
down	le	leh
early	korán	koran
late	késő	kayshur
entrance	bejárat	beh-yarut
exit	kijárat	ki-yarut
toilet	WC	vaytsay
free/unoccupied	szabad	sobbod
free/no charge	ingyen	injen

Making a Telephone Call

Can I call abroad from here?	Telefonálhatok innen külföldre?	telefonalhutok inen kewlfurldreh
I would like to call collect	Szeretnék egy R-beszélgetést lebonyolítani	seretnayk ed-yuh er-bessaylgetaysht lebon-yoleetuni
local call	helyi beszélgetés	hayee bessaylgetaysht
I'll ring back later	Visszahívom később	vissuh-heevom kayshurb
Could I leave a message?	Hagyhatnék egy üzenetet?	hud-yuhutnayk ed-yuh ewzenetet
Hold on	Várjon!	vahr-yon
Could you speak up a little please?	kicsit hangosabban, kérem!	kichit hungosh-shob-bon kayrem

Shopping

How much is this?	Ez mennyibe kerül?	ez menn-yibeh kerewl
I would like ...	Szeretnék egy ...-t	seretnayk ed-yuh ...-t
Do you have ...?	Kapható önöknél ...?	kuphutaw urnurknayl
I'm just looking	Csak körülnézek	chuk kur-rewlnayzek
Do you take credit cards?	Elfogadják a hitelkártyákat?	elfogud-yak uh hitelkart-yakut
What time do you open?	Hány kor nyitnak?	Hahn kor nyitnak?
What time do you close?	Hány kor zárnak??	Hahn kor zárnak
this one	ez	ez
that one	az	oz
expensive	drága	drahga
cheap	olcsó	olchow
size	méret	mayret
white	fehér	feheer
black	fekete	feketeh
red	piros	pirosh
yellow	sárga	sharga
green	zöld	zurld
blue	kék	cake
brown	barna	borna

Types of Shop

antique dealer	antikvárius	ontikvahrioosh
baker's	pékség	paykshayg
bank	bank	bonk
bookshop	könyvesbolt	kurn-yuveshbolt
cake shop	cukrászda	tsookrassduh
chemist	patika	putikuh
department store	áruház	aroo-haz
florist	virágüzlet	vi rag-ewzlet
greengrocer	zöldséges	zurld-shaygesh
market	piac	pi-uts
newsagent	újságos	oo-yushagosh
post office	postahivatal	poshta-hivatal
shoe shop	cipőbolt	tsipurbolt
souvenir shop	ajándékbolt	uy-yandaykbolt
supermarket	ábécé/ABC	abaytsay
travel agent	utazási iroda	ootuzashi iroduh

Staying in a Hotel

Have you any vacancies?	Van kiadó szobájuk?	vun ki-udaw soba-yook
double room with double bed	francia-ágyas szoba	frontsia-ahjosh sobuh
twin room	kétágyas szoba	kaytad-yush sobuh
single room	egyágyas szoba	ed-yad-yush sobuh
room with a bath/shower	fürdőszobás/zuhanyzós szoba	fewrdur-sobahsh/zoohonzahsh soba
porter	portás	portahsh
key	kulcs	koolch
I have a reservation	Foglaltam egy szobát	foglultum ed-yuh sobat

Sightseeing

bus	autóbusz	owtawbooss
tram	villamos	villumosh
trolley bus	troli(busz)	troli(booss)
train	vonat	vonut
underground	metró	metraw
bus stop	buszmegálló	boossmegallaw
tram stop	villamosmegálló	villomosh-megahllaw
art gallery	képcsarnok	kayp-chornok
palace	palota	polola
cathedral	székesegyház	saykesh-ejhajz
church	templom	templom
garden	kert	kert
library	könyvtár	kurnvtar
museum	múzeum	moozayoom
tourist information	turista információ	toorishta informatzeeo
train station	vasútállomás	vashootallawmash
closed for public holiday	ünnepnap zárva	ewn-nepnap zarva

Eating Out

A table for ... please	Egy asztalt szeretnék... személyre	ed-yuh usstult seretnayk ... semayreh
I want to reserve a table	Szeretnék egy asztalt foglalni	seretnayk ed-yuh usstultfoglolni
The bill please	Kérem a számlát	kayrem uh samlat
I am a vegetarian	Vegetáriánnus vagyok	vegetari-ahnoosh vojok
I'd like ...	Szeret nék egy ...-t	seret nayk ed-yuh ...-t
waiter/waitress	pincér/pincérnő	pintsayr/pintsayrnur
menu	étlap	aytlup
wine list	itallap	itullup
chef's special	konyhafőnök ajánlata	konha-furnurt oyahu-lotta
tip	borravaló	borovolo
glass	pohár	pohar
bottle	üveg	ewveg
knife	kés	kaysh
fork	villa	villuh
spoon	kanál	kunal
breakfast	reggeli	reg-geli
lunch	ebéd	ebayd
dinner	vacsora	vochora
main courses	főételek	fur-aytelek
starters	előételek	elur-aytelek
vegetables	zöldség	zurld-shayg
desserts	édességek	aydesh-shaydek
rare	angolosan	ongoloshan
well done	átsütve	ahtshewtveh

Menu Decoder

alma	olma	apple
ásványvíz	ahshvahnveez	mineral water
bab	bob	beans
banán	bonahn	banana
barack	borotsk	apricot
bárány	bahrahn	lamb
bors	borsh	pepper
csirke	cheerkeh	chicken
csokoládé	chokolahday	chocolate
cukor	tsookor	sugar
ecet	etset	vinegar
fagylalt	fodyuhloot	ice cream
fehérbor	feheerbor	white wine
fokhagyma	fokhodyuhma	garlic
főtt	furt	boiled
gomba	gomba	mushrooms
gulyás	gooyahsh	goulash
gyümölcs	dyewmurlch	fruit
gyümölcslé	dyewmurlch-lay	fruit juice
hagyma	hojma	onions
hal	hol	fish
hús	hoosh	meat

kávé	kavay	coffee
kenyér	ken-yeer	bread
krumpli	kroompli	potatoes
kolbász	kolbahss	sausage
leves	levesh	soup
máj	my	liver
marha	marha	beef
mustár	mooshtahr	mustard
narancs	noronch	orange
olaj	oloy	oil
paradicsom	porodichom	tomatoes
párolt	pahrolt	steamed
pite	piteh	pie
sertéshús	shertaysh-hoosh	pork
rántott	rahntsott	fried in batter
rizs	rizh	rice
rostélyos szelet	bifstek	steak
roston	roshton-	grilled
sajt	shoyt	cheese
saláta	sholahta	salad
só	shaw	salt
sonka	shonka	ham
sör	shur	beer
sült	shewlt	fried/roasted
sült burgonya	shewlt boorgonya	chips
sütemény	shewtemayn-yuh	cake, pastry
szendvics	sendvich	sandwich
szósz	sowss	sauce
tea	tay-uh	tea
tej	tay	milk
tejszín	taysseen	cream
tengeri hal	tengeri hol	seafood
tojás	toyahsh	egg
töltött	turlturt	stuffed
vörösbor	vur-rurshbor	red wine
zsemle	zhemleh	roll
zsemlegombóc	zhemleh-gombowts	dumplings

Numbers

0	nulla	noolluh
1	egy	ed-yuh
2	kettő, két	kettur, kayt
3	három	harom
4	négy	nayd-yuh
5	öt	urt
6	hat	hut
7	hét	hayt
8	nyolc	n-yolts
9	kilenc	kilents
10	tíz	teez
11	tizenegy	tizened-yuh
12	tizenkettő	tizenkettur
13	tizenhárom	tizenharom
14	tizennégy	tizen-nayd-yuh
15	tizenöt	tizenurt
16	tizenhat	tizenhut
17	tizenhét	tizenhayt
18	tizennyolc	tizenn-yolts
19	tizenkilenc	tizenkilents
20	húsz	hooss
21	huszonegy	hoossoned-yuh
22	huszonkettő	hoossonkettur
30	harminc	hurmints
31	harmincegy	hurmintsed-yuh
32	harminckettő	hurmintskettur
40	negyven	ned-yuven
50	ötven	urtven
60	hatvan	hutvun
70	hetven	hetven
80	nyolcvan	n-yoltsvun
90	kilencven	kilentsven
100	száz	saz
200	kétszáz	kayt-saz
300	háromszáz	haromssaz
1000	ezer	ezer
10,000	tízezer	teezezer
1,000,000	millió	milliaw

Time

one minute	egy perc	ed-yuh perts
hour	óra	awruh
half an hour	félóra	faylawruh
Sunday	vasárnap	vusharnup
Monday	hétfő	haytfur
Tuesday	kedd	kedd
Wednesday	szerda	serduh
Thursday	csütörtök	chewturturk
Friday	péntek	payntek
Saturday	szombat	sombat